50 Years of EU Economic Dynamics

Richard Tilly · Paul J. J. Welfens
Michael Heise

(Editors)

50 Years
of EU Economic
Dynamics

Integration, Financial Markets
and Innovations

Dedicated to Jacques Delors – A Leading Spirit of European Integration

 Springer

Professor Dr. Richard Tilly
University of Münster
Institut für Wirtschafts- und Sozialgeschichte
Domplatz 20-22
48143 Münster
Germany
burhop@uni-muenster.de

Professor Dr. Paul J. J. Welfens
University of Wuppertal
EIIW – European Institute
for International Economic Relations
Rainer-Gruenter-Straße 21
42119 Wuppertal
Germany
welfens@eiiw.uni-wuppertal.de

Dr. Michael Heise
Allianz Group
Gallusanlage 8
60301 Frankfurt
Germany
michael.heise@dresdner-bank.com

Library of Congress Control Number: 2007934935

ISBN 978-3-540-74054-4 Springer Berlin Heidelberg New York

Springer is a part of Springer Science+Business Media

springer.com

Production: LE-TeX Jelonek, Schmidt & Vöckler GbR, Leipzig
Cover-design: WMX Design GmbH, Heidelberg

SPIN 12102921   43/3180YL - 5 4 3 2 1 0   Printed on acid-free paper

Table of Contents

Introduction

The European Union will celebrate its 50th anniversary in 2007. Europe can be proud of half a century of peaceful economic and political cooperation. The integration process triggered in 1957 has turned out to be not without problems, but the inherent dynamics of liberalization and cooperation have brought about a prosperous and growing community with continuing liberalization in many fields and with several rounds of enlargements. Thus the specific approach of combining multilateral regional policy cooperation and the activity of a supranational policy layer – with the European Commission, the European Parliament, the European Court of Justice and the European Council as the four pillars – has worked. In addition to the traditional nation-state, there is a new political organization: a hybrid institutional setup. Major European personalities such as Jean Monnet, Paul-Henri Spaak, Walter Hallstein, Jacques Delors, Romano Prodi, Willem Duisenberg and many others have contributed to building the EU house.

The European counter-approach of the free trade area without much cooperation, the EFTA, has witnessed a long term decline as the modest free trade agenda obviously was not attractive enough to keep most of its founding members on board for more than four decades. Rather the EU has absorbed most former EFTA member countries.

The EU has been rather ambitious in terms of enlargements, and the eastern enlargement of 2004 – with ten new member countries – has stretched the Community almost to the limit. With close to 500 million people from 27 countries cooperating on the basis of shared values and common institutions, the EU signifies a unique historical achievement. It certainly has its problems, but it cannot only draw on rich resources and a large variety of institutions and actors but, in addition, on a (short) history of successes and failures which both lend themselves as a basis for institutional learning and adjusting in a dynamic future.

The EU has not only achieved a single market with four basic freedoms – free trade of goods, free trade of services, free capital flows and free movement of labour – it also has contributed to the liberalization of global trade. Firms and consumers have benefited from increasing regional specialization and growing innovation. Compared to the costs of integration, namely contributions of member countries to the EU budget which sums to slightly more than 1% of GDP, the benefits are large. Those benefits, however, are not clearly visible for the people in the EU since they accrue in the form of specialization and income gains; and in the form of millions of goods which are cheaper by a few percent compared to the case of non-integration. The European Commission has claimed in a rather conservative assessment that benefits from the single market within the first decade amounted to 1.8 percentage points of EU GDP, namely € 165 bill. or € 5,700 per household; exports to third countries have increased from 6.9% of GDP to almost 12% in 2002, and foreign direct investment inflows relative to GDP have more than doubled. It is also noteworthy that the European Commission has been the driver of liberalization of network industries, including fixed-network telecommunications, gas and electricity.

While the EU has achieved sustained growth in past decades, one cannot overlook the fact that several EU member countries have suffered from high unemployment, with France, Germany, Italy and Spain at the top (Spain, however, has made considerable progress since joining the EU, mainly through combining EU impulses with domestic liberalization and market opening up with higher investment in education and infrastructure). At the beginning of the 21st century, France and Germany as well as other EU countries have made new efforts to adopt reforms which could help bolster economic growth and employment on the one hand and help overcome the problems in financing social security in ageing societies on the other. Small open economies, however, have often been more successful in facing the economic challenges through comprehensive reforms.

The number of EU countries has increased from six in 1957 to 27 in 2007, which is a success in terms of widening the membership. At the same time, however, this widening has created problems related to the community´s greater heterogeneity. This could be a temporary problem if economic catching-up dynamics in the relatively poor countries in Eastern Europe resemble the earlier experience of Spain, Portugal and Greece in the context of Southern EU enlargement. As regards the position of the EU relative to the US one may emphasize that per capita income of the EU12 represented a successful economic catching-up process in the 1970s and early 1980s (with the EU reaching about 85% of US per capita GDP), but since the late 1980s the transatlantic income gap has increased. The gap is not as dramatic as it seems at first glance since people in the EU enjoy – according to official statistics – more leisure time than in the US (note, however, that the shadow economy in Europe is about twice as large in the US where it is estimated to be close to 10% of official value-added).

The creation of the Euro zone represented an ambitious project of EU deepening whose success is still uncertain, although one certainly will welcome the expansion of Euro bond markets, the rising share of the Euro in global currency reserves and the successful ECB policy which has achieved a low inflation rate and considerable credibility as well. Moreover, reduced real interest rates in Euroarea countries – except for Germany, the Netherlands and Austria which already had low interest rates prior to the start of the Euro and ECB – have translated into considerable capital gains.

The Lisbon Agenda of the EU which aims at making the EU the most competitive economy by 2010 has emphasized the goals of higher employment and higher growth in the Community; particularly by placing emphasis on the role of information and communication technology in a knowledge society. The initially envisaged top-down approach has not worked well so that the European Commission has decided to adjust the strategy after a mid-term review: National governments of member countries are expected to implement programmes and projects for higher growth and employment; the peer group pressure within the EU club has worked indeed, and all countries have adopted new measures along the lines of the Lisbon Agenda. While peer group pressure within the club is likely to be weaker than in the small group of the founding member countries – free riding and cheating is more difficult to monitor in a larger group than in a small group – it is remarkable that the EU indeed can still exploit this mechanism in a useful way. Here the EU has developed a political mechanism which also could be important in other integration clubs in the world economy. The supranational policy layer of the EU – the European Commission and the European Council – is, however, a rather unique institution which has not been adopted in any other integration club. The biggest success in economic terms has been the creation of the EU single market – surely a unique case of successful liberalization in the history of Europe.

Besides elements of success in EU integration, there is considerable criticism vis-à-vis Brussels: Excessive bureaucracy, the high expenditures on agriculture and unrealistic setting of goals (e.g., the Lisbon Agenda). Here and in other fields the Commission has shown a strong commitment to bringing long term economic challenges onto the political agenda of the EU and its member countries. At the beginning at the 21st century the new challenges in the field of energy policy and climate policy are crucial, and the European Council indeed made clear in early 2007 that the EU will try to be an international leader in this field. Another very serious long term policy field for all EU countries is the ageing of societies and the problems posed for social security systems and public finances in the long run. Here the European Commission has made a number of important suggestions which could help in achieving the twin goals of sustainable public finances and reforming social security.

The biggest problem the Community faces is the failure of the EU with respect to the constitution, which was defeated in two referenda in France and – massively – in the Netherlands. Those two countries obviously deserve special attention for economic and political reasons, and the whole topic of an EU constitution is a key challenge for the survival of the EU in the 21st century. The options for reviving the constitutional process might be limited and one should indeed study the contributions of major economists in this field which is at the interface between Economics and Political Science.

The papers presented in Frankfurt on the occasion of an EIIW conference organized by the European Institute for International Economic Relations (EIIW by its German acronym) and hosted by Dresdner Bank, cover a broad array of topics which aims to look back, take stock of achievements thus far, and examine future challenges. The key focus is on integration patterns, economic growth, financial market dynamics and the economic as well as political innovations which may be required in the future.

Richard Tilly takes a look at the historical dynamics of the EU and emphasizes that economic nationalism has been largely overcome by the Community. He argues that post-1945 European economic integration has been built on the principle of supra-national policy coordination ("Monnetism") as well as the integration of Germany as a pivot of trade and economic nationalism. This latter factor to some extent shaped the patterns of integration achieved and largely reflected the pressure of national interest groups on the respective governments. Tilly draws a line from the European Payments Union to the creation of the European Community for Steel and Coal. He emphasizes that the Federal

Republic of Germany – supported by the US – used the economic integration process in the ECSC and the EU to become an important political player in Europe again. This was the political achievement which motivated West Germany in 1957 to accept the costs of continued protectionism in some of the other member countries. Moreover, the rapid growth of the large German economy which gave sustained impetus to a growing trading network in Western Europe continued after 1957, thus rewarding the FRG economically as well. EU agricultural protectionism, by far the economically least defensible component of European integration, had, as Tilly points out, a long history dating back to the economic problems of the 1930s. Politically speaking, however, its acceptance was a *conditio sine qua non* for the Treaty of Rome. Defence of national interests, powerfully restrained by EU rules and the principle of "ever closer union" – that is the uneasy balance that went into the Treaty of Rome and which is still present. In Tilly's view, the long term challenge boils down to the question of the extent to which national policymakers are really willing to further transfer political power to the supranational level.

European integration is an important element of economic internationalization which is embedded in the broader development of economic globalization. Thomas Gries examines the present dynamics in the world economy and the role of the EU in various fields more closely. For decades the world economy was mono-centric with a periphery. With the successful economic and political unification of Europe, a second economic centre appeared on the world economic map. While in the last decades of the 20th century the EU had begun to become nearly as important as the U.S, in these same decades a third region began to appear in the Far East. Asia has since then become an even more significant part of the world economy. The emergence of a second (EU) and even a potentially third centre of economic activities placed in Asia – with China playing a major role – has challenged the notion of a clear hub of the world economy located in US. "Global Shift" signifies this fundamental change in the world map of economic activities, and the EU is facing considerable challenges in this respect. Europe could benefit considerably from global economic dynamics, yet whether the overall EU27 or the Euro area will be able to achieve sustained growth in the long run is an open question.

We now turn to the individual contributions which confront this basic challenge. The contribution of Lucas Papademos reviews the main factors explaining the growth performance of the euro area as a whole and of its member countries over the past decade using a growth accounting framework. In this context, it also discusses the observed differentials among euro area countries in terms of growth, inflation, competitiveness, and their underlying causes. The appropriate means to address these divergencies, and to put the euro area economy on a higher sustainable growth path, he argues, is a determined implementation of structural reforms as outlined in the revised and re-focused Lisbon strategy of the European Union.

Financial market integration has made considerable progress in the EU. The European Commission, however, has identified a rather long list of obstacles to be overcome for full integration. In the Euroarea the integration of financial markets has deepened considerably and there are major benefits to be realized in this context. The conduct of monetary policy in such a setting, however, requires certain adjustments. In this context Hans-Helmut Kotz presents a broad set of statistics and important insights into the working of financial markets and the conduct of monetary policy. Europe is characterized by still some significant heterogeneity of its financial markets. In providing differential mechanism of transmission of monetary policies, they complicate, to a degree, the task of the ECB. At the same time, this institutional variety reflects national compromises, in which these rules are deeply embedded. Hence, those features are most plausibly to change only slowly (or up to persist). Nonetheless, as the ECB has shown, monetary policy can, quite evidently, perform its functions remarkably successfully. Therefore, while further integration would make, no doubt, monetary policy less difficult, this is not the decisive clincher why financial markets should be integrated. A lexicographic ordering is very clear – monetary policy is, with regard to the dynamics behind change, of second order only (in terms of politics but of policies as well). In any case, the limits to integration (or arbitrage) are, with the ever stronger utilization of derivatives, however, shrinking rapidly.

As regards the Ansgar Belke und Daniel Gros examine the dynamics in the Euro area, discussing key aspects of monetary policy and structural reforms. There is a potential for instabilities in the Eurozone stemming from an insufficient interplay between monetary policy and reform effort on the one hand and the emergence of intra-Euro area divergences on the other hand. The authors discuss the effects of European Monetary Union (EMU) on structural reform and investigate this question with an examination of the relationship between fixed exchange rates and reform in two wider samples of countries. Belke and Gros also point out that risks for EMU are not only increasing as a result of longer-term disequilibria which have become evident in fiscal and monetary policy, but also because serious divergences are now appearing within the Euro area which threaten its long-term cohesiveness. The most manifest example of this threat comes from what promises to be a long-term divergence between Germany and Italy, which for the time being was offset by asynchronous developments of housing prices in both countries. Belke and Gros then construct a simple formal model in order to investigate whether the EMU is in danger from internal tensions which could lead to severe instabilities. The experience thus far suggests that some countries are continuously losing competitiveness. Is this a structural problem in the sense that these countries simply have problems in keeping inflation at a level that does not imply a continuing loss of competitiveness? Or is the persistence of higher inflation observed in some countries due to the internal dynamics of a monetary union in which any country starting with a higher inflation rate also has a lower real interest rate, thereby stimulating demand and thus potentially leading to even more inflation.

David Dickinson takes a closer look at financial markets and global integration. A puzzle in the literature on financial globalisation has been that the benefits from this process ` not appear to have been fully exploited. This paper identifies three types of financial integration and analyses the benefits of each in the context of financial market roles, to allow intertemporal substitution and risk-sharing and to provide corporate governance mechanisms. Whilst the effects of integration on the first two of these roles is most likely to be positive, the impact on corporate governance is less obvious and may well be negative, at least in the short run. The paper then goes on to consider the impact of financial integration when it is recognised that individual behaviour is not fully rational. When this is taken into consideration, it is clear that the benefits of integration will come through more slowly and there may be adverse consequences as a result of the transmission of irrationality from one market to another and the failure of market participants to exploit opportunities available. In the long-run, however, the benefits should be fully realised, particularly if foreign financial institutions are allowed to operate without restriction in domestic financial markets.

Michael Heise takes up the topic of financial market integration from a banker's perspective. Integration of financial markets in the Euro area is part and parcel of single market integration. Heise argues that sustained efforts towards financial integration are clearly worth the effort; the case for creating an integrated and open European financial market that can not only match the size, but also the efficiency of the US market is indeed strong. Encouragingly, considerable progress has been made in recent years. While the introduction of the euro has given integration of the wholesale European financial markets a huge fillip, integration of retail markets — which still have strong national features — is far from complete. One should continue to encourage the establishment of European enterprises and to do away with all forms of protectionism. Further steps towards integration and harmonization of the European supervisory systems have to be taken.

Freddy van den Spiegel emphasizes a broader European perspective of financial market integration and points out that the EU first started to encourage financial market integration in the late 1980s and that the top-down approach of harmonization has gradually been supported by bottom-up dynamics from the business community. Furthermore, the Financial Services Action Plan has transformed the regulatory framework of financial markets and institutions. This initiative has improved information across markets and countries. Furthermore, EU rules have brought about greater transparency and a more level playing field in many financial markets. The "Lamfalussy Process" has also been useful. Finally, however, Van den Spiegel argues that integration at the level of retail businesses is still rather weak and that there are considerable unnecessary costs imposed on cross-border banking activities.

A major driver of economic growth in OECD countries has been information and communication technology (ICT), which affects not only the dynamics of outsourcing but also financial markets and the adjustment patterns in the overall economy. Paul J.J. Welfens takes a closer look at outsourcing dynamics in Europe and in the context of economic globalization, emphasizing that ICT capital accumulation and enhanced digital networks contribute to sustained output expansion in Europe. The author also shows that EU countries vary in terms of ICT investment and ICT innovation patterns. It is shown that structural adjustment in EU countries is partly shaped by an increased role of technology-intensive and knowledge-intensive industries, and the ICT sector itself plays, of course, a major role in this context. Finally, the author highlights changes in the adjustment dynamics of a modified Dornbusch model, whose dynamics are influenced by ICT-induced shifts of the speed of learning – read: expectation formation – and the interest elasticity of the demand of money. The policy implications of the changing adjustment dynamics are explored.

Axel Pols puts the analytical and policy focus on the ICT sector. In the EU, modern Information and Communications Technology (ICT) has not led to productivity improvements and economic growth to the same extent as it has in the US, thus pointing to one reason for the comparatively weaker economic performance of the EU. The empirical evidence shows that the EU's challenge is to reap the benefits of both ICT production and ICT adoption, with significant intra-EU variations. According to Axel Pols, policymakers in Brussels and across Europe have acknowledged this situation and reacted with a number of policy initiatives at both the EU and national level. From an industry perspective, these initiatives are welcome. They need to be improved and properly implemented, however, in order to give appropriate attention to a number of important policy challenges, including for example convergence and digital rights management. Moreover, this article stresses the need to complement policy initiatives focusing on ICT with structural reform policies such as labour market and education reforms. Those reforms will typically benefit both ICT production and ICT adoption at the same time.

Three short contributions put the analytical focus on a country experience. France, the Netherlands and Greece all demonstrate important developments. France and the Netherlands are two founding member countries of the EU whose populations have disapproved of the EU constitution in a popular referendum; at the same time both countries illustrate alternative directions of economic modernization.

Alain Chappert analyses the links between growth, employment dynamics and structural reforms in France. This country has sometimes given the impression that structural reform was almost impossible, which has recently been the case with respect to the failure of the so-called "contrat nouvelles embouches/CNE". However, the reality is a little more complex than this seemingly simple story suggests. The calculations presented by the author indeed shed new light on this important French – and European – debate, and there are considerable arguments that successful reforms could be implemented in the long run.

Kees van Paridon presents his thoughts on Dutch economic and political dynamics. During the past 30 years a remarkable change has occurred regarding the impact of economic policy. With sometimes impressive budget cuts, deregulation, privatisation and many other measures, the role of the government in most Western countries seems to have been considerably reduced. It is not, however, only reduced, but also changed. Much more than in the past, the economic well-being of a country has become increasingly dependent on the adequate functioning and appropriate arrangements of the labour, social security and product markets. This article deals with the way subsequent Dutch governments have been able to accomplish these adjustments after 1983, considerably improving the performance of the Dutch economy. Several arguments regarding the (absence of) structural reforms are discussed and applied for the Dutch situation. The analysis reveals that even a government in a small, very open economy can decisively influence its pattern of economic development.

Greece has been a latecomer with respect to internal liberalization after EU accession, but one which achieved marked growth in the 1990s when new policies were adopted. Greece is also the first new member country to join the original 11 starter countries of the Euro area. The contribution by Daphne Nicolitsas – with a focus on Greece – suggests that certain product market reforms could contribute to decreasing the gap in per capita income between Greece and the EU-15. In particular, four types of reforms could strengthen productivity and increase the employment rate: (a) reducing administrative burdens, (b) enhancing competition, (c) providing incentives to increase firm size and (d) setting the preconditions for the diffusion of Information and Communication Technology (ICT). It is thought that these reforms will contribute to sustaining the robust rates of growth that have been observed in the last 10 years or so in the face of challenges such as the ongoing technological progress, globalization and workforce ageing.

EU Eastern enlargement is a major step for the Community but also brings enormous adjustments and changes in the accession countries, whose policymakers aim at a long term economic catching-up process. In the context of catching-up and monetary policy, the Balassa-Samuelson effect has traditionally been a major aspect of relative price and inflation dynamics. Empirical insights, however, have been missing, in particular into the process of adjustment with respect to output prices and the prices of assets and real capital – here with an emphasis on housing. Balázs Égert sheds new light on some of the key issues involved. He provides a comprehensive overview of the factors that potentially determine price levels and inflation rates in Central and Eastern European countries. His focus is also on structural factors relating to economic catching-up that may have an influence on market services, regulated prices, residential property prices and goods prices. Furthermore, the analysis sketches the role of cyclical and external factors. Finally, the author discusses the potential mismatch between price level convergence and inflation differentials in fast-growing economies.

From the panel discussion, "The Future of the EU: Economic and Political Challenges", we present three views. Andrew Hughes-Hallett takes a look at key strategic economic policy issues of the European Union. These are the three problems that have presented the European Union with its greatest challenges over the past thirty years: the constitutional issue, enlargement, and the problem of settling on a coherent economic policy framework. Christian Müller highlights why Switzerland has neither joined the EU nor the European Economic Area and argues that bilateral treaties have brought major economic benefits for Switzerland while allowing the country to pursue a rather autonomous policy. He argues that EU as well as Swiss citizens are concerned about adequate federalism and that progress with the EU constitution – including a successful referendum – will be crucial not only for the Union but also for improved cooperation between Switzerland and the Community. András Inotai takes a closer look at the future challenges of the European Union. He argues that there is a need for a European identity, a long term vision for the integration process and clear leadership. He also integrates some of the external forces affecting EU integration dynamics into his study. Finally, the author suggests key reforms related to economic globalization, a shifting internal balance in the enlarged Community and the issue of Euro area enlargement, all of which are of considerable significance to eastern European access countries.

For long term prosperity in Europe, innovation dynamics are crucial. In the Lisbon Agenda the European Council has emphasized how important innovation and growth should be for a prosperous and stable Community. The contribution by Horst Hanusch and Andreas Pyka shows that "Comprehensive Neo-Schumpeterian Economics" (CNSE) is an adequate theoretical approach accompanying the enforcement of the aims of the Lisbon Agenda. The CNSE approach as well as the Lisbon Agenda is based on the principle of innovation as a competitive driving force and the idea of future orientation penetrating all spheres of economics which can be summarized in three domains of economic life: industry, finance and public sector (the 3-pillars of CNSE). The CNSE approach is applied to an empirical study of 14 EU member countries using a three-step procedure. The country patterns of pillars are first identified in a cluster analysis. This gives a fine-grained picture of institutional and structural set-ups for the countries under study. In the second step, a performance analysis is exercised within the pillar clusters in order to rank the countries. Because of the similarities of countries within a cluster, such a comparative analysis can be done; for countries belonging to different clusters, this comparison would lead to misleading conclusions. Next, the cluster composition is sorted by the average growth rates of the economies as a first representation of macro-economic success. This allows a first correlation of pillar composition and growth performance. In the final step, pattern dynamics are investigated by a comparison of the two periods, 1996 to 2000 and 2001 to 2005.

Ageing and economic growth are interrelated, and both are crucial for long term systemic pension reform in Europe. Werner Roeger's contribution projects the macroeconomic and budgetary effects up to 2050 of retaining the current pay-as-you-go system of EU countries and analyses two alternative strategies for avoiding an increase in non-wage labour costs, namely debt financing and a partial move to a funded system. For both options, the model analyses the macroeconomic and budgetary consequences. Special emphasis is given to the question of whether a partial move to a funded system is a feasible option. At least during a transition period, budgetary costs appear to be rather large. In an alternative scenario, the author highlights the debt explosion associated with a move to debt financing of additional pension expenditures. The reader thereby finds some key insights into one of the most important economic challenges the EU faces.

An important challenge concerns the long term energy policy issues and problems of global warming, which are both crucial for Europe and the world economy. Raimund Bleischwitz and Katrin Fuhrmann discuss the EU emission trading system and the sustainability of its impact on European industry. The authors explain the mechanism of the EU Emission Trading System and highlight the political background of this system. Moreover, the authors focus on developments since the inception of the system in 2005 and analyse some key effects on energy-intensive industries. Finally, the authors take a closer look at a radical innovation scenario based on the case of a hydrogen economy. In this contribution the reader finds key aspects of the long term debate on the modernisation of the energy system and the overall economy, including options for CO_2 emission reduction policies.

The most important long term challenge for the EU concerns the adoption of a new European Constitution. Here Friedrich Schneider – with a long record of research in European integration in general and in EU constitutional issues in particular – presents his analysis, which provides many interesting insights based on Public Choice Analysis. His contribution (presented at the workshop in the form of a dinner speech) comes up with some crucial arguments and key considerations. In order to guarantee a successful functioning of the enlarged European Union, a European Constitution is proposed which contains six basic elements: the European Commission should be turned into a European government and the European legislation should consist of a two chamber system with full responsibility over all federal items. Three further key elements are the subsidiarity principle, federalism and the right of secession. A final important element is application of "direct democracy", which provides the possibility for European voters to actively participate in political decision-making and to thus restrain the power of political and interest group cartels.

This book is part of a wider EIIW project on EU financial and real economic dynamics, but it also reflects sustained analytical cooperation between the European Institute for International Economics and partner institutions in Belgium, France, the Netherlands, the UK and several EU accession countries (European Network on Economic Analysis, ENEA). In a bit more than a decade of EIIW research, the Institute has organized about 30 international workshops and conferences with a broad network of partners and has also supported outstanding research by young economists, several of whom received scientific recognition. The EIIW will continue to be an active interface between scholars in Economics, outstanding experts from the business community and leading policymakers in Europe and worldwide.

We greatly appreciate the organizational support by Edeltraut Friese and Christian Schröder (EIIW) and the editorial assistance provided by Michael Agner, Odense, Deniz Erdem and Zornitsa Kutlina (EIIW/Wuppertal).

Wuppertal and Brussels, Münster and Frankfurt, April 2007

Paul J.J. Welfens, Richard Tilly and Michael Heise

A. The European Union 50 Years On: Some Comments on Its Early History

Richard Tilly

A.1. Introduction

The approaching 50th anniversary of the EU promises to be an ambivalent event. For it is at once an occasion for rejoicing, and for worry. For rejoicing, because the EU has not only survived for 50 years, but also grown in size and economic weight; and survival and growth, after all, represent frequently used criteria of success in economic life. Worry is also justified due to a number of dispiriting features of the EU´s recent past:

- its slow economic growth,
- its high unemployment,
- the spread of popular fears about globalization, and
- weakened support of supra-national ties.

These features, to be sure, are not uniformly distributed across all 25 EU nation-states: they are surely most concentrated among the older larger members. Nevertheless, taking the EU as a whole, the idea of "ever closer union" – the guiding principle of the Treaty of Rome – sounds less apt these days than it once did. In part, perhaps, this follows from the fact that it collides with EU expansion, with what one might see as a newer principle of "ever more members" i.e. growth in membership.

Be that as it may, this paper makes no attempt to review the current malaise or its possible causes. Instead it returns to the Union´s beginnings, a little more than fifty years ago, and speculates in retrospect about why and how integration got started. Before turning to the first post-1945 steps, however, it offers a few reflections on that integration´s historical background. These are largely about economic nationalism, because I believe that that concept, properly understood, is an important key to understanding the history of post-1945 European integration.

A.2. Historical Background and Economic Nationalism

As an economic historian I have spent most of my professional career trying to understand two disciplines: economics and history; and in both of these disciplines, the phenomenon "economic nationalism" has had a place. In economics the concept of economic nationalism has always featured as a destructive historical force, as a source of market barriers, rather like a disease, in this case to be overcome by openness, and through international integration. In

history, in contrast, economic nationalism is and has been a fact of life that one cannot ignore. In history, national economies are usually the principle subject, rather than the utility-maximizing individuals of economics. This is not the place for deeper discussion of that interes
ting contrast.[1] The following comments merely attempt to suggest their relevance for understanding European economic integration.

The standard big picture story of the interwar period compares it with the pre-1914 era of globalization. It emphasizes disintegration of the world economy, the failure of international cooperation – and the rise of economic nationalism (LANDES: 1968, Ch. 6; LEWIS: 1957, Chs. XI and XII; PINDER: 1986, Pp. 377–411; POLLARD: 1981, Ch. 8). Artefacts of that era are well known: disharmony related to war reparations, U.S. demands for repayment of the war loans made to its allies, the collapse of the gold standard, competitive beggar-thy-neighbour currency devaluations, high tariffs, quantitative import restrictions, and so on.

There is a more sophisticated variant of the story. It confirms the failure of international cooperation, but sees that as a reflection of a changed political economy in many countries, the need to adjust to more democratic rules, broader suffrage rights, political parties and governments as coalitions reflecting compromises among competing socio-economic groups (EICHENGREEN, 1992). WWI caused governments to demand sacrifices from their citizens and thus made those governments, in effect, more dependent on a domestic political consensus. The World Economic Crisis of the 1930s reinforced this tendency. It also strengthened popular demands for government actions to reduce economic insecurity. This meant that insofar as international economic relations affected economic security of a nation's population, its government had the obligation to intervene and exercise influence on those relations. That is how one needs to see 20th-century economic nationalism. It represented a major shift in policy orientation – away from classical liberalism. In the 1930s, however, national governments intervened without paying much attention to the international repercussions of their policies. They reacted to interdependence by trying to reduce it, rather than by attempts at integration.

---

[1] It surely has to do with the historical links between economics, on the one hand, and the development of capitalism and classical liberalism, on the other. The Marxist historian, Eric HOBSBAWM, offers an extreme statement of the nexus: He describes the revival of economic nationalism in the late-19th century as a reflection of "the strange schizophrenia of the capitalist world economy" in which the global logic of capitalism conflicted with the nation states, for "such an economy recognized no frontiers, for it functioned best where nothing interfered with the free movement of the factors of production. Capitalism was thus not merely international in practice, but internationalist in theory. The ideal of its theorists was an international division of labour which ensured the maximum growth of the economy." HOBSBAWM (1987), Pp. 40-41. Until very recently, mainstream economics has retained its "broken relationship" to nation-states.

A.3. Post-1945 European Economic Integration

It will be useful to bear these reflections in mind as we turn to the question of post-1945 European economic integration. For that historical development rested in my opinion on three interrelated forces, one of which we may term "economic nationalism". Figure 1 below depicts this relationship.

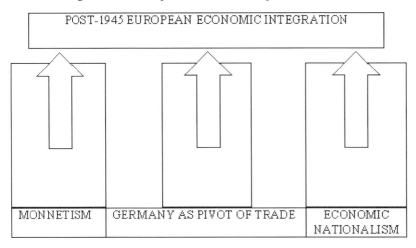

Fig. A1. The Three Pillars of Post-1945 European Economic Integration.

Moving from left to right, the pillars represent the role played by the idea of integration, the economic advantages it promised, and the political constraints it faced, respectively.

I begin with the role played by that "founding father" of European integration, Jean Monnet. Following the historian Gillingham, I call this "Monnetism" (GILLINGHAM, 2003, p. 18).

A.3.1. "Monnetism" and the European Coal and Steel Community

I use this term to suggest three formative forces Monnet embodied and which reflected his experience in the 1930s and 1940s. First, the emphasis on strong government vis-à-vis private enterprise and sectoral interests to maintain competition and stimulate, and even to coordinate investment. French *planification* offers an example of what Monnet had in mind. Second, the stress on the need for a supra-national authority to police, restrain and coordinate the interests and ambitions of the individual European nation-states. He was a "federalist" in the American sense, interested in centralizing power. Third, he had close ties to the U.S. political elite and thus represented the interest that the U.S. expressed in these years in a strong France leading the way to a strong and integrated Western Europe, an interest which grew step in step with the deepening of the Cold War divide.

Monnet´s predilection for strong government corresponded to the weakness of Western Europe´s political economies, which seemed far from ready for liberal market solutions; but what truly gave him leverage in post-war Europe was the combination of close ties to U.S. political leaders – as "the Frenchman Washington trusted most" – and his quasi-religious commitment to the goal of a European union guided by a strong supra-national authority. The former facilitated the provision of "start capital" for Western European reconstruction – Monnet played a major role in the funnelling of Marshall Plan aid to France – while the strength of his commitment to European integration inspired others to work for the same goal. This combination is what enabled Monnet to force the first step toward a reconciliation of French and German interests – the key to that European integration.

For when in May 1950 the French foreign minister, Robert Schuman, publicly announced what became known as the "Schuman Plan", he was presenting Monnet´s blueprint for the creation of "The European Coal and Steel Community" (ECSC), the first major step toward European integration. That this first step should focus on coal and steel is not surprising, given the strategic importance of coal and steel for Western European economies in the early post-war period. That was particularly true of France, whose industrial modernization Monnet believed to depend on assured access to German coal. West Germany, pulled on by its francophile Chancellor Adenauer, seized the chance for international acceptance, trading, in effect, the country´s heavy industrial advantages in exchange for its treatment as an equal power. At this point, the Korean War enhanced Cold War sentiments and made West Germany still more important as a building block of Western Europe, especially for the United States, which now pushed hard for West German rearmament, a feature which made that country´s integration in western Europe still more urgent and clearly added support to Monnet´s project (BERGHAHN, 1984; BERGHAHN, 1993).[2] Nevertheless, the negotiations which followed proved difficult. For one thing, Adenauer had to override resistance of the Steel Konzerne to divestiture of their coal mines (BÜHRER, 1986, Pp. 41ff).[3] For another, interest groups in Belgium became a stumbling block. Its high-cost coal producers demanded protection and steel producers objected to the Schuman Plan´s intended restrictions on its associations – restrictions which were actually aimed at German industrial organization (MILWARD, 1992, Pp. 46ff).[4] In the end, Monnet had to back down on some of his governance aims, and West Germany carried most of the burden of subsidizing Belgian coal. Even after the

---

[2] Berghahn´s biographical study of FRIEDRICH, O. (1993) offers valuable insights into the forces shaping post-1945 West German economic policies.

[3] Bührer´s study of the role of Ruhr steel interests and their organizations in the formation of the Coal and Steel Community is one of the most authoritative of its kind.

[4] Here MILWARD shows how subsidies to coal mining, especially in southern Belgium, became an important political issue in Belgium – and for European integration – by the early 1950s.

Treaty of Paris (April, 1951) had launched the ECSC, resistance to Monnet and the "High Authority" "intrusions" into national governance arrangements continued, but, as Alan Milward has pointed out, Belgian governments in fact found the ECSC to be convenient, both as a scapegoat to be blamed, and as a source of financial support, for its declining coal industry.

Monnetism no doubt helped get the economic integration of Western Europe moving. This did not follow from Monnet´s leadership as the first President of the ECSC High Authority, however, for he was notoriously ineffective. It derived from his ability to spread the idea of European economic union as a desirable and achievable political end. Ideas, after all, are important. As Keynes once said (at the end of The General Theory) (KEYNES, 1965, p. 383):

"The ideas of of economists and political philosophers, both when they are right and when they are wrong, are more powerful than is commonly understood. Indeed the world is ruled by little else. Practical men, who believe themselves to be quite exempt from any intellectual influences, are usually the slaves of some defunct economist."

Keynes, indeed, had been an early advocate of European integration centered on German heavy industry and may have supplied some of Monnet´s ideas.[5]

A.3.2. The Role of West German Trade

Monnetism alone, however, would have produced little more than an interesting chapter in the history of doctrine and ideology. In several respects it was the pivotal role of the German economy in Western Europe which proved decisive (MILWARD, 1992).[6] On the one hand, in spite of war- and postwar-related limits on its capacity, in the 1950s West Germany soon became the principal single supplier of capital goods to the rapidly growing Western European countries, thus reassuming the role it had played historically (MILWARD, 1992, Pp. 134ff). By 1956 the two categories "machinery" and "metals" alone – crude proxies for capital goods – accounted for nearly 40 percent of all West German exports, and a good share went to the smaller, more "open" Western European countries. In 1950–51 they took between one third and one half of all West Germany´s exports; and in the crucial 1954–57 period nearly three times the value exported to the bigger, more protectionist economies of France, Italy and the U.K. This gave German producers incentives to intensify their trading links, not only to the smaller economies but to the bigger ones as well. On the other hand, the West German economy grew in tandem and became an important market for Western Europe. Table One illustrates this point indirectly by comparing those countries´ exports to the Federal Republic in 1950 and 1957. In a sense, therefore, they must

---

[5]   MONNET, present at the Versailles Peace negotiations, will have been familiar with the "bombshell" that Keynes´ *Economic Consequences of the Peace (1919)* – an attack on the Versailles Peace Conference and an early plea for European economic integration – was to become.

[6]   MILWARD´s book contains the most convincing discussion of that role I have read.

have felt at this time the "need" for closer ties to the latter as much as that country did.

Table A1. Exports to Western Germany as Percent of Total Exports in 1950 and 1957.

Country	1950	1957
Austria	14.3	23.8
Belgium-Luxembourg	6.8	10.2
Denmark	17.4	19.5
France	7.8	10.9
Italy	5.9	14.0
Netherlands	20.9	18.5
Norway	11.3	13.3
Sweden	9.3	14.2
United Kingdom	2.0	3.2

Source: MILWARD, The European Rescue of the Nation-State, Ch. 4.

The already high relative share of intra-ECSC trade rose still more in the 1950s, but largely because of exports to the Federal Republic. Table 2 shows this development.

Table A2. Exports to ECSC Countries as Share of Total Exports and W. German Share (in %).

Countries	1951	1956	Difference	Due to W.Ger.
Belgium-Luxbg.	35.2	44.5	9.3	4.1
France	15.4	24.8	10.4	5.6
Italy	21.1	25.3	4.2	5.6
Netherlands	34.4	40.7	6.3	4.1

Source: MILWARD, The European Rescue of the Nation-State, Ch. 4.

Another way of making the same point is to show "relative export integration" as normalized by the world import share of the trade partners (LINDLAR/ HOLTFRERICH, 1999) and (Table 3).

These tables are a way of telling the story that strong economic and commercial ties centered on West Germany were a powerful force leading toward integration; but they also suggest that commercial union with the five other ECSC countries was not costless for the Federal Republic – whose ties with "outside" countries could weaken as a result (GIERSCH/PAQUE/SCHMIEDING, 1992, Pp. 166 ff).[7]

---

[7] These authors emphasize "the economic division of Western Europe" into EEC and EFTA countries which emerged after 1957.

Table A3. Relative Export Integration of West European Countries, Average of 1953–59*.

From/To	W.Ger.	France	Italy	Benelux	Austria/CH	Scandinav	U.K.
W.Ger.		1.5	1.8	2.4	4.1	2.5	0.4
France	1.6		1.3	1.5	1.9	0.8	0.6
Italy	2.2	1.2		0.7	4.2	0.9	0.7
Belg-Lux	1.8	2.0	0.8	6.3	1.4	1.4	0.6
NL	2.9	1.0	0.8	5.0	1.3	1.9	1.1
Austria	4.0	0.6	5.9	0.8	3.0	0.7	0.3
CH	2.8	1.4	2.8	1.2	3.4	1.3	0.6
Denmark	2.9	0.5	1.5	0.6	0.8	3.3	3.2
Norway	2.0	0.8	0.9	1.1	0.7	4.3	2.0
Sweden	2.2	1.0	1.1	1.6	0.8	5.7	1.8

*The value 1 = importing country´s share in world imports.
Source: LINDLAR/HOLTFRERICH, "Germany´s Export Boom", p. 169.

Both Monnetism and West German trade developed within the context of broader attempts, promoted especially by the U.S., to build a liberal but cooperative international economy. Currency convertibility was to replace exchange controls, relatively free multilateral trade to reduce bilateralism and high trade barriers. Bretton Woods, the International Monetary Fund and G.A.T.T. followed from these efforts. To soften the adjustment of Europe´s war-ridden economies to a more liberal regime, regionally limited measures were undertaken, e.g., reduction of import quotas under the auspices of the Marshall Plan and the O.E.E.C., or partial restoration of convertibility via the European Payments Union, or, as has been already mentioned, a kind of sectoral union, the ECSC.[8] By some criteria these measures proved highly successful. The volume of trade governed by bilateral trading agreements, for example, declined relative to overall European trade (BUCHHEIM, 1990). Liberalization went furthest and fastest in West Germany, where Erhard pushed through several unilateral tariff reductions and from whence as early as 1955 the demand for restoration of full convertibility emanated (GILLINGHAM, 2003, Pp. 41–2; GIERSCH/PAQUE/SCHMIEDING, 1992, Pp. 108–14). Even before then, to be sure, European political leaders had begun to discuss the possibility of yet another regional measure – a customs union.

---

[8] This may be an appropriate place to mention that in the discussion of this paper, several conference participants felt that U.S. influence on postwar European integration was greater than the paper suggested. Following Alan Milward´s interpretation – which emphasized European origins – it focused on European negotiations. When Milward was writing, "endogenous" European forces had been largely neglected.

A.3.3. Birth of the European Economic Community

Nevertheless, the road from these "successes" and from ECSC to the EEC led through difficult political terrain, ran into detours; and in 1952 its end was not in sight. For one thing, leaders of European integration such as Monnet or a Belgian kindred soul, Paul-Henri Spaak, placed supra-national political and administrative organization, rather than economic interests, in the center of their efforts. Both, interestingly, initially enjoyed strong support from U.S. political leaders and diplomats; but both began to lose influence over European integration as American influence in Europe receded (MILWARD, 1992, Pp. 319–27).[9] Their plan to extend the bureaucratic ECSC "model" to other sectors failed to come to grip with economic interests; and Monnet's project for a "European Defence Community" (EDC), launched in 1952, failed to win support in his own country, France, for whose leadership it had been designed, partly because in the meantime the West German government, under U.S. pressure, decided to rearm. Before the failure of EDC had become definitive, a Dutch initiative to convert the supra-national political accompaniment to the EDC, the "European Political Community" into a customs union had been added – which became known as the "Beyen Plan", bearing the name of the Dutch politician who had authored it. Political security, it was argued, depended less upon a Western Europe's military build-up than on its prosperity. The initial details are less significant than the Dutch insistence, maintained to the end of negotiations, that any treaty had to stipulate "from the outset automatic and irrevocable procedures for its completion."(MILWARD, 1992, P. 189).

The customs union project built upon both Monnetism and the trade network dominated by West Germany, but necessarily had to take account of a much greater number and variety of special interests in the individual countries than the ECSC. Oversimplifying somewhat, these can be summarized as follows (MILWARD, 1992, Pp. 197ff). France sought a way out of the high protectionism of its recent past and, given the need to accept U.S. policy of West German rehabilitation, access to that country's markets. West Germany, in turn, sought equal political status as a nation-state and secure access to West European markets, especially the relatively large French and Italian ones. The Benelux countries together feared a bilateral Franco-German commercial and economic agreement which left them out, but, in addition, the Netherlands sought protected access to the German market while Belgium sought a harmonization of European economic and social policies which would protect its relatively high-wage levels. Italy, finally, hoped for insured access to West German markets as well as labor mobility within the community, which would help it absorb its underemployed labour. France raised the greatest difficulties. These turned on its demand for higher common tariffs than most of the other countries, especially Germany, thought desirable, and its demand for upward "harmonization" of wages and social security costs. Even after the Messina meeting of the ECSC foreign ministers in

---

[9]   SPAAK, however, had shown awareness of the importance of economic interests to successful integration through his association with the formation of Benelux.

May, 1955, had signalled readiness to reach an agreement by empowering the high-level "Spaak Committee" to prepare a concrete proposal, France held out. According to MILWARD, by late-1956 French leaders were ready to agree, but "needed" nominal concessions by the others on several issues to get the agreement through parliament. The boom years of 1954–56 had revealed that France was internationally more competitive; and also that economic growth in West Germany pushed up wages and social benefits faster than had been thought back in 1954. French tactics paid off. The Treaty of Rome conceded almost everything they had demanded: the commitment to harmonization of welfare levels, flexibility on the timetable for tariff reductions, the relative weakness of the supra-national authority (mainly the European Commission), the agreement to guarantee long-term purchases of French agricultural products over the first stage of tariff harmonization and until a common agricultural policy had been achieved, and the inclusion of French overseas territories in the common market. In return, France had accepted the irreversibility of union. The result was economic union, and thus went beyond the customs union originally planned. The collective winners were the European nation-states, who had discovered in the common market an institutional means capable of helping their populations to the prosperity and security they felt no longer able to provide as individual countries.

The most obvious consequence of the EEC was a shift in trade away from EFTA countries. The Tables 4 and 5 offer one measure of this change. As expected, West German export shares changed least, though EFTA countries experienced a sharp reduction in the share of their exports to that country after EEC rules had gone into effect. France, somewhat surprisingly, attracted the greatest shifts in export shares of EEC countries.

Table A4. Relative Export Integration of West European Countries, Average of 1967–73*.

From/To	W. Ger.	France	Italy	Benelux	Austria/CH	Scandinavia	U.K.
W.Ger.		1.9	1.7	2.2	3.1	1.5	0.6
France	2.1		2.3	2.1	1.8	0.6	0.7
Italy	2.3	2.2		1.1	2.1	0.6	0.6
Belg-Lux	2.5	3,2	1.0	4.7	0.9	0.8	0.6
NL	3.4	1.7	1.1	3.8	0.9	1.0	1.1
Austria	2.5	0.4	2.7	0.6	5.4	1.7	1.0
CH	1.6	1.4	1.9	0.6	4.8	1.4	1.1
Denmark	1.4	0.5	0.9	0.5	1.3	6.4	2.9
Norway	1.5	0.5	0.6	0.7	0.6	6.3	2.7
Sweden	1.2	0.8	0.7	1.0	1.4	8.2	2.0

*The value 1 = importing country´s share in world imports.
Source: LINDLAR/HOLTFRERICH, "Germany´s Export Boom", p. 169.

Table A5. Change in Relative Interdependence* of Selected EEC Countries, 1953/59–1967/73.

Country	EEC Countries	EFTA Countries
West Germany, Exports	+0.1	-0.9
West Ger., Imports**	+1.8	-5.4
France, Exports	+2.1	-0.4
France, Imports	+3.3	-1.1
Italy, Exports	+1.5	-2.5
Italy, Imports	+1.4	-5.6

*Based on Share of World Trade Norm = 1.0. Source: as in Table 3.
**Based on share of other countries´ exports to these EEC countries/their world imp. share.

The Treaty of Rome focused almost exclusively on the manufacturing sector, thus leaving many questions open: agriculture, services, regional disparities and policies, and social policies, just to mention the most important. In retrospect, this left two negative legacies: first, the high costs of agricultural subsidies (universally condemned by economists); and a series of political crises concerning the degree of centralization of EEC decision-making power. Walter Hallstein, the EC´s first president and a Monnet disciple, saw the Treaty omissions as an opportunity to centralize power. In Gillingham´s interpretation, Hallstein succeeded in only one area: making regional policy an important part of the EC´s work (GILLINGHAM, 2003, Pp. 55ff). In other areas his success consisted mainly of more bureaucracy and eventually led to severe conflict with the member states, whose direct power concentrated in the Council of Ministers. In 1965, finally, France (under De Gaulle) led a "revolt" of the Council – marked by the famous "policy of empty chairs" – which reasserted its powers and eventually (in 1967) led to Hallstein´s resignation (GILLINGHAM, 2003). [10]

A.3.4. The Legacy of Agricultural Protectionism

Agriculture, though left out of the Treaty of Rome, played a major role in the EU´s early history. It is therefore fitting to conclude this paper with some comments on that role. In all of the EEC countries agriculture had become a policy problem area early in the 20th century. Agricultural incomes had lagged behind those of manufacturing since the nineteenth century but by the early twentieth century, overseas competition had enhanced the problem and governments – increasingly based on popular consensus – felt obligated to soften the effects of market forces through tariff protection and subsidies (MILWARD, 1992, Ch. 5; TILLY, 1999).[11] The economic crisis of the 1930s in part reflected the maladjustments and world wide overproduction of agriculture but it also

---

[10] It was indirectly related to the EEC program "Common Agricultural Policy" (CAP) and that program´s prospective EC budget.

[11] TILLY´s paper points out that only in Britain, whose agricultural sector was unusually small and landownership highly concentrated, did a significant movement toward agrarian protectionism fail to take place before 1914.

magnified the difficulties and motivated further government intervention. World War II temporarily transformed the problem into one of extreme scarcity; but in the post-war period, the growing prosperity of the EEC countries was marked, once again, by the problem of lagging agricultural incomes and government attempts to overcome it with subsidies, price supports and other means – all at the expense of the consumer.

These developments, nota bene, characterized the post-war but pre-EEC era. European governments everywhere felt impelled to maintain and even strengthen support of agriculture. These policies promoted an unprecedented increase in productivity and output, probably a higher rate of increase in incomes than would have come about without them. Even so, they failed to maintain income parity with manufacturing employment and the decline of agriculture accelerated after 1950. They did succeed in maintaining prices for comparable products (especially grains) which were significantly higher than those on world markets. That represented not only a redistribution of income away from European consumers but also the beginnings of the problem of agricultural surpluses – the problem which led the way to the Common Agricultural Policy (CAP).

Its story is as follows. Individual countries all subsidized and protected their agricultural sectors; none could alone cope with the surpluses they tended to generate MILWARD, 1992).[12] EU-historiography has tended to single out France as the driving force behind CAP. Early on, French policy showed the extent to which it was willing to make economic sacrifices for its agriculture, for example, in the subsidies extended to exports (between 1954 and 1958 from 15–16 to 45 % of the realized export prices for wheat) (MILWARD, 1992, P. 272). France, however, would have been satisfied with the concession made to her intra-EEC exports in the Treaty of Rome. The other signatories were not. What the Dutch realized at the time was that the EEC timetable for tariff reduction could not apply to agriculture, since it was insulated from market forces by non-tariff barriers; and to create the envisaged common market in agriculture would mean a merging of the six national policies. In particular, the Netherlands insisted on an agreement leading to common policies and common prices, which would permit individual countries to maintain lower prices for their own domestic markets, but with a commitment to attain common prices within a 10-year period, eventually agreed as the "prices which should not be fixed below the German level, which was generally the highest." (MILWARD, 1992, P. 313). The Netherlands, in addition, pushed for the CAP because as part of the EEC it would protect its important agricultural exports from Danish competition. Agreements were reached in 1960 and 1964 which then set the timetable for the beginning of the CAP in 1967. This became then far more than the sum of its six parts, living on beyond and with more political power at the European level than it had ever had in the member countries, mainly because agricultural political blocs in the late 1950s still held decisive blocking minorities in France, the Netherlands, even in West Germany,

---

[12] This was partly because those policies included investment modernization subsidies which increased productivity, but though this facilitated the shrinkage of agriculture its chief effect was more output.

whose assent was essential to launch the EEC project. As MILWARD writes: "The Common Agricultural Policy has lumbered on like some clumsy prehistoric mastodon, incapable of evolution into the present world where the political influence of agriculture on parliamentary systems is small indeed, an awesome reminder of the strength which integration could add to the rescue of the nation-state." (MILWARD, 1992, P. 317).

A.4. Conclusion

That quote offers a welcome opportunity to end the paper. For in a sense, the CAP concluded the first phase of EEC development. It was a phase marked by an historically unprecedented step toward European economic integration. I have argued that it was carried forward by three historical forces: Monnetism, the economic advantages of an intra-European trade network based on West Germany, and what I have called "economic nationalism", which determined the specific form of integration achieved. This had to do with the need of the six national governments to accommodate domestic interest groups and a related determination to limit the powers delegated to the supra-national authority. Since then, there have been a few further such steps, more powers have been delegated (EMS, SEA, ECB); but the same basic need of those governments seems to be still with us. It remains to be seen whether and to what extent – and why – member governments will decide that satisfying that national need requires further delegation of powers to the supra-national authority. Should such delegation take place, and a U.S. of Europe emerge, it would be the first time in history that an important new national state had ever come into existence by peaceful means! That sounds improbable, perhaps utopian, but it is a possibility with considerable appeal, one worth keeping in mind.

References

BERGHAHN, V. (1985), Unternehmer und Politik in der Bundesrepublik, Frankfurt/Main.
BERGHAHN, V.; FRIEDRICH, P. J. (1993), Otto A. Friedrich, ein politischer Unternehmer, Frankfurt/Main, New York.
BUCHHEIM, C. (1990), Die Wiedereingliederung Westdeutschlands in die Weltwirtschaft 1945–58, Munich.
BÜHRER, W. (1986), Ruhrstahl und Europa: die Wirtschaftsvereinigung Eisen- und Stahlindustrie und die Anfänge der europäischen Integration, Munich.
EICHENGREEN, B. (1992), Golden Fetters. The Gold Standard and the Great Depression, 1919–1939, New York.
GIERSCH, H.; PAQUÉ, K.-H.; SCHMIEDING, H. (1992), The Fading Miracle. Four Decades of Market Economy in Germany, Cambridge (Eng.).
GILLINGHAM, J. (2003), European Integration 1950–2003: Superstate or New Market Economy, Cambridge.

HOBSBAWM, E. (1987), The Age of Empire. London: Weidenfeld and Nicolson, P. 40–41.

KEYNES, J. M. (1919), The Economic Consequences of the Peace, London, MacMillan.

KEYNES, J. M. (1965), The General Theory, New York, etc: Harcourt,Brace, 1965.

LANDES, D. (1968), The Unbound Prometheus, Cambridge (Mass.).

LEWIS, W. A. (1957), Economic Survey 1919–39, London.

LINDLAR, L.; HOLTFRERICH, C. (1999), Germany´s Export Boom at Fifty – An Enduring Success Story?, in: Brady, J., Crawford, B. and Wiliarty, S. E. (Eds.): "The Postwar Transformation of Germany. Democracy, Prosperity and Nationhood", Ann Arbor, University of Michigan Press.

MILWARD, A. (1992), The European Rescue of the Nation-State, London, Methuen.

POLLARD, S. (1981), Peaceful Conquest. The Industrialization of Europe 1760–1970, Oxford.

PINDER, J. (1986), Europa in der Weltwirtschaft, in: Cipolla, C. and Borchardt, K. (Eds.), Europäische Wirtschaftsgeschichte, Vol. 5, Stuttgart, N.Y.

TILLY, R. (1999), Globalisierung in historischer Perspektive: Lehren aus der Geschichte?, *Kölner Vorträge zur Sozial- und Wirtschaftsgeschichte*, Nr. 41, Cologne, 1999.

B. Global Shift – The European Union, the United States, and the Emergence of China

Thomas Gries

B.1. Introduction

In the 1960s the world economy had only one clear center. The US economy was the largest (in absolute terms) and richest (in per capita terms) economy and dominated the world economy. The economic world was mono-centric with a periphery. In the present context an economic center is an economically integrated region of the world, which can substantially affect others as well as the world economy.

With the successful economic and political unification of Europe a second economic center appeared on the world economic map. In the second half of the 20th century European integration and the ongoing process of enlargement of the EU transformed a number of medium sized (but each small compared to the US economy) economies to a second center of the world economy.

While in the last decades of 20th century the EU started to become almost equally important, a third region began to appear in the far east of the world map. Starting with Japan in the 70s and 80s, followed by the emerging of China, Asia has become a significant part of the world economy. The emergence of a second (EU) and even a potentially third center of economic activities placed in Asia has challenged the notion of a clear hub of the world economy located in US.

Global Shift stands for a fundamental change in the world map of economic activities. As described by DICKEN (2003) there are many dimensions of the Global Shift which might be worthwhile to look at for a better understanding of the development of the world economy.[1] The discussion of this contribution is focusing on the last 50 years and four major aspects:

- Despite a good performance of the US economy the United States will be of decreasing importance for the world economy. While the US used to be the only economic center, within only a few decades the US economy will be just one -and not even the largest- of several centers. Even if the US had a substantial population growth and over-performed with respect to economic success, there are other even larger fully integrated world regions which are potentially outperforming the US economy.
- Despite a lower performance of individual countries in Europe, the process of European unification and enlargement will make the EU one of the global economic centers, both in real and monetary terms.

---

[1] Recently BERGSTEN (2005) collected a number of contributions to discuss the effects of global shift on the US foreign and economic policy.

- A significant number of medium sized emerging market economies, especially in Asia and Eastern Europe add up to make a substantial contribution to world GDP, trade and financial activities. Other less developed countries become less important.
- The emergence of China and India as super-large countries in terms of population will potentially lead to an additional, i.e. at least a third fully, integrated economic center in the world economy.

Since a comprehensive discussion of the large number of medium sized economies mentioned above is beyond the scope of this paper, we would like to put a light on some very long term stylized aggregate developments most likely leading from a mono-centric to a poly-centric world with at least three or even more economic centers. Increasingly this contribution is focusing on the emergence of China because China is the one of the two Giants exhibiting the most rapid development.[2] A fast development of such a giant will change the map substantially and could shift the economic hub of the world. Hence, *Global Shift* is a term that clearly understates one of the most important changes in economic history.

So far a center of the world economy is identified by the pure absolute size of economic activities. Why is it interesting to look at these huge integrated economic regions? Because in some respect size matters. There are several dimensions where size plays a role for economic activities. Large economies:

- can realize scale economies in the domestic market and advantages for large scale production processes.
- can function as a gravity center.[3]
- have bargaining power in trade- currency, exchange rate and environmental policy and can define and enforce legal, technical and economic norms. [4]
- can provide a diversified technical infrastructure for high end research.
- dominate world business cycles.
- can realize seigniorage if the currency is a substantial fraction of international reserves

Apart from these pure economic advantages, the political advantages are obvious. Absolute economic size will eventually provide the resources for the ability to enforce political concepts and advantages. Looking at the pure absolute economic size is not enough. Per capita income and welfare is a second important dimension for identifying economic centers. High per capita income often is closely linked with technical capabilities and high endowments of human capital. Hence absolute and to a certain extend also per capita values are investigated. However, this paper is not going to focus on the effects of having these

[2] For a discussion of the general appearance of large emerging market economies. see BOYER/TRUMAN (2005).
[3] For contributions in this context see e.g. TINBERGEN (1962), PÖYHÖHEN (1963) LINNEMANN (1966), ANDERSON (1979), or more recently OGULEDO/MACPHEE (1994) and BAYOUMI/EICHENGREEN (1997).
[4] See e.g. SMITH (1999) or GLICK/ROSE (2001).

economically dominating centers. The intention of the paper is just to show that these centers are presently shifting rapidly from the western side of the global map to the eastern side.

The discussion of Global Shift and the emergence of additional centers in the world economy will follow 3 steps.

1. A precondition for becoming a center of the world economy is a sufficiently large population (chapter 2 *Population*). Population size defines the potential economic size.
2. Only if large population is combined with economic success can population size transform into economic size. However, the combination of population size and increasing economic success can very rapidly turn a rather small economy in an economic giant (chapter 3 *Economic activities*).
3. In order to be relevant for the rest of the world an economic center must be integrated in the world economy. Only a sufficient integration in trade and financial markets and hence mutual dependences will make a large economy relevant for the rest of the world. (chapter 4 *International trade and economic integration* and chapter 5 *International finance and economic integration*)

In this discussion we focus on China, as China is a very likely candidate for the emergence of a third huge world economic center located in Asia.[5] Even if Japan is a big single economy the population size of Japan is too small to develop the potential of such a global center comparable with the EU the US or the potential of China. We will basically look at the stylized developments and will not focus on analyzing reasons or implications. However, some interpretations of the stylized facts implicitly use long term neoclassical ideas for explanation.

B.2. Population

Population is the driving force for potentials. Population is the fundamental determinant of the potential size of a country or global region. Only a region with a substantial population size has the potential for developing into a global center, high population is a necessary, although not a sufficient condition for a region to become a center. However, before we may have a look at the economic activities we will look at the development of the population as the fundamental driving force.

---

[5]   See LARDY (2005).

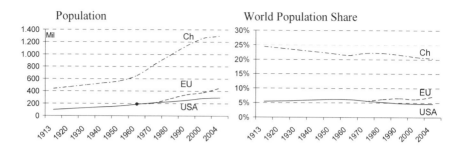

Fig. B1.a. Population. [6]

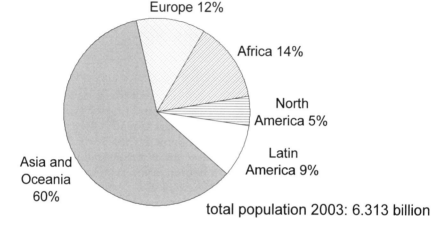

Source: TODARO/SMITH (2006), S. 267.

Fig. B1.b. Population Share of the World in 2003.

As we can see from figure 1a and b the development of the population has led to only a minor shift of the world population map. While at the beginning of the 20th century Western Europe and North America together still hosted more than 25% of world population the picture at the end of the century has changed. A hundred years later the population share of Europe and North America is about 17%. Moreover, Asia and Oceania with a share of about 60% are clearly hosting most of the world population. Moreover, this distribution of world population weights illustrates the momentum of the driving forces of the economic shift and eventually also the shift of political power.

6   Source: Population of the hole world for the period 1950-2004: U.S. Census Bureau; Population of China, India, Japan, US and EU countries for the period 1950-2004; Penn World Table, Population historical statistical data for the years 1870, 1913: AGNUS MADDISON (2006), The World Economy, Development Centre Studies, OECD Publishing. Data from 1913 until 1950 were generated by extrapolation.

Pure population size does not necessarily lead to economic success or size. However, once the take off process is successful and the countries start to develop, population size rapidly transforms into economic size.[7] The large (in terms of population), but poor countries now begin to develop successfully and turn there potentials into real economic values of gigantic size.

B.3. Economic Activities

Economic success is needed to transform potentials into relevant economic activities and finally into a notable center. Looking at the development of per capita income as the most general indicator for economic success, we can still see the traditional picture of the world. The US is the most successful economy followed by Japan and the EU (represented by Germany) (figure 2a). There has not been a dramatic shift in terms of per capita income.

Real GDP per Capita, international $ (PPP)   Human Development Index (HDI)

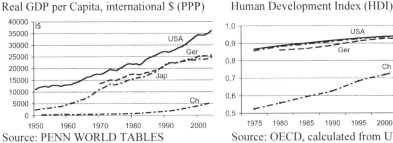

Source: PENN WORLD TABLES   Source: OECD, calculated from UN
                                              Statistics, extrapolation between 1995
                                              and 2003.

Fig. B2.a. Per Capita HDI and GDP.

The development of the Human Development Index (HDI) gives a similar result (see figure 2a). Even if China could catch up quite dramatically, there remains a large gap to the US and Europe.

---

[7] If this process takes place or not is beyond the scope of the paper, the path leading to population traps or to economic miracles seems to lie close together.

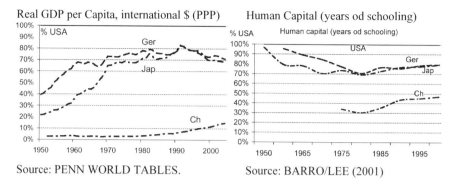

Source: PENN WORLD TABLES.   Source: BARRO/LEE (2001)

Fig. B2.b. Per Capita GDP and Human Capital Relative to the US.

This picture also does not change if the most important determinants of success are considered. Many theoretical and empirical studies like BARRO/LEE (1994), AGHION/HOWITT (1998), TEMPLE (1999), DURLAUF/QUAH (1998) and GROSSMAN/HALPMAN (1994) or BARRO/SALA I MARTIN (2004) tried to identify the main sources of growth. They have shown that capital accumulation, the level of technology, and openness in terms of trade and FDI often have a positive effect on economic growth. FUJITA/KRUGMAN (2004) also attach great importance to geographic factors. However, in most contributions, educational attainment proved to be a major source of growth, convergence and catching up (see also BENHABIB/SPIEGEL, (1994) and DE LA FUENTE, (2002)). Hence, economic success is bound to people and the abilities of the people. If the potentials of countries with large populations can be used (via accumulation of human capital) for economic development, highly populated countries have the potential for a high level of economic activity. While the people in the US or in Europe historically enjoy a good education, and hence are endowed with high productive human capital, the people in most developing economies do not have comparable human capital (figure 2b). However, while the endowments in Europe and Japan are stagnating, China is catching up.

Further, by making use of their high human capital endowment, the most successful economies are also the most innovative economies. Figure 3 illustrates that there are three innovative centers in world, the US, the EU and Japan. Global technological progress is generated in these technological cores. High productivity and strong innovative power are strong determinants of success at the higher end of the income ladder.

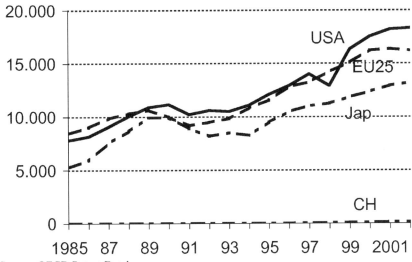

Source: OECD Patent Database.

Fig. B3. Number of Patents, Innovations.

In contrast, a lack of productivity leads to economies with large populations living under rather poor conditions. Population size did not transform into economic size or even a global economic center. Until the last decade of the 20th century the two countries with the largest population, China and India could not develop their potentials. They were both living under rather poor conditions. At the beginning of the 90s, China could not reach Germany's level of total economic activity even if the population was 20 times as high.

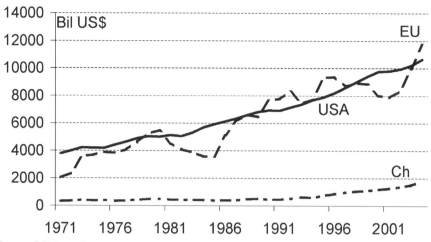

Source: PENN WORLD TABLES, base year 2000.

Fig. B4.a. Absolute Real GDP Current Exchange Rates.

While the population was huge, absolute GDP in these countries was comparatively small. This picture changes slightly if China's rapid growth process during the 90s is considered. Figure 4a shows the development of real GDP in current exchange rates. According to this figure China is still far away from the two other almost equally large centers.

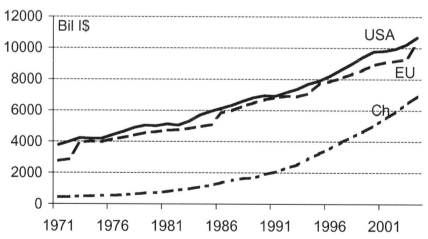

Source: PENN WORLD TABLES, base year 2000.

Fig. B4.b. Absolute GDP PPP (Purchasing Power Parity) Exchange Rates.

However, measured in purchasing power parity (PPP) values, the economic take off of China changed this traditional picture within less than a decade. China had passed all G7 countries except the US at the turn of the century. Looking at the absolute level of economic activities, we can now identify three global regions (see figure 4b). Two of almost equal size and one close behind. Taking total GDP, the EU is presently of almost equal size to the US followed by China. With the emergence of China a third huge center is apparent. Note Japan is the economic global center in Asia. Japan's population size is not sufficient. With the rapid growth of China, the potential of China's large population is transforming China into a global economic center. This is even more obvious, if the fact is taken into account that most of the development in China has taken place in the coastal belt hosting a population of about the size of the US. The rapid absolute growth of the Chinese economy is driven by the large population multiplier. A small increase in per capita productivity driven by technological catching up is multiplying into huge absolute growth rates. Even if the per capita income will remain low and grow slowly, there is no doubt, that China and potentially India will be one of the global economic centers in Asia much more important than Japan during the last 2 decades. In Europe, more than in the US, the awareness of this shift process is limited. The waking up of a giant in the east is not sufficiently related to their own situation and position. The huge distance between China and Europe and the still relatively small per capita income seems to lead to an underestimation of the importance of Asia and China in global economic relations.

B.4. International Trade and Economic Integration

Pure economic size does not make a global economic center. Integration in the global economy is another precondition for being a center of importance to the world. If an economic unit is isolated from the rest of the world like the COMECON, it exists, but does not matter for the world economy. A global economic center must be integrated significantly in the economic activities of the rest of the world. There must be a significant contribution to world trade and financial streams in order to be relevant for the global economy. Looking at the structure of world trade, international transactions traditionally were dominated by the EU countries, the US and Japan.

34   Thomas Gries

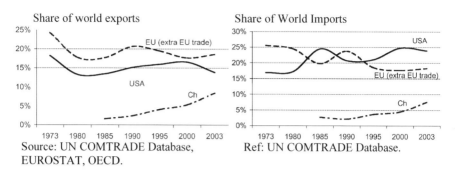

Share of world exports

Source: UN COMTRADE Database,
EUROSTAT, OECD.

Share of World Imports

Ref: UN COMTRADE Database.

Fig. B5. Global Trade Shares.

Recently this picture changed substantially. Apart from a significant number of medium sized catching up countries the emergence of China in international markets is the most important process during the last two decades.

Since the beginning of the "Open Door Policy" at the end of the 70s three waves of international integration have been introduced to the Chinese economy. TUAN/NG (2004) identifies three waves of integration policy. These waves are characterized by preferential policies that were introduced sequentially to different regions.

The first wave was defined by the introduction of Special Economic Zones (SEZs). All these SEZ were located in the coastal belt. The geographic advantages of the coast (BAO et al., 2002) and preferential policy (DEMURGER et al., 2002) were used to reduce international transaction costs for exports and international investors. (WEI, X., 2000).Overseas Chinese were attracted as international investors. These inflowing FDI were transformed into a successful growth process in the coastal regions. "Export and FDI have been causing the Chinese economy to grow faster, while at the same time the highly uneven distribution of trade and FDI has caused regional disparity to increase greatly." (FUJITA/HU, 2001, p.31, see also CHEN/FLEISHER, 1996).

Since 1992 the experiment of international integration facilitating deregulation has been extended to more locations. This second wave of integration was still highly controlled, both in terms of instruments and affected locations. This period of broader but still limited liberalization led to the tremendous success-story of the coastal belt in the 90s. FDI and the ability to export seem to be a major determinant of successful development.

With the adjustment to WTO accession the third wave of international integration has begun. Accession to the WTO has required a change in economic rules in a large number of regulatory areas. Preferential policies had to be abolished. Hence, in contrast to the first and second wave, accession to the WTO does not systematically prefer certain locations. WTO accession may push convergence of economic rules across regions. Broad liberalization (via WTO rules), together with the "Go West Policy", is expected to trigger a broad wave of development in the formerly less privileged regions (see e.g. XIAOJUAN, 2001).

China's fast growth is driven by and is leading to a rapid penetration of world markets.

Hence, within less than a decade China became one of the major exporting and importing countries, passing even Japan. With a share of almost 10% of todays world exports China does not yet reach the importance of the EU with about 20% (see figure 5). However, China is not too far from the 14% of US export share. Absolute GDP (measured in PPP) trade shares indicate the rapid emergence of a third global center. Rapid penetration of world markets by Chinese activities affects the other economies in two ways. First, a new huge competitor has emerged on the markets for raw materials, energy and financial resources. Second, Chinese firms are competing in markets for industrial products. Even more significant than smaller countries like Korea, Taiwan or Thailand, in an increasing number of markets China is much more than a marginal supplier.

In figure 6 we can see how fast a potentially large country like China can penetrate markets. Within less than five years China doubled its share in EU trade and became, with almost 13% of EU imports, as important as the US. In the US the development of the Chinese import share is almost identical. In the US only Canada and the EU have a higher import share (figure 6). If this development goes on for some years, China will clearly be the most important trading partner for both the US and the EU.

EU 25 Import Shares (extra trade)   US Import Shares

Source: EUROSTAT, EU-15, and since   Ref.: UN COMTRADE Database
2003 EU-25.

Fig. B6. Import Share of Major Trading Partners for the US and the EU.

These potentials in absolute terms can also be indicated by the net trade flows of merchandise trade between the global regions. As we can see in figure 7a gross merchandise trade is already higher between Asia and the US and Asia and the EU than merchandise trade between the US and the EU. Asia is the region with a huge trade surplus both, towards the US and the EU (figure 7b). The emergence of Asian's large economies has a clear impact on international trade relations.

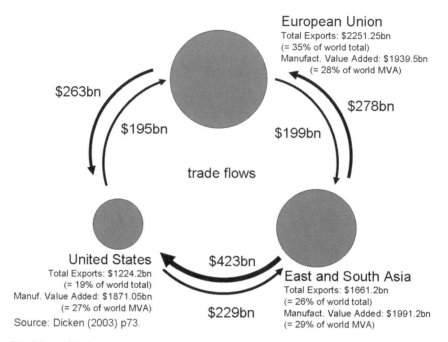

Fig. B7.a. Global Gross Trade Flows Between Major Regions.

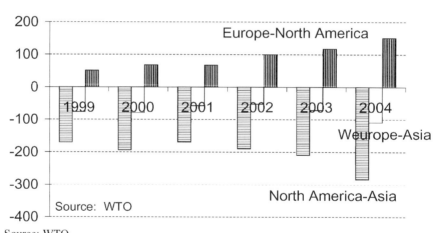

Source: WTO.

Fig. B7.b. Global Net Trade Flows Between Major Regions.

The internationalization of the value chain has led to a global production process. An important reason for higher growth rates in merchandise trade than in world GDP growth is global sourcing of the value chain. Figuratively speaking the intermediates of a final product have circulated the globe several times before they reach the final consumer. Furthermore, decomposing the value chain has led to a highly specialized allocation of each component of the value chain according to the comparative advantages of locations. A substantial part of the development strategy of China was to take advantage of this process. Integration policy and producing according to comparative advantages has led to industrial clustering in several coastal regions (WEN, 2003). Even if this rapid industrialization is still limited to a small number of regions, the successful development of these provinces has now led to a shift in comparative advantages. China has gained competitiveness in industries, which were traditionally reserved for highly developed economies like the US or the EU.

The importance of China being a major competitor in world goods markets can be analyzed by looking at the development of the Revealed Comparative Advantages (RCA)[8] as indicators for international competitiveness in major industries. RCAs are defined as a country's share of world exports of a certain industry divided by its share of total world exports. Hence a country has comparative advantages if an industry exhibits a higher share in the countries exports than in world exports.

Figures 8a, b and c gives the RCA-values for major industries and indicates the current pattern of comparative advantages as well as the development of the specialization pattern. In figure 8 industries are classified according to the groups of UN Standard International Trade Classification (SITC). The RCA definition used is the relative gross export performance. Values larger than 1 indicate a relative comparative advantage.

The profile of comparative advantages shows that there are still industries where China is not able to compete with high income competitors, that is where China still has no revealed comparative advantages. Going through the merchandise trade we will start with SITC group 5, *Chemicals.* We can see from figure 8a that even if China has advantages in *Pyrotechnical Products* (SITC 57) there are still disadvantages over the whole range of *Chemicals* (SITC 5).

---

[8] We use the measure of relative export performance by country and industry, defined as a country's share of world exports of a good divided by its share of total world exports (BALASSA, 1965). The index for country i good j is $RCA_{ij} = (X_{ij}/X_{wj})/(X_{it}/X_{wt})$ where X_{ab} is exports by country a (w=world) of good b (t=total for all goods).

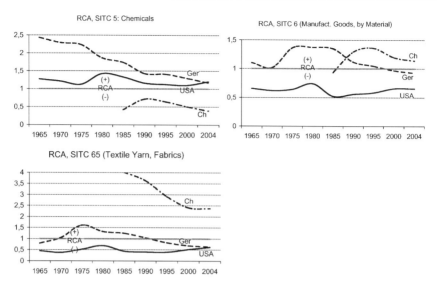

Fig. B8.a. RCA Values for SITC group 5 and 6.

This picture changes dramatically if we look at the SITC group 6, *Manufactured Goods by material*. SITC 65, *Textile Yarn, Fabrics* etc. gives a good example for a typical industry in this product group. For the total group China developed advantages during the 90s, while the US and even recently Germany revealed disadvantages. However, group 6 stands for an industry where firms of catching-up countries successfully compete and displace traditional suppliers located in higher income countries. As group 6 on average does not stand for high technology human capital intensive goods, the observed picture can be expected.

A similar pattern of comparative advantages holds for SITC group 8, *Commodities*. On average products of this group are also not characterized as high technology or human capital intensive goods (figure 8b). Typical subgroups are *Travel Good, Handbags* etc (SITC 83) or *Clothing* (SITC 84). As can be seen from figure 8b, China's comparative advantages are extremely high in these industries. For a catching-up economy this pattern is not unexpected. However, China is already moving out of this pattern of specialization. As for SITC 65, RCA values for SITC 83 and SITC 84 are still very high, but already clearly decreasing. Moreover, in the more advanced SITC group 86[9], *Scientific & Control instruments, Photogr. Goods, Clocks* etc, China is rapidly developing towards a position of comparative advantage.

---

[9]   In this group are still low technology and labor intensive industry-subgroups.

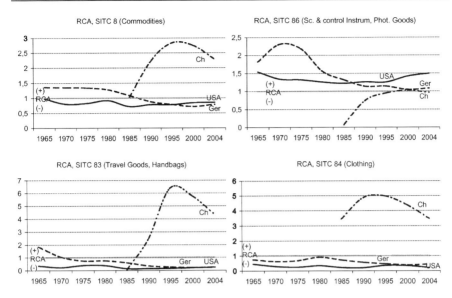

Fig. B8.b. RCA Values for SITC group 8.

The change in specialization becomes even more apparent if SITC group 7, *Machinery and Transport* is taken into account. Unlike SITC groups 6 and 8, SITC 7 is regarded as the major domain of comparative advantages for the high income countries. Even if the original disadvantages of China's less developed machinery industry during the first phase of the open door policy and international market integration is apparent from figure 8c, the catching-up of competitiveness in this industry (SITC 7) is dramatic. While in SITC 72, Electrical *machinery, apparatus etc.* China passed Germany in 90s and the US at the beginning of this decade, China reached Germany and the US just recently at the SITC group 71, *Machinery other than electrical*. The only Industry on the two digit level where China could not catch up substantially is transport equipment (SITC 73). Although the pictures show an increasing competitiveness in these aggregate industry groups there is a number of subgroups where China is still not competitive.

However, gaining comparative advantages in industries which are less typical for low income economies is an indicator of the rapid technological development. While the major volume of trade is still in the expected industries, the speed of advance is dramatic. This holds even more as China is a potentially large competitor. Today only a part, namely the cost belt with about 300 mil inhabitants, is involved in export activities. If China's development process can be extended to the inland and western regions, China will massively penetrate industry sectors traditionally dominated by high income economies like the US, Japan or the EU.

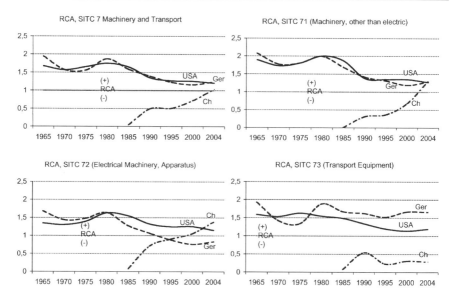

Fig. B8.c. RCA Values for SITC group 7.

B.5. International Finance and Economic Integration

In the previous section we looked at the gross and net trade flows in order to investigate total international trading activities. In this section we would like to look at international financial streams. Both the gross and net streams are considered in order to identify the development of financial interconnection of the large centers. The overall picture of financial streams is similar to the picture for trade.

Looking at the different types of financial streams, FDI is of particular interest, as it indicates the direct allocations of real economic firm activities over the globe. Traditionally FDI was executed almost only between the high income countries in Europe and North America. During the last 15 years China has become one of the major receivers of FDI (figure 9). Even if the stock of foreign investments has not yet reached the level of the EU or US, China is a major destination of FDI.

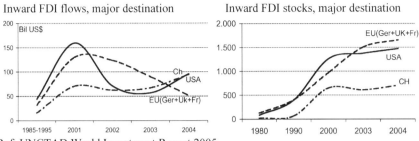

Ref: UNCTAD World Investment Report 2005.

Fig. B9. Major destination of FDI.

Looking at today's general financial streams the importance of Asia and China becomes even more obvious if the net streams are considered. While the current account of the EU is almost balanced (figure 10), the current account of the US shows a huge deficit and Asia exhibits a huge surplus. Even more, the huge deficit of the US economy is not a short term phenomenon.[10] For decades and with increasing speed the US accumulated an international debtor position which was mainly financed by Asian countries, first by Japan and recently by China. There seems to be a global imbalance in which Asia with an increasing share of China is financing the US deficit. With this development, Europe is replaced as a major financial resource for the US by Japan and in particular by China. China is becoming one of the major creditors of the US. Hence, Asia is today already the most important source of financial resources.

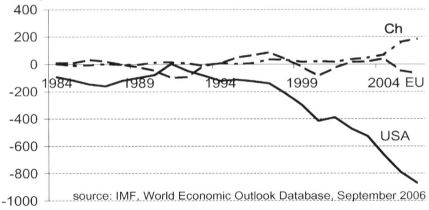

Source: IMF, World Economic Outlook Database, September 2006.

Fig. B10. Net financial streams: Current account.

However, the importance of Asia in international trade and finance is not reflected yet in the use of Asian currencies as international reserve currency (figure 11). The decomposition of present allocated official foreign reserves shows

---

[10] For a recent discussion see MUSSA (2005).

that the US$ still counts for 2/3 of international reserves. The Euro has a share of 25% and all other currencies together add up to not even 10%. The only issue in international economic relations where China has not yet appeared as major center is as supplier of an international reserve currency (figure 11).

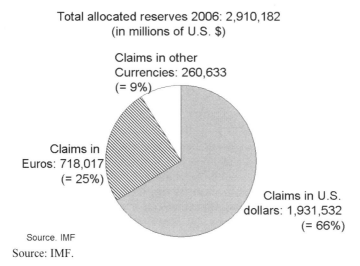

Source: IMF.

Fig. B11. Decomposition of Allocated Official Foreign Reserves.

B.6. Summary and Conclusions

The economic world was mono-centric with a periphery. With the successful economic and political unification of Europe a second economic center appeared on the world economic map. While in the last decades of 20th century the EU started to become almost equally important, a third region began to appear in the far east of the world map. Asia has become a significant part of the world economy. The emergence of a second (EU) and even a potentially third center of economic activities placed in Asia has challenged the notion of a clear hub of the world economy located in US. *Global Shift* stands for this fundamental change in the world map of economic activities.

The discussion of Global Shift is following 3 steps.

1. A sufficiently large population is a precondition for becoming a center of the world economy. Population size defines the potential economic size of a country. During the last 50 years the distribution of world population with respect to the USA, the EU (growing through enlargement) and China did not change dramatically.
2. Only if a large population is combined with economic success can population size transform into economic size. Once a huge population starts to become economically successful, a rather small economy is very rapidly turned in an

economic giant. This process is currently happening in China. Even if average per capita income is still small, the significant growth of per capita income multiplies into a large absolute size. Measured in PPP China is already the third largest integrated economic region in the world.

3. In order to be relevant for the rest of the world an economic center must be integrated in the world economy. China's speed of integration into the world economy is even more rapid than GDP growth. Today, China's trade share is the third largest in the world and in the EU and the US China is one of the three most important trading partners. China's comparative advantages are already moving towards more sophisticated, human capital intensive products. With increasing and already large current account surpluses during the last decade, China has also become one of the major world financial sources financing the huge US deficit.

The described fast development of China has already made China the third potential center of the world economy. An ongoing development of such a giant will change the map substantially. *Global Shift* means the shifting of the economic hub of the world.

References

AGHION, P.; HOWITT, P. (1998), Capital Accumulation and Innovation as Complementary Factors in Long-Run Growth, *Journal of Economic Growth*, 3, pp.111–130.

ANDERSON, J.E. (1979), A Theoretical Foundation for the Gravity Equation, *American Economic Review* 69, 106–116.

BALASSA, BELA. (1965), Trade Liberalization and 'Revealed' Comparative Advantage, Manchester School 33, pp. 99–123.

BAO, S.; CHANG, G.H.; SACHS, J.D.; WOO, W.T. (2002), Geographic Factors and China's Regional Development under Market Reforms, *China Economic Review* 13, pp. 89–111.

BAYOUMI, T.; EICHENGREEN, B. (1997), Is Regionalism Simply a Diversion? Evidence from the Evolution of the EC and EFTA, in T. Ito and A.O. Krueger, Eds., Regionalism versus Multilateral Trade Arrangement, University of Chicago Press.

BARRO, R.; LEE, J. (1994), Sources of economic growth, Carnegie-Rochester Conference Series on Public Policy, v40, pp. 1–46.

BARRO, R.J., LEE, J-W. (2001), International Data on Educational Attainment – Updates and Implications, Oxford Economic Papers, 3, pp.541–563.pdf.

BARRO, J., SALA-I-MARTIN, X. (2004), Economic Growth, 2ed, MIT Press.

BENHABIB J.; SPIEGEL, M.M. (1994), The Role of Human Capital in Economic Development. Evidence from Aggregate Cross-country Data, *Journal of Monetary Economics*, v.34, iss. 2, pp. 143–173.

BERGSTEN, C.F., (2005), The United States and the World Economy: Foreign Economic Policy for the Next Decade, Institute for International Economics, 28, 2005.

BOYER, J.E., TRUMAN, E.M. (2005), The United States and the Large Emerging-Market Economies: Competitors or Partners?, in: Bergsten, C.F., (2005), The United States and the World Economy: Foreign Economic Policy for the Next Decade, Institute for International Economics, 28, 2005.

CHEN, J.; FLEISHER, B.M. (1996), Regional Income Inequality and Economic Growth in China, *Journal of Comparative Economics,* Vol. 22, pp. 141–164.

DE LA FUENTE, A. (2002), On the Sources of Convergence: a Close Look at the Spanish Regions, *European Economic Review*, 46, pp. 569–599.

DEMURGER, S. (2001), Infrastructure Development and Economic Growth – An explanation for Regional Disparities in China?, *Journal of Comparative Economics* 29, pp. 95–117.

DICKEN, P (2003), Global Shift: reshaping the global economic map in the 21st century, The Guilford Press.

DURLAUF, S.; QUAH, D. (1998) The New Empirics of Economic Growth, *NBER Working Papers* 6422, National Bureau of Economic Research, Inc.

FUJITA, M.; HU, D. (2001), Regional Disparity in China 1985–1994 – The effects of Globalization and Economic Liberalization, *The Annals of Regional Science* 35, pp. 3–37.

FUJITA, M., KRUGMAN, P. (2004), The New Economic Geography – Past, Present And the Future, *Papers in Regional Science*, 83, pp.139–164.

GLICK, R.;. ROSE, A.K (2001), Does the Currency Union Affects Trade? The Time Series Evidence. National Bureau of Economic research, NBER Working Paper No. 8396,

GROSSMANN, G.M.; HELPMAN, E. (1991), Innovation and Growth in the Global Economy, Cambridge (USA), MIT Press

LARDY, N.R. (2005) China The Great New Economic Challenge?, in Bergsten, C.F., (2005), The United States and the World Economy: Foreign Economic Policy for the Next Decade, Institute for International Economics, 28, 2005.

LINNEMANN, H. (1966), An Econometric Study of International Trade Flows, Amsterdam: North-Holland.

MUSSA, M. (2005), Sustaining Growth while Reducing External Imbalance, in: Bergsten, C.F., (2005), The United States and the World Economy: Foreign Economic Policy for the Next Decade, Institute for International Economics, 28, 2005.

OGULEDO, V.I.; MACPHEE, C.R. (1994), Gravity Models: A Reformulation and an Application to Discriminatory Trade Arrangements. Applied Economics, 26(2), pp.107–20.

PENN WORLD TABLE; HESTON A.; SUMMERS R.; ATEN B.; PENN WORLD TABLE VERSION 6.2, Center for International Comparisons of Production, Income and Prices at the University of Pennsylvania, September 2006.

PÖYHÖNEN, P. (1963), A Tentative Model for the Volume of Trade Between Countries, *Weltwirtschaftliches Achive* 90, pp. 93–100.

SMITH, P.J. (1999), Are Weak Patent Rights a Barrier to U.S. Exports?, *Journal of International Economics,* 48(1), pp. 151–77.

TEMPLE, J. (1999), A Positive Effect of Human Capital on Growth, Economics Letters, 65, pp.131–134.

TINBERGEN, J. (1962), Shaping the World Economy – Suggestions for an International Economic Policy, The Twentieth Century Fund.

TODARO, M.; SMITH, C. (2006), Economic Development, 9ed, Pearsson.

TUAN, C.; NG, L. F.Y. (2004), Manufacturing agglomeration as incentives to Asian FDI in China after WTO, *Journal of Asian Econmics*, Vol. 15, pp. 673–693.

WEN, M. (2003), Relocation and Agglomeration of Chinese Industry, *Journal of Development Economics* 73, pp. 329–347.

WEI, X. (2000), Acquisition of Technological Capability through Special Economic Zones, Industry and Innovation, Volume 7, No. 2, pp. 199–221.

XIAOJUAN, J. (2001), The New Regional Patterns of FDI Inflow, OECD China Conference, 11–12 October 2001, Xi'an, China, pp.1–18.

C. Growth and Competitiveness in Euro Area Economies

Lucas Papademos*

C.1. Introduction

> *"Two nations who traffic with each other become reciprocally dependent; for if one has an interest in buying, the other has an interest in selling; and thus their union is founded on mutual necessities."*
>
> Montesquieu, 1748

What was true in the eightteenth century is still relevant today, and especially in the European Union (EU), where the economic links between the EU Member States can be expected to strengthen further as a result of the increasing integration of all markets in the Union. For the member countries of European Economic and Monetary Union[1], the single European currency implies a particular, unique and irreversible connection and interdependencies between their economies implied by their.

Trade, investment and financial transactions between countries foster growth and prosperity. Clearly, however, the overall economic performance of the national economies of euro area countries will in the future also depend crucially on the evolution of the economic environment within which they operate. This environment has been undergoing rapid and profound changes as a result of technological advances and the globalisation of markets. Moreover, in Europe, the gradual completion of the internal market, the enlargement of the European Union and the introduction of the European single currency have further intensified competition; these factors have also fundamentally influenced monetary and financial conditions and imposed constraints on national economic policies.

Technological advances, market globalisation and European integration are transforming the environment within which the economies of the EU countries function. This new environment not only offers opportunities, but also poses challenges for the euro area economy and the individual Member States. This

---

[*] Lucas Papademos is the Vice-President of the European Central Bank. This article is based on a keynote speech delivered at the General Assembly of the German-Hellenic Chamber of Industry and Commerce in Athens on 22 September 2005.

[1] On 1 January 2007, Slovenia joined euro area, so that the single currency area now comprises 13 member countries. Since the analysis in this article and the relevant data mostly relate to period until 2006, the references to the euro area concern the euro area of 12 EU Member States, i.e. excluding Slovenia.

observation is not new. To say that the rapidly evolving economic environment provides opportunities and poses challenges may sound somewhat clichéd. But this does not make it less true. Indeed, it is more valid than ever. Therefore, the growth and prosperity of the European economies depend on their ability to effectively address the challenges and take advantage of the opportunities. This requires that conditions and institutions be established internally that foster growth and adopt policies and market practices that allow European economies to successfully compete in the global market.

How can the internal sources and forces of growth be strengthened, in the euro area and the individual Member States? And how can, simultaneously, their international competitiveness be enhanced? More specifically: What are the necessary conditions and key policies that can effectively foster stronger sustainable growth in the euro area in the increasingly competitive global environment? The answers to these questions have aspects that pertain to the euro area as a whole and to the individual Member States. These aspects, of course, overlap and are interconnected, as the euro area economies are highly integrated and function under certain constraints imposed by the single currency. These constraints seem not to be fully understood or sufficiently appreciated by all market participants, social partners and economic authorities in some euro area countries.

In discussing the two broad issues of growth and competitiveness in the euro area, a number of specific questions concerning the economic performance of the countries of the European monetary union need to be addressed:

- Have the economies of the 12 euro area countries converged sufficiently to thrive under the European single monetary policy, which is geared towards the maintenance of price stability in the euro area as a whole?
- Are the observed divergences in growth, inflation and competitiveness across the euro area unusually large? Are they a cause for concern?
- What are the main determinants of the relative growth performance of individual Member States?
- Are these divergences likely to be temporary or are they likely to persist?
- What can be done to reduce these divergences in the direction of price stability and higher sustainable growth?

C.2. Conditions and Policies for Higher Euro Area Growth

It is no secret that the growth performance of the euro area has not been satisfactory and has repeatedly proved to be below expectations. From the mid-1990s in particular the annual growth rate in the 12 euro area countries averaged 2.1% (1995–2004). During the six-year period following the introduction of the euro (1999–2004), real GDP in the euro area grew on average by slightly less, namely 1.9%. More recently, the recovery in economic activity following the trough reached in 2001 has been moderate and hesitant at times. This disappointing performance reflects the combined influence of several factors and shocks that, on the one hand, have adversely affected aggregate demand and, on the other hand, have constrained the expansion of aggregate supply.

Taking a long-term perspective, the determinants of potential output define an economy's trend growth performance. Various studies have estimated that potential growth in the euro area is within a range of 2% to 2.5%. And some suggest that the lower limit of the estimated range of potential growth rates is a more realistic figure and more representative of present reality, given demographic trends and prevailing market structures and practices, and under the presumption of unchanged economic policies.

What are the fundamental causes of this unsatisfactory low trend growth in the euro area? The answers can be found by looking at the factors that determine potential or long-term economic growth: demographic trends, productivity growth and the degree of labour utilisation in the economy. The latter concept – the extent to which the labour potentially available in the economy is effectively utilised – depends in turn on the share of the working age population that enters the labour force (the labour force participation rate), the percentage of the labour force that is employed and the average number of hours worked by each person.

Europe's long-term growth performance has been constrained by: *(1)* the low rate of increase of its population and the ageing of its society; *(2)* the deceleration of labour productivity growth since the mid-1990s, despite the fact that the level of labour productivity per hour is still very high in a number of countries; and *(3)* a low degree of labour utilisation, despite some improvement in the utilisation of labour in recent years. Without wanting to go into detail, a few basic facts will help illustrate why growth in Europe is so subdued, especially when compared with the United States (see also ECB, 2004). Over the past decade, Europe's population has been growing at a rate of just 0.3% per year; the United States' population has been growing at a rate of 1.3%. Productivity growth in the United States is between 0.5 and 1 percentage point higher than on this side of the Atlantic, depending on the sector of the economy and the period chosen. Only around 70% of Europeans of working age participate in the labour market – compared with over 80% of Americans. Unemployment in the euro area is almost 9%, three percentage points higher than in the United States. Moreover, those who are employed work fewer hours. Europeans work, on average, around 300 hours less per year than Americans.

These facts reflect the influence of a variety of factors affecting the demand for and supply of labour and the ability of the European economy to further increase the efficiency with which goods and services are produced. It has been argued by a number of economists (e.g. BLANCHARD, 2004) that some of these facts simply reflect a preference on the part of Europeans for more leisure time, rather than seeking additional income – in other words, that Europeans rather enjoy *la dolce vita*, while people in other societies, influenced by different work ethics and/or a more materialistic attitude to life, work harder. That may be an appealing explanation, but reality is more complex. For example, the incentives for companies to hire staff and for people to take up work are also influenced by tax and benefit policies. More generally, productivity growth and the functioning of labour markets are affected by a host of sometimes interacting factors –

institutions, regulations, traditions, preferences – which can be influenced, or even radically changed, by appropriate policies and reforms that can help to boost productivity growth and employment creation.

Supply-side reforms are undoubtedly of crucial importance for enhancing the long-term growth prospects and the competitiveness of the European economy, as will be elaborated further below. What should be stressed in parallel is that the maintenance of a stable macroeconomic environment is also essential. This is a necessary condition for sustained growth. The European single monetary policy has as its primary objective the preservation of price stability in the euro area. To achieve this objective, the ECB aims to maintain inflation at a rate close to but below 2% over the medium term for the euro area as a whole. During the six years (1999–2004) following the introduction of the euro, annual inflation in the euro area averaged 2%. So the ECB has succeeded in maintaining a high degree of price stability in an unfavourable environment characterised by many adverse inflationary shocks, including the continuous and substantial increase in oil prices over the last two years. More importantly, the credibility of the stability-oriented monetary policy has anchored long-term inflation expectations at levels consistent with price stability and this has helped to maintain bond yields at historically low levels. Indeed, the very low level of interest rates across the entire maturity spectrum has provided considerable and continuous support to economic growth over the past few years.

C.3. Output Growth Differentials in the Euro Area Countries

Naturally, the aggregate data for the euro area disguise certain differences that exist between individual euro area countries as regards their growth and inflation performance. Much has been said and written about the sluggish growth in the large economies at the core of Europe, contrasting them with the "tiger economies" on the fringes. However, a careful look at the data shows that the differences in growth rates are not exceptionally large and have not increased in recent years. The dispersion of annual real GDP growth rates across euro area countries since the introduction of the euro is no greater than before. It is more or less the same as it was 30 years ago – around 2 percentage points on average. Indeed, contrary to some perceptions, the dispersion of annual growth rates has declined somewhat. It is also interesting to note that growth differentials across the euro area countries do not seem to be significantly different to those observed across regions or states within the United States.

C. Growth and Competitiveness in Euro Area Economies   51

Dispersion of real GDP growth rates (annual averages) within the euro und US*
(Unweighted standard deviation in percentage points)

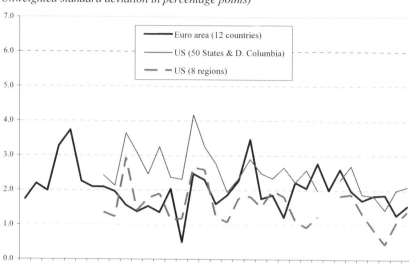

* There is a statistical break in the US regional data in 1998. In the US states and regions, the data refer to Gross State Product (GSP). The 8 regions by BEA covering the whole country.
Sources: European Commission (AMECO database and US Bureau of economic Analysis (BEA).

Fig. C1. Growth Dispersion within the Euro area and the United States.

Of course, real GDP growth has a cyclical and a trend component, and recent analyses produced at the ECB show that the cyclical component has had a relatively limited influence on growth dispersion since the early 1990s (see BENALAL et al., 2006). This indicates that the observed dispersion can be largely explained by differences in trend output growth, which are relatively long-lasting – hence the fairly stable profile of growth dispersion in the last few years. These differences in trend output growth rates might reflect structural factors, including reforms implemented in recent years.

Differences in trend growth caused by structural factors may, at least in part, reflect demographic trends or normal and healthy catching-up processes in some countries. Such growth differentials should not be a cause for concern. Catching-up processes seem to have been underway in Spain, Greece and Ireland for several years, and output growth in these countries has persistently exceeded the euro area average. In terms of cumulated GDP per capita, the cumulative rate of growth of these countries since 1999 has been much higher than the euro area average.

However, growth differentials may indeed be a cause for concern if they reflect rigidities and inefficiencies in product and labour markets resulting from insufficient structural reforms, or if they are caused by losses in competitiveness in some countries. Since the mid-1990s Germany and Italy have persistently been growing at rates below the average observed across the rest of the euro area, which might reflect some long-lasting structural problems in these countries. In Germany, a rigid labour market with low employment growth has prevented a pick-up in domestic demand. In the case of Italy, a strong deterioration in its price and non-price competitiveness in the context of increasing competition from the new EU Member States and from non-EU countries (especially from China), may have dampened real activity, particularly real exports. This observation leads over to the next issue: the divergence across euro area countries in terms of competitiveness.

C.4. Competitiveness of the Euro Area Countries

Competitiveness developments are of crucial importance to the real economy, and to real export performance in particular. Price competitiveness is a somewhat complex concept to define because it involves several elements. First of all, nominal exchange rate developments play a key role in determining the price of euro area exports abroad, expressed in foreign currencies. But the nominal exchange rate is not, of course, the only determinant of price competitiveness. The fact that there is a single euro exchange rate for all euro area countries is the very essence of a monetary union. This means that a period of exchange rate depreciation or appreciation represents a common shock for all euro area countries. However, countries do not all cope with this shock in the same way.

During a period of euro appreciation, euro area exporters try to lower their prices in euro terms. But the individual euro area countries have not all been equally successful in lowering their export prices in euro terms and thus maintaining their export performance. For instance, whereas German exporters have managed to significantly reduce their export prices in euro – thus staying competitive and maintaining or even expanding their market shares – Italian and Greek exporters have been less successful in reducing their export prices, partly as a result of domestic cost pressures. The differences in the evolution of domestic costs per unit produced has been a key factor helping German real exports to rise far more rapidly than Greek and Italian real exports over this period (see also ECB, 2006). Thus, some countries have been unable to respond in a competitive manner to external challenges, partly as a result of product and labour market rigidities that have prevented swift and adequate adjustments to relative prices and wages.

Needless to say, the international competitiveness of an economy is a broader concept than price competitiveness. It depends on the range and quality of the goods and services a country can produce and export and, correspondingly, on the way markets, institutions and policies support and promote the other aspects of the competitiveness of the country's products. Nevertheless, the export performance of the euro area countries does depend on price competitiveness, which can be substantially affected by the cumulative differences in inflation and cost developments across euro area countries over a period of time, as has been the case during the six years since the launch of the euro.

C.5. Inflation and Cost Differentials Across the Euro Area Countries

Looking at the evolution of inflation rates across euro area countries over time, we observe a remarkable convergence since the early 1990s. Specifically, inflation dispersion across the 12 euro area countries declined substantially, by around 5%, between the early 1990s and 1998. Since the start of Economic and Monetary Union in 1999, inflation differentials have remained fairly stable. A measure of dispersion, the unweighted standard deviation of inflation differentials from the average euro area inflation rate has oscillated around 1 percentage point.[2] Moreover, inflation dispersion within the euro area since the launch of the single currency is no greater than in the United States.[3] It is also no greater than among regions within individual euro area countries, such as Germany and Spain.[4]

What is distinctive about the euro area is the fact that these differences in inflation rates are more persistent than elsewhere. Persistence in this context means that in some euro area countries inflation is systematically either above or below the average inflation rate in the euro area as a whole. In six out of the twelve euro area countries, such persistence in differentials could be observed since 1999. Specifically, inflation has, over this period, persistently been above the euro area average in Ireland, Spain, Portugal and Greece and below the average in Germany and Austria.

---

[2] During the ten years before the introduction of the single currency, this measure of dispersion stood at around 2.9 percentage points.

[3] Compared with the differences in inflation rates among the 14 US metropolitan statistical areas typically used to measure such phenomena.

[4] When comparing inflation dispersion within the euro area with that within individual countries, we need to be cautious for various reasons. For instance, the methods used to calculate these differences or the definition of the number and size of the geographical regions within a Member State may differ.

Dispersion of annual inflation across euro area countries, the 14 US Metropolitan Statistical Areas (MSAs) and the 4 US census regions
(unweighted standard deviation in percentage points)

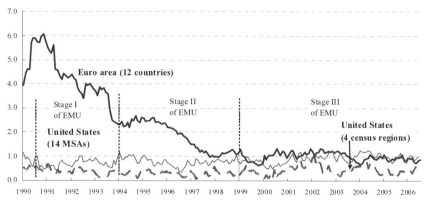

Sources: EUROSTAT and US Bureau of Labor Statistics.
Euro area data up to Jul 2006. US data up to Jun 2006.

Fig. C2. Inflation Dispersion in the Euro Area and in the United States.

What are the reasons for different inflation rates in different euro area countries, and why have they not converged (or have converged only partly), now that there is a single currency and a single monetary policy? The reasons are manifold. Some inflation differentials are simply a normal and even desirable feature of a monetary union that help to correct country-specific imbalances when national monetary and exchange rate policies are no longer available options. Such inflation differentials may reflect, inter alia, adjustments to shocks or catching-up processes. National fiscal policies, resulting in different changes to indirect taxes or administrative prices, also seem to explain part of the inflation differentials. Even though some of these factors have indeed contributed to the persistence of inflation differentials, they should not automatically be considered a cause for concern.

However, other factors, such as rigidities in price-setting mechanisms or excessive wage developments, leading to strong rises in unit labour costs in some countries, may give rise to inflation differentials that could be of concern. These factors may delay the necessary adjustment of relative prices to economic shocks and amplify fluctuations of the business cycle. According to recent research by the ECB, domestic factors, such as diverging unit labour costs, seem to be of key importance in explaining inflation differentials within the euro area (ECB, 2005).

Some developments in unit labour costs across the euro area reflect wage changes relative to productivity gains. Since the introduction of the euro, unit labour cost developments have, indeed, differed markedly across the euro area countries. During this period the cumulative increase in unit labour costs has in some euro area countries, such as Portugal, Spain, the Netherlands, Italy, Ireland and Greece, been significantly higher than the euro area average. As mentioned before, these are also economies where inflation has been persistently above the euro area average. On the other hand, countries such as Germany and Austria are among those with very limited cumulative unit labour cost increases over the same period, and inflation in these countries has been lower than in the rest of the euro area.

Real effective exchange rates against 11 other Member States
(based on Unit Labor Costs; smoothed with four-period moving average)

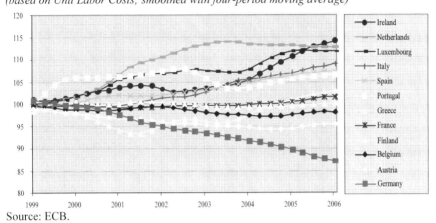

Source: ECB.

Fig. C3. Competitiveness of Euro Area Countries (1999–2006).

When discussing these facts, one should keep in mind that unit labour cost developments in the economy as a whole can mask different developments across sectors. For instance, looking only at the manufacturing industry – which constitutes, on average, around 20% of the whole economy – unit labour cost developments seem much more benign than is the case for the economy as a whole in many countries. This, of course, implies that unit labour cost growth is stronger in the non-manufacturing sector of the economy, especially in the services sector, which is less exposed to international competition. This seems to confirm that inflation differentials are primarily explained by domestic cost factors.

Decomposing the cumulative change in unit labour costs for the whole economy over the period 1999–2004 shows that cross-country differentials appear to stem primarily from differences in developments in compensation per employee across countries, while changes in labour productivity have been more homogeneous.

With a single currency, cost developments in individual countries, as captured by unit labour costs, play a key role in determining changes in competitiveness across the euro area countries. If a country's unit labour costs persistently rise by more than the euro area average, this will obviously have a negative impact on its competitiveness vis-à-vis the other euro area countries as well as vis-à-vis other (non-euro area) countries that are competitors in world markets. Remaining competitive by favourably influencing domestic cost developments is, therefore, crucially important for economic activity and employment. Of course, this is not the only way to maintain and enhance competitiveness, but it is an essential way.

This analysis of the causes and implications of growth, inflation and competitiveness differentials raises certain pertinent questions, namely what *should* be done about these differentials, and what *can* be done about them? The short answer, containing the core message, is this: higher long-term growth and improved competitiveness for the euro area and its member countries are urgently needed and are indeed possible. The way to achieve them is through the determined implementation of the necessary structural reforms in an environment of price stability.

C.6. Structural Reforms for Higher Growth and Improved Competitiveness

This message about the urgent need for structural reforms has been repeated time and again. And by now there is indeed a large consensus in Europe about the kind of remedies that are needed to bring European economies on a sustainably higher growth path. The Lisbon agenda, as recently refined and refocused in response to the analysis contained the Kok Report (EUROPEAN COMMUNITIES, 2004) – and endorsed by all 25 EU Member States – is evidence of this broad support. The next urgent step is to focus on implementation. Europeans have to move from *recognising* what is necessary to *doing* what is necessary. It would be beyond the scope of this paper to address the appropriate structural reforms in detail. However, it is worthwhile to mention a few areas in labour and product markets where further progress is most urgently needed.

Structural reforms in labour markets are vital so as to make them more flexible and adaptable, in order to support the creation of new jobs and to increase labour utilisation. The institutional framework and wage-setting mechanisms, including wage indexation, also need to be reviewed. A sufficient degree of wage differentiation is important to ensure that wage adjustments reflect differences in regional and sectoral productivity. The institutional framework of the labour market should contribute to the reduction in the rate of unemployment, which is especially high in Europe, and should not be limited to securing the interests of those who already have jobs. The ultimate objective of all these reforms should be to increase employment by strengthening the incentives for job creation on the basis of market mechanisms in a way compatible with and supportive of the necessary improvement in a country's competitiveness.

At the same time, labour market policies should go hand in hand with structural reforms resulting in enhanced competition in goods and services markets. This in turn requires measures aimed at increasing the number of potential players in the market. There are significant productivity gains to be reaped in Europe by removing the considerable barriers to competition that still remain at the national and EU levels. Further efforts should therefore be made to reduce firms' entry costs, such as the administrative burden on start-ups, and – more generally – to reduce red tape. In this context, specific emphasis should be placed on enhancing competition within and across the EU economies by liberalising trade in services – which account for almost seven out of ten jobs in the Union. Ensuring an institutional environment that encourages business creation and expansion should therefore be among the key priorities, together with supporting innovation and the diffusion of technological progress. In order to successfully harness technological advancements – and thus to compete in world markets on the basis of superior quality and scientific and technological edge – a continuous improvement in human capital is crucial. As economic activity becomes increasingly knowledge-based and jobs shift from low to high-skilled workers through the process of Schumpeterian "creative destruction", sustained investment in education and in research and development becomes indispensable.

To plead for all this is not "to dream the impossible dream". That it can be done successfully is shown in the Nordic countries, which have undergone such structural reforms in the past decade – and have done so without abandoning the basic features of what might be referred to as the European social model. These countries are now reaping the benefits of these reforms in terms of growth, employment and technological excellence. The cooperation within the EU provides a forum where policy-makers can learn from each other, analyse what works and what does not, and adapt suitable policies to local conditions. In so doing, unnecessary regulation or bureaucratic procedures that might be well-meant, but end up stifling growth, should be avoided.

In these efforts to enhance the growth performance of the European economies, fiscal policy plays a crucial role. Sound fiscal policies are not only necessary to support the stability-oriented single monetary policy; healthy public finances are a key element in shoring up the confidence of investors, businesses and consumers. Moreover, public expenditure should aim to deliver efficient and competitive public services. A reformed public sector can also play an important role as a catalyst in stimulating the ongoing restructuring of the private sector, eliminating rigidities and dismantling structures that impede competition, efficiency and the adaptability of the economy. Finally, fiscal policy should not only aim to reduce the fiscal burden resulting from excessive budget deficits, but also give due regard to the "quality of public finances", i.e. the structure and character of public expenditure.

C.7. Conclusions

There are plenty of challenges ahead in seeking to cope with the impact of globalisation and technological change. Not just for the euro area as a whole, but also for its individual member countries – especially those whose level of international competitiveness is relatively low and which may have been adversely affected in recent years. While Monetary Union in Europe has been an effective – and hugely successful – response to globalisation for the euro area countries, it has also placed those countries under a specific constraint – that there is only one single monetary policy, geared towards price stability in the euro area as a whole. That said, the policy framework and tools to address these challenges and achieve faster growth and enhanced competitiveness are already in place: the Lisbon strategy, as refocused and reaffirmed by the European Council in 2004. The tasks ahead are demanding, but there is also reason for optimism.

References

BENALAL, N.; DIAZ DEL HOYO, J.L.; PIERLUIGI, B.; VIDALIS, N. (2006), Output growth differentials across the euro area countries: some stylised facts, *ECB Occasional Paper* No. 45, May, Frankfurt am Main: European Central Bank.

BLANCHARD, O. (2004), The economic future of Europe, *Journal of Economic Perspectives*, pp3–26.

EUROPEAN CENTRAL BANK (2004), Labour productivity developments in the euro area: aggregate trends and sectoral patterns, ECB Monthly Bulletin, July, pp. 47–58.

EUROPEAN CENTRAL BANK (2005), Monetary policy and inflation differentials in a heterogeneous currency area, ECB Monthly Bulletin, May, pp. 61–78.

EUROPEAN CENTRAL BANK (2006), Competitiveness and export performance of the euro area, ECB Monthly Bulletin, July, pp. 69–79.

EUROPEAN COMMUNITIES (2004), Facing the Challenge: The Lisbon strategy for growth and Employment, Report from the High Level Group chaired by Wim Kok, November, Luxembourg: Office for Official Publications of the European Communities.

MONTESQUIEU, Charles de Secondat, Baron de (1748), Spirit of Laws, trans. Thomas Nugent, rev. J.V. Prichard, vol. 35 of The Great Books of the Western World, ed. Mortimer Adler (Chicago: Encyclopedia Britannica, 1990), pp. 146.

D. Financial Market Integration and Monetary Policy

Hans-Helmut Kotz[*]

> *"The more nearly perfect a market is, the stronger is the tendency for the same price to be paid for the same thing at the same time in all parts of the market..."*
>
> Marshall, Principles, 1920

D.1. Filling the Gaps in the Chain of Substitution

...is, in the pertinent (and marvelous) wording of the Joan Robinson, what integration or, for that matter, globalization is all about. And this is, almost by definition, welfare enhancing. Moreover, following classical welfare economics, further integration is acceptable or, one might say, palatable, when losers could be compensated out of the surplus generated (Kaldor-Hicks criterion). And those losing ground do, most evidently, exist. In any case, Europe, that *grand projet* of Schumann, Monnet, de Gasperi and Adenauer, being viewed at from different angles in this conference (book), has been, from a purely economist's view, simply about reducing barriers to exchange. Be they in goods, services or capital markets. In fact, this is the order in which those issues appeared on the political agenda, rather protractedly, but as well quite effectively. Who, 50 years back, or even only 25 years ago, could have imagined the level of effective integration of their markets Europeans enjoy today?

But economics only makes, of course, for a very limited or, more precisely: poor, perspective on Europe's integration. While it is fading out of perception, the decisive result of "50 years of EU Dynamics" is, ultimately, the achievement of a lasting peace in Europe. This point bears reiterating. The following remarks, however, focuses on a much narrower issue. That is, the evolution towards the integration of financial markets within Europe and the pursuant consequences for monetary policy are to be dealt with. But, to repeat, it would be an incomplete perspective if one would assess Europe only from this perspective.

---

[*] Deutsche Bundesbank; paper written, in a purely personal capacity, for a book to be edited by Richard Tilly, Michael Heise and Paul Welfens. I do thank Paul Welfens for critical remarks (as well as his patience). Thomas Gehrig (Freiburg University), via a jointly offered course in the summer term 2005, has been influential, as has been Stefan Collignon (LSE), again via a joint seminar, and my long-term collaborators Hans-Hermann Francke and Harald Nitsch (both of Freiburg University). Finally, I owe a debt of gratitude to Sandra Haasis and Martin Beck for help with the data; as concerns errors I do have, unfortunately, undiluted property rights.

Before going in *medias res*, it is sensible to briefly outline why the integration of financial markets is relevant for the general public, why it could be a public policy issue. At the same time, it is most important to become clear about the vocabulary, i.e. what does integration really mean. This is not about definitional quibbles but has, as is to be shown, a substantial (or political) relevance. We illustrate the degree of integration with regard to European money, bond and stock markets – mainly evaluating integration through the lens of price dispersion (for almost the same products). The third part of this note deals, against the background of traditional mechanisms of the transmission of monetary policy, with the possible relations between the degree of financial market integration and the consequences for the implementation of monetary policy. To put it simply: Less heterogeneity (greater homogeneity) makes for a less complicated operation of monetary policy. Therefore, central bankers are, as much as they are conservatives with regard to inflation containment, as well, almost by way of occupation, natural harmonizers. Some of the homogeneization, however, is coming about, as is argued in section four, by the force of arbitrage. In particular the instruments to trade and price credit risk – the credit risk transfer mechanisms in their various guises – narrow the bounds to arbitrage, i.e. lead to a reduced dispersion of prices for substitutes. This is, obviously, tantamount to a deeper integration of financial markets through credit derivatives.

D.2. Integration of Financial Markets:
Concepts and Indicators

An environment which allows for a frictionless flow of goods and services as well as factors of production fosters the efficient allocation of resources. This holds true for financial intermediation as well. A larger market, as an upshot of the removal of impediments to cross-border exchange, allows for reaping the benefits of scale (i.e. fixed costs spread over a larger output). In addition, with the market horizon widened, opportunities to diversify and spread risks are concurrently enhanced. Again, this should encourage additional capital expenditures, support innovation and, ultimately, underwrite value creation.

Such a completion of markets in a geographical dimension is in addition of interest to the public, thus: a policy issue, since it should reinforce, at the same time, the resilience of financial relations. Not unlike a reliable infrastructure this spells more stability. While an increased resilience supports the implementation of monetary policy, a higher degree of robustness is conducive in a second dimension: it simultaneously strengthens the effective channeling of resources, ultimately fostering the creation of value added. In any case, diverging set-ups of financial structures amount to a complication for monetary policy. This holds true in both its macro, inflation containing, as well as in its micro, financial-market stability underwriting dimension. Those are the decisive reasons why central banks profess a desire for homogeneity. Less heterogeneity would ameliorate the difficulties emanating from the differential thrust of an identical change in the policy instrument.

But then, at least up to today, the ECB had to make do with substantial differences in the underlying structure of financial markets, mainly differentiated along national lines. Nonetheless, judging from its ultimate target, namely keeping inflation at bar, it did it rather successfully. Therefore, the current degree of financial diversity did not prevent monetary policy from being by and large effective. Nonetheless, the strive for making finance over the European domain more similar, as it became forcefully evidenced in the *Financial Services Action Plan*, was not only largely greeted with affirmation on the side of the ECB but also defined as an objective to pursue.

What does integration, as a matter of fact, actually mean. There are two perspectives from which indicators have been constructed.[1] The first is, to look at cross-border flows. The higher the transaction volumes the stronger is the integration of markets. Capital accounts or tabulations of cross-border M&A volumes, for example, do translate this perception. The second angle is to view at the dispersion of prices for near or close substitutes, that is, financial claims being characterized by the same attributes: the same thing fetching the same price. Here we will illustrate the level of integration mainly by alluding to these latter – the Marshallian – indicators.

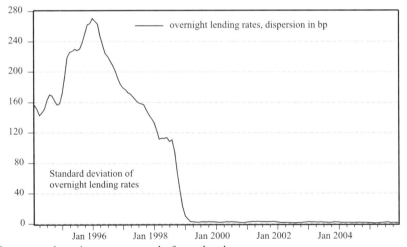

60-day centered moving averages, end-of-month values;
Source: ECB, Indicators of financial integration in the euro area.

Fig. D1.a. MM Integration 1: Overnight Lending Rates.

---

[1] In the following, I simply borrow data as provided by the ECB in its report on "Indicators of financial integration in the Euro area", September 2006, http://www.ecb.int/stats/finint/html/index.en.html.

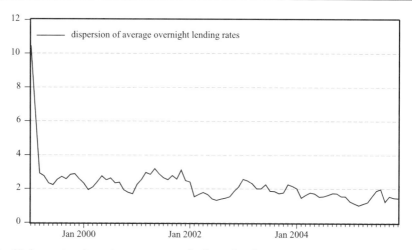

Basis, 60-day centered moving averages, end-of-month values;
Source: ECB, Indicators of financial integration in the euro area.

Fig. D1.b. MM Integration 1: Overnight Lending Rates.

Money markets, as Fig. 1a and 1b illustrate, have been essentially integrated, ever since the beginning of the monetary union. Spreads on overnight lending rates hover about 2 bp only – see Fig. 1b (note the change in scaling), which portrays the EMU period only. Such integration could also be documented for the secured repo markets. Price dispersion here is very low and by and large the upshot of (almost negligible) technical impediments to arbitrage. In this domain, markets are indeed (almost) perfectly integrated. And it is here, at the short end, where monetary policy through its operating target for funding rates wields its initial and most powerful influence.

To a degree, this holds true for bond markets as well. Today, bonds of EMU member states are traded at premia very significantly below their historical averages. Before EMU, spreads between paper issued by Canadian provinces appeared to be a sensible benchmark (at least to the present author). In fact, this counterfactual was – directionally – instructive, but intra-EMU spreads presently are even below those we do see in Canada. Italian government bonds, for example, which were up to 700 bp above German Bunds now just pay a premium of only 30 bp. This reduction is, most evidently, substantial (see Fig. 2 a on the very significantly reduced dispersion of spreads). And it is to a large degree a direct consequence of EMU, namely, the upshot of the devaluation risk gone. But it tells us also that markets do read credit risks (default premia) differently now – as they might against the background of all the institutional change in Europe. Moreover, since the beginning of EMU there is essentially a one-to-one response between a shock to the German bond yield and the reaction of other European government bond yields. (This is what Fig. 2 b shows us – individual beta coefficients, measuring the contemporaneous response to a change in German bond yields, are very close to one.)

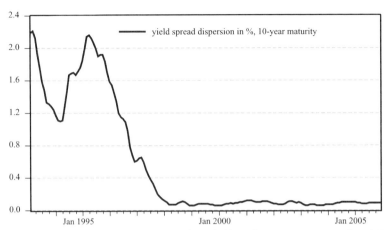

Note: For the bond yield spreads determination, yield on German government bonds have been taken as the benchmark. Greece enters the calculation of standard deviations with its date of entry into EMU.
Source: ECB, Indicators of Financial Integration in the Euro area.

Fig. D2.a. Bond Market Integration: Spreads.

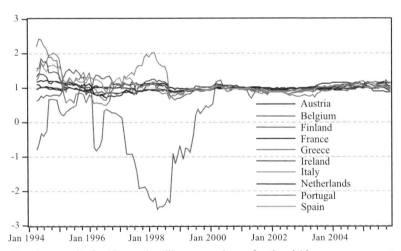

Note: Based on results for 18-month rolling regressions of national 10-year government bond yield changes on charges of benchmark German 10-government bond yields.

Fig. D2.b. BM Integration 2: Beta Coefficients.

Corporate bond markets barely existed in Germany before EMU – not so much as a result of impeding regulation but because of a lack of economic attractiveness, i.e. mainly too high user costs. Meanwhile, the corporate bond market has really taken off. The larger domain of the market has made it comparatively more appealing, from an all-in-cost perspective, to tap the bond market for larger companies. And, again, the common factor or the underlying market is the EMU area, with differentiation in terms of conditions taking place along sector lines (see Fig. 3 a: from top to bottom, the ordering is based on 1998)

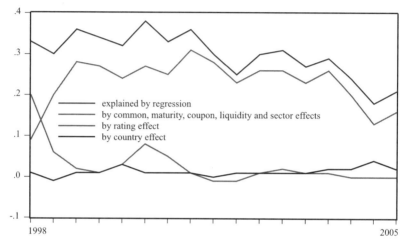

Note: Based on regressions of yield spreads of corporate bonds on commen effects, maturity, coupon, liquidity, sector, rating, and country effects. Values are for 6-month averages, given in percentages.

Fig. D3.a. Bond Market Integration: Corporates.

The EMU-dimension gained ground in particular with regard to equity markets. Here, until the launch of the common currency, European stock markets where characterized by a significant national component, largely dominating the sector dimension (HELG et al., 1995). EMU, or Europeanization, implied a new reference or market portfolio, a new home market (KOTZ, 1998). And, indeed, today companies do not evolve along national trajectories but are judged against the respective sectors to which they belong. Illustrative of this point is that indicators of dispersion along national lines, see the above Fig. 3 b, have been going down ever since the introduction of the Euro.

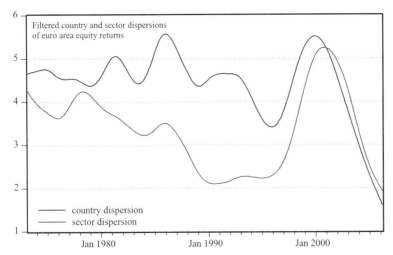

Note: The chart shows Hodrick-Prescott filtered cross-sectional dispersions of monthly
euro area country and sector equity returns. Values are in percentages.
Source: ECB, Indicators of financial integration in the euro area.

Fig. D3.b. Equity Market Integration.

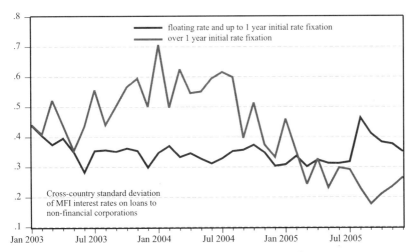

Note: Measurement based on MFI interest rates on new loan business.
Source: ECB, Indicators of financial integration in the euro area.

Fig. D4.a. Banking Market Integration 1.

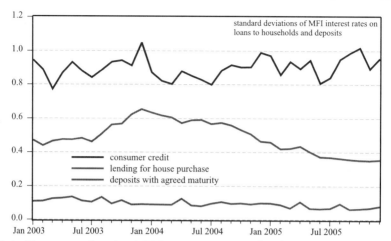

Note: Measurement based on MFI interest rates on new loan business. Deposits with agreed maturity include deposits from non-financial corporations and households.
Source: ECB, Indicators of financial integration in the euro area.

Fig. D4b. Banking Market Integration 2.

Banking markets are least integrated. While the dispersion of interest rates on new loans taken out to corporate sector entities has been decreasing, the correspondence between retail markets is much less complete (see Fig. 4 a and b: in 4a top line is for over one year initial rate fixation). Here, price dispersion is still in evidence. But this holds true for the intra-national or sub-European dimension as well. (In fact, as a glance at tabulations in the press shows, even if one goes at the city level, one does see some remarkable differences between, for example, the conditions of mortgages.) In any case, the degree of dispersion is highest for consumer credit and lowest with regard to mortgage financing conditions.

Quite obviously, however, price dispersion is not exclusively the upshot of regulatory impediments to trade or barriers to entry. In fact, we know that for infrequently purchased goods as well as less expensive items prices do stray more widely around their mean – because, for individual consumers, search costs relative to marginal benefits are comparatively high. With joint products, consumers' response to price changes is even more reduced. For economically rational reasons: At the margin, it would simply be too costly to constantly search for the best bargain. Moreover, in addition to switching costs, the all-else-equal assumption is difficult to make with regard to a number of financial products. In fact, here we have to do with monopolistically competitive markets where suppliers do set prices and, most importantly, differentiate products (terms and conditions, service level etc.). In addition, banking relations are experience goods. They are about developing trust and relationships. They thrive on soft-information and non-standardized procedures. Many clients prefer the convenience of one-stop banking because they do not have to constantly re-tell their story. And this, quite evidently, implies inertia – perfectly rational of the side of individual clients.[2] On the other hand, such slow-response behavior, as a result of strong ties, gives suppliers some leeway in price discrimination. But only up to a point. Even pure monopolists see their market power limited by some elasticity of demand – there's a threshold beyond which prices induce customers to completely abstain from a product. And this effect of a reduction of barriers to entry and the concurrent limitation of suppliers' power is, arguably, the most beneficial economic effect of the integration of European markets: It increases consumers' choice sets and contains suppliers' influence.

But here we want to stress, that trying to achieve complete homogeneity would be a vain target. Proximity has value to many consumers. This introduces a home or even a regional bias (see FRANKEL 2000, p. 13). Distance, on the other hand, implies transaction costs. To these distance-producing institutions belongs language as well as legislation (consumer protection laws, information disclosure requirements etc.). In creating information hurdles, they raise barriers and at the same time widen the bands of arbitrage. That is why the geographical dimension of banking markets is often not national. In the U.S., for example, for anti-trust policy purposes (to delineate the base for concentration indices), "banking markets are defined to be relatively small geographical areas" (MOORE 1998, p. 2). While distance – in all its dimensions – might lose in importance, it is still very much relevant. And this, quite naturally, entails – heterogeneity.

D.3. Financial Markets Heterogeneity: Consequences for Monetary Policy

Non-homogeneous financial markets imply that identical monetary impulses will be translated differentially to the real economy – bearing witness to the respective financial context. As concerns monetary policy's macro dimension, this means mainly varying speeds of adjustment. To be brief: capital-market oriented systems do transmit a given interest rate impulse more rapidly than bank-oriented systems (where intermediaries' balance sheets provide a buffer which produces some viscosity, slowing-down the adjustment). In this vein, differential effects potentially raise problems for monetary policy, which can only deliver one interest rate – which has to fit in all parts – regions – of the market.

The second dimension in which a different set-up of financial structures could have an impact has to do with financial stability issues. Capital-market oriented systems appear to be more prone to volatile valuations of assets, claims on future income streams. At the same time, they do seem to be less restrictive in underwriting new ventures. Here, however, we concentrate on the monetary policy issues in their macro guise.

---

[2] Moreover, in particular in financial markets, individuals are not always behaving as *homo oeconomicus* would do; see for example FRANK, R. (1994), pp. 281-307.

A natural conceptual starting point to think about varying impacts of monetary policy would be to consider sub-EMU interest rate channels.[3] (In the following, we obviously take our guiding questions from Mishkin's concise overview article of 1995.) Put very simply, this is the subject of sub-EMU IS-LM constellations, more precisely: their possibly differing slopes along national lines. In a bank-oriented, hence less responsive, system the LM curve should be steeper. The central bank therefore would have to apply its instrument more forcefully in order to generate the intended impact because banks, unlike capital markets, blunt to a degree monetary impulses. On the sides of banks this inertia or stickiness is an endogenous reaction to an environment in which they are price setters and where they do compete with their services, quite obviously, on quality attributes as well. At the same, the IS curve is implied since differences in financial structure do impact on the availability (possibility of credit rationing) as well as the user cost of capital. Bank-oriented systems do economize on transactions costs emanating from an unequal distribution of pertinent information. They ameliorate market access problems, in particular for small and medium-sized companies. Thus, they ultimately could have a bearing on the level as well as responsiveness of capital expenditures.

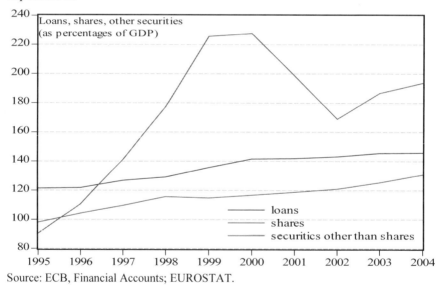

Source: ECB, Financial Accounts; EUROSTAT.

Fig. D5.a. Euro Area's Financial Structure.

[3] One frequently taken approach to handle that question was to run VAR-Systems on a national basis and determine from the impulse-response functions whether EMU policy impacts differently along these lines.

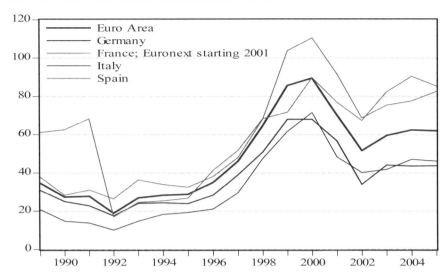

Source: DAI FACTBOOK, online.

Fig. D5.b. Stock Market Capitalization (as Percentages of GDP).

Our main point to be made here bears reiteration: We are reasoning in terms of a differential argument. That is, we raise the question: Do nationally defined financial systems produce significantly different policy outcomes in response to an identical monetary policy impulse? We do not try answering this question empirically but simply refer to a substantial research effort on the part of a network of researchers within the European System of Central Banks. Their conclusion, using elaborate approaches, is in the negative. ANGELONI et al. (2003, p. 410–11) sum up their main observations in writing: "that the [interest rate channel], while not playing an exclusive role, is clearly a prominent channel of transmission in the euro area....interest rate effects are always sizeable, and sometimes the virtually unique, source of investment movements."

Still, this approach to dealing with the transmission of monetary impulses, however, is rather frugal. It does not, obviously, capture the much richer structure of actual financial markets. Financial factors, as ANGELONI et al. stress correctly as well, do play a role "in several important ways" (p. 411). It is here, where as a consequence of information asymmetries and agency problems a complementary channel of influence comes in: the credit channel (see for a concise overview BERNANKE/GERTLER, 1995). It comes in two guises – as bank lending as well as balance sheet channel. Banks do play a special role, in particular for small and medium-sized companies. They are important for the supply of loanable funds – and, as a consequence of information imperfections, loan markets cannot be assimilated with auction markets. Instead, they do rely on intimate knowledge, "the information relevant for providing the credit [being] highly specific" (STIGLITZ/ GREENWALD 2003, p. 30). As a result of these information problems, credit rationing arises. Those effects could be attenuated, depending on the net worth of prospective debtors. (Net worth usually serves as collateral, as a cushion to absorb shocks to cash-flow. The willingness to lend is obviously increasing with this buffer – as is therefore the capacity to fund capital expenditures (BERNANKE/GERTLER 1995, p. 40.) And this rationing could be different – will most probably be – depending on the characteristics of the relevant jurisdiction.

The for our question relevant point is whether, as a consequence of differences in financial structure, this complementary ways of impacting do make a substantial difference in monetary policy's final outcome. To put a judgment on that: in our eyes, after quite significant changes in financial rules (Financial Services Action Plan), these differential effects will be even less detectable than they were in the ANGELONI et al. study, relying in fact on pre-EMU data.

Still, we could have – and currently most probably do observe – as a result of segmentation or fragmentation in retail mortgage markets differential effects in residential construction. They might have provided the background scenario for rather divergent developments in terms of house prices. Most evidently, housing sector developments are local indeed. Nonetheless, national differences in typical mortgage products (variable vs. fixed rates; standard loan to value ratios, taxation: deductibility of interest rates; prepayment options: who pays the premium?; enforcement institutions) do seem to have contributed to ratios of market value written over replacement costs (Tobin-q perspective) which show substantial differences across institutional set-ups or jurisdictions. As a consequence of the attendant wealth effects, being higher with housing, this could have a macro effect, i.e. result in differential growth rates and some persistent economic divergence. It would, hence, complicate monetary policy – wielding a one-size instrument only. Further integration, in terms of opening markets and giving consumers more possibilities to choose from, possibly along the White Paper's mutual recognition line, would be an appropriate response. Still, from a largely macro-perspective, and since those issues have a mainly national dimension, deploying national tax instruments would be the first line of attack.

D.4. Pushing Back Limits to Arbitrage – Integration Through Markets

Banks, in a traditional understanding, are mainly in the business of pooling of funds and transforming risk and maturity since they have a comparative advantage in dealing with the incompleteness of information. Moreover, by investing in long-term relations with borrowers, they are not only better judges of proposed business projects, but also able to convince debtors to employ borrowed funds in less risky ways. While the evaluation of business projects – credit assessment – is costly, in contested markets, which obviously favor customers, the ties between client and intermediary are loosened. With the benefits of such relationships diminishing, it becomes increasingly less attractive for banks to "compile information," all the more so if the processing of credit evaluations becomes public knowledge (PETERSEN/RAJAN, 1995). All of this, inexorably, fosters more arms' length financial relations.

In fact, the bulk of finance is still handled in an intermediated way. Nonetheless, the "auction market" domain of finance, as described so convincingly by Arthur Okun, has been rapidly gaining in importance. We see a substantial increase in importance of capital markets. This means in particular that for all of those financial products whose idiosyncrasies are diminishing in importance, the trend is to migrate from intermediaries to markets. As standardization creates lower transaction costs, it implies the re-packaging and selling of loans or other claims on future cash flows – and hence more liquidity and trading. All of this is made possible by analytical tools, relying largely on pricing contingent claims, which allow for a cost-effective unbundling and repackaging of products (HULL 2003). Thus, separating out distinct functions that were formerly perceived as unalterably joined has become ever easier to achieve. This separation along functional lines – origination, funding (securitization), and processing, in particular in the U.S. mortgage business – has served MERTON/BODIE (1995) as a prime example for their "functional finance" perspective.

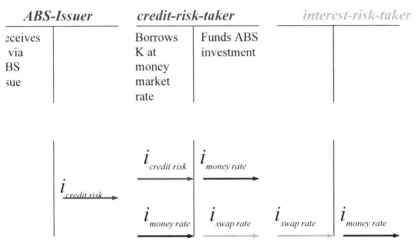

Fig. D6. Risk Dynamics.

Breaking-Up the Risk Chain

Bank issues a bond, covered by loans; taker of credit risk borrows funds in money market and buys asset-backed security; to hedge interest-rate risk, enters into a swap with interest risk taker, who receives fixed rate and pays variable money market rate; source BRENDER/PISANI (2003).

A particularly instructive example is portrayed in the above shown schematic, taken from Anton Brender and Florence Pisani's very instructive book on the increasing relevance of capital markets for the U.S. case. The bottom-line is that the swap rate, i.e. the rate a payer is prepared to offer (the average of the bid-offer of fixed rates), has been becoming the basic or common factor from which individual credit risk is priced. And this common factor is determined ever more in an integrated or EMU dimension. Therefore, monetary policy wields its decisive influence through its impact on the swap rate (and the respective yield curve). With loans being ever more securitized, in fact, being already originated with the intention to take them on a bank's balance sheet at best only temporary, the cushioning effect – viscosity – of banks is significantly reduced. In other words, bank-oriented systems become ever closer aligned with capital market developments. As an aside, the binary perspective on financial systems is less operational than it used to be a decade ago.

Apparently, banks seem to be dis-intermediating themselves out of the credit-risk business. Loan sales, loan syndication, and the entire spectrum of credit derivatives and collateralized debt obligations unambiguously point in this direction. Credit or default risk, being of a long-term nature, is reduced to a short-term or market risk. Disaggregating risk into narrower time-buckets, in equilibrium, implies that investors do rationally account for the risk over the whole life-time of the claim. In well-working markets, there is, hence, no difference between (short-term) market and (long-term) default risk.

Against this backdrop, daily – or even continuous – price quotes for credit exposures seem to become complete substitute for banks in their risk transformation function. To a degree, this is not unlike the puzzle posed by Grossman: if markets make instantly available all the pertinent information to handle or price default risk – where are the incentives to produce those evaluations. In this case, the paradox is possibly even a bit more vexing, since evaluation and lending used to be joint products. Now, while risk can be more jointly shared with the help of the new instruments, incentives to generate robust credit evaluation might, at the same time, have diminished (RAJAN, 2005).

This could become problematic for central banks not so much in discharging their macro duty, but in their responsibility for underwriting financial stability. The point, however, we wanted to stress here is that market integration – the production of a common factor for monetary policy – has been significantly, though almost in an unnoticed way, advanced via markets in derivatives which, by exploiting no-arbitrage conditions, have further shrunken, the gaps in the chain of substitution. The impact of derivatives markets on the transmission of monetary policy impulses is still not completely acknowledged. In our case, it probably means that markets are more homogenous in their response than one would assume at first blush.

D.5. By Way of Concluding – Variety Is Manageable

To be sure, EMU is still characterized by significant heterogeneity. This could make monetary policy more cumbersome, even less effective. Though, in light of actual performance, doubts are well founded. Nonetheless, a removal of impediments to intra-European exchange in financial markets (negative integration) is, for good reasons, high on the agenda.

At the same time, the rather diverse set of region-specific national rules and approaches reflects quite a variation in views about how the financial world should work. Thus, while the progressive integration of European markets reinforces the need for joint policy action, the multitude of underlying conceptions (as well as hard fought-out national compromises) complicates exactly that task.

Obviously, remaining institutional differences are deeply rooted in regional preferences. The variety in approaches to financial issues is the upshot of national political compromises and, as a consequence, strongly influential on the superstructure of laws and institutions. In other words, those rules are not simply up for change – only to make the conduct of monetary policy an easier task.

As consequence, the ECB will have to live with variety up to a degree (as does the Fed) – which, ultimately, is for sure not simplifying its job, but the legitimate result of a diversity of preferences as well as their reflection in sub-European democratic processes of which Europe – principle of subsidiarity – is rightly fond of.

References

BERNANKE, B.; GERTLER, M. (1995), Inside the Black Box: The Credit Channel of Monetary Policy Transmission, in: *Journal of Economic Perspectives*, vol. 9, no. 4, pp 27–48.
BRENDER, A.; PISANI, F. (2004), *La nouvelle économie américaine*, Paris: Economica.
FRANK, R. (1994), Microeconomics and Behavior, McGraw-Hill, New York.
FRANKEL, J. (2000), Globalization of the Economy, *NBER Working Paper* 7858.
HULL, J. (2000), Options, Futures and Other Derivatives, Prentice-Hall: Upper Saddle River.
KOTZ, H.-H. (1998), Binnenmarkt und Währungsunion: Verknüpfungslogik, Mikro- und Makrofolgen, in: Paul J.J. Welfens et al. (eds.): Euro – Neues Geld für Europa, Campus: Frankfurt, S. 117–128.
KRAHNEN, J. (2005), Der Handel von Kreditrisiken: Eine neue Dimension des Kapitalmarktes, in: *Perspektiven der Wirtschaftspolitik*, vol. 6, no. 4, pp. 499–519
MERTON, R.; BODIE, Z. (1995), A Conceptual Framework for Analyzing the Financial Environment, in: David Crane et al. (eds.): The Global Financial System. A Functional Perspective, Boston, HBS,
MERTON, R.; BODIE, Z. (2004), The Design of Financial Systems: Towards a Synthesis of Function and Structure, *NBER Working Paper* 10620.
MISHKIN, F. (1995), Symposion on the Monetary Transmission Mechanism, in: *Journal of Economic Perspectives*, vol. 9, no. 4, pp 3–10.
MOORE, R. (1998), Concentration, Technology, and Market Power in Banking: Is Distance Dead? , in: Federal Reserve Bank of Dallas, *Financial Industry Studies*, December, pp. 1–10.
PETERSEN, M.; RAJAN R. (1995), The Effect of Credit Market Competition on Lending Relationships, in: *Quarterly Journal of Economics*, vol. 110 (May), pp. 407–44.

RAJAN, R. (2005), Has Financial Development Made the World Riskier? , *NBER Working Paper* 11728.

STIGLITZ, J.; GREENWALD B. (2003), Towards a New Paradigm in Monetary Economics, Cambridge UP: Cambridge

TOBIN, J.; GOLUB S. (1998), Money, Credit and Capital, McGraw-Hill: Boston.

E. Instability of the Eurozone? On Monetary Policy, House Prices and Structural Reforms

Ansgar Belke and Daniel Gros[*]

E.1. Introduction

This paper deals with potential instabilities in the Eurozone stemming from an insufficient interplay between monetary policy and reform effort on the one hand and the emergence of intra-Euro area divergences on the other hand. As a first step, we assess the effect of European Monetary Union (EMU) on structural reform and investigate this question by an examination of the relationship between fixed exchange rates and reform in two wider samples of countries. We also stress that loose monetary conditions, which prevailed until some months ago, can also manifest themselves in asset price inflation, notably in the housing market. When these bubbles burst (e.g., when housing prices stop rising) this often leads to a prolonged period of economic instability and weakness rather than consumer price inflation.

As a second step, we point out that risks for EMU are not only increasing because longer-term disequilibria become evident in fiscal and monetary policy, but also because serious divergences are now appearing within the Euro area which threaten its long-term cohesiveness. The most manifest example of this threat comes from what promises to be a long-term divergence between Germany and Italy, which for the time being was offset by asynchronous developments of house prices in both countries. There are still large differences within the Euro area, with the small countries performing much better than the large ones on almost every indicator. This suggests that better policies can make a large difference even if monetary policy is the same for everybody.

Finally, we construct a simple formal model in order to investigate whether EMU is in danger from internal tensions which could lead to severe instabilities. The experience so far has shown that some countries are continuously losing competitiveness. Is this a structural problem in the sense that these countries just have problems in keeping inflation at a level that does not imply a continuing loss of competitiveness? Or is the persistence of higher inflation one can observe in some countries due to the internal dynamics of a monetary union in which any country that starts with a higher inflation rate also has a lower real interest rate, thereby stimulating demand and thus potentially leading to even more inflation.

[*] Corresponding author: Professor Dr. Ansgar Belke.
Acknowledgements: We are grateful to Michael Frenkel for his valuable comments and to Funda Celikel and Arne Breuer for their excellent research assistance.

The purpose of our theoretical section is to discuss the main factors which could lead to such diverging cycles.

In the first years of EMU, neither the degree of economic flexibility nor the stability of the fiscal framework or the independence of the ECB was severely tested. However, as growth has faded, tensions have increased. Optimists hoped that economic tensions would eventually break the existing structural rigidities. Unfortunately, it seems as if the rigidities are prevailing while fiscal policy discipline is giving way. Since this will certainly not keep growth going, it would be a nearly safe bet to forecast that political pressure will increasingly be brought to bear on the ECB to support economic activity in the short run by weakening the Euro both internally and externally. Hence, we raise three questions in order to tackle the primary question of the paper: Is there a significant menace of instability of the Euro area?

Part 2:
Can monetary policy serve as a driver of structural reforms?; and
Part 3:
What kind of monetary policy is suitable for a Slow Growth Economy?; and
Part 4:
How should European monetary policy look like in a large and diversified economic zone?

Of course, there are many other dimensions of instabilities which could have been discussed here. Among them are evident and pressing topics like the menace of de-synchronization of regional business cycles, the question of whether the ECB only follows the Fed, the problems of decision making in monetary policy and other related policy areas caused by EU Eastern Enlargement, EMU exit considerations by politicians like Berlusconi and their feedbacks on the Euro area economies, impact differentials of Euro-EXR movements among Euro area countries, the challenges to the Euro due to the Asian countries' endeavor to increase the share of the Euro in their currency baskets and the recent treatment of the stability pact (see, e.g., WYPLOSZ, 2006).[1]

In principle, the topic of this paper is not as trivial as it looks: What is meant by instability? Generally, we could define instability in several dimensions, for example instability in terms of the risk that EMU breaks apart, instability in terms of high inflation (internal stability of the Euro), or instability in terms of high exchange rate volatility and misalignments (external stability of the Euro).

In this paper, we look at the most current set of issues at the time the paper was written, namely structural reforms, monetary policy, real estate market developments, and business cycle divergence. While there are numerous important issues within EMU, only parts of the topics of instability can be addressed here due to the space constraint.

---

[1]   BELKE (2002) examines whether wage policies in EMU have been destabilizing factors as was feared by opponents to EMU. It is argued that labor market reforms are important prerequisites of moderate wage agreements.

The remainder of the paper is structured as follows. Section 2 reflects on the question of whether EMU has fostered reform efforts in the countries of the Euro area. Here, we strictly refer to the more general relationship between monetary policy autonomy and structural reforms in open economies as the most promising guideline. In section 3, we analyze in more detail a longer-term aspect of monetary policy that has gained in importance since the start of EMU and almost certainly should have a bearing for the question whether there is internal instability of the Eurozone, namely the consequences of allowing a liquidity overhang to build up. We only note that money and credit growth that cannot be explained as responding to the needs of an economy growing at potential and a desired rate of inflation should alert us to potential future risks to price and/or financial stability and make us question the appropriateness of the stance of monetary policy.

In section 4, we argue that the emergence of widening intra-area divergences could severely test the resolve of the Euroland authorities to support the value of the Euro, which could degenerate in a process of gradual 'lira-isation' of the Euro – again a potential source of large instability of the Eurozone. Section 5 summarizes and draws some policy conclusions with an eye on some promising ways of avoiding future instabilities in the Euro area in the future.

E.2. Monetary Policy for a Slow Growth Economy and Structural Reforms in Europe

EMU might tend to lower instabilities on continental European labor markets if it leads to more reform efforts due to its character as an irrevocably fixed peg than in the case of its counterfactual – flexible exchange rates among European economies (POSEN/POPOV GOULD, 2006). But can we really expect any impact of the degree of monetary policy autonomy on the solution of the reform deadlock especially in some larger continental European economies?

E.2.1. Monetary Policy as a Driver of Structural Reforms?

Recently, the economics of structural reforms has attracted increasing attention in the academic literature (ABIAD/MODY, 2005; HELBLING et al., 2004; for a survey see HEINEMANN, 2004 and 2005). This ongoing research is driven by the fact that for a number of EU countries, the speed of structural change lags behind what is necessary given high structural unemployment and imminent demographic change. Policy fields for which a striking contrast between needs and deeds of institutional change has been identified are, for instance, labor markets, product markets, social security and tax systems.

Although the existing empirical literature has started to identify important drivers and obstacles of reforms with regard to different policy fields, the interplay of structural reforms and monetary policy has been neglected thus far. While the theoretical literature has formulated some hypotheses of how monetary policy may act as a catalyst for reform processes, thorough empirical studies based on the experience of a large number of industrial countries are only scarcely available. This is all the more valid with respect to European Monetary Union, since any effort to estimate the impact of EMU on the degree of reforms must empirically suffer from the lack of degrees of freedom.

A recent paper by BELKE/HERZ/VOGEL (2006) which we would like to address here asks if and how monetary policy can contribute to increasing the likelihood of reform and to safeguarding the continuation and successful implementation of beginning reform processes. The empirical work uses a panel of OECD countries and sophisticated measures of reform events and the monetary stance, distinguishing between reforms of labor markets, financial markets, product markets and the tax system.

E.2.1.1. Structural Reforms and European Monetary Union – What Can We Learn from the Data?

BELKE/HERZ/VOGEL (2006) avoid the problem with the limited degrees of freedom by examining the relationship between fixed exchange rates and reform in two wider samples of countries. Based on these results, it then tries to infer the implications for EMU as a variant of irrevocably fixed exchange rates from the perspective of an individual EMU member country.

A further important distinction of our study concerns the exchange rate regime: Necessarily, the link between national reform processes and monetary policy must be relatively loose where, for instance, fixed exchange rate regimes restrict monetary policy (CALMFORS, 1998, 2001; DUVAL/ELMESKOV, 2005). Hence, we start from the empirical puzzle laid open by HERZ/VOGEL (2005) that more open economies do not reform more than less open ones and focus on different exchange rate arrangements as one of the main determinants of monetary policy autonomy.

However, the first-best solution to the problem of high structural unemployment in isolation (without any look at the degree of monetary policy autonomy) is to remove labor market rigidities, the fundamental cause of high structural unemployment (SVENSSON, 1997, p. 104 and p. 109; DUVAL/ELMESKOV, 2005, p. 5).[2] Yet, such a proposal could be regarded as rather naive from a public choice perspective which emphasizes that labor market institutions, as an outcome of rational political choice, must be implemented in the loss function of politicians. Hence, what is the role for monetary policy in this context?

Cross-country event studies are one obvious approach to empirically examine the impact of monetary policy strategies on the degree of economic reform.

---

[2]   OECD (2005) applies a consistent procedure to derive policy priorities to foster growth across OECD countries and identifies labor market reforms as being particularly important, for example in the Euro area. However, this does not at all imply that reforms in other areas are unimportant. Hence, BELKE/HERZ/VOGEL (2006) analyze a variety of different reform measures in the empirical part of the paper.

However, there are severe limitations to this approach since evidence is ambiguous. The United States, for instance, is a monetary union with labor market institutions that encourage a low natural rate of unemployment. The EMS commitment was extremely helpful in fostering the reform process in the Netherlands and Denmark. The same holds for Austria under the DM peg (HOCHREITER/TAVLAS, 2005). In contrast, the U.K. experienced extensive labor market reforms without adhering to an international exchange rate arrangement. Several other countries outside EMU have also experienced that monetary policy changes had no fundamental effect on labor market flexibility. In Canada, for example, changes in monetary policy strategy in the early 1990s did not increase wage flexibility or unemployment. Neither could New Zealand, despite a sharp turn-around in its monetary policy towards inflation targeting, nor Argentina, through its adoption of a currency board, achieve higher wage or labor market flexibility. This suggests that it is probably highly unrealistic to expect that the ECB can exert any significant effect on the degree of structural reforms in the Euro area.

Hence, BELKE/HERZ/VOGEL (2006) choose an econometric analysis for a large sample of countries in order to include country variance which would not be available if one only concentrates on the EMU irrevocably fixed exchange rate case. Hence, one should clearly go beyond the EMU case studies by VAN POECK/BORGHIJS (2001), BERTOLA/BOERI (2001), and IMF (2004) which are rare examples of empirical investigations in this field.

VAN POECK/BORGHIJS (2001) argue that the prospect of qualifying for EMU should provide as big an incentive for labor-market reform as EMU membership itself. They conclude that EMU countries did not reform more than other countries and, unlike elsewhere, their progress on reform seemed unrelated to the initial level of unemployment. For a period from the early 1990s up to 1999, BERTOLA/BOERI (2001) only focus on cash transfers to people of working age (e.g., unemployment benefits and on-job protection). They arrive at exactly opposite conclusions, namely reforms accelerated more in the Euro area than outside.

The IMF (2004) looks at the impact of a range of factors including macroeconomic conditions, political institutions, reform design and variables aimed at capturing attitudes towards structural reform on different policy areas across OECD countries from the mid-1970s up to the late 1990s. It finds that EU membership leads to faster moves towards liberalization of product markets. However, it does not clarify whether this represents an effect of EMU and/or policies to prepare for EMU (see also DUVAL/ELMESKOV, 2005, p. 10).

E.2.1.2. Monetary Policy Autonomy and Structural Reforms: The Case of European Monetary Union

The discussion about whether EMU has fostered reform efforts in the countries of the Euro area, i.e. the relation between the degree of monetary policy autonomy and structural reforms, is characterized by a wide spectrum of conflicting views.

However, note that it is always demanding though not impossible to identify and specify the counterfactual, i.e. the impacts of non-EMU on reform effort.[3]

We start with a sketch of the literature on monetary policy autonomy and reforms and throughout refer to a prominent example of the loss of monetary autonomy, i.e. the irrevocable fixing of exchange rates EMU.

In the run-up to EMU, a number of studies tried to assess the incentive effects of alternative monetary policy strategies on labor market reforms. According to the proponents of a liberal view, EMU, as a classical variant of a rule-based monetary policy, should have a disciplinary impact on national labor markets.[4] In the first place, EMU enhances the credibility of monetary policy and thereby lowers inflation expectations. Negative employment effects as a result of (too) high wage claims can no longer be accommodated by discretionary monetary policy. The responsibility of wage setters for unemployment increases significantly, because they no longer negotiate about nominal wage but, instead, about real wage growth. The responsibility for existing unemployment is more transparently assigned to the parties which negotiate the relative price of labor. In contrast, autonomous discretionary monetary policy makes it more difficult to remove market rigidities, because there is still the option to solve or at least to shift the unemployment problem onto third parties (i.e., to an expansionary monetary policy).

Insofar as the single currency increases transparency, the costs of structural rigidities, as reflected in relative prices, become more evident. Lower trading costs and higher transparency jointly tend to foster competition in goods markets, which in turn reduces the available product market rents. If these rents are smaller, the incentive to resist reforms that prevent such rents to be captured are smaller as well.

Overall, the incentives for extensive reforms of goods, labor, and capital markets increase under a regime of EMU, i.e. irrevocably fixed exchange rates.[5] If changes in monetary policy and the nominal exchange rate are not available, and if labor is immobile as is the case in most parts of the Euro area, there is no other option than to undertake reforms in order to facilitate the market-based adjustment to shocks. Hence, credible currency pegging in general and EMU in particular has often been interpreted as a version of Mrs. Thatcher's There-Is-No-Alternative (TINA) strategy.[6] In their paper, BELKE/HERZ/VOGEL (2006) generalize this striking TINA argument empirically and extend it also to countries beyond the narrow focus of the Euro area, which is what for instance DUVAL/ELMESKOV (2005) concentrate on. However, there are also important arguments against a

---

[3] We owe this comment to David Mayes, Western Economic Association Annual Meeting, San Diego/CA, June 29th to July 4th 2006.

[4] For a recent survey of the arguments see DUVAL/ELMESKOV (2005) and HOCHREITER/TAVLAS (2005).

[5] See ALOGOSKOUFIS (1994), CALMFORS (1998), DUVAL/ELMESKOV (2005, p. 6), MÉLITZ (1997) and SIBERT/SUTHERLAND (1997).

[6] See, BEAN (1998), CALMFORS (1998, p. 28); DUVAL/ELMESKOV (2005, p. 5) and SAINT-PAUL/BENTOLILA (2000).

positive impact of monetary rules on economic reform which can be applied to EMU as a specific monetary rule as well. It is thus ultimately an empirical question.

E.2.2. Main Pattern of Empirical Results and Stylized Facts

BELKE/HERZ/VOGEL (2006) are interested in examining the effect of EMU on structural reform and investigate this with an examination of the relationship between fixed exchange rates and reform in two wider samples of countries. Their results indicate that – in the context of OECD countries and with respect to reform beyond money and banking – EMU should not have been clearly expected to encourage structural reform.

They estimated and tested the relationship between exchange rate regimes and the degree of economic reforms by estimating panel regressions partly also via GMM. As dependent variable they use the degree of market-oriented reforms. As independent variables they include indicators of the flexibility of the exchange rate system, the stability of monetary policy and further control variables like economic performance as a proxy of reform pressure and institutional impediments to further reform. The results of their empirical analysis suggest that the adoption of an exchange rate rule like EMU is positively correlated with market-oriented reforms only in a broad world sample and with reforms in the money and banking sector in particular.

For the government sector and for market regulation, they do not find a robust significant effect, however. The impact of exchange rate policy on economic reforms is not significant in the sample of OECD countries. The use of an alternative indicator of monetary policy commitment supports these findings.

Seen on the whole, these results do not confirm the implications of Calmfors-type models, namely that one should observe a higher degree of reforms under monetary policy autonomy, i.e. outside EMU. However, the empirical results at least partly confirm the TINA argument that limiting monetary policy autonomy (like a common monetary policy under EMU from the perspective of a single EMU-in country) tends to raise the probability of the implementation of structural reforms / liberalization steps. The seemingly irrevocable elimination of the exchange rate option seems to extend the incentives for painful but long-term beneficial institutional adjustments on labor and product markets for developing countries and emerging markets, but not for OECD countries. If one subsumes Euro area countries among the latter, it becomes immediately clear that the disappointing reform experience in some larger EMU member countries is totally consistent with our estimations.

Finally, the exchange rate regime often turned out to be insignificant when the authors apply it to reforms in areas other than the money and banking system. Instead, the usual suspects like the so-called problem pressure variable as measured by the initial degree of freedom dominate the regressions. These results imply that a higher initial level of economic freedom leads to a lower scope for further liberali ation and a higher conditional policy convergence. If the exchange rate regime is significant, these coefficients are around three times as high as the coefficients measuring exchange rate flexibility. In a sense, one could even argue that a change in a nominal variable such as the exchange rate regime appears to have mainly effects on other nominal variables like the monetary and banking system, a view often condemned as too pessimistic in the discussions during the run-up to the Euro.

Hence, the upshot of the study is that one should not exaggerate the impact of monetary policy autonomy and the exchange rate regime on economic freedom in view of a large status-quo bias and path-dependence of reform intensity. There seems to be no empirical base for the argument that discretionary monetary policy is favorable because it gives more incentives for structural reforms. This insight probably represents the most robust result of the contribution by BELKE/HERZ/ VOGEL (2006).

From this perspective, the estimation results are strikingly similar to the huge amount of non-results which DUVAL/ELMESKOV (2005) found for their sample of Euro area countries. Moreover, the results are compatible with the widely held prior that EMU was not at all important for incentives to reforms in Europe. They can also explain why the Euro neither proved to be a job machine nor a job killer, as claimed by politicians before the start of EMU. Instabilities of the Eurozone could arise because (a) a lack of reforms might hamper labor market flexibility which becomes necessary in a currency union in case of asymmetric shocks and, hence, global competitiveness of the Euro area (BELKE/GROS, 1999), and (b) the shift in the monetary regime towards the Euro did not necessarily have the same impact on the reform intensity in all Eurozone member countries' economies (if instability is interpreted in an inter-country phenomenon). In general, it is unclear whether a monetary union itself increases the probability of asymmetric shocks. Not only labor market rigidities or flexibility matters, but also differences in labor market flexibility between European countries. However, what matters is the combination of asymmetric shocks and labor market flexibility. The net effect might, for instance, depend on the pre-existing degree of unionization, on the extent of centralization and coordination of wage-bargaining and the relative size of a country within the currency union (BELKE/GROS, 1999, and POSEN/ POPOV GOULD, 2006).

We now become less specific and turn to our second question and ask what kind of monetary policy suits a slow growth economy like the Eurozone and whether actual monetary policy has behaved like that. If not, this might have contributed to the emergence of instabilities in the Eurozone.

E.3. What Kind of Monetary Policy for a Slow Growth Economy?

It has often been argued that the ECB has been much less activist in its policy than the Federal Reserve (see, e.g., BELKE/GROS, 2005). Could it have done more? We start by showing that cutting interest rates to 1% in 2003 would have offset the tightening of conditions induced by the appreciation of the Euro, but it would not have qualitatively changed the assessment of the relative inaction with respect to the United States.

After these more short-run considerations, this section analyses in more detail a longer-term aspect of monetary policy that has gained in importance since the start of EMU, namely the consequences of allowing a liquidity overhang to build up. Some economists may perhaps argue that 'liquidity overhang', or 'excessive credit growth', is a meaningless concept. Money and credit growth simply reflect real economic and price growth without exerting any influence on these variables. We do not want to enter here into the causality of money and prices. We only note that money and credit growth, which cannot be explained as responding to the needs of an economy growing at potential, and a desired rate of inflation should alert us to potential future risks to price and/or financial stability (note again the title of this paper which is "Instability of the Eurozone?") and make us question the appropriateness of the stance of monetary policy. Thus, we subscribe to the conventional wisdom that, in the long run, inflation is a monetary phenomenon, and that central banks should always keep an eye on the long run. The most recent meeting of the "ECB and its Watchers" Conference in Frankfurt has again shown that this view has emerged as a consensus among the different ECB watchers (PILL/RAUTANEN, 2006).

The temptation to look at the short-run becomes especially strong when price stability seems assured 'as far as the eye can see', i.e. for the next few years. This explains the strength of the pressure on the ECB to 'get the economy moving'. However, it can be shown that a monetary policy that focuses on the output gap (because price stability seems assured) is liable to make serious errors as well, because estimates of the output gap are also subject to a wide margin of uncertainty. This is particularly the case for the Euro area, as is documented in chapter 1 of GROS et al. (2005). The persistent uncertainty about the growth potential for the Eurozone thus suggests that the ECB is justified in placing less emphasis on cyclical stabilization policy. The example of the Federal Reserve is misleading in this area as well, because the growth potential of the US seems to have been much more stable.

E.3.1. Not Enough Loosening?

The ECB held rates at a historically low level for two and a half years until December 6th, 2005. However, this does not seem to have been enough to get the Euroland economy going. One explanation of this apparent failure might be that the appreciation of the Euro led to a tightening of monetary conditions despite the constant low level of interest rates. This leads to the question: Could the ECB have done more to support the Eurozone economy?

It is true that monetary policy could have been even more accommodative, as it failed to offset the impact of the strengthening currency. But how much could the ECB have achieved? Figure 1. below shows a counterfactual exercise, whereby the ECB cut interest rates to 1% in 2003 and kept them stable until now. That move would have offset the appreciation of the Euro during the period and prevented monetary conditions from tightening, providing a final level of monetary conditions similar to that of the US. Nevertheless, the ECB would still have been a less activist central bank than the Federal Reserve over the period (see GROS et al., 2005).

The exercise undertaken here assumes that the exchange rate would have moved in the same fashion despite the lower level of interest rates in the EU. Although this runs against economic intuition, it might not be far from what might have happened. The strong downward trend of the dollar of the last two years is widely perceived as a corollary of the huge US current account imbalance. This imbalance would probably not have been materially affected by a loosening of policy in Euroland. It might actually have worsened if one believes the major macroeconomic models.

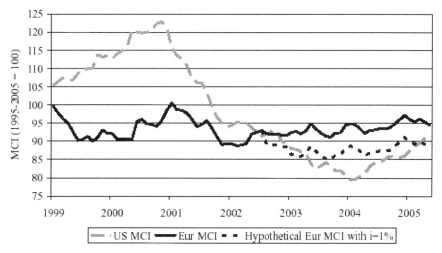

Source: Deutsche Bank, Global Market Research.

Fig. E1. Comparison of the Monetary Conditions Index: US vs. Eurozone.

Thus, with the benefit of hindsight, the ECB failed to anticipate, or to react promptly to the tightening of monetary conditions that was induced by the persistent appreciation of the Euro over the two years until the midst of 2005. As we will explore below, conflicting short- and longer-term objectives probably lie at the heart of this apparent inaction.

E.3.2. Between Two Pillars

Even if to a lesser extent than the Federal Reserve, the ECB maintained an expansionary monetary policy stance in the period until the second half of 2005, stimulating the real economy (and thus giving policy makers ample room to implement economic reforms and consolidate government finances). Against the background of its long-standing opposition against a monetary policy aimed at supporting growth and against ex-ante coordination with fiscal and structural policy, the ECB's accommodating monetary policy stance (which we advocated last year) at that time is noteworthy. Unfortunately, the policy had none of the desired effects: growth remained lackluster and governments neither exerted fiscal discipline nor progressed much with structural reform (see part 2 and 3 of this paper).

Despite this shortage of progress in reform and accelerating liquidity growth, the ECB (at the time of the 7th Annual Report of the CEPS Macroeconomic Policy Group by GROS et al., 2005, going to publication, namely June 2005) still shied away from fading out the strong monetary stimulus. The simple reason for this was that growth remained weak and inflation low.

The ECB has thus been caught between a rock and a hard place. The rock consisted of continuing sluggish real growth and subdued goods and wage inflation. The economic analysis within the ECB's monetary policy strategy thus argued for unchanged or lower interest rates. The hard place consisted of dynamic money and credit growth (which has raised housing prices). The monetary analysis was arguing for higher rates (see, e.g., the ECB Observer Report by BELKE et al., 2005). With the two pillars of the strategy sending different signals, the ECB apparently has been in a dither about rate cuts or hikes for the last 15 months before June 2005. At that time, this was beginning to raise questions about the credibility of its monetary policy strategy.

With the two pillars giving conflicting signals, the communications strategy has been severely tested. The ECB has preferred not to admit openly that it is in a quandary. Instead, it has simply vacillated from one stance to another: when economic conditions seemed to pick up it has seemed to lean towards a rate increase, only to change track when current conditions deteriorated.

E.3.3. What Happened to the Monetary Pillar?

When the ECB started to be responsible for monetary policy, it emphasized that the first pillar for its decisions on monetary policy had to be an analysis of monetary policy conditions and accordingly set a 'reference' value for the rate of growth of the main monetary aggregate on which it chose to concentrate, i.e. M3. Everything else being equal, growth rates of M3 above this reference value (4.5%) were meant to signal a need for tightening policy. Since the start of EMU, however, actual growth of both money and credit has consistently been above the reference rates as shown in Figure 2. below.

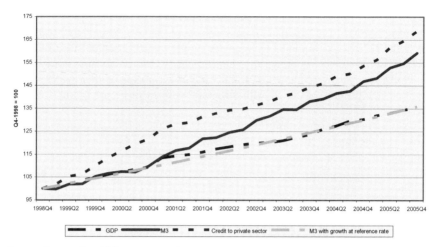

Source: International Monetary Fund.

Fig. E2. Money and Credit in the Eurozone.

Nominal Gross Domestic Product (GDP) grew over this seven-year period by more than 30%, which is very close to the compound growth M3 would have had if the reference rate had been observed over this period. In reality, however, the stock of money is now almost 25 percentage points above this level.

One might argue that less emphasis should be placed on monetary and credit aggregates in a time of rapid evolution of the financial markets, but upon closer inspection, this argument is much less convincing. It was widely expected that the introduction of the Euro would trigger a process of disintermediation whereby economies of scale in securitized markets would allow firms to finance themselves without recourse to bank credit. Moreover, households would then have a much wider range of investments available, which would induce them to hold a smaller share of their assets in bank accounts. Both arguments suggest that the structural changes coming with the Euro would actually reduce the ratio of credit and money relative to GDP. The expectation was that the Eurozone would move closer to the US model in which banks play a much smaller role in the financing of corporate investment and in the US the ratio of both credit and money to GDP is much lower than in the Eurozone. As Figure 2. shows, however, both money and credit actually increased trend-wise relative to GDP with the result that the ratio of both money and credit to GDP increased by about 20 to 25%.

A transatlantic comparison is again instructive. Figure 3. shows the evolution of the ratio of money and credit to GDP also for the US since 1998. It is apparent that on this metric, there is a slight difference. While the change in credit per GDP is 24.2% and the change in M3 per GDP amounts to 17.2% for the Euro area, the relevant figures are 22.6% and 17.5% for the US. The popular image of the Federal Reserve flooding the US economy with liquidity compared to a much stingier ECB that at least constantly talks about the need to keep money growth in check was thus wrong. Monetary policy on (bank) credit expansion could even be seen as having been slightly more expansionary in the Euro area than in the US.

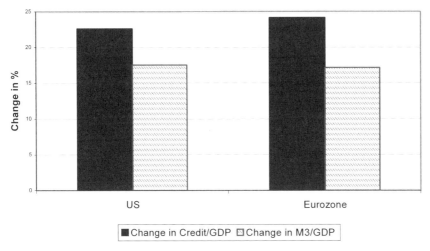

Source: International Monetary Fund.

Fig. E3. A Transatlantic Comparison of Excess Liquidity (2005, yoy).

E.3.4. The Costs of Ignoring the Monetary Pillar

At first glance, money and credit growth above earlier-desired levels do not seem to have exacted any costs on the economy. Between January 1999 and April 2005, the harmonized yearly consumer price inflation rate averaged 2%. This appears to be close enough to qualify as meeting the ECB's goal of keeping inflation below, but close to 2% over the medium term.

This does not mean, however, that one can ignore money and credit developments. We have learned from past experience that the lag between monetary policy and its effects on inflation can be long and variable (PILL/ RAUTANEN, 2006). Money growth above the rate absorbed by money demand will at some point raise prices, be they for goods, services or assets. Hence, even if consumer price inflation has remained well-behaved so far and there are no signs of an imminent rise, it is too early to dismiss all risks resulting from liquidity growth.

One potential warning sign comes from housing prices. While it is true that price increases for real estate Euro area average have not been alarming in any single year (e.g., 7.2% in 2004), a longer run view reveals a trend that gives rise to concern.

Indeed, it seems that the Euro area housing index shows the same longer run development as that of the US, confirming the similarity in the expansion of monetary and credit aggregates. This can be verified immediately from a simple plot of the data in Figure 4. which shows the average Euro area index constructed from OECD data together with that of the US.[7] The transatlantic correlation seems quite strong, not only for the most recent history, but also over a much longer period of time. House prices thus seem to be important even within the Euro zone. How large is the risk that markets turn around in the US and the Euro area at the same time? Figure 4. suggests on a very stylized level that the Euro area seems to follow the US with a lag of about 2 years, suggesting that, if this relationship continues to hold, the Euro area would still have two years of higher real estate prices to go.

Real House Prices in a long run perspective: Euroarea (GDP weighted) and US compared

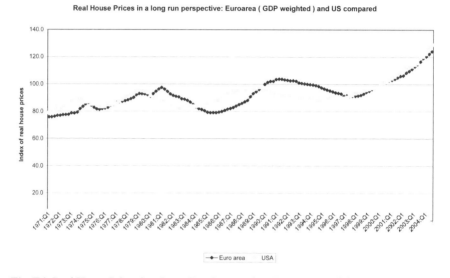

Fig. E4. Real House Prices in a Long-Run Perspective: Euro Area and the US Compared.

The simple fact illustrated here is that the Euro area has experienced a similar development as the US over the last decade (BELKE/WIEDMANN, 2005). This is not yet widely enough appreciated. ECB President Trichet has over the last year drawn some comfort from the contained level of house price inflation in the Euro area average during 2005. However, what seems worrisome is not so much the increase during last year, but the cumulative increase over the last decade and the acceleration over the last decade, which has brought the index to beat all previous records as can easily be verified in Figure 4.

Many seem reluctant to look at the Euro area average for real estate prices, but this is not appropriate. Real estate market developments are always heavily

---

[7] Real estate market developments have always been heavily influenced by regional supply and demand conditions and price bubbles have tended to be concentrated in certain regions. This is as true for the US as for Europe. The depressed state of real estate in Germany is not too dissimilar to that of the Midwest of the US. Hence, it is as useful to look at the Euro area average as it is to look at the US average. See BELKE and WIEDMANN (2005).

influenced by regional supply and demand conditions, and price bubbles have tended to be concentrated in certain regions. At the same time, however, the deflation of regional price bubbles, given a critical size of the affected region, has tended to have supra-regional effects. Two examples may suffice to illustrate the point.

First, in the late 1980s, there was a property price boom in many parts of the US, particularly in states like Texas and California, fuelled by strong lending growth by savings and loan banks. While the property price booms were localized, the entire US savings and loans industry was severely shaken when the bubble burst. To help the sector recover, the Federal Reserve kept interest rates at very low levels for an extended period of time. When they eventually raised rates in 1994, they induced a severe correction in world bond markets (BELKE/ WIEDMANN, 2005).

Second, in the early 1990s, following the fall of the Berlin Wall and German unification, property prices rose strongly in eastern Germany. Construction investment and mortgage lending boomed, until overbuilding caused prices to collapse in the mid-1990s. The implosion of property prices weakened German consumption, investment and GDP growth. Although prices have now stabilized, the collapse of the building industry caused severe economic problems given the limited flexibility of the German labor market. Moreover, the stagnation of house prices certainly contributed to the ongoing weakness of consumption in Germany. Given the weight of the economy in the Eurozone, the housing market collapse was a major reason why the ECB had to keep interest rates at relatively low levels for a long time. These and other examples from economic history suggest that regional property-price cycles can have supra-regional effects. Recently, property prices have increased especially rapidly in France and Spain (FERNÁNDEZ-KRANZ/HON, 2006, and GIROURARD et al., 2006). These countries are certainly large enough to cause Euro area wide problems should a housing price bubble suddenly deflate (see Fig. 5)[8].

---

[8] Even if a house price bubble exists in, say, Spain, the main research question remains whether this triggers indeed Euro area wide problems, especially with an eye on different financing structures, different potential for extracting one's equity investment in housing (which is much lower in most Euro area countries than in the US) and different degrees of "foreign" ownership. The effects could be more isolated than in the case of the different states in the US or the different Laender in Germany after the reunification. This debate is open for further research. See FERNÁNDEZ-KRANZ/HON (2006), GIULIODORI (2005), and GROS (2006).

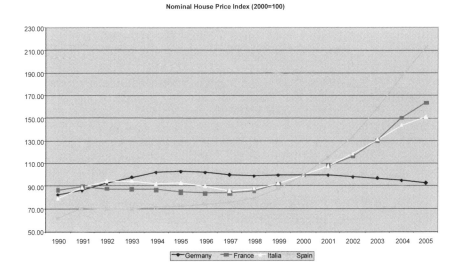

Fig. E5. Development of Nominal House Prices in Selected OECD Countries.

What are the consequences of real estate booms? The key reason US house prices have attracted so much attention is that a property price crash, or just a deceleration of the rate of increase of house prices, in the US would almost certainly weaken private consumption through wealth effects and increased uncertainty about the economic outlook (BELKE/WIEDMANN, 2005). This is well known, but the data presented here implies that the same danger exists for the Euro area. In the Euro area the wealth effect might be less strong and consumers might be less indebted, but a fall in house prices could instead also lead to an abrupt fall of new construction investment.[9] Moreover, a fall in house prices may impair a part of the outstanding loans of the banking sector and force banks to raise reserves. This could reduce their willingness to extend credit to businesses and consumers. A slump in demand in the countries suffering from housing price deflation could spill over to other Euro area countries and, in the worst case, pull the entire Euro area into recession or even deflation. While the exact details of the transmission mechanism are different on the two sides of the Atlantic, it is clear that both sides face a quite similar risk.

Figure 6.a. below illustrates the close link that existed between house prices and consumption (the correlation coefficient is about 0.80) in the year 2004. Figure 6.b. suggests a similar pattern also for the year 2005.

---

[9] For more details of estimated housing wealth effects in several countries and the relative importance of mortgage loans see CATTE et al. (2006), GIULIODORI (2005), PEEK/WILCOX (2006), and SELOSSE/SCHREFLER (2005, p. 13).

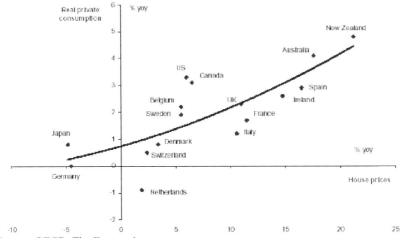

Source: OECD, The Economist.

Fig. E6.a. House Prices and Consumption.

The development of house prices in Euroland also matters with respect to the current account position of the Euro zone member countries. The importance of housing prices in influencing domestic demand even in continental Europe where re-financing of mortgages is more costly and where house ownership is often much lower (GIULIODORI, 2005) can be illustrated by simply comparing house prices and the current account across Euro area members. (Euro area members share the same exchange rate; most of any divergence in current accounts should thus be due to divergences in domestic demand.) As Figure 7. shows, there is a rather close correlation between the current account and real house prices, with the latter explaining 80 % of the variance of the former.

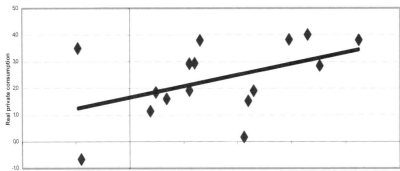

Source: Economist June 2005 and OECD, (2005a).

Fig. E6.b. Housing Prices and Consumption in the Year 2005.

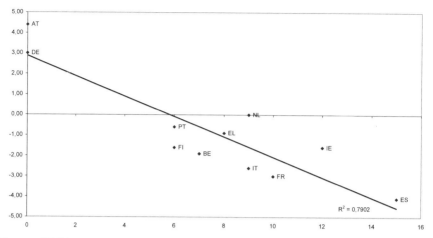

Source: OECD.

Fig. E7. House Prices and the Current Account (1998–2004): the Experience of Eurozone Members

Thus, excessive money and credit growth raises risks to price stability from two sides: it could stoke consumer price inflation in the longer run, or cause consumer price deflation by creating a negative asset price bubble.

The fact that an asset price bubble does not lead to consumer price inflation while it is building up and might even lead to deflation once it bursts explains why even longer term inflation expectations might not be a good guide to policy. The cost of letting these bubbles emerge do not come in the form of higher inflation, but of a misallocation of resources (empty houses) and prolonged economic weakness. According to Figure 4., house prices seem to move in long-term cycles and are much smoother than stock markets. The Euro area aggregate index of real house prices has risen almost as much as that of the US and is now (together with that of the US) about 40% above its 30 year average. This is almost exactly equal to the overvaluation of Japanese real estate at the height of the Japanese bubble, which was then followed by a decade of decline (POSEN, 2003). However, with an eye also on Figure 4., there is no doubt that (real) house prices have a clear tendency to revert to their mean (SHILLER, 2005). Hence, it would be wrong to expect a sudden 'crash' in the real estate market. Sharp declines in stock prices have indeed corrected excesses in more than one occasion, but real estate prices tend to move much more smoothly, in part because households seem reluctant to accept lower nominal prices and prefer to hold on to their house even if real prices continue to decline for an extended period. This does not imply that the EU (or the US) will have to expect a similar economic performance than Japan over the last decade, but it does imply that a serious and long drawn out correction in house prices cannot be ruled out. It is the latter that is the most relevant danger for Euroland and could give rise to significant instabilities, given Euroland's still quite low overall degree of flexibility (see part 2 and 3 of this paper).

Is the Anglo-Saxon experience a reason to relax? The UK and Australia, to name just two Anglo-Saxon countries, have also experienced massive run-ups in their housing markets. Although the markets have slowed down considerably over the last year, their economies have not collapsed. It is thus tempting to use the experience of the UK and Australia as a counter example to the thesis that housing prices have reached a worrisome level in the Euro zone (and the US). One might be tempted to infer from the relatively good performance of the UK and Australian economies after the end of their respective housing booms that 'resilience' to housing booms and busts has increased. However, there are several reasons why it is clearly too early to conclude that housing booms can pass without any negative effects. The first reason is simply that too little time has passed since the peak was reached in these two countries. As emphasized above, the decline in house prices following a period of overvaluation tends to be stretched over a long period. Second, both the UK and Australia have strongly benefited over the last year (their first year without real estate price increases, but yet no fall) from a significant terms of trade gain due to higher raw material prices which might have prevented negative effects from materializing.

A longer-term perspective is again useful to measure the scale of the monetary overhang at present (see, extensively, PILL/RAUTANEN, 2006). Figure 8. shows that the scale of the present divergence between money growth and inflation had only one precedent, namely the early 1990s, when a scissor opened between accelerating money growth and inflation which was on a downwards trend. The scissors closed in the middle of the decade, with only a slight acceleration of inflation. The main event that led to the two series to convergence was the strong deceleration of money growth which preceded the recession of 1995 (and a subsequent period of slow growth). The deceleration in money growth was in turn due first to a tightening by the Bundesbank, which saw German inflation rising and then a considerable increase in interest rates as the central banks of those countries under speculative attack tried to maintain price stability in the face of large devaluations.

There is another parallel between the current situation and that of the early 1990s (see also part 4). At the time, exchange rates were kept fixed within the ERM, although some countries were continuously losing competitiveness vis-à-vis the core of the ERM, Germany. That this situation was unsustainable became clear only in the currency crisis that started in late 1992, precipitated by the combination of a tightening by the Bundesbank and the uncertainty surrounding a French referendum. Part 4 of this paper will analyze the dangers inherent in the present situation in more detail. The latter might lead to instabilities of the Eurozone, again from two angles. First, the bursting of a bubble might be problematic per se, and second, all the Eurozone economies might be impacted differently.

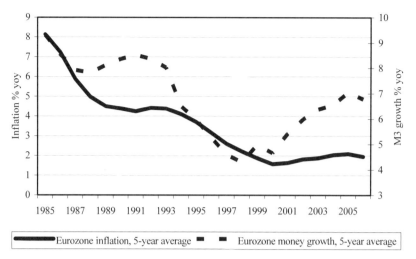

Source: EUROPEAN COMMISSION, BUNDESBANK.

Fig. E8. Inflation – A Monetary Phenomenon.

E.4. The European Monetary Policy in a Large and Diversified Economic Zone

E.4.1. EMU's Coming Stress Test

From the time perspective of June 2005, GROS et al. (2005) have documented in their recent Macroeconomic Policy Group report the inability of the usual macroeconomic levers to get the Euroland economy on a sustainable growth path, as longer-term considerations limited the extent to which both fiscal and monetary policy could perform a stabilization role. Pressured by persistently weak growth, a choice was made in favor of 'short-termism': In the fiscal field, the key disciplinary device, the Stability Pact, has already effectively been emasculated by the politicians. In the monetary field, the ECB has initially ignored but more recently taken into account medium-term warning signals stemming from the acceleration in money and credit growth. In fact, in the midst of 2005 and before the most recent interest rate hikes, it still looked to some observers as if fears of political pressures were inducing the ECB to focus on short-term growth considerations at the cost of neglecting long-term stability risks (again a close reminder of the main topic of the paper, instabilities of the Eurozone).

    In the end, neither short-term demand has been boosted nor long-term discipline maintained. The result of this failed attempt to stimulate demand in the face of very sluggish supply is that Euroland is now faced with rising public debt/GDP ratios and a large monetary overhang. The latter has not led to incipient inflationary pressures so far, and the current state of labor markets suggests that inflation is likely to remain under control in the near term. Additionally, financial markets do not seem to care, although public debt is indeed very different between EMU countries (see most recent data). Despite this, growing fiscal deficits combined with a rising monetary overhang in the face of considerable cost and price rigidities constitute a threat to future price and financial stability in the Euro area.

Seen on the whole, the European monetary policy in a large and diversified economic zone has functioned remarkably well in the first years of EMU. However, in this final section we would like to add some water to the wine and argue that this will not necessarily be the case in the future, because EMU will almost certainly come under stress in the near future due to its diversity. The emergence of widening intra-area divergences could severely test the resolve of the Euroland authorities to support the value of the Euro, which could degenerate in a process of gradual 'lira-isation' of the Euro.

E.4.1.1. EMU's Potential Breaking Points Resurface

In the earlier debates about the requirements for economic and monetary union, many participants – including senior policy-makers – argued that monetary union would not be stable and could not survive in the long run if it were not accompanied by more economic flexibility and closer political union. The former was seen as necessary to allow for better adjustment in the absence of country-specific interest and exchange rate changes; the latter was seen as necessary to establish democratic legitimization for a stability oriented monetary policy and the conditions for a fiscal policy consistent with this type of monetary policy. Without closer political union and the emergence of a European public will, it was feared that the ECB could come under irresistible pressure from national governments to conduct a softer monetary policy and that fiscal policy would lack the necessary discipline to ensure price stability in the long run. In other words, governments could pursue their narrow interests at the expense of the public good of price stability.

As preparations for EMU progressed and prospects for closer political union faded into the background, it was argued that the statutory independence of the ECB would shield it against political influence. Moreover, to ensure some fiscal policy discipline, the Stability and Growth Pact was agreed at the Amsterdam European Council meeting in 1997.

In the first few years of EMU, neither the degree of economic flexibility nor the stability of the fiscal framework or the independence of the ECB was severely tested. However, as growth has faded, tensions have increased. Optimists hoped that economic tensions would eventually break the existing structural rigidities. Unfortunately, it seems that the rigidities are prevailing while fiscal policy discipline is giving way. Since this will not keep growth going, political pressure will increasingly be brought to bear on the ECB to support economic activity in the short-term by weakening the Euro internally and externally.

E.4.1.2. A New Element: Intra-Area Divergences

Growth differentials among EMU member countries have so far been rather limited and at a stable level (BENALAL et al., 2006). The weighted standard deviation of the growth rates of the Euro area members has barely moved between 1999 and 2004, as the large three Euro area members tended to move broadly together. As documented below, the two main laggards in the Eurozone were Germany and Italy, with France falling somewhat in between them and the more dynamic smaller countries ("small is beautiful" also with respect to deficits, see GROS et al., 2005, chapter 2, and FELDERER, 2006, for details, excluding current Portugal and Greece).

Table E1. "Small is beautiful" in Macroeconomic Terms (Averages 2000 to 2005).

Large vs. small (averages, 2000–2005)	Big-3*	Small-8 **	France	Germany	Italy	NMS	US	Eurozone
Real GDP growth	1.42	2.91	1.99	1.14	1.13	4.77	2.76	1.79
Fiscal balance	-2.82	-0.45	-2.83	-2.70	-2.93	-3.43	-2.68	-2.07
Labor productivity growth	2.34	4.08	2.76	1.69	2.58	8.82	1.97	2.76
Share of industry	19.82	17.42	15.52	21.20	21.99	23.58	14.85	19.03
Unit labor cost	1.58	2.46	1.65	0.30	2.78	2.96	2.06	1.59
Change in share of exports in Eurozone	0.01	0.40	-2.26	1.15	1.15	7.43	n.a.	n.a.

* Big 3= DE, IT, FR
** Small 8= BE,AT,PT,GRE,NL,LU,FI,IE
Source: Own calculations based on AMECO data.

However, any apparent similarity between developments in Italy and Germany has been superficial. It is now becoming clear that a chasm has opened up between them under the surface.

Germany entered EMU with an overvalued exchange rate, but it has regained competitiveness through a process that used to be called 'competitive deflation'. By contrast, Italy has continuously lost competitiveness and hence market shares. These large relative movements in competitive positions did not translate earlier into different growth rates because of the offsetting tendencies in the housing markets. As documented above, the low interest rate environment fostered by the ECB's policy and global developments led to a housing boom in a number of countries, including Italy. This has thus far sustained consumption in Italy, while overbuilding especially in the eastern part of the country during the early 1990s lead to persistent weakness in the real estate market and consumption in Germany. However, the cumulated loss in Italian competitiveness has become so severe that its negative effects can no longer be offset by the housing boom. Hence, we foresee that Italy is likely to provide the first stress test for EMU. Below, we would like to develop some arguments underlining our hypothesis from the time perspective of the 7th Annual Report of the CEPS Macroeconomic Policy Group in June 2005. We feel legitimized in doing so, since things have not changed dramatically since then.

E.4.1.3. Italy Moving Towards the Brink

The Italian economy has slipped back into recession in 2004Q4–2005Q1. However, in contrast to developments in 2003, the most recent downturn has been more pronounced, and there are presently no signs of a bottoming out of this contraction in the near future. As a consequence, Italian real GDP could now drop in 2005 in a recession almost as deep as that of 1993, when real GDP contracted by 0.9%.

As mentioned above, a key reason for Italy's economic weakening has been a pronounced loss in external competitiveness. With unit labor costs in Italy rising by 1.3 percentage points faster than in the Euroland average – and by 2.5 percentage points faster than in Germany – in 1999–2004, Italy's real effective exchange rate (based on relative export prices) rose by 15.6% between 1999 and 2004, compared to a 1.7% increase in Germany and a 1.3% drop in France. This, in combination with the accompanying deterioration in business and investor confidence, has led to a sharp decline in growth since 2000 and, most likely, recession in 2005.

When Italy fell into recession in 1993, the lira depreciated substantially. It fell by altogether 34% against the Ecu – the predecessor of the Euro – between 1992 and 1995. Producer price inflation accelerated from 1.9% in 1992 to 7.8% in 1995, but the total increase in prices by 16% between 1992 and 1995 was much less than the depreciation of the exchange rate. As a result, Italy regained competitiveness. This gain in competitiveness was large enough to overcome the negative impact of the increase in interest rates so that GDP growth recovered after an initial fall to 2.3% in 1994 and 3.0% in 1995.

This time, Italy cannot regain competitiveness – and stimulate economic growth – through nominal exchange rate depreciation. What is needed is real exchange rate depreciation through cost and price cuts. This is how Germany improved its external competitiveness and raised economic growth in recent years (while many economists and market participants misinterpreted these developments as deflation). Thus, German unit labor costs increased by only 0.4% in the annual average of 1999–2004, with a substantial drop by 0.7% yoy occurring in 2004. Aided by increased competitiveness, net exports rose and the German economy recovered from stagnation in 2003. However in contrast to their German counterparts, which learned to live with a hard currency and fierce competition in the past, Italian companies and trade unions have little experience in rigorous cost and price controls in a highly competitive economic environment.

They operate in an environment characterized by significant restrictions on competition and a soft currency.

Moreover, while they tend to concentrate more on the production of medium-quality, price sensitive goods and services, they have made less progress than their German counterparts in outsourcing production to low-cost locations. All this suggests that it will take Italian companies much longer than their German counterparts to improve their competitive position. As a result, the medium-term outlook for the Italian economy is rather bleak.

On top of the loss of competitiveness, one has to ask how long the housing boom in Italy will last. Should housing prices stop increasing, or even decline, domestic demand would fall even further. The economic situation in Italy thus has the potential to develop into a full-blown crisis. Moreover, as both the loss of competitiveness and any post-bubble housing market weakness require considerable time to be corrected, it is likely that the Italian economy will experience a long period of economic stagnation or even contraction (GROS, 2006a).

Table E2. Italy: All Competitiveness Indicators Point in the Same Direction.

1999–2004	EU 12	Germany	France	Italy
Labour Productivity(*)	0.0	0.9	1.1	0.0
ULC(*)	1.6	0.4	1.6	2.9
Change in the share of exports over eurozone (national accounts)	--	+9.3%	-5.6	-14.4
Exports(customs) (*)	6.7	7.4	7.4	4.6
Competitiveness ranking (2004–05)	---	13	27	47
REER (ULC)	12.5	-4.8	1.7	10.9
REER (X prices)	9.2	1.7	-1.3	15.6

* This the year average of the %yoy rate. The changes in REERs refer to the wholw period, as the change in the share of exports.
Note: X stands for exports. In the case of EU 12; REER is computed against the rest of the world. In the case of individual countries, it is against their main 34 trade partners.
Source: HAVER, EUROPEAN COMMISSION, WORLD ECONOMIC FORUM and NATIONAL STATISTICAL INSTITUTES.

E.4.1.4. Some More Formal Considerations:
Instability in a Monetary Union?

The decisive question now with respect to the title of our paper runs as follows: Is EMU in danger from internal tensions? The experience so far has shown that some countries are continuously losing competitiveness. Is this a structural problem in the sense that these countries just have problems in keeping inflation at a level that does not imply a continuing loss of competitiveness? Or is the persistence of higher inflation in some countries due to the internal dynamics of a monetary union in which any country that starts with higher inflation rates also has a lower real interest rate, which stimulates demand, and thus leads potentially to even more inflation. In other words, does a monetary union always lead to diverging cycles?

The purpose of this brief section is to discuss an extremely simplified model that can allow one to see what factors could lead to such diverging cycles at present. This representation has just two building blocks that describe the two main channels through which output and price interact in a monetary union:

$$y_t - y_{t-1} = -\varphi(i_t - (p_t - p_{t-1})) - \gamma p_t + g_t \tag{1}$$

$$p_t - p_{t-1} = \beta^{-1}(y_t - y_{t-1}) + u_t \tag{2}$$

Where the usual notation applies: y stands for output, i the nominal interest rate, p the price level. The shocks to the demand equation and the Philips curve are denoted by g and u, respectively. The first equation says that output (growth) depends on the real interest rate and the level of the real exchange rate, which in EMU is given by the domestic prices level. The second equation is just a standard Philips curve.

The parameters have a straightforward interpretation: γ should increase with the degree of openness (to intra Euro area trade); it should thus be higher for small countries (and for Germany where exports amount to over 40 % of GDP) than for Italy, France or Spain (where exports are around 25 % of GDP). The parameter φ denotes the impact of interest rate conditions on demand and should thus be related to the financing structure of the economy, e.g. the importance of external finance for investment and the mortgage sector for household consumption (and investment in housing). Finally, β denotes the inverse of the slope of the Philips curve.

The dynamics of the system are determined by the difference equation which results from simply inserting the second into the first equation:

$$\beta(p_t - p_{t-1} - u_t) = -\varphi(i_t - (p_t - p_{t-1})) - \gamma p_t + g_t \tag{3}$$

$$p_t = \{-\varphi i_t + (\beta - \varphi)p_{t-1} + g_t + \beta u_t\}/(\beta + \gamma - \varphi) \tag{4}$$

Stability of the system requires that

$$-1 < (\beta - \varphi)/(\beta + \gamma - \varphi) < 1 \quad \text{or} \quad \beta + \gamma > \varphi \tag{5}$$

This suggests that the bigger φ is relative to γ (for example the case of Spain which combines a relatively low degree of openness with a relatively strong financial sector), the more likely it is that the country will experience large deviations of its price level from the equilibrium value. More generally, a higher degree of openness makes it more likely that the stability condition is satisfied. More openness should thus stabilize the price level (and hence also output) in a monetary union.

Figure 9. below shows the root of the difference equation as a function of the parameter φ for two particular values of β and γ (both equal to 30). This figure illustrates a general pattern: For small values of φ, the system is always stable and adjustment becomes initially quicker until $\varphi = \beta$. At this point the root is zero and inflation is no longer influenced by its own past (and thus driven only by the shocks). If φ is greater than β the root becomes negative, implying that the system will exhibit cycles. These cycles will converge as long as φ< β + 0.5*γ. If φ is greater than β + 0.5*γ, the system becomes instable (but remains cyclical provided that φ is smaller than β + γ).

For an alternative with competitiveness having a lagged instead of an immediate impact on output, see our annex.

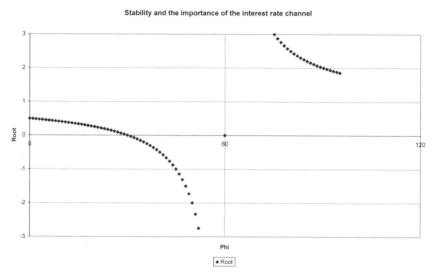

Fig. E9. Relevance of the Interest Rate Channel

E.4.2. The Stress Test in Action

Unfortunately, Italy is not the only country to experience the combination of a strong loss of competitiveness whose effect has so far been covered by a housing boom; Portugal and Greece are in a similar situation. These two countries are also running the highest government budget deficits in the Euro area – in the case of Greece even before growth is likely to turn down under the impact of a slowing housing market and the ongoing loss of competitiveness. Even a strong performer like Spain masks a deteriorating competitive position under the strong growth that, were its housing market to slow down, would put its economic performance at risk. Thus, the list of countries at risk is increasing and could easily become a majority soon. At that point, a key political question will have to be answered: Does the majority want to undergo the painful process of regaining competitiveness through cost and wage control, or is a weaker currency preferable?

Given the aversion of especially the large member countries to painful structural reform, which was documented above in section 4, and in view of the likely persistence of the economic difficulties, the political systems in the weaker countries – at first probably Italy – are likely to abandon fiscal policy discipline. The European Commission hopes that the Council of Finance Ministers (ECOFIN) will demonstrate that the Stability and Growth Pact still exerts a disciplinary influence on EMU members after its recent revision. We doubt this. With France and Germany also experiencing severe strains in government finances, and Portugal and Greece among its 'compagni di sventura', Italy can count on powerful and numerous allies in its likely course towards higher fiscal deficits.

However, it is crucial to understand that fiscal policy cannot address Italy's long-term competitiveness problem and is hence unlikely to engineer the desired economic revival – in the same way that past devaluations of the lira only provided temporary respite. Therefore, Italian policy-makers are very likely to step up pressure on the ECB to pursue an even more expansionary monetary policy, especially as they would have to bear the largest fiscal burden should interest rates increase substantially. French and German politicians may not stand in the way of efforts to coax the ECB into an easier monetary policy as they have been unable to engineer a reduction of unemployment through labor market reform.

Without European political union, the ECB lacks a public constituency supporting its monetary policy stance in the face of political pressure. Public support was a cornerstone for the German Bundesbank's ability to pursue a low-inflation, hard currency policy. It remains to be seen whether the ECB can do the same without strong backing from the general public. Should the ECB yield to inevitable political pressures, the switches would be set for a higher-inflation, softer-currency EMU. Monetary union is thus likely to undergo a major stress test, which should not come as a surprise. Many economists had predicted severe stress before the start of EMU and warned that this could result in a softening of the common currency or even an eventual demise of EMU. What is perhaps surprising is how unprepared economic policy-makers, including those at the ECB, presently appear in dealing with the stress.

The debate preceding the referendum in France (even more than its outcome) showed the severe stress under which policy-makers have come throughout the EU. One argument used against the Constitutional Treaty was that it validated an excessively liberal economic approach, based on 'Anglo-Saxon' principles. Formally, this argument was wrong in that the draft Constitutional Treaty would not have changed the economic constitution of the EU. However, this argument does have a basis: the EU, and especially EMU, has been a catalyst for reforms in many areas (finance, central bank independence, etc.), which more often than not have been presented by national policy-makers as constraints imposed by 'Brussels'. Moreover, at the European Council of Lisbon, national leaders united to proclaim solemnly that the EU would deliver the "most competitive knowledge-based economy". However, as documented amply in previous analyses (and official documents), the so-called 'Lisbon process' has led to reform inflation with many promises and little action. This failure to deliver – combined with the constant sniping against EU rules that were perceived either as too liberal (services directive) or too constraining (limits on state aids, limits on fiscal deficits) – has undermined the legitimacy of the EU in general. It appears to be only a question of time before this general dissatisfaction also reaches the ECB.

E.5. Policy Conclusions

In this paper we have demonstrated how tensions between short-term and long-term policy objectives seemed to have delivered the worst of all possible outcomes for the Eurozone, lack of cyclical support and a weakening of long-term discipline. With growth now slowly picking up there is no longer an excuse for structural policy to shelve important reforms. It should now also become easier to tighten fiscal policy by cutting expenditures and for monetary policy to continue to refrain from turning a blind eye to accelerating money and credit growth.

While the Eurozone average seems to slowly be coming out of hibernation, important internal divergences have appeared. The key question is whether these stark divergences in performance are the result of divergent policies or of diverging economic fortunes. The answer is probably both: inside a monetary union, diverging economic fortunes will lead to diverging economic paths, especially if policy responses diverge. Our analysis suggests that countries that have learned to live with a hard currency in the past should be able to adjust within EMU. This applies primarily to some of the smaller countries, but also to the same extent to Germany which has regained competitiveness through rigorous price and cost control. According to section 4, however, this is valid only for German firms, but not to the same extent for the labor market, which still suffers from severe mismatch problems.

Which lessons can be drawn from the history of European integration in order to assess the probability of instabilities within the Eurozone? The first attempt to form a monetary union in Europe started in the early 1970s (the so-called Werner Plan to reach EMU by 1980). It ended in total failure because of intra-area differences which show, mutatis mutandis, very similar elements to today's situation. At the time, the main reason for divergence was a difference in the reaction to the oil shock of 1973. Germany chose the hard-currency approach, whereas most other countries tried to inflate their way out. Needless to say, the attempt to inflate away a terms-of-trade loss was not successful. The hard currency model thus led over time to much better economic performance. Monetary union became possible only once this lesson had been learned and, at least on the surface, there was broad agreement on the hard-currency approach. The list of countries that have successfully absolved a national stress test of the hard-currency approach is not long:

- Germany after 1967, following the rise of the DM against the dollar and again in 1973;
- The Netherlands following break-up of the Bretton-Woods system in 1974, in the 'snake' with the DM;
- Austria in the early 1980s, after adoption of the hard-shilling policy;

- France in the early 1990s, following adoption of the franc fort policy in the late 1980s; and
- Germany over the last decade following the reunification boom and bust especially in its real estate market.

By contrast, none of the Southern European countries have maintained a hard currency policy over an entire business cycle. Today, the main threat no longer comes from trade-unions that demand double-digit wage increases. Rather, the main danger lies in the swelling ranks of retirees who demand 'only' their acquired rights in the face of shrinking resources. As GROS et al. (2005) have documented, the resources available for distribution have shrunk due to lower productivity growth and ongoing demographic decline. Today, as 30 years ago, policy-makers are at first trying to ignore the long-term constraint.

Acceptance of the long-term constraints on fiscal policy is made more difficult by the fact that financial markets can provide immediate signals only as long as there is – as was the case before EMU – a national currency to sell. Countries like Italy (and France at some point) learned from first-hand experience that bad fiscal policy led immediately to large pressures on the currency and interest rates. Under EMU, the long-term constraints appear now in the form of man-made rules, like the Stability Pact, which is increasingly perceived as an unwarranted intrusion of the EU into national policy-making. In the 1970s, the 'gnomes from Zurich' were the favorite bogeymen for the leftwing Italian press. Today, the 'accountants from Brussels' have a similar image.

Under EMU, it is the ECB's task to perform this job for those countries that have not had this education. This means that the ECB will have to downgrade its short-term concern about cyclical economic developments and pursue a monetary policy with the goal of hardening the Euro in the long run. It also means that the hard-currency countries will have to return to fiscal discipline, setting an example and exerting pressure on the previous soft-currency countries to do the same. The importance of this point cannot be exaggerated: only credible fiscal discipline leads to a comfortable position by the beginning of the next downturn and to the necessary moral and political authority to prevent much more serious excesses in Italy and other countries under stress.

However, the ECB will not be able to keep the Euro hard if it lacks political support. But it has no natural constituency it can appeal to over the heads of politicians for a stability-oriented monetary policy. Hence, EMU can only survive as a hard-currency union, if ECB policy makers muster the courage to pursue a monetary policy that may become very unpopular in the short-run and if the governments of previous hard-currency countries support the ECB in this endeavor. If these conditions are not fulfilled, we fear that the Euro will descend into a soft currency.

The 'lira-isation' of the Euro can no longer be excluded. The 'Euro-isation' of Italy is also possible, and by far the more desirable scenario; it will however require a strong commitment by the ECB, and all institutions in general, to force through the painful but necessary adjustments in Italy and elsewhere.

What can we learn from our analysis? While instability in terms of exchange rate volatility is not perceived as an important issue, instability exists in terms of absorption capacities of economies given structural problems including market rigidities. More specifically, there is primarily a no-result regarding the effect of the exchange rate regime or the monetary policy autonomy on the degree of structural reforms. Second, the ECB has allowed a liquidity overhang to build up, but no negative consequences have (yet?) resulted from it. Third, house price developments in the Euro area have – on average – not been very different from the US involving risk from a possible bursting of a house price bubble. Fourth, developments particularly in Italy, but also in Greece and Portugal, are likely to cause a stress test to EMU. This will eventually lead to either a "Euro-isation" of Italy or a "lira-isation" of the Euro area. Sixth and finally, the different real interest rates are part of the convergence mechanism. Yet as our model shows, they have the potential to lead to cycles or instability.

The real risks for EMU seem to arise from the lack of shock absorption capacities of economies. In this context, possible tensions can be expected resulting from real appreciation in some countries (e.g., Italy, Portugal and Greece). Problems of global competitiveness could arise related to the political economy of structural reforms not only in connection with labor markets, but also with ageing, health reforms, the lack of innovation, and education policies.

Appendix E.1

In the following we develop an alternative with competitiveness not having an immediate impact on output. Given the well known lagged effects in trade equations it could also be assumed that output growth responds only with a lag to changes in the price level, which here are equivalent to changes in competitiveness.

$$y_t - y_{t-1} = -\varphi(i_t - (p_t - p_{t-1})) - \gamma p_{t-1} + g_t$$
$$p_t - p_{t-1} = \beta^{-1}(y_t - y_{t-1}) + u_t$$

With the same substitution as above this yields:

$$\beta(p_t - p_{t-1} + u_t) = -\varphi(i_t - (p_t - p_{t-1})) - \gamma p_{t-1} + g_t$$
$$p_t = \{-\varphi i_t + (\beta + \varphi - \gamma)p_{t-1} + g_t + \beta u_t\}/(\beta - \varphi)$$

Stability of the system requires now that :

$$-1 < (\beta + \varphi - \gamma)/(\beta - \varphi) < 1 \quad \text{or} \quad \gamma < 2\varphi \text{ , with } \beta > \varphi \text{ or } \gamma > 2\varphi \text{ , with } \beta < \varphi$$

In this case it is not always true that a higher degree of openness is stabilizing. If it is too high it might destabilize.

List of Abbreviations

CEPS: Centre for European Policy Studies
ECB: European Central Bank
ECOFIN: Economic and Financial Affairs Council
EMS: European Monetary System
EMU: European Monetary Union

EU: European Union
EXR: Exchange Rate
GDP: Gross Domestic Product
GMM: Generalized Method of Moments
IMF: International Monetary Fund
n.a.: not available
NMS: New Member States
OECD: Organisation for Economic Cooperation and Development
REER: Real Effective Exchange Rate
TINA: There-Is-No-Alternative
ULC: Unit Labor Cost
Yoy: year over year

Explanation for Table 1

AT: Austria
BE: Belgium
DE: Germany
FI: Finland
FR: France
GRE: Greece
IE: Spain
IT: Italy
LU: Luxemburg
NL: Netherlands
PT:Portugal

References

ABIAD, A.; MODY, A. (2005), Financial Reform: What Shakes It? What Shapes It?, *American Economic Review,* Vol. 95, 66–88.

ALOGOSKOUFIS, G. S. (1994), On Inflation, Unemployment and the Optimal Exchange Rate Regime, in: F. Van Der Ploeg (ed.), The Handbook of International Macroeconomics, Blackwell, Cambridge, Oxford, 192–223.

BEAN, C. (1998), The Interaction of Aggregate-Demand Policies and Labour Market Reforms, *Swedish Economic Policy Review*, Vol. 5, 352–382.

BELKE, A. (2002), Wage Policy in European Economic and Monetary Union – Stabilizing or Destabilizing Factor?, in: Caesar, R. and H.-E. Scharrer (eds.), European Economic and Monetary Union: An Initial Assessment, Veröffentlichungen des HWWA-Instituts für Wirtschaftsforschung, No. 68, Nomos, Baden-Baden, 207–248.

BELKE, A.; GROS, D. (1999), Estimating the Costs and Benefits of EMU: The Impact of External Shocks on Labor Markets, *Weltwirtschaftliches Archiv,* Vol. 135, 1–48.

BELKE, A.; GROS, D. (2005), Asymmetries in Trans-Atlantic Monetary Policy Making: Does the ECB Follow the Fed?, in: *Journal of Common Market Studies*, Vol. 43, 921–946.

BELKE, A.; HERZ, B. ; VOGEL, L. (2006), Structural Reforms and European Monetary Union What Can a Panel Analysis for the World versus OECD Countries Tell Us?, Paper presented at the Money, Macro & Finance Research Group and University Association for Contemporary European Studies Conference on "The Travails of the Eurozone," Edinburgh, March 24, 2006.

BELKE, A., KÖSTERS, W., LESCHKE, M.; POLLEIT, T., ECB Observer, various issues, web: http://www.ecb-observer.com.

BELKE, A.; WIEDMANN, M. (2005), Boom or Bubble in the US Real Estate Market?, in: Intereconomics – *Review of International Trade and Development*, Vol. 40, 273–284.

BENALAL, N.; DIAZ DEL HOYO, J.L.; PIERLUIGI, B.; VIDALIS, N. (2006), Output Growth Differentials across the Euro Area Countries – Some Stylized Facts, *ECB Occasional Paper Series*, No. 45, European Central Bank, Frankfurt/Main, May.

BERTOLA, G.; T. BOERI (2001), EMU Labor Markets Two Years On: Microeconomic Tensions and Institutional Evolution, paper presented at the Workshop `The Functioning of EMU: Challenges of the Early Years´ organized by the Directorate General for Economic and Financial Affairs, European Commission, Brussels, 21–22 March 2001, 27 April 2001 version.

CALMFORS, L. (1998), Macroeconomic Policy, Wage Setting and Employment – What Difference Does the EMU Make?, *Oxford Economic Policy Review*, Vol. 14, 125–151.

CALMFORS, L. (2001), Unemployment, Labor-Market Reform and Monetary Union, *Journal of Labor Economics*, Vol. 19, 265–289.

CATTE, P.; GIROUARD, N.; PRICE, R.; CHRISTOPHE, A. (2006), Housing Markets, Wealth and the Business Cycle, *OECD Economics Department Working Papers* No. 394, Paris, January.

DUVAL, R.; ELMESKOV, J. (2005), The Effects of EMU on Structural Reforms in Labour and Product Markets, *OECD Economics Department Working Paper,* No. 438, Paris.

FELDERER, B. (2006), Small Is Beautiful, in: Festschrift für Professor Bodenhöfer, Institut für Höhere Studien (IHS), Vienna.

FERNÁNDEZ-KRANZ, D.; HON, M.T. (2006), A Cross-Section Analysis of the Income Elasticity of Housing Demand in Spain: Is There A Real Estate Bubble?, in: *Journal of Real Estate Finance and Economics*, Vol. 32, 449–470.

GIROURARD, N.; KENNEDY, M.; VAN DEN NOORD, P.; ANDRÉ, C. (2006), Recent House Price Developments: the Role of Fundamentals, *OECD Economics Department Papers* No. 475, Paris, January.

GIULIODORI, M. (2005), The Role of House Prices in the Monetary Transmission Mechanism across European Countries, in: *Scottish Journal of Political Economy*, Vol. 52, 519–543.

GROS, D. (2006), Bubbles in Real Estate? A Longer-term Comparative Analysis of Housing Prices in Europe and the US, CEPS Working Document No. 239, Centre for European Policy Studies, Brussels, February.

GROS, D. (2006a), Italy and Germany – Convergence or Divergence for the Euro Laggards, Centre for European Policy Studies, July, Brussels, mimeo.

GROS, D.; MAYER, T.; UBIDE, A. (2005), EMU at Risk, 7th Annual Report of the CEPS Macroeconomic Policy Group, Centre for European Policy Studies (CEPS), Brussels.

HEINEMANN, F. (2004), Explaining Reform Deadlocks, *Applied Economics Quarterly Supplement*, Vol. 55, 9–26.

HEINEMANN, F. (2005), How Distant is Lisbon from Maastricht? The Short-run Link between Structural Reforms and Budgetary Performance, mimeo, prepared for the DG ECFIN Workshop 'Budgetary Implications of Structural Reforms', Brussels, 2 December.

HELBLING, T.; HAKURA, D.; X. DEBRUN (2004), Fostering Structural Reforms in Industrial Countries, in: World Economic Outlook 2004, chapter III, 103–146.

HERZ, B.; VOGEL, L. (2005), Bestimmungsgründe marktorientierter Reformen: eine empirische Analyse, in: W. Schaefer (ed.), Institutionelle Grundlagen effizienter Wirtschaftspolitik, Schriften des Vereins für Socialpolitik, N.F. 304, Berlin, 2005, 25–49.

HOCHREITER, E.; TAVLAS, G. S. (2005), The Two Roads to the Euro: The Monetary Experiences of Austria and Greece, in: S. SCHADLER (ed.), Euro Adoption in Central and Eastern Europe – Opportunities and Challenges, International Monetary Fund, Washington/DC.

INTERNATIONAL MONETARY FUND (2004), Fostering Structural Reforms in Industrial Countries, chapter III, in World Economic Outlook. Advancing Structural Reforms, International Monetary Fund, Washington D.C. (2004).

MÉLITZ, J. (1997), The Evidence about the Costs and Benefits of EMU, in: *Swedish Economic Policy Review*, Vol. 4, 191–234.

ORGANIZATION FOR ECONOMIC COOPERATION AND DEVELOPMENT (2005), Economic Policy Reforms – Going for Growth, OECD (2005a): Economic Outlook November, Paris.

PEEK, J.; WILCOX, J.A. (2006), Housing, Credit Constraints, and Macro Stability – The Secondary Mortgage Market and Reduced Cyclicality of Residential Investment, in: *American Economic Review* – Papers ands Proceedings, Vol. 96, 135–140.

PILL, H.; RAUTANEN, T. (2006), Monetary Analysis – The ECB Experience, Paper presented at the 8th The ECB and Its Watchers Conference, Session ECB Watch – Review of the ECB's Strategy and Alternative Approaches, May 5th, Frankfurt/Main.

POSEN, A. (2003), It Takes More than a Bubble to Become Japan, Institute for International Economics, Working Paper No. 03.09, Washington, D.C., October.

POSEN, A.; POPOV GOULD, D. (2006), Has EMU Had any Impact on the Degree of Wage Restraint?, Paper presented at the Money, Macro & Finance Research Group and University Association for Contemporary European Studies Conference on "The Travails of the Eurozone," Edinburgh, March 24, 2006.

SAINT-PAUL, G.; BENTOLILA, S. (2000), Will EMU Increase Eurosclerosis?, International Macroeconomics and Labor Economics, *CEPR Discussion Paper* No: 2423, April, London.

SELOSSE, SCHREFLER, C. L. (2005), Consumer Credit and Lending to Households in Europe, European Credit Research Institute (ECRI), Brussels.

SHILLER, R. (2005), Irrational Exuberance, Princeton University Press, second edition.

SIBERT, A.C., SUTHERLAND, A. (1997), Monetary Regimes and Labor Market Reform, *CEPR Discussion Paper* No: 1731, London, November.

SVENSSON, L. (1997), Optimal Inflation Targets, "Conservative" Central Banks, and Linear Inflation Contracts`, in: *American Economic Review*, Vol. 87, 98–114.

VAN POECK, A.; BORGHIJS, A. (2001), EMU and Labor Market Reform: Needs, Incentives and Realisations, Blackwell, Oxford, Cambridge Publishers.

WYPLOSZ, C. (2006), European Monetary Union – the Dark Sides of a Major Success, with comments from Stephen Nickell and Martin Wolf, *Economic Policy,* Vol. 21 P. 207–261.

F. Financial Markets and Global Integration

David Dickinson

F.1. Introduction

The process of economic globalisation is offering increasing opportunities to individual consumers and producers through trade in goods and services and the internationalisation of production, particularly via multinational companies. Since the Second World War we have seen increasing liberalisation of domestic financial markets (towards the open system seen during the 19th and early 20th century), a process which has generated opportunities for greater trade in financial assets and increasing integration of financial markets. This paper asks a number of questions about the latter process, often termed Financial Globalisation.

There is substantial evidence that the process of financial integration does not provide all the gains that are theoretically possible. Specifically, capital does not seem to flow sufficiently towards less developed economies given that returns will be significantly higher in such markets and the degree of risk-sharing (by diversifying wealth across different financial markets) that individuals undertake appear to be sub-optimal. Explanations for this behaviour range from imperfections in markets to irrationality of investors.

To consider this issue we shall begin by considering the ways in which financial markets can become integrated. We shall then turn to the reasons why financial markets and institutions exist, and consider the extent to which the process of financial integration can achieve benefits for savers and borrowers. We shall then consider why financial integration may not deliver the benefits that are expected by focusing upon the possibility that investors do not behave in a manner consistent with the model of the rational economic agent. We conclude with some thoughts on what the future holds as financial globalisation proceeds.

F.2. Levels of Financial Integration

In describing the process of financial market integration we can identify three processes. Firstly, domestic financial markets may be opened to trade in financial assets. In this way domestic residents can buy foreign financial assets and foreign residents can purchase domestic financial assets. Such a process of liberalisation is often termed Capital Account Liberalisation in that restrictions on trade in foreign currency holdings is removed for any (legal) trade in financial assets. It is equivalent to the Current Account Liberalisation which opens the way for free trade in goods and services. During this process, which has taken place in most developed countries in the last 60 years, we may observe some restriction on trading (on inflows or outflows of capital) but in broad terms the developed world and many developing countries have already fully liberalised their capital accounts. However this process does not always come without costs, particularly if the resulting liberalisation brings with it unstable capital inflows and the potential for sudden withdrawals (we will discuss this point later).

By opening up the capital account, an economy is allowing domestic residents to purchase (and sell, or borrow via) foreign currency assets. A second stage of this process of liberalisation is to allow foreign firms (financial institutions) to do business in domestic currency. This is where the process of financial market integration differs from that involving trade in goods and services in that a financial asset is different because it is denominated in a different currency. Clearly a particular good is the same good everywhere in the world, whatever currency is used for prices. In other words opening up the capital account does not imply that individuals can buy domestic financial assets from foreign institutions without restrictions. Many countries have pursued this second type of liberalisation, although countries have seen the protection of their domestic financial firms as taking precedent, for example, if they believe that allowing foreign entry will bring instability to the financial markets. Often the process of allowing foreign entry into domestic currency business is a slow and disjointed one, with some favoured institutions being allowed entry while others are blocked. There is no single legal mechanism imposing this sort of restriction and it can be related to the regulatory regime in that foreign financial firms may be required to adopt unprofitable capital requirements in order to gain entry to domestic currency business. Membership of the WTO (specifically of GATS) is often associated with a major change in policy towards the entry of foreign financial firms.

The third, and potentially most complete, type of financial integration occurs when we introduce a single currency across a number of economies. Clearly this removes any capital account barriers and should also imply that there is a single market for financial services and assets across the currency area. As a result any financial firm operating within the single currency region has the opportunity to offer products to any consumer within the single market. However there may still be barriers to market penetration as a result of legal restraints (e.g. due to differences of legal systems across the currency area), informational and other costs. One alternative to the process of currency union is to move to adopting another currency to circulate within the domestic financial system. Another possibility is to adopt a currency board, which, if used in its purest form, means that the domestic currency becomes a perfect substitute for the international currency used to define the currency board. In less official ways this process, often referred to as dollarisation for the obvious reason that it typically involves the US dollar, effectively leads to the international currency usurping the domestic currency in the domestic financial markets. In either case we should observe integration of the domestic financial system into that of the foreign currency.

In describing these levels of financial market integration it should be noted that there is no a priori reason why one should follow the other. It would be feasible to adopt a single currency without allowing foreign financial institutions into domestic financial markets. However I have chosen this ordering since in practice this is the way in which liberalisation has proceeded and there are good reasons for it.

Typically countries have introduced current account convertibility as a first step into entry into the global economic order. After some time, and usually associated with attempts to improve the efficiency of the domestic financial system, capital account liberalisation follows. This is typically a response to both an increase in demand for financial capital from domestic firms and a desire for domestic investors to diversify and reduce risk. The choice of exchange rate system is also crucial and can be the source of potential problems. The countries of South East Asia experienced the unpleasantness of liberalisation in 1997 and 1998 as a result of the withdrawal of foreign capital and collapse of their pegged exchange rate regimes. It can be argued that a country cannot introduce capital account convertibility until its domestic financial institutions (including regulatory bodies) are able to ensure a stable and orderly response to the resulting surge in capital inflows.

The introduction of foreign financial institutions into domestic financial markets can result in significant improvements in the efficiency of the domestic financial institutions as a result of the competitive pressures created. However, in order for the domestic financial markets to take advantage of this process they must be in a position to compete which requires a degree of preparation even greater than when opening up the capital account. Hence there is normally only limited penetration of domestic financial markets by foreign institutions prior to capital market liberalisation. In the light of previous discussion this might seem to be getting the liberalisation the wrong way round, since you need to encourage domestic financial market and institution development prior to introducing capital account convertibility. However it may be difficult to encourage foreign financial firms into the domestic markets if they anticipate having problems with removing capital and profits at some point of time in the future. Improvements in regulation may be a requirement for foreign firms to enter and this can be an important by-product of entry. And finally foreign firms are unlikely to enter unless some macroeconomic stability has been achieved so a decision to open-up domestic financial markets may put pressure on the policy makers to achieve low inflation. It needs to be recognised that allowing foreign financial institutions into domestic markets also raises the possibility of ownership of domestic institutions transferring to these foreign firms. Although this is a natural consequence of the process and often a driving force behind the improvement in efficiency, scale and scope of the domestic financial system, there is often significant political resistance to such developments. As a result the decision to allow large scale entry of financial firms is often delayed, although there will always be some small scale penetration.

The decision to move to a single market for financial services and products supported by introducing a single currency is the most complete way of ensuring that domestic financial markets become integrated with each other. However without the legal structures in place to ensure that there is, truly, a single market, barriers may still exist that prevent financial institutions doing business across the whole of the single currency area. For example, arguments about the need to have national champions can be an impediment to progress towards a single market in financial services. Often foreign financial institutions enter the domestic market through take-over rather than direct entry and this can be viewed as an example of the importance of having a market presence to successfully penetrate a new market. For financial markets, physical presence in the domestic economy should be less important. In a single currency area the most efficient (lowest cost) market will prevail. But it is feasible for countries to erect barriers to trade, for example, by blocking mergers and encouraging the formation of large domestic financial institutions to compete on a global basis. Conversely it can be argued that takeover of foreign firms may be easier outside a single market since the gains from having domestic producers are lower in a small domestic market than a much larger single market spanning several economies. Furthermore financial markets are increasingly becoming global and the most competitive will prevail by offering products in a multitude of different currencies. For both markets and institutions the creation of single currency zones creates the potential for domestic (to the currency zone) institutions to develop and grow, exploiting economies of scale and scope and becoming competitive enough to operate at the global level in a fully integrated financial system.

To summarise, the process of financial globalisation can take a number of different forms. For it to be complete we need to have not only unrestricted capital flows across different domestic financial markets but also the ability of foreign financial institutions to compete in domestic currency business. Only by allowing this to happen will we see the full benefits of financial market integration at the domestic level. The creation of currency zones provides the impetus for the formation of institutions and markets which have the market presence to compete on a global scale.

F.3. Benefits of Financial Integration

We now turn to consider why the integration of domestic financial markets into a global market place is a good thing. In order to approach this question we will consider the main roles of financial markets and how these are improved by financial market integration. First we can observe that there is increasing evidence that financial market growth generates economic growth (LEVINE 1997, 1999) provides in-depth reviews and identifies a number of reasons. There are three basic roles of financial markets on which we shall focus that can be identified with providing reasons for economic growth and hence providing a link between financial sector and economic development. These are Intertemporal Substitution, Risk Sharing and Corporate Governance.

Financial markets provide the mechanism for individuals to equate the marginal rate of intertemporal substitution to the marginal productivity of capital. If individuals do not have access to financial markets they may be constrained to consume all income when it is earned, or use inefficient intertemporal production opportunities (e.g. they may be forced to acquire more capital then is optimal to achieve their desired consumption over time). When we have heterogeneous agents (in terms of intertemporal substitutability and opportunities) then the range of financial assets which are traded will reflect this heterogeneity given the costs of setting up financial markets. The key idea behind intertemporal substitution is that individuals like to smooth consumption over time (DEATON, 1991). This implies that the volatility of the marginal utility of consumption does not vary significantly through time (in present value terms). When consumption opportunities are very different across time individuals will have a strong desire to substitute consumption intertemporally. Financial markets provide the mechanism for achieving this desired position. The ability to smooth consumption over time provides mechanism for economic growth. Given that individuals spend the latter part of their lifetime not working, they will need to transfer consumption from their early lives to later lives by saving. The more developed are financial markets the better use the economy makes of these savings, thus increasing growth rates.

In the case of risk-sharing we assume heterogeneity across individuals in the risks that are faced measured by consumption possibilities. Financial assets reflect the risks of their issuer. Consequently by holding assets with different risk characteristics individuals can achieve a utility improving distribution of stochastic consumption opportunities (see DEATON, 1991). Given that individuals are risk averse they will wish to smooth consumption profiles over different states of the world and hence reduce the potential volatility of consumption. The underlying argument is similar to that for intertemporal substitution. Individuals will prefer to have relatively small variation in marginal utility of consumption across different states of the world. The effect on economic growth is less clear since better risk-sharing may actually reduce savings. However if improved risk-sharing from financial development allows for a more diverse range of risk-sharing opportunities it is likely that the overall expected return from financial markets will increase, from a more efficient choice of risky projects, implying higher growth rates.

If owners were also managers and all investors had full information then there would be no need for financial markets to play any corporate governance role. However typically managers and owners are not the same individuals and those who manage have more information about the firm than those who own. The resulting principal/agent and moral hazard/adverse selection problems which arise can be (partially) solved by financial markets. For example, much work has been done on how the debt/equity ratio, paying of dividends, monitoring by debt holders, market for takeovers, can ameliorate the agency costs arising from the asymmetry of information and separation of ownership and control. JENSEN/MECKLING (1976) identified how ownership structure can provide corporate control and hence lower the agency costs. ANG/COLE/LIU (2000) provide an analysis of how these agency costs are related to the separation of ownership and control, but can be reduced if mangers own shares and increases if ownership is dispersed. See SHLEIFER/VISHNY (2005) for a thorough review of issues relating to corporate governance.

The impact of financial development on growth is clear if it improves corporate governance. If firms make value maximising decisions, growth of the economy will be at its optimum. However, for example, if managers use free cash flow for their own objectives (see JENSEN, 1986) then firms will no longer maximise value and resources will be diverted for manager's own use resulting in inefficient outcomes.

What then are the benefits of financial integration given these roles for financial markets? We start with the case where a country removes controls on capital flows. We need to find benefits in terms of improved efficiency of capital and opportunities for savings. The basic argument for the benefits from financial globalisation is that capital will flow from the rich countries with relatively low productivity of capital to labour-rich poorer economies with much higher productivity. This will have two effects. Firstly individuals in rich countries will be able to achieve higher utility since they are net savers and will achieve a higher return by buying foreign financial assets; secondly individuals, who are net borrowers, in poorer countries will be able to fund projects which are utility enhancing that were previously not undertaken. The result will be increased growth in the global economy. In terms of risk sharing, opening the capital account increases opportunities. As long as economic activity across different economies is not perfectly synchronised then diversification into foreign financial asset will offer the possibility of smoothing consumption more effectively.

In the context of corporate governance the effects of opening of the capital account are ambiguous. What domestic residents want to see is an improvement in control of managers. If the market is relatively underdeveloped, and hence governance does not operate well (compounded by a poor functioning legal and regulatory structure), opening the market to foreign capital inflows could improve this aspect since professional foreign investors will demand proper corporate governance mechanisms. However there is a countervailing influence that typically international capital flows will bring increasingly dispersed ownership. It is well-known that concentrated ownership is one way of mitigating the problems which arise from asymmetric information. Furthermore if there is significant political influence on domestic enterprises then it may well be that corporate governance problems increase as a domestic economy enters the global financial system (see STULTZ, 2005, 2006 who argues that corporate governance issues will limit the extent of financial integration).

Moving on now to consider the effects of the entry of foreign financial institutions into the domestic markets, there are a number of benefits. Firstly, for markets that are relatively under-developed, the move of global financial institutions can provide an impetus to growth in the scope and scale of financial markets. As the depth of financial markets increases we would expect to see increasing opportunities for intertemporal substitution and greater ability to share risks. This occurs because of the introduction of new products as well as the possibilities that global financial institutions offer since they do business across a range of economies. The introduction of foreign institutions will increase competition in the domestic financial system implying an improvement in the efficiency of the system as a whole generating utility enhancement as savers and borrowers get a better deal. If foreign financial institutions enter the domestic markets through takeovers and other direct acquisition methods then we may see some countervailing forces where the degree of competition could be potentially reduced in the case where the domestic financial markets are dominated by a few large market suppliers. However foreign firms can impart improved skills and knowledge into domestic financial markets through such entry and hence the impact on efficiency should still be positive. If foreign financial institutions require better corporate governance mechanisms then this aspect will also improve. They may also have better internal risk management and encourage tighter regulatory control of domestic institutions since otherwise domestic investors will go to the lower risk foreign institutions.

Finally we consider the development of a single currency area. The scale of domestic financial markets should now become less important that that of the single currency area as a whole. Whether this is the case depends upon restrictions on doing business in domestic financial markets for firms within the single currency area (KLEIMEIER/SANDER, 2000 find that there is only limited evidence of segmentation in retail banking markets in the EU despite some years of operation of a single market). Although typically a single currency area should provide support for the single market in all goods and services, there may be restrictions on doing business and to protect domestic financial institutions against foreign takeover. Of course, single currency areas (or other arrangements such as currency boards) are not necessarily set up to support single markets but to provide exchange rate stability across a number of different economies and hence we may not see major impacts on financial market operation. However if a single currency area works fully we would expect to see improved risk-sharing and intertemporal substitution possibilities since exchange rate risk should no longer be an issue. Risk-sharing can also improve if non-fundamental exchange rate risk is eliminated and this may improve economic performance. AGHION et al. (2006) find that exchange rate volatility reduces growth for economies with relatively low levels of financial development while it has no effect on economies with more developed financial systems which suggests that risk-sharing effects are non-linear, such that economies which do not have many risk-sharing opportunities benefit significantly when risk is reduced. Beyond this, the adoption of a single currency to support a single market can allow for markets, which previously did not exist, to be set-up. The easiest way of seeing this is to assume that such markets have very high set-up costs (for example needing high levels of knowledge and skills to operate) and hence require a large market base to be worthwhile entering as a supplier.

If the development of single market for financial services occurs it will be necessary to ensure that regulatory and legal systems are flexible enough to keep pace. This is also important in order to ensure that corporate governance mechanisms work properly. We would expect to see both a more dispersed ownership of equity as a result of a single currency area (LA PORTA et al., 1999 observe that ownership tends to be concentrated except in the US/UK which have market-based financial systems). Furthermore the monitoring function of banks may be diminished as a result of more distant lending relationships. There appears to be a relationship between legal systems and the optimal corporate governance mechanisms (see LA PORTA et al. 1998, 2002), a link which can be broken if the impact of a single currency area is to bring financial markets operating with different legal systems and hence corporate governance mechanisms into a single market for financial services. Furthermore if there is a desire to enhance areas of the financial markets which are relatively less developed there may be implications for the operation of the legal system. Recent work by LA PORTA et al. (2006) has found that information disclosure by equity issuers and laws which support private enforcement of liability are beneficial to the operation of stock markets. HALE et al. (2006) observe that stock markets are less volatile when creditor rights are strongly protected, suggesting that the relationship between legal structure and financial system operation is a complex one. In addition there is an increasing risk of fraudulent activity which will require mechanisms across the single market and beyond given that a large market is attractive to criminals outside as well as inside the single currency area.

Overall we can see that financial integration has potential for both positive and negative consequences for the operation of domestic financial markets. There are benefits in terms of improved risk-sharing and intertemporal substitution possibilities. The scale, scope and efficiency of financial markets should rise although the effect on market competitiveness may be negative, in the case where a single global institution becomes dominant in a particular market. The impact on corporate governance is much less clear. The possibility of capital outflows should lead to improved governance since investors can choose to move their wealth overseas if they are unhappy with the performance of domestic assets. Similarly introduction of foreign financial institutions that are used to use financial systems to monitor and control firms should improve domestic corporate governance mechanisms. Within a single currency area there is a danger that legal and regulatory systems do not keep pace with the integration of financial markets and hence corporate governance systems will be less efficient. Also the increasingly dispersed ownership of shares will generate a negative influence on corporate governance which may imply there is a limit to the degree to which financial systems can become integrated.

F.4. Financial Market Integration and Investor Behaviour

In the last two sections we have considered why financial market integration generates benefits to economies which fully embrace the global financial system. However, when we observe the actual results of financial globalisation we are left to conclude that the resulting gains are significantly below what would be expected. In particular we may note that there appears to be less flow of capital from developed to developing countries than would be justified and that risk-sharing does not reach levels consistent with theoretical considerations of the gains from doing so (see OBSTFELD/TAYLOR, 2003). Also it has been observed that investors do not seem to take the benefits of international diversification. The home equity bias (see LEWIS, 1999), that investors hold too high a proportion of domestic assets in their portfolios, is a well-known result. Furthermore studies of the correlation between output and consumption across countries has found there to be an inefficient level of risk-sharing (see AMBLER et al., 2004, ASDRUBALI/KIM, 2004). Note that ATHANASOULIS/VAN WINCOOP (2000) have identified significant increases in growth resulting from a move to optimum risk-sharing and hence there seem to be large unexploited gains still available from the process of financial integration.

So now we consider why it is that financial market integration has not had the expected benefits and hence whether we can expect to see increasing benefits. We start by observing that changes in exchange rates should reflect the difference in (log of) the stochastic discount factors across economies. We know that, in order to explain the equity premium, we require very volatile stochastic discount factors (e.g. COCHRANE, 2001). This implies either that exchange rates should be very volatile (to reflect the variation in stochastic discount factor implied by the equity premium) or that, if they are not very volatile then there is not large differences between stochastic discount factor across economies i.e. risk-sharing is high (see BRANDT et al., 2005, who also discuss reasons why risk-sharing may not be complete as a result of transactions costs on goods and incomplete financial markets).

We diverge from this argument by observing that there is increasing evidence that financial market behaviour is not completely described by the rational economic agent model which lies at the heart of the above analysis. Specifically there is increasing evidence that individuals do not make decisions by maximising expected utility under rational expectations (see BARBERIS/THALER, 2005 for a survey of the behavioural finance literature which uses this idea as a starting point). We will consider a number of the significant developments which have been introduced by the behavioural finance research agenda to explain financial market performance. We will use them to consider why financial integration does not appear to have generated the benefits which would be expected. In so doing we hope to provide a better understanding of the way in which globalisation offers opportunities to individuals to achieve value improving outcomes.

Firstly we may note that financial markets do not seem to behave consistently even when they are trading the same asset. FROOT/DABORA (1999) document persistent price differences for the same assets traded in different markets (so-called 'twin stocks'). In particular they find that local prices are heavily influenced by the local stock index and hence if there is a twin stock traded on US and UK markets and, say, the US market is rising quickly while the UK market is flat, the price in New York will move higher relative to that traded in the UK market. Dollar appreciation against sterling would have similar effects. They do not find that information or transaction costs can explain this since such twin stocks represent global companies which are traded in highly liquid markets. Similarly tax rules do not explain all of the observed price differences. They argue that local market noise (from irrational traders) may impact more than foreign market noise on stocks traded locally and this can explain the difference in price. They also point out that domestic fund managers may have controls on their behaviour so that it is easier for investors to identify whether they have performed well or not and that this can explain the differences in price. However neither of these explanations seem to definitively explain the observation.

We now turn to consider what type of investor behaviour will impact upon the effects of financial integration. We consider three aspects which have been highlighted in the literature on behavioural finance: a). framing of investment b). the desire of individuals to avoid ambiguity and c) representativeness and conservatism which indicates how individual's form expectations. In so doing we will identify how such behaviour will impact upon investor's reaction to an extension of choice of financial assets as will be seen in the process of financial globalisation.

The behavioural heuristic known as 'framing' argues that the way in which individuals are presented with a problem influences their decisions. BENARTZI/ THALER (1995) present the idea of narrow framing where individuals work on short-term time horizons (allied to loss aversion) to explain the equity premium. If we extend this idea to increasingly integrated financial markets then we can observe that narrow framing can imply that individuals concetrate on a narrow set of financial assets. This may well mean that they focus more on domestic than foreign financial assets and hence we can explain the limited amount of international risk-sharing and the home equity bias. The failure to take opportunity of the better intertemporal substitution possibilities offered by extending asset choice internationally is also consistent with the concept of narrow framing. If fund managers are judged according to domestic benchmarks (as may well happen with narrow framing by investors) then there is an incentive for them to favour domestic over foreign assets.

Ambiguity aversion relates to the idea that individuals prefer situations in which they feel competent. HEATH/TVERSKY (1991) argue that this aversion is particular relevant to how competent individuals feel in assessing risky situations. Thus an individual will prefer situations where they feel comfortable with assessing the risk. As financial globalisation proceeds then we would expect such ambiguity aversion to hold back individual's desire to invest internationally. Individual investors will concentrate on situations with which they are familiar. They may invest some wealth abroad but it will take time for the benefits of a globalised financial system to be fully exploited since only by becoming more familiar with foreign markets will investors feel willing to invest heavily. In them

Representativeness and conservatism heuristics have been used to explain why individual's adjust slowly in their expectations to new events. Individuals prefer to characterise new risky events in the context of situations with which they are familiar. Thus a move towards financial market integration may not influence individual's assessment of asset returns since they regard it simply as an extension of assets with similar characteristics with which they are familiar. Hence we would not expect to see significant changes in capital flows. The impact of conservatism is that expectations do not adjust quickly to new information. Hence it takes time for individuals to adjust to the effects of financial market integration. This may explain why, for example, after the Asian Financial Crisis it has taken international investors considerable time to engage in capital flows to the affected territories. That there was such a major negative event may well have entered into an unfavourable assessment of the risks of international investment which caused individuals to switch to developed financial markets.

The final behavioural aspect we highlight is that of excessive optimism. However rather than applying this to investors we can consider how it affects financial institution behaviour. HEATON (2002) has argued that managers are prone to this behavioural attribute. The concept means that individuals are likely to overestimate good performance and underestimate bad performance. However it is observed that this optimism impacts more over outcomes which agents feel they have control. Secondly optimism is related positively to outcomes for which they feel commitment. Such behaviour can be used to explain the impact of financial globalisation. If managers of financial institutions are optimistic about outcomes over which they have control this suggests a preference for domestic financial assets. Similarly given that managers may well see domestic business as core business they will feel more optimistic about investing domestically. As we have discussed a number of times this sort of behaviour is likely to result in a slow adjustment to new opportunities which appear as a result of financial globalisation rather than no response. However a further implication is that once foreign markets become familiar and are regarded as core business we shall see a large change in behaviour. The excessive capital inflows into the economies of South East Asia in the mid 1990s were probably driven by a sudden shift in the optimism of international banks.

The above discussion represents a limited view of the impact of behavioural finance research on the modelling of investor and financial market decision-making. However we can note that the aspects we have identified provide reasons why investors have not fully grasped the opportunities to them as financial markets have become more integrated. However the explanations above do not imply that this will not eventually happen but that the process will take time. There is evidence that while financial globalisation has not been fully exploited investors are taking advantage of the opportunities offered. Our observations are consistent with this conjecture. Furthermore we have also identified reasons why sudden shifts in capital flows can be observed as a result of excessive optimism followed by excessive pessimism. Whilst financial integration can bring significant benefits it can impose large costs induced by inflows and then outflows of capital.

F.5. The Future for Financial Market Integration

We conclude by offering some perspectives on the effect of continuing integration of financial markets. There are a number of issues to emphasise. Firstly there are still significant developing economies, particularly China which need to open their capital account. This liberalisation will bring additional funds into the global financial markets and open up increasing possibilities for international investment. Secondly we are likely to see increasing consolidation of the financial services industries as domestic economies allow more foreign firms full entry into their markets. This will have the advantages of both reducing the informational differences between domestic and international financial markets and encouraging more diversified investment. It will have the further effect of increasing the efficiency of domestic financial markets and institutions which have been protected. Thirdly there may be further moves towards currency union as economies prefer the security of removing exchange rate volatility to the benefits associated with a flexible monetary policy.

These developments will have positive effects on investment opportunities but our analysis of investor behaviour suggests that these will take time to come to fruition. Further globalisation of financial markets will generate unfamiliarity to which investors will take time to respond. For example, representativeness implies that individual investors will dislike the unfamiliarity of the structural changes in financial markets which will be observed over the next few years. As unfamiliar assets continue to out-perform those which are the staple of investors, conservatism will hinder the speed at which investors will adjust their expectations. To some extent financial institutions can mitigate these effects by putting their global presence at the heart of their investment strategy. However as we have seen this may imply that managers of institutions will be too optimistic and hence over-invest, creating the risk of another financial crises.

The continuing internationalisation of financial markets will lead, most likely to a dilution of ownership concentration. The implications for corporate governance are generally negative since ownership concentration is a key method for many financial markets to exert control over managers and reduce agency costs. A response to this trend will be to move towards the use of takeovers as a way of penalising managers who pursue their own interests. However for many markets this is a relatively unused mechanism of control and hence there will need to be some change in culture for such activities to emerge.

Furthermore we have also identified that legal systems are a key explanation for how the financial system operates. The process of financial globalisation implies that institutions and investors used to one type of system will operate in markets controlled by the other type of legal structure. Whilst it is not impossible that we may have two different types of financial systems it is more likely that financial globalisation will lead to convergence to single model. But then legal systems will need to adapt to provide support for such convergence and this may well generate further delays to the process. The possibility for political interference and the capture of rents will also create impediments. It will be important to ensure that the legal infrastructure keeps pace with financial sector developments.

A more difficult issue to resolve relates to the cultural influences on the operation of financial services. STULTZ/WILLIAMSON (2003) provide evidence that culture and particularly religious tradition has an effect on the way the financial system operates and its impact on economic growth. This further complicates the way on which integration will impact upon different financial systems and their resulting operation. In addition there is evidence that informal mechanisms for enforcement are as powerful as legal structures. ALLEN/QIAN/QIAN (2003) highlight that the extraordinary economic growth of

China has occurred despite the failure to properly develop financial and legal systems. This may well be an indication that in some economies, at least, networking effects can replace more formal legal and institutional structures. As economies from different social, cultural and legal backgrounds become more financially integrated then we may need a convergence of enforcement systems which is just not feasible. Hence we may find that the process of globalisation does have limits (as STULZ, 2005, suggests).

However if we go back to the classification of types of liberalisation which introduced this paper, we are left to conclude that allowing foreign institutions into domestic markets may be the most effective way of bringing the benefits of financial integration. Irrespective of legal and cultural constraints, the impact of foreign financial institutions should be positive. They bring knowledge, skills and products. They improve the efficiency of the domestic financial system and with it the domestic financial institutions and markets. They will ensure that regulatory authorities adopt international standards to improve the operation of the domestic markets. It may well be that risk-sharing and intertemporal substitution opportunities will not be fully exploited. But the increased competition brought by integration will still have major effects which will benefit domestic investors and give an impetus to economic growth.

References

AGHION, P.; BACCHETTA, P.; RANCIERE, R.; ROGOFF, K. (2006), Exchange rate volatility and productivity growth: the role of financial development, *NBER Working Paper*, 12117.

ALLEN, F.; QIAN, J.; QIAN, M. (2003), Law, Finance and growth in China, *Research Paper 03–21*, ILE, University of Pennsylvania Law School.

AMBLER, S.; CARDIA, E.; ZIMMERMAN, C. (2004), International Business Cycles: What are the facts?, *Journal of Monetary Economics*, 51, 257–76.

ANG, J. S.; COLE, R. A.; LIN, J. W. (2000), Agency costs and ownership structure, *Journal of Finance*, 55, 81–106.

ASDRUBALI, P.; KIM, S. (2004), Dynamic risksharing in the United States and Europe, *Journal of Monetary Economics*, 21, 809–836.

ATHANASOULIS, S.G.; VAN WINCOOP, E. (2000), Growth, uncertainty and risksharing, *Journal of Monetary Economics*, 45, 477–505.

BARBERIS, N.; THALER, R. H. (2005), A survey of behavioural finance, Ch. 1 in R.H THALER (ed.) Advances in Behavioural Finance Vol. II, Russell Sage Foundation, Princeton University Press.

BENARTZI, S.; THALER, R. H. (1995), Myopic loss aversion and the equity premium puzzle, *Quarterly Journal of Economics*, 110, 73–92.

BRANDT, M.W.; COCHRANE, J. H.; SAMTA-CLARA, P. (2005), International risk-sharing is better than you think, or exchange rates are too smooth, mimeo.

COCHRANE, J. (2001), Asset Pricing, Princeton University Press.

DEATON, A., Understanding Consumption (1991), Oxford Univeristy Press, Oxford.

FROOT, K. A.; DABORA, E. M. (1999), How are stocks affected by the location of trade?, *Journal of Financial Economics*, 53, 189–216.

HALE, G.; RAZIN, A.; TONG, H. (2006), Institutional Weakness and stock price volatility, *NBER Working Paper*, 12127.

HEATH, C.; TVERSKY, A. (1991), Preference and belief: ambiguity and competence in choice under uncertainty, *Journal of Risk and Uncertainty*, 4, 5–28.

HEATON, J. B. (2002), Managerial optimism and corporate finance, *Financial Management*, 31, 33–45.

JENSEN, M. C. (1986), Agency costs of free cash flow, corporate finance and takeovers, *American Economic Review*, 76, 323–29.

JENSEN, M. C.; MECKLING, W. H. (1976), Theory of the firm: managerial behaviour, agency costs and capital structure, *Journal of Financial Economics*, 3, 305–60.

KLEIMEIER, S.; SANDER, H. (2000), Regionalisation versus globalisation in European Financial Market Integration: Evidence from cointegration analysis, *Journal of Banking and Finance*, 24, 1005–1043.

LA PORTA, R.; LOPEZ-DE SILANES, F.; SHEIFER, A. (1999), Corporate ownership around the World, *Journal of Finance*, 54, 471–517.

LA PORTA, R.; LOPEZ-DE SILANES, F.; SHEIFER, A. (2006), What works in securities Laws?, *Journal of Finance*, 61, 1–32.

LEVINE, R. (1997), Financial development and economic growth: views and agenda, *Journal of Economic Literature*, 35, 688–726.

LEVINE, R. (1999), Law, finance and economic growth, *Journal of Financial Intermediation*, 8, 8–35.

LEWIS, K. (1999), Trying to explain home bias in equities and consumption, *Journal of Economic Literature*, 37, 571–608.

OBSTFELD, M.; TAYLOR A. M. (2003), Globalisation and capital markets in M.D. Bordo, A. Taylor, M. and Williamson, J.G,.Globalisation in Historical Perspective, *NBER*, Chicago University Press.

SHLEIFER, A.; VISHNY, R.W. (1997), A survey of corporate governance, *Journal of Finance*, 52, 737–83.

STULTZ, R. M. (2005), The Limits of Financial Globalisation, *Journal of Finance*, 60, 1595- 1683.

STULTZ, R. M. (2006), Financial globalisation, corporate governance and Eastern Europe, *NBER Working Paper*, 11912.

STULTZ, R. M.; R. WILLIAMSON (2003), Culture, openness and Finance, *Journal of Financial Economics*, 70, 313–49.

G. Banking, Financial Market Dynamics and Growth in the EU Single Market

Michael Heise

G.1. The Importance of Financial Markets to Economic Growth

Financial markets play a vital role for the economy as a whole. They lead capital to its most efficient investment. And, of course, the financial services industry is a large sector of the economy in itself : net output and employment are high.

There are also significant indirect effects of financial markets on growth. Well-developed financial markets encourage innovative medium-sized businesses; existing companies are better prepared to withstand fluctuations in the economy because of sounder equity ratios and easier access to credit. Generally speaking, an improved allocation of funds and a cut in transaction costs have a positive impact on businesses' investment activities, and thus on productivity trends in the economy.[1]

Without any doubt, Europe's financial markets are already huge. According to the IMF (IMF, 2006), the total value of the EU's financial assets – including bank assets, public and private debt, and equities – stood at roughly 50 trillion US-dollars at the end of 2004. This accounts for one third of the world's financial stock and is on a par with the US.

Sheer size is no longer an important issue for European financial markets. But what about efficiency? Is it already justified to talk about the "European financial market" in the same sense that we refer to the US market? An obvious difference is that the euro, the so-called "common currency", is actually not yet really common in the enlarged EU: Just half of the current Member States use the euro as the official currency.

For those countries that have introduced the euro, it has been a catalyst for real and financial market integration:

- There has been a significant increase in intra and extra-euro area trade in goods and services since the launch of the euro.
- Foreign direct investment has grown considerably particularly within the countries of the euro zone. Whereas overall growth since 1998 has been 180 % in nominal terms, intra-euro FDI grew by over 240 %.
- On financial markets, the euro has been a remarkable catalyst, particularly in market segments close to the single monetary policy. Interest rate convergence has been impressive.

---

[1] On the positive effects of financial markets on growth see LEVINE, R. and DEMIRGUC-KUNT, A. (2001).

Besides the working of the euro there have of course been various political steps to foster financial integration. European legislators have made great efforts and spent considerable time and resources in the quest to advance European financial integration.

The most evident outcome is the Financial Services Action Plan (FSAP), an unparalleled legislative *tour de force* which since 1999 has set more than 40 regulatory and other measures on their way, and the Lamfalussy-process, which streamlined the European regulatory and supervisory framework.

While the positive effects of deeper and broader financial markets on the economy cannot be calculated precisely, there are some rough estimates. For example, on the basis of previous empirical analyses one study (LONDON ECONOMICS, 2002) for example concluded that fully integrated markets would increase the GDP-level over a time horizon of ten years by 1.1 %.

For Germany, the Initiative Finanzstandort Deutschland expects – by the implementation of its objectives (scaling up the stock of capital for financial provisioning, a better financing base for companies and added value in the financial services industry) – a growth stimulus worth around EUR 100bn or a good 4.5 % increase in gross domestic product up to 2015 (INITIATIVE FINANZSTANDORT DEUTSCHLAND, 2005, p. 19).

Also there is a clear – and beneficial – trend towards capital market financing in virtually all major European countries. The advantage of capital market orientation is obvious in that risks can be better diversified and the accumulation of corporate risks in banks' balance sheets avoided. Capital market financing has special importance from a German angle: on average, the capital base of small and medium-sized companies in Germany is traditionally weak. So, with the implementation of Basel II, the German Mittelstand must aim at a healthy financing mix of equity, debt and innovative capital market products such as mezzanine capital.

Summing up, efforts towards financial integration are clearly worth the effort; the case for creating an integrated and open European financial market that can not only match the size, but also the efficiency of the US market is indeed strong. Encouragingly, considerable progress has been made in recent years.

G.2. The Euro and the Wholesale Market

First, introduction of the euro has given integration of the wholesale European financial markets a huge fillip. With the single monetary policy, virtually overnight a single (unsecured) money market emerged and, over time, yields on government bonds converged enormously (EUROPEAN CENTRAL BANK, 2005a).

The market for euro-denominated corporate bonds has also become highly integrated. Liquidity has increased and issuing fees in Europe have come down to the US level. That means decreasing costs of capital as had been anticipated prior to the monetary union.

As a consequence of these developments, the international market for debt securities denominated in euros has registered headlong growth. Today, the volume of international debt securities outstanding in euros is as high as that of dollar-denominated paper: About 50 % of all long and short-term debt securities are currently (first quarter of 2006) denominated in euros. Since the beginning of the monetary union the euro has thus expanded its share of these markets by more than 20 percentage points (helped also by the appreciation of the euro).

On stock markets the speed of integration has been somewhat slower. But here too, the "home bias" in stock portfolios has decreased, and prices increasingly react to "European news".[2]

G.3. Retail Markets Still Domestically Focused

How about retail financial markets? Markets for the individual retail customer, such as bank lending or deposits and life or non-life insurance markets, have mainly kept their local character (ALLIANZ DRESDNER ECONOMIC RESEARCH, 2005).

Integrating the retail markets undoubtedly poses a huge challenge. Language, culture and longstanding financial habits play a far greater part on these markets than on the market for wholesale customers.

There are several indications for the still incomplete integration of retail markets. In some retail banking segments, interest rate differences show some remaining fragmentation along national borders. The variation coefficients for some selected retail interest rates in the EU 15 show that following the distinct compression of interest rate spreads in the run-up to the launch of the euro this process has stagnated since 2002; indeed, in some cases – with loans for private housing construction as one example – it is pointing in the opposite direction again (EUROPEAN COMMISSION, 2006).

The prices of everyday banking services such as account management and payments still also vary considerably in the EU. A price range from € 25 a year for the Netherlands to € 113 for Italy indicates that even within the monetary union banking prices are to a significant extent still national prices (CAPGEMINI, ING, EFMA, 2005). Also (primary) insurance markets are not integrated and insurance companies provide local products in local markets.

In asset management there has been rapid growth of cross-border funds in recent years. However, comparing the EU asset management industry with the US, the benchmark for a fully integrated market, reveals striking differences: There are more than three times as many funds in the EU than in the US and, consequently, the average size of EU funds is significantly smaller (roughly one fifth of the US

---

[2] A comprehensive overview of the state of play in financial integration can be found in the annual Financial Integration Monitor by the European Comission (EUROPEAN COMMISSION, 2004, 2005a, 2006).

size). Economies of scale are not fully exploited, leading to higher costs for investors (EUROPEAN COMMISSION, 2005a).

Opening up the still largely domestically focused retail markets requires the removal of all kinds of artificial obstacles. Economic theory clearly lays down that retail financial integration is to the benefit of both consumers and financial services suppliers. While consumers benefit from increased product choice and falling prices, suppliers realize economies of scale, profit from a diversification of risks and benefit from new market opportunities. On the whole, these effects are assumed to greatly outweigh the costs of retail market integration and will stimulate economic growth

It is simply wrong to assume that the fragmentation of retail financial services markets is caused by consumers' preferences that are irreversibly tied to local financial services providers. Empirical data clearly demonstrates that a steadily increasing number of products are already sold across borders. For example, 5% of EU-citizens have already obtained a bank account in another member state. The proportion of EU-citizens intending to purchase cross-border retail finance is even larger, e.g. up to 15% of EU-citizens intend to acquire a bank account in another member state (EUROPEAN COMMISSION, 2003). Current legislative initiatives are expected to raise these figures even more in the medium term, as further retail market segments will be gradually harmonized, e.g. UCITS, mortgages, payments or consumer credit. Besides these considerations, even if only five percent of EU citizens engage in cross-border retail transactions this would constitute a market of around 23 million citizens.

This process is supported by the fact that customers have become more and more familiar with modern and cheap telecommunication and internet services. As retail products are offered through various sales channels (multi-channel access), the historically prominent role of branches as primary points of sale shrinks constantly, e.g. over 40% of citizens ordered a product on the telephone and over 20% used the internet for this purpose.

G.4. Conclusion

What can be undertaken in order to enhance financial market integration and, hence, economic growth in Europe?

1. It is necessary to foster integration of the retail markets which still have strong national features. This does not necessarily mean harmonization of all regulations, it may also take the form of mutual recognition, i.e. accepting existing differences.
2. We must encourage the establishment of European enterprises and do away with any kind of protectionism. This is because the harmonization of market standards is fostered by pan-European corporations.
3. Further steps towards integration and harmonization of the European supervisory systems have to be taken; this is indispensable to complete an integrated European financial market.

4. A common European stock exchange would be extremely helpful for an integrated financial market. My impression is that, at the moment, Europeans underestimate this point.

These conclusions are reinforced by taking a global view. Given the size that US financial services providers have reached, it seems only a matter of time before they abandon the restraint and become more active in financial M&A in Europe. The longer Europeans persist in thinking in national categories, the more likely it becomes that Europeans get themselves relegated from the premier league of global players.

Finally, further integration of retail markets is not only advantageous from a consumer's viewpoint since it strengthens competition and tends to reduce prices. The integration of banking and insurance markets also has relevance for monetary policy. Given the differences in e.g. national mortgage markets or markets for consumer and corporate credit, the transmission of monetary impulses differs widely from one country to another. This is the reason why monetary developments – measured by credit volumes and monetary aggregates – vary significantly within the EU. Thus, the ECB's interest rate policy produces different effects in different countries. The integration of financial markets would reduce these differences so that it would be advantageous for the single monetary policy as well.

References

ALLIANZ DRESDNER ECONOMIC RESEARCH (2005), European Financial Market Integration and Banking Consolidation, Economy & Markets 09/2005 (author: A. Holzhausen).

CAPGEMINI, ING, EFMA (2005), World Retail Banking Report 2005.

CECCHINI, P; HEINEMANN, F.; JOPP, M. (ed.) (2002), The incomplete European market for financial services, *Publication Series ZEW Economic Studies*.

EUROPEAN CENTRAL BANK (2003), The Integration of Europe's Financial Markets, Monthly Bulletin, October 2003.

EUROPEAN CENTRAL BANK (2005a), Indicators of Financial Integration in the Euro area.

EUROPEAN CENTRAL BANK (2005a), EU Banking Sector Stability.

EUROPEAN CENTRAL BANK (2005a), EU Banking Strucutres.

EUROPEAN CENTRAL BANK (2006), The Contribution of the ECB and the Eurosystem to European Financial Integration, Monthly Bulletin, May 2006.

EUROPEAN COMMISSION (2003), Eurobarometer May 2003.

EUROPEAN COMMISSION (2004), Financial Integration Monitor 2004, *Commission Staff Working Document*.

EUROPEAN COMMISSION (2005a), Financial Integration Monitor 2005, *Commission Staff Working Document*.

EUROPEAN COMMISSION (2005b), Cross-border consolidation in the EU financial sector, *Commission Staff Working Document*.

EUROPEAN COMMISSION (2005c), Green Paper on Financial Services Policy 2005 – 2010.

EUROPEAN COMMISSION (2005d), White Paper on Financial Services Policy 2005 – 2010.

EUROPEAN COMMISSION (2006), Financial Integration Monitor 2006, *Commission Staff Working Document*.

IMF (2006), Global Financial Stability Report, Washington.

INITIATIVE FINANZSTANDORT DEUTSCHLAND (2005), Report on Finanzstandort Deutschland No. 1, Frankfurt.

LEVINE, R.; DEMIRGUC-KUNT, A. (2001), Financial structure and economic growth, MIT Press.

LONDON ECONOMICS (2002), Quantification of the Macro-Economic Impact of Integration of EU Financial Markets, Report to the European Commission, London.

TRICHET, J.-C. (2005), Remarks on the European financial integration and on the management of inflation expectations by the European Central Bank, Speech at the ECB Conference, New York.

WEBER, A. (2006), European Financial Integration and (its implications for) monetary policy, Keynote address at the AGM Foreign Bankers' Association in the Netherlands.

H. Banking, Financial Market Structures and Growth in the EU Single Market

Freddy van den Spiegel[*]

H.1. Evolution of Financial Integration in the EU

There is a broad belief that integration in the financial sector is lagging behind the integration of other economic sectors within the EU. That situation is seen as detrimental to economic growth. Recent research points to the fact that fully integrated financial markets would lower costs and increase EU GDP by more than one percent, which is significant. Given the ambitious Lisbon agenda, it is clear that action has to be taken to boost financial integration. But the problem was, and remains, how to decide on the political priorities for achieving optimal integration.

The first point worth noting is that financial integration was not seen as a priority until the end of the 1980s. This changed dramatically, however, thereafter.

The most important catalyst for financial integration was without any doubt the Monetary Union, and the resultant single currency. Money lies at the heart of all financial systems, and most financial markets are naturally organised and regulated around a currency, that of a single country and its government. However, where several countries use a common currency, financial markets have a natural tendency to expand and integrate in line with the currency zone. Regulatory divergences between member states are then increasingly perceived as unjustified hurdles for further integration. The difficult work of harmonisation – required for further integration – is no longer only a top-down process imposed by policy makers, but has also become a bottom-up process supported by pressure from the business community.

The second important step towards financial integration was the Financial Services Action Plan (FSAP). A thorough analysis of the reasons for the lack of financial integration, by a group of "wise men" under the chairmanship of Alexander Lamfalussy, resulted in an inventory of more than 40 regulatory projects to further streamline and harmonise financial regulation in the EU. The FSAP achieved the necessary political support, and all European Institutions – Commission, Council and Parliament – worked within tight deadlines to get all the projects done between 1999 and 2004. The FSAP fundamentally transformed the regulatory framework of the financial markets and institutions. Full harmonisation was seldom achieved, but the impact of the FSAP is huge, as can be illustrated by just looking at some of the major projects:

---

[*] Chief Economist – Fortis.

- IFRS (International Financial Reporting Standards), setting EU standards for financial reporting by listed companies;
- CRD (Capital Requirements Directive), transposing the Basel II Accord on harmonised solvency rules for banks throughout the EU;
- Solvency II, creating pan-EU capital requirements for insurance companies;
- MIFID (Markets in Financial Instruments Directive), creating a European framework for investment services.

Furthermore, as part of the FSAP, the "Lamfalussy Process" was set up as an institutional framework for improving the speed and quality of EU financial regulation:
- Basic regulation, called "Level I" is developed in the traditional way, with involvement of the three European institutions;
- regulation of technical details is delegated to 'Level II" committees, consisting of specialised representatives of the Member States;
- supervisors and regulators sit together in "Level III" committees. They provide advice to the "Level II" committees, and work towards smooth implementation of the rules in all Member States, convergence of supervisory practices and the development of EU-wide best practices in the field of supervision.

While the "Lamfalussy Process" does not always deliver the progress anticipated, it receives broad support from politicians and the industry, as it has improved the transparency and the quality of rulemaking.

However, it is difficult to accurately assess the results of these initiatives. Some of the major FSAP directives, such as Solvency II, have still not been finalised; others, like the CRD or MIFID, are more or less finalised but have not yet been implemented. Still other directives have been implemented but have not yet achieved their full impact on business practices. It is therefore too early to determine whether the FSAP has been successful or has failed to create an integrated market. There is indeed a significant risk that politicians, frustrated by slow pace of change, might decide on new regulations that could be detrimental to the smooth process of integration, and therefore impose an excessive burden on the financial markets. The decision of the Commission not to launch a new FSAP seems to be the right approach. Regulation should create the right framework and eliminate unjustified hurdles, but business decisions should drive the process of integration, and that will take some time.

This does not, however, mean that nothing should be done. In certain fields, new initiatives are necessary to eliminate remaining key hurdles, but regulation must be selective, with clear targets.

H.2. Integration of Wholesale Markets

In general, integration of wholesale markets has made good progress. This process of integration is not restricted solely to the EU, but is a worldwide phenomenon. Certainly for the euro, issuing and underwriting has become a global activity, with even US investment banks serving as major players. Prices and spreads have converged, and the "nationality" of the issuer or the intermediary is no longer a major feature of an issue. However, a major handicap for the EU wholesale markets is the fragmentation of back office activities, such as custody, clearing and settlement, which increases costs for users and reduces liquidity. Improvements to the efficiency of these activities remains a priority for the Commission, but a directive will not resolve the problem. A lot of work has to be done at the level of the Member States to remove a wide range of administrative and tax problems, which are the true hurdles for further integration.

H.3. Integration of Retail Markets

For retail markets, integration remains at a much lower level. Retail customers stick to the high-street banks in their neighbourhood, despite the possibility of "freedom of delivery of services" within the EU and e-business. Cross-border distribution of retail products continues to be virtually impossible because of different consumer protection rules and taxation structures. Full integration of retail markets would require harmonisation of all these aspects, but this is an extremely difficult exercise. Harmonising consumer protection seems almost impossible since it is a highly sensitive issue and current practices diverge significantly. This is not only a question of the level of consumer protection, but also of the style: some Member States rely more on principles, on consumer education, information requirements and a code of conduct for the intermediaries, giving consumers greater choice and greater accountability. Other Member States focus on direct rules and detailed product descriptions. For countries with rigorous and stringent consumer protection rules, local pressures make it impossible to agree on more open standards. For countries adopting a more principle-based approach or with lower standards, it is difficult to accept stricter rules since these are seen as limiting consumer choice and increasing costs.

Different solutions have been tested to open up the EU market in retail financial products:
- There have been proposals to put in place a "26th Regime" governing certain retail products EU-wide. This regime would exist alongside current domestic rules. Products complying with this regime would get access to all EU markets. However, the Regime could be confusing for consumers since similar products would have a different legal basis;
- More recently, with the Consumer Credit Directive, the Commission tried the so-called "full targeted harmonisation," meaning that essential features of the product would be fully harmonised, while less important elements would remain local, but without restricting access to other Member States. Member States do not agree on what the "essential" features are, however, nor do they agree on giving access to foreign products which do not fully comply with local rules.

The fundamental question to be asked is whether the objective and emotional cost of achieving fully harmonised retail products is justified, given that consumers seem to be relatively happy with their local rules, and the economic benefits of fully harmonised products are not always particularly clear. Cost-benefit analyses and impact assessments are therefore essential before taking regulatory initiatives.

H.4. Integration of Infrastructures

An integrated market requires open and accessible infrastructures. For the financial markets, these infrastructures consist of custody, clearing and settlement systems – which have already been mentioned before – and payment systems. The Commission, together with the ECB, is keen on creating a fully integrated payment system for the Euro zone and harmonised rules about payment products for the whole EU.

SEPA (Single Euro Payments Area) is a major project which aims at replacing all existing payment systems – organised by the Member States – with new, pan-Euro systems. The cost is huge, and the effect for the consumer will be small, and might even be negative on occasion, since payment systems in some advanced countries have already achieved a level of efficiency which is not within the reach of the Euro zone as a whole in the short term.

One of the key questions in this respect is who will pay the bill. Building the new framework and organising the transition of all existing payment systems will cost some €10 billion according to some estimates. There is a general expectation that the banking sector will finance the whole project. However, there is no economic incentive for banks, as the new framework will increase competition and probably lower margins for banks in most Member States. In those Member States where prices are already extremely low (sometimes below cost), there is a clear political message that the transition cannot lead to increased costs for payment services. This means that this project is essentially of a political nature and that the economic grounds and incentives are not clear, increasing the risk of sub-optimal developments.

H.5. Institutional Integration

Institutional integration is making progress, but relatively slowly. In the case of stock exchanges, certain projects with pan-EU objectives, like Euronext, have been developed successfully. However, in the case of projects involving major exchanges, the debate becomes far more complicated with nationalistic and power play arguments clearly dominating. A merger of the London Stock Exchange (LSE), Deutsche Börse and/or Euronext has been the subject of debate for several years now. There are surprising signs that LSE could become a partner of the

NASDAQ, while Euronext might join the NYSE. This illustrates the fact that EU financial integration is only part of a wider process of globalisation. It is questionable, therefore, whether the EU needs an EU stock market or whether it would be better to participate in projects with a global ambit.

Cross-border integration of banks and insurance companies is far slower than in other economic sectors. The Commission has launched consultations to pinpoint the reasons for this. These seem to be twofold:

First, banks from other Member States are not welcomed as acquirers of domestic banks. This may take the form of total rejection of an acquisition by the domestic supervisory body, as was the case when ABN-Amro tried to take over the Italian Antonveneta bank. The transaction was made possible only after the intervention of the Commission. A more subtle version of this lack of welcome consists of a hostile environment in which the risk of regulatory hell is considered a serious threat and a reason for not proceeding to a merger or acquisition. Some Member States implicitly or explicitly seem to have the creation of "national financial champions" as a specific goal. Any foreign takeover then becomes a threat to this nationalistic policy.

The second reason for the low volume of cross-border mergers and acquisitions (M&A) is that they are seen as riskier and the potential synergies (economies of scale and scope) are just not there.

Despite the huge amount of harmonisation work within the EU, potential synergies through cross-border activities are partly eliminated because of certain remaining hurdles.

Some of these hurdles are the result of clear local preferences and potentially, consumer protection. If there are clear local consumer preferences, leading to specific local consumer protection rules, the same products cannot be sold across the whole territory, which reduces potential synergies. In such cases, any political action to remove the hurdle would be highly unwelcome.

Other hurdles have, however, nothing to do with the interest or preferences of consumers, but are the result of outdated historical situations, which are not justifiable in the actual circumstances. Take, for example, the VAT regime for banks. The most natural thing, when building an integrated pan-EU bank, would be to set up centralised functions for the whole group operating out of one place. Such functions could include risk management, auditing, and also back office functions for securities or payments. Such localised centres of expertise would bring about important synergies of scale. However, for cross-border banks, this structure leads to cross-border services delivered from one subsidiary to another. The resultant cross-border invoices lead to VAT costs of 20%. This means that an occasional cost synergy of 20% is immediately offset by additional tax.

Another major hurdle for the functioning of cross-border banks is the organisation of prudential supervision, which is still based on a country model, a clearly outdated situation in an integrated EU market. That aspect is further discussed in Point 6.

H.6. Integration of Prudential Supervision

Prudential supervision of financial institutions is justified by the fact that these institutions have access to the savings of the public at large. This access is only given if institutions follow specific rules in order to reduce the risk of bankruptcy. In the event of problems, governments often step in to resolve the situation with taxpayer's money. That explains why capital adequacy rules are the core element of prudential supervision. It also explains why supervision of financial institutions is essentially the responsibility of Member States in the EU.

Within the EU, financial institutions active in several Member States have to comply fully with the specific rules in each Member State, which, despite common directives, differ significantly between them. Today, a pan-European financial institution would have to cope with more than 50 supervisors, each asking for specific reporting and adding local requirements. On top of that, for any such institution, supplementary supervision at the consolidated level would be organised by the supervisor for the mother company. This situation increases the administrative burden unnecessarily and destroys a significant proportion of potential synergies. In some cases, the requirements of different supervisors are not even compatible or coherent, creating possibilities of regulatory arbitrage or pure conflicts. The situation worsens if financial institutions integrate more comprehensively across borders, organising certain key functions at the central level. In that case, a local supervisor cannot really understand what is happening within his country without looking at the overall picture. If each local supervisor develops his own ideas about how the group as a whole should be organised, however, conflicting views of supervisors could make management impossible. This would impact not only on costs, but also on the stability of the institution concerned.

In the event of a crisis, there would be total chaos since the central banks, deposit guarantee schemes and Government Treasuries from various countries would be involved. The lack of a framework for a clear and coherent cross border approach to crisis management of all these stakeholders is a real threat to financial stability.

Some measures have been taken to improve the situation:
- The Capital Requirements Directive for banks is quite detailed, leaving relatively little room to manoeuvre for local implementation;
- The task of Lamfalussy Level III Committees is to ensure coherent implementation of directives and to develop EU best practices for supervision;
- The Capital Requirement Directive for banks establishes a specific role for the consolidating supervisor, who has the power to approve risk management models for the group as a whole, including subsidiaries in other Member States;
- Supervisors, central banks and government treasuries are concluding on memoranda of understandings (MOUs) on crisis management.

However, all these initiatives do not completely overcome the lack of an efficient and effective supervisory framework. The solution for the future could be to set-up a pan-EU supervisory agency, but this is not politically feasible at the moment. In the short run, supervisors have to be encouraged to "act as one." A practical solution to achieve this would be to appoint a "lead supervisor" for each cross-border group. That lead supervisor – in principle, the supervisor for the parent company – would be responsible for all aspects of prudential supervision of the group and its subsidiaries as a whole. This lead supervisor would be assisted by a "college of supervisors concerned," within which information about the group would be exchanged and in which the practical supervisory activities would be organised. While the lead supervisor would be in charge of the whole process of supervision, the practicalities – such as on-site inspections – could be delegated to the host supervisors. In the event of disagreement within the college, a dispute resolution mechanism (mediation, arbitrage) would have to be organised.

Such prudential supervision would be possible within the current EU regulatory framework, but requires further work to determine how crises would be handled and how the burden would be split between the various Member States in which the financial institution concerned is active.

H.7. Certain Conclusions

Integration of financial markets in the EU is clearly progressing. The speed of integration varies, however, depending on the financial market segment concerned.

In deciding what political and regulatory EU initiatives should be taken in the future to boost further integration, a number of important issues must be taken into account:
- There is a time lag between regulation and the visible effects on the industry. Not taking this time lag into account could lead to overshooting regulation;
- For wholesale markets, a lot has already been achieved;
- For retail markets, integration is slow but new initiatives should be carefully selected on the basis of their feasibility and a thorough cost-benefit analysis;
- Integration of infrastructures is a priority but should be based on realistic assumptions and fair distribution of the burden;
- There are a number of clearly identified and outdated regulatory hurdles for cross-border M&As of financial firms;
- The supervisory framework of the EU has to be adapted to the reality of an integrated market for reasons of efficiency and effectiveness.

Fully integrated financial markets would help the economic growth of the EU. However, the path towards integration is difficult and requires a lot of effort and financial means. A change in behaviour is required of all stakeholders – industry, consumers and supervisors. Therefore, realistic timing and selective new political initiatives are essential to success.

I. Information and Communication Technology: Dynamics, Integration and Economic Stability

Paul J.J. Welfens

I.1. Introduction

The sector of information and communication technology (ICT) is a major driver of the economy in the 21st century. ICT represents a rising share of investment and R&D in OECD countries and thus is of particular relevance for growth and economic competitiveness. From a EU25 perspective, it also is crucial to note that the expansion of ICT is associated with the growth of a networked society in which the flow of information and technology on the one hand is accelerating; at the same time both ICT and digital networking facilitate international outsourcing and offshoring. Offshoring involves foreign direct investment while international outsourcing occurs through trade and arm's length market transactions.

In the context of the Lisbon Agenda of the European Community, the growth-enhancing aspect of ICT is quite important; at the same time one may anticipate impulses for:

- Structural change: as the relative price of ICT capital goods is expected to continue to fall sectors using ICT capital will intensively expand.
- Shifts in employment demand: as skilled labor is complementary to ICT capital the demand for skilled labor will rise while the relative demand for unskilled labor will fall; this will require transitorily higher wage differentials and indeed could imply that wages of unskilled workers will have to fall if rising unemployment rates are to be avoided.
- Digital education: In the European Learning Space – as defined by the Community – there will be new opportunities to embark upon digital learning/teaching projects which could be quite useful in meeting key challenges in the field of human capital building and productivity growth in an ageing EU society.
- Enhanced economic globalization through both trade and foreign direct investment as trading costs – relevant for international outsourcing – are reduced in a digitally networked economy on the one hand; on the other hand firm-internal transaction costs are falling due to modern ICT so that larger multinational companies can be established in larger international markets. The share of intra-company trade might rise in this context – reflecting increased offshoring – although the pressure for national and international outsourcing is a counter-balancing effect.
- The increasing use of ICT facilitates the creation, processing and storing of information, which should affect adjustment parameters in goods markets and financial markets; for example, the learning speed in the formation of exchange

rate expectations might increase and information about international availability of liquid assets could become more easily accessible so that the interest elasticity in the demand for money would rise – both parameters are relevant in the Dornbusch model with its focus on the problem of exchange rate overshooting.

Many economists have classified ICT as a general purpose technology which affects productivity in almost all sectors as the use of ICT is associated with considerable technological progress and facilitates innovation dynamics in many sectors. HEMPELL (2006) has emphasized that the concept of ICT as an "enabling technology" means that productivity increases are contingent on adequate company strategies and complementary efforts – this includes an impulse for human capital formation, as skilled labor is complementary to ICT investment. The implication is that the diffusion of ICT will increase the trend growth rate in many countries. At the same time, one must consider the potential problem that ICT capital accumulation will primarily increase the demand for skilled labor and thus could bring about a relative rise in the skill premium in wages. If the wages of unskilled labor were insufficiently flexible (and if progress is labor-augmenting with respect to unskilled labor), a rising unemployment rate among unskilled workers might result in the medium term. However, as regards the long run, one should also consider the challenge of retraining and education, as the share of unskilled workers in Europe – or the US – is not exogenous. This then, points to the issue of adequate policies, including tax policies that stimulate human capital formation and retraining.

The share of high technology imports (with the degree of technological sophistication assumed to correspond to skill intensity) in global imports increased from 18% in 1992 to 22.4% in 2003 – of which ICT represented 12.8% and 17.9%, respectively; the share of medium-high technology trade remained rather stable at around 37% (ECFIN, 2005, p.63). If one classifies global trade rather according to factor intensity, one finds that the share of R&D intensive goods has increased in global trade: the share of easy to imitate research goods stood at 14.3% in 1992, but at 18.3% in 2003. The share of difficult to imitate research goods was 24.6% in 1992 and 26.2% in 2003.

ICT goods production is not only technology intensive, it is also largely scale intensive so that the creation of the (enlarged) EU single market should reinforce the competitiveness of EU firms in this sector. One may measure the change in international competitiveness by regional or global indicators of revealed comparative advantage (RCA). Traditionally the Balassa-Samuelson RCA is used for RCA analysis where the definition of traditional RCA puts the focus on the sectoral export-import ratio relative to the aggregate export-import ratio. In this perspective, a ratio above unity indicates a comparative advantage ("positive specialization"). This indicator might be used in a trade-balance corrected form which takes into account any bias related to an aggregate surplus or deficit position (see, e.g., ECFIN, 2005). Alternatively one can focus on modified RCA, which is the ratio of sectoral exports to aggregate exports of country i relative to the same ratio for a benchmarking group of countries in the same target market (e.g., EU15 market). This concept has been developed by BORBÉLY (2005) who compares EU accession countries' normal sectoral export performance with various groups of sectors (e.g., labor intensive or technology intensive) in the EU15 market. Instead of focusing on the EU15 market, one could focus on the world market. Due to data problems, however, the more narrow EU15 single market is often considered.

While it is true that each country naturally is positively specialized in some sectors and negatively specialized in other sectors, one should note that the type of positive specialization is crucial with respect to economic growth, as was shown for the EU15 by JUNGMITTAG (2004; 2006):

- If a country is positively specialized in high-technology sectors ("Ricardian specialization"), this will significantly contribute to economic growth.
- Smithian specialization naturally will occur in the process of competition and trade in open economies, but it does not contribute to growth in EU15 countries. One should not rule out that in certain manufacturing sectors import competition could be a particular driver for productivity growth. (For positive evidence in the case of the US but negative for the case of Germany, see MANN, 2000.)

The EU Economy 2005 Review (ECFIN, 2005) emphasizes several important developments:

- there is a growing global tendency towards trade in intermediate products and hence to flexible international networked production
- the EU's trade position is rather weak in ICT, which is considered a high-technology sector; based on traditional RCA and with respect to the world market the EU15 has structural deficits in five of the 20 export groups which grow most quickly among the 3-digit product classification groups. In the five negative RCA sectors of the EU15, there are three ICT related industries (semiconductors, computers, parts and accessories for computers) as well as clothing and electrical machinery (ECFIN, 2005, p. 73). East Asian countries – including China and India – have gained considerable market shares in ICT.
- Across all sectors the EU(15) has lost ground in low- and medium-quality products but not in the top-of-the-range product groups; upmarket products accounted at the beginning of the 21st century for 48% of EU15 exports, for 52% of exports in the case of Japan and for 41% of exports in the case of the US (ECFIN, 2005, p. 74)
- ICT is facilitating the international fragmentation of the value-added chain, namely both in the manufacturing industry and services sector. The latter thus also raises new challenges for skilled labor (MANN, 2003) which so far has been under rather limited pressure from outsourcing and offshoring. The European Commission notes (ECFIN, 2005, p. 15): "ICT is affecting production structures: International specialization according to Ricardo's comparative advantage applies increasingly to segments of the product cycle rather than to complete products. The growing share of part and components in world trade…indicates the increasing fragmentation of manufacturing production. ICT has been a fundamental contributor to the dramatically

changed tradability of goods and services...Services are affected: While modularity and fragmentation of manufacturing production is not a new phenomenon, it is now also applied to services. Many jobs previously considered as non-tradable are suddenly exposed to international competition and may risk being dislocated."

The fact that tradability has increased implies that the costs of international fragmentation have fallen, which has to be further explored in basic models of fragmentation. To the extent that services become more tradable – see the case of digital products and services – one may also expect economies of scale to become more important in the services sector.

Internationalization of industries is a consistent phenomenon of economic globalization which mainly suggests a rising role for both foreign direct investment and international trade, particularly since the expansion of the internet has increased the digital cross-border diffusion of information and knowledge. Globalization and the above described developments have to be explained in theoretical terms, namely

- in order to get a better understanding of the international and national economic dynamics
- to develop rational policy options with the aim of increasing economic welfare, maintaining economic stability and reinforcing cooperation among partners in the EU integration club as well as outside the EU.

Globalization also concerns the aspect that more and more countries have opened up for trade and capital flows, which in turn has facilitated international outsourcing and trade with intermediate products on the one hand and with differentiated final products on the other, the latter being a crucial part of intra-industrial trade. In this perspective, the expansion of ICT and accumulation of ICT capital in Europe is crucial as it

- helps to create new markets and thus stimulates product cycle trade in ICT goods
- affects relative factor abundance (as measured by the share of ICT-capital in overall capital) and thus stimulates internationalization of goods and services along the lines of a modified Heckscher-Ohlin approach; countries which have relatively high ICT capital intensities will specialize in ICT-capital-intensive goods and record high shares of the respective export category
- creates new opportunities for outsourcing at the national level and the international level; international outsourcing is stimulated relatively strongly in industries with opportunities for digital outsourcing, since the liberalization of telecommunications markets in EU15 after 1998 has brought with it the steepest fall in prices in international telecommunications (as regards accession countries there are several special developments, including transition periods to full international liberalization in telecommunications which imply that digital international outsourcing opportunities will improve in EU25/Eastern European accession countries more slowly than in EU15); national long distance prices

have also fallen considerably, while the decline of local prices was modest in the first stage of liberalization.

- ICT reduces firm internal transaction costs and thus facilitates management in large companies which in turn implies new opportunities for foreign direct investment (FDI); in the context of product cycle trade FDI can be expected to play a particularly strong role in scale intensive goods. The new tendencies towards fragmentation – facilitated by ICT – allow even for the possibility to relocate production of high-technology components so that offshoring-dynamics increase. To the extent that ICT-expansion creates larger markets, the typical positive correlation between market size and firm size also implies increased FDI and offshoring.

From an EU15 perspective, EU eastern enlargement has strongly risen interest in off-shoring – defined as international outsourcing involving foreign direct investment – as new low-wage countries have entered the EU single market. Assuming that not only cheap unskilled labor in eastern Europe is found but also relatively cheap skilled labor is available in accession countries, one may anticipate considerable pressure for off-shoring. If there is off-shoring through a subsidiary abroad, rising management costs associated with a more complex (international) organization of the respective multinational company must be more than offset by a cost advantage in production or the provision of services – or by improved access to the host country markets. If there is off-shoring to a foreign firm there will be quality uncertainties, so that the cost savings should more than offset the increasing cost of quality verification in the buying of intermediate inputs of uncertain quality.

Policymakers are to some extent worried that international outsourcing could lead to considerable job losses. This fear is not only relevant with respect to (ICT) manufacturing but also with respect to services which typically are more skill-intensive than the manufacturing industry. Thus international outsourcing of services could mean that jobs requiring skilled labor (representing relatively high wages and incomes) may be relocated internationally. Taking into account that a considerable share of international outsourcing does indeed improve the global competitiveness of EU firms – say EU software firms outsourcing to Asia so that cost competitiveness of EU firms in US markets is improved – the basic equation could reveal that in a triangular trading perspective, one should not worry about outsourcing. The situation with ICT, however, is special to some extent since the ICT sector is a Schumpeterian sector with high innovation dynamics. Between 15–25% of patents from firms in leading EU countries concern the ICT sector in the early 21st century.

Section 2 takes a look at ICT characteristics and international outsourcing dynamics on the one hand and on ICT on the other to get a better understanding of the role of ICT for Europe. Section 3 considers the role of ICT and foreign direct investment in the context of a modified Dornbusch model to offer a better idea about the nature of overshooting problems in a digital economy with ICT. Section 4 puts the focus on some regulatory policy issues and key aspects of life-long learning in the EU.

I.2. Economic Development, Adjustment and Outsourcing

I.2.1. Traits of the ICT Sector and Economic Dynamics

The ICT sector has been part and parcel of the international outsourcing process. ICT sector dynamics have broad economic significance; they affect many sectors, as so many use ICT products or ICT services, which implies strong competition and in turn stimulates the cost-cutting reorganization of industries and national or international outsourcing dynamics – part of which concerns the ICT sector itself. Moreover, one may expect four impulses for rising internationalization in the sense of growing trade:

- the ICT sector is an expanding field in its own right, as novel digital products and services are created in a dynamic networked world economy; the internationalization of the ICT sector thus has to be analyzed not in the least from the perspective of the product cycle trade approach (VERNON, 1966); a special ICT issue concerns the question as to whether ICT contributes to an accelerated innovation race, possibly induced through faster diffusion of new knowledge in an increasingly networked world economy
- part of the ICT sector (e.g., software, a sub-sector of digital services) is characterized by network effects, which amounts to a kind of unusual endogenous growth impulse coming from the demand side. To the extent that this raises both output and per capita income, one faces a trade creation effect
- since part of the ICT sector expansion amounts to cutting international transaction costs – relative to domestic transaction costs – there is an indirect trade creation effect which will influence not only the ICT sector itself but other sectors as well
- since ICT is particularly characterized by high R&D intensity and since in technology-based ownership specific advantages are considered as the basis for successful international investment, one should expect that expansion of the R&D sector will stimulate foreign direct investment.

Since the 1990s information and communication technology (ICT) has been a major driver of economic growth in OECD countries. There is broad consensus in the literature that ICT production (mainly due to high rates of process innovations) is contributing to this growth. Moreover, there is also some support for the argument that ICT use contributes to increases in output (VAN ARK, 2001; AUDRETSCH/WELFENS, 2002 BARFIELD/HEIDUK/WELFENS, 2003; WELFENS, 2005). There is considerable evidence that ICT plays an important role for the growth differential US vs. EU15: JORGENSON/STIROH (2000), COLECCHIA/SCHREYER (2002), OLINER/SICHEL (2002), STIROH (2001), and INKLAR ET AL. (2003) have argued that ICT production and the use of ICT (that is, cumulated ICT investment) are important drivers of productivity growth. More cautious about the link between ICT and growth is GORDON (2004). As regards Eastern Europe, VAN ARK/PIATKOWSKI (2004) find some evidence that ICT significantly affects productivity and output growth. WELFENS/

PONDER (2003) and PONDER/MARKOVA (2005) have shown that Eastern European countries have considerably caught up in the field of telecommunications, however Russia lags behind EU accession countries.

Comparing the periods 1995–2000 to 1979–1995, the INKLAAR et al. analysis of labor productivity growth in the US and EU-4 finds a rise of 1.25 percentage points in the US and a fall of 0.27 points in the EU. The growth accounting estimates show that labor quality changes have reduced labor productivity in both the US and the EU-4. The employment reallocation effect in the US was positive at + 0.05 points, but in the EU-4 the figure was -0.06 points. ICT producing industries generated similar impacts on productivity growth in the US and the EU, namely 0.04 and 0.03 percentage points. As regards the impact of ICT-using industries, the EU did not reach even half the increase of the US which was 0.29 points, the main effect stemming from financial services (0.17 in the US; 0.02 in EU-4). Non-ICT capital deepening contributed to 0.08 points in the US and -.45 points in the EU. Total factor productivity contributed 0.79 points in the US, but only 0.13 points in the EU-4. The impact from ICT producing industries was rather similar on both sides of the Atlantic (0.36 in the US vs. 0.24 in the EU), but in ICT using industries there were many larger differences; in particular wholesale trade, retail trade and financial services seem to be problem areas for Western Europe. Weak EU15 productivity increases and slow growth are all the more unsatisfactory, since Germany, France, Italy and Spain suffer from high unemployment rates and since slow growth from 2000 to 2005 seems to indicate that the ambitious goals of the EU Lisbon Agenda (aiming at higher growth and employment by 2010) will not be achieved. However, there is a range of reports from the European Commission which analyze the dynamics of the information society developments and suggest policy options for stimulating digital modernization in EU eastern accession countries (BOGDANOWICZ/CENTENO/ BURGELMAN, 2004; BOGDANOWICZ/ BURGELMAN/ CENTENO/ GOUROVA/ CARAT, 2003; GOUROVA/BURGELMAN/BOGDANOWICZ/ HERRMANN, 2002).

A growth accounting analysis by SAKELLARIS/VIJSELAAR (2005) for the Euro zone has tried to take into account the role of quality changes in capital formation and in output (unfortunately this SOLOW-type growth accounting exercise does not consider labor quality aspects – and the analysis might suffer from methodological problems since focus is on the Euro zone with its high unemployment figures, which would rather suggest relying on data envelopment analysis). This leads to an upward correction of output growth figures for 1982– 1990 and for 1991–2000 by about 0.5 percentage points in both periods. The role of capital growth, based on quality adjusted figures, rises by 0.33 in the first period and by 0.45 points in the second period. Among the sub-categories IT hardware, software, communication equipment, other machinery and equipment, transport equipment and non residential construction, the combined contribution of IT hardware, software and communication equipment amounted to 0.26 percentage points in the first period and 0.2 percentage points in the second period (reflecting a modest upward revision from quality-unadjusted figures; as regards software, quality adjustment brought no change in the assessment). Total factor productivity growth accounted for 2.2 points in the first period and 1.46 in the second period which had shown a deceleration of growth (2.34 % growth of GDP compared to 2.97% in the first period; both quality-adjusted figures are 0.6 percentage points higher than the figures without quality adjustment). The increase in total factor productivity growth is decomposed in equipment and software as well as "rest"; equipment contributed 0.59 percentage points in the first period and 0.63 percentage points in the second period. This suggests that ICT dynamics have a triple importance for the Euro zone as well as for other countries:

- quality adjustment of output;
- contribution to capital growth;
- growth of total factor productivity growth;

In the 1990s, the overall contribution to growth in leading OECD countries was – according to OECD figures – between 0.5 and 0.8 percentage points, which is rather impressive for a sector which hardly accounted for 10% of aggregate output at the beginning of the 21st century (and for 15–35% of investment). ICT is a broad field which contains computers & software, telecommunications and modern digital services, all of which are inputs in every sector of the economy. ICT is also crucial for innovation since a rising share of R&D expenditures is accounted for by the ICT sector. Nevertheless one cannot argue that ICT expansion has stimulated growth in a rather homogeneous way across OECD countries, and indeed very few OECD countries have experienced a considerable increase in labor productivity or technological progress in the context of the growth of ICT. PILAT (2005) argues that only a few countries have witnessed an upsurge in labor or multi-factor productivity growth in those sectors that have invested most in ICT. Among the factors explaining this – according to PILAT – are differences in the countries' respective uptake of ICT (OECD, 2003; 2004). ICT investment rose from less than 15% of total non-residential investment in the early 1980s to a range of 15–30% at the beginning of the 21st century; the share of ICT investment was relatively high in the US, the UK, Sweden, the Netherlands, Canada and Australia (OECD, 2004), where the uptake of ICT is partly linked to differences in the direct costs of ICT (ICT equipment, telecommunications, installations of e-commerce systems etc.). These costs still differ across OECD countries despite rising ICT trade and the liberalization of telecommunications. Moreover, countries differ in the degree of competition in ICT markets and in their respective ability to absorb ICT and use this technology effectively, which in turn is related to the availability of know-how and skilled labor. There also could be some impediment on complementary process innovations in Europe which explains the relatively modest productivity gains in some continental EU countries, and a lack of new firm creation in ICT-using services could play a role.

HEMPELL (2006) has emphasized that ICT is not a panacea for productivity gains; rather ICT raises productivity mainly by acting as a catalyst of innovation and upgrading of skills. He basically suggests several conclusions based on a large sample of German firms and findings for the Netherlands (HEMPELL et al. 2004). ICT use stimulates productivity; a 10% increase in the firm's ICT capital stock raises company productivity by roughly 0.6%. Given relative factor endowments in the sample of firms considered, annual returns to ICT investment are likely to exceed its user costs for many years to come. A crucial element of ICT productivity reflects improved quality of output. Quality improvements are quite important. Productive ICT use is complemented by innovation dynamics and innovative activities. Successful use of computers and internet requires companies to introduce their own innovations. Innovation history is important; service firms that have introduced innovations in the past are found to be better in using ICT productively than firms that have not, and the empirical results point to a major role of process innovation as a basic source of experience for ICT use. ICT productivity is contingent on the skills of workers and employees: the higher the share of highly-skilled workers in firms, the greater the productivity contribution of ICT.

- For the medium term, HEMPELL (2006, p. 182) sees two partially-opposed ICT developments. ICT access will become simplified and ubiquitous and innovation opportunities more complex and expensive from ICT use.
- On the one hand, falling computer prices and increasingly standardized software will make ICT more ubiquitous and simpler so that ICT could become less important for the sustained competitive advantage of firms. This implies that ICT will diffuse in the world economy.
- Technological progress in ICT hardware and software imply new options for a growing range of ever more complex innovations, including novel types of knowledge management. This includes ICT-based new tools and broadband internet access, which will facilitate collaboration of R&D teams scattered around the world (FRAUNHOFER-GESELLSCHAFT, 2004). The implication is that the internationalization of ICT as a high-technology field will be concentrated in advanced countries endowed with highly skilled labor and which have made investments in modern broadband e-communications networks. North America, Europe, Japan and a few Asian countries will fall into this category.

With the economic opening up of China and the transformation of the former Soviet Union and east European countries, a large part of the world economy (richly endowed with labor in the case of China and with labor and human capital in the case of Eastern Europe and Russia) has become integrated into the global economy. Both growing trade and rising FDI flows – mainly inflows – play a role for Eastern Europe and China/Asean countries. China and East Asian countries have become a major export region for ICT goods; however, considering Asia a natural winner in the process of modern globalization would be an overstatement (ECFIN, 2005).

I.2.2. Financial Markets and ICT

Banks are top users of ICT and also are heavy users of digital services. For international banks, communication costs represent a high share of costs and with sustained competition in telecommunications and continuing technological digital progress, banks will be able to strongly benefit from ICT dynamics. One particular aspect is eBanking, which offers a broad range of new digital banking services to national and international customers. However, apparent security problems indicate that there is no easy way to achieve long term growth in eBanking and other digital financial services. At the same time, one may point out that the US has developed internet-based venture capital funds which create larger funds, offer better transparency and stimulate reputation building.

In a broader perspective, there are also other links between the financial market system and ICT; the most interesting are the following:

- Banks, insurance companies and other financial services firms are among the heavy ICT investors so that this sector has been characterized by high ICT-based productivity growth. The financial services sectors in the UK and the US have been quite strong in pushing ICT.
- Prudential supervision in the Basel II framework eliminates most of the traditional continental European relationship banking and puts strong emphasis on computerized monitoring of clients and debtors. The expansion of digital networks will reinforce the ability of banks to put all major financial activities of clients permanently on the radar screen.
- Data protection in the financial and personal sphere becomes increasingly important with ICT expansion. Problems of government in effectively taxing transactions over the internet will generate pressure for tax authorities to increasingly peek into internet users' e-commerce transaction. Moreover, internet-based advertising will become more personalized, which leads to the issue of consumer protection and data protection in a sensitive area. While customers have certain benefits from getting personalized advertisement, there is also the problem that the consumer is relatively losing control over the advertisement presented to him or her. Digital bonus programs further reinforce some of the problems with firms generally being happy to exploit data mining in a broad form. (Customers who regularly spend lavishly on products might never see the cheapest offer of some internet services companies as the customer's profile points to low price sensitivity.)
- The expansion of ICT will create particular problems for the bank-dominated financial systems to finance the growth of ICT. Since ICT often is characterized by a high intensity of immaterial assets – or the use of assets whose price is falling rapidly – banks will find it rather difficult to finance the expansion of young ICT firms. This will generate pressure to reform the financial system in continental EU countries and to reinforce the role of stock markets. As the US is the global leader of the stock markets, the EU markets could become dominated by these markets.
- ICT expansion will affect adjustment parameters in goods markets and financial markets and thereby influence the equilibrium solution in any standard macro model; for example, price adjustment speed in all markets will increase and collecting, processing and storing information should become easier so that the formation of expectations is thereby influenced.

To the extent that ICT expansion helps to create greater transparency in markets and to reduce the risk of overshooting, there will be positive external effects from firms' ICT investment. If there should be reduced volatility of asset prices, this would reduce the effective costs of capital and could thus raise the investment-output ratio and hence the level of the growth path.

I.2.3. Growth, Competitiveness and Outsourcing Dynamics

Achieving sustained economic growth is a key challenge for industrialized countries which rely on the accumulation of capital, human capital formation, technological progress and positive spillovers to generate growth. Analytically, spillovers have played a prominent role in endogenous growth models which rely on constant returns to a sufficiently broad concept of capital accumulated over time (ROMER, 1986; 1987; LUCAS, 1988; REBELO, 1991). Complementary approaches to endogenous growth are the R&D based models of ROMER (1990) and GROSSMAN/HELPMAN (1991a, 1991b), who emphasize accumulation and product upgrading. The emphasis in AGHION/HOWITT (1997a, 1997b) is on combining R&D and capital accumulation. MARREWIJK (1999) presents an interesting and important extension as he integrates the expansion of product variety rather than quality improvements (vertical differentiation as opposed to horizontal differentiation). He then looks at knowledge spillovers as well as learning, before finally considering different production technologies in the R&D sector and in the final goods sector. He thus departs from the standard assumption of identical technologies in these two sectors (RIVERA-BATIZ/ROMER, 1991; BARRO/SALA-I-MARTIN (1995), AGHION/HOWITT (1997a, 1997b).

Rising trade (in intermediate products) will lead to different results if we consider neoclassical trade theory and modern trade theory (typically with a simple focus on two countries):

- Traditional neoclassical trade theory suggests that more trade should contribute to international price equalization and hence to factor price equalization, which in turn reinforces economic convergence.
- Modern trade theory offers models with skilled and unskilled labor (FEENSTRA, 2004) where introducing trade with intermediate products leads to a relative increase in the demand of skilled labor in both countries. If wages are not fully flexible in both countries, a key result will be unemployment in one of the countries or in both. If one country has full employment and the other structural unemployment of unskilled workers, it is clear that factor price convergence and hence convergence of real per capita income will slow down.

I.2.4. ICT, Outsourcing and R&D

The EU adopted a strong focus on ICT in the 6th and 7th framework programme, thereby stimulating cross-border ICT research in the EU. However, it is unclear whether the Community adequately emphasizes the ICT sector and if the interplay between national R&D policies and supranational R&D policy is optimal. R&D policy is optimal if positive external effects are internalized efficiently. National external effects can be internalized mainly at the national level. International external effects could be internalized through R&D policy in partner countries or through adequate supranational policy. If there is insufficient international cooperation (within the EU or within the OECD), the level of innovation policy will be sub-optimal. From the perspective of the respective government, it is clear that positive growth effects and the associated additional tax revenues provide an incentive for R&D promotion.

R&D intensities in the EU do not seem to converge across countries; only for a subgroup of early leading EU countries and Finland can a convergence be observed. At the same time, empirical evidence exists for a convergence of trade structure among EU15 (JUNGMITTAG, 2006). It is, however, unclear what convergence really means here. One may state the hypothesis that through increasing vertical trade – within industries – there is some structural convergence in the EU (or in the world economy). If convergence is to mean that intermediate products with low profit rates are more and more concentrated in Spain and Portugal while final goods production is in Germany, France, the UK and the Benelux group as well as Scandinavian countries and Ireland, one would not really expect economic convergence in terms of per capita income. The main reason for non-convergence or divergence is that final goods producers in technology-intensive industries will appropriate a Schumpeterian rent in their respective profit rates. In a Heckscher-Ohlin approach to international trade, technologies are the same across countries. For this reason, Schumpeterian profit differentials across countries cannot play a role. In reality Schumpeterian profits indeed play a crucial role; this holds not only for countries with high patent intensities but also for countries with a specialization in sectors shaped by high progress rates. ICT is such a sector; the OECD (2002) has emphasized that it is one of the most important fields of innovation dynamics in the US and other OECD countries.

I.2.4.1. ICT Dynamics: Outsourcing and Insourcing

ICT facilitates national and international outsourcing (WELFENS, 2005) and also raises the range of tradability in the services sector; the N-sector shrinks (see the figure: dashed line in country II) while the T-sector grows. The firm T_1 considered in country I can outsource tradable goods and services domestically – say to firms T_{11} and T_{12} – or to the domestic N-sector. As regards intermediate tradables, there is potential competition with suppliers abroad; the split between outsourcing to domestic suppliers and foreign suppliers typically will be determined along the lines of the Heckscher-Ohlin-Samuelson approach. As countries I and II differ in terms of relative factor endowment, international outsourcing will be favored with respect to those components which use the factors intensively which are relatively abundant in country II.

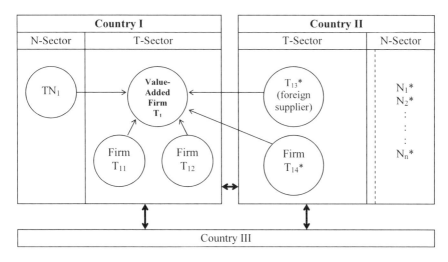

Fig. 11. National and International Outsourcing/Fragmentation of ICT Production (T is tradables sector; N is nontradables sector).

A large share of ICT is strongly technology intensive and therefore international outsourcing is often in the form of offshoring. Offshoring allows not only for cutting costs by importing from foreign subsidiaries in the tradables sector, but in principle there is also the option that ICT offshoring take place in the foreign non-tradables sector (case of special ICT services). Intermediate inputs from foreign subsidiaries go into production of firm T_1 in country I; however, part of valued-added in foreign subsidiaries could be sold directly on the world market (country III). As the R&D intensity of ICT is expected to grow over time, one should expect offshoring to increase in importance in the long run.

In some ICT sectors network effects are relevant; to the extent that those effects are international, outsourcing dynamics could be influenced. From a theoretical perspective, international network effects are of particular importance in ICT innovations in certain fields. Network effects are positive demand-side externalities, which are rather unusual. ICT R&D is likely to have positive cross-sector spillover effects. One also may anticipate considerable international spillovers, either in the ICT sector itself or through increasing use of ICT capital in other sectors. One should, however, carefully distinguish sub-sectors of ICT. For example, chip production is scale intensive and knowledge intensive (referring to the overall product not the rather simple chip production as such) as is software. However, many digital services have to be very customer specific so that economies of scale play a limited role. To some extent economies of scale can be exploited for the basic product – say the core algorithm – while customization requires specific adjustment involving the employment of skilled labor.

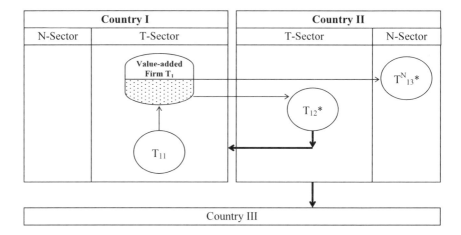

Fig. I2. ICT and International Offshoring Opportunities *(including direction of sales from subsidiary* ➔ *)*.

While ICT facilitates international outsourcing, it is not true that leading OECD countries are natural losers from outsourcing. Indeed, international outsourcing can stimulate structural adjustment in a way which increases productivity, competitiveness and growth. Moreover, international outsourcing from the EU to Eastern Europe, Asia or elsewhere goes along with insourcing in the sense that firms from Asia and other regions of the world economy can conquer markets in EU countries/OECD countries only if they set up marketing centers and R&D facilities in those countries (which have a comparative advantage in relevant R&D fields). Two important studies can be found in this context:

- BAILEY/LAWRENCE (2005) have shown that the US software sector internationally outsourced some 100,000 jobs in the period from 2000 to 2003. However, the overall number of software personnel in the US increased in that period. Mostly, rather simple programming jobs were outsourced, often to Asian countries. This suggests that the international outsourcing of standardized services will allow advanced countries with a relative abundance of skilled workers to specialize increasingly in advanced services. The EU15 should also benefit in a similar way, as leading software firms become more globally competitive by outsourcing to Eastern Europe or Asia.

- As regards the outsourcing of services, a broader picture is obtained if one takes into account data on the largest absolute insourcers, the principal world relative insourcers (for business services and computer & information services) and the biggest surplus and deficit countries (AMITI/WEI, 2005a; 2005b). In 2002, the top insourcers in business services were the US, the UK, Germany, France, the Netherlands, India, Japan, China and Russia; as regards computer & information services No. 1 was Ireland followed – with the exception of Spain – roughly by the same list of countries.

As regards the outsourcing of services in Europe, the study by AMITI/WEI (2005a) is quite interesting. They follow the study of FEENSTRA/HANSON (1996, 1999) – their focus was on material inputs outsourcing of the US – in their definition of outsourcing. Defining Y, J and X as production, imports and exports, respectively, the outsourcing intensity Ω of sector i is defined as:

Ω_i = (Input purchase of service by i/total nonenergy inputs used by i) $(J_i/[Y_i+J_i-X_i])$

In the AMITI/WEI study, the denominator includes all non-energy material inputs as well as the five business service industries: communication, financial services, insurance, other business services, computing and information. The authors only report figures for the UK where the figures are rough estimates, as no sectoral data on imported services inputs are available; instead the economy-wide import share is applied to each industry (the UK imported 6.6% of business services in 2001; it thus is assumed that each industry – in manufacturing and services – imports 6.6% of the business services used in that year; as the ratio of business services to total non-energy material inputs is 15%, the outsourcing intensity of business services is 0.15*0.066 = 1%.). The authors aggregate across the five service inputs and thereby obtain the average service outsourcing intensity in each industry. Unfortunately AMITI/WEI do not provide a split of imports according to intra-EU service imports and extra-EU services imports. They also do not look into the topic of transfer pricing which, however, might be rather important in the context of outsourcing of services in countries with considerable inward or outward stocks of foreign direct investment. The figures for the UK for 1992 and 2001 show that there has been a modest increase in international outsourcing of services, except in the case of communications services. The latter finding can probably be explained through the fall of telecommunications prices in the 1990s triggered by increasing competition in EU countries and technological progress. This shows that it can be quite important to carefully split purchase figures into prices and quantities.

152   Paul J.J. Welfens

Services	Share of Service		Import of service j
	Mean	Std Dev	
1992			
Communication	0.0153	0.0373	0.0587
Financial	0.0330	0.0247	0.0173
Insurance	0.0137	0.0103	0.0186
Other business service	0.1261	0.1615	0.0503
Computer and Information	0.0112	0.0185	0.0148
2001			
Communication	0.0158	0.0393	0.0547
Financial	0.0306	0.0198	0.0420
Insurance	0.0123	0.0060	0.0230
Other business service	0.1536	0.1872	0.0659
Computer and Information	0.0211	0.0302	0.0283

Source: AMITI/WEI, 2005a, p. 319.

Fig. I3. UK: Outsourcing of Services.

The average outsourcing of services – relative to GDP – has increased in the UK (from 1.4% in 1992 to 2.6% in 2001) and the US (0.6 and 0.9%, respectively) (AMITI/WEI, 2005a; 2005b). By contrast, material outsourcing intensities are much higher in both the US and the UK. At the beginning of the 21st century, it was about 27% in the UK and 11% in the US; the figure for the UK peaked in 1996. In the US, the outsourcing of material inputs is a sustained phenomenon, although in the period from 1992 to 2001 the growth rate was lower than in services.

The leading 10 exporters in the field of computer and information services are Ireland (14 bill. in 2003; this includes revenues from software sales), India, the US, the UK, Germany, Israel, Spain, Canada, Netherlands and Sweden (2 bill.); the global figure is 75.1 bill, to which the EU has accounted for an impressive 40.7 bill. (WTO, 2005). Israel and Spain are two interesting newcomer countries in the export of computer and information services. The "effective US surplus" of 2.4 bill. – defined not geographically but on a company basis – is certainly higher than the US figure indicates, as more than one-half of the Irish figure is likely to represent activities of US subsidiaries.

The relatively biggest insourcers of business services (relative to local GDP) were Vanuatu, Singapore, Hong Kong, Papua New Guinea and Luxembourg, which recorded business services outsourcing in the range of 17% to 10% of GDP; rank 21 is for India, 33 for the UK, 50 for France, 54 for Germany, 79 for China, 88 for Russia, 90 for the US, and 95 for Japan. The average share of the UK (2.35%), France (1.45%) and Germany (1.40%) was more than twice as high as the share of the US of 0.58% of GDP; hence even under the assumption that leading EU countries' insourcing represents one-half of the insourcing from other

EU countries, the combined position of the UK/France/Germany is favorable. As regards computer and information services Ireland, Cyprus, Luxembourg, Costa Rica and Belgium were the top 5 (with a rang of 8.5% to 0.8%), rank 17 was for the UK, 24 for Germany, 42 for France, 49 for the US. Thus one may state that for some of the small open economies in the EU, there has been relatively successful insourcing which reflects a particular specialization in ICT services. As regards large countries, it is not surprising that insourcing figures are rather small relative to GDP, as most regional outsourcing in a large economy is regional insourcing; this is in contrast to small open economies.

Rank	Country	Business services	Rank	Country	Computer& information services
1	United States	58.794	1	Ireland	10.426
2	United Kingdom	36.740	2	United Kingdom	5.675
3	Germany	27.907	3	United States	5.431
4	France	20.864	4	Germany	5.185
5	Netherlands	20.074	5	Spain	2.487
6	India	18.630	10	France	1.191
8	Japan	17.401	11	Japan	1.140
14	China, P.R.	10.419	12	China, P.R.	638
29	Russia	2.012	25	Russia	137

Source: AMITI/WEI (2005a), p. 324.

Fig. 14. Biggest Absolute Insourcers in the World Economy, (Business Services and Computer & Information Services), 2002.

Rank	Economy	Business services	Rank	Economy	Computer and information services
A. Ratio to Local GDP (%)					
1	Vanuatu	17,13	1	Ireland	8,54
2	Singapore	14,98	2	Cyprus	2,19
3	Hong Kong SAR	11,53	3	Luxembourg	1,09
4	Papua New Guinea	10,55	4	Costa Rica	0,91
5	Luxembourg	9,78	5	Belgium	0,76
21	India	3,79	17	United Kingdom	0,36
33	United Kingdom	2,35	24	Germany	0,26
50	France	1,45	42	France	0,08
54	Germany	1,40	49	United States	0,05
79	China, P.R.	0,82	51	China, P.R.	0,05
88	Russia	0,58	54	Russia	0,04
90	United States	0,56	59	Japan	0,03
95	Japan	0,44			
B. Ratio to Value-added of Local Service Sector (%)					
1	Papua New Guinea	32,92	1	Ireland	15,64
2	Vanuatu	23,85	2	Guyana	1,50
3	Singapore	21,93	3	Costa Rica	1,46
4	Swaziland	16,06	4	Luxembourg	1,40
5	Hong Kong SAR	13,46	5	Armenia	1,09
13	India	7,82	18	United Kingdom	0,51
44	United Kingdom	3,28	24	Germany	0,38
53	China, P.R.	2,45	38	China, P.R.	0,15
64	Germany	2,07	42	France	0,12
66	France	2,03	51	Russia	0,07
87	Russia	1,04	52	United States	0,07
91	United States	0,76	60	Japan	0,04
94	Japan	0,66			

Source: AMITI/WEI (2005a), p. 325.

Fig. 15. Biggest Relative Insourcers in the World Economy (Business Services and Computer & Information Services), 2002.

Rank	Economy	Business services	Rank	Economy	Computer and information services
Surplus countries			**Surplus countries**		
1	United Kingdom	20.555,96	1	Ireland	9.882,71
2	United States	17.864,30	2	United States	3.884,00
3	Hong Kong SAR	15.424,54	3	United Kingdom	3.072,72
4	India	6.813,44	4	Canada	1.077,12
5	Singapore	3.826,12	5	Spain	914,65
6	China, P.R.	2.462,05	9	France	41,39
10	France	1.752,32	10		
Deficit countries			**Deficit countries**		
135	Russia	-2.570,90	95	Russia	-454,30
139	Korea	-4.450,90	96	China, P.R.	-494,85
140	Japan	-7.313,51	97	Italy	-674,85
141	Indonesia	-7.985,71	98	Germany	-939,29
142	Germany	-11.205,43	99	Japan	-1.007,74
143	Ireland	-13.882,01	100	Brazil	-1.118,10

Source: AMITI/WEI (2005a), p. 327.

Fig. 16. Biggest Services Trade Surplus Countries (Business Services and Computer & Information Services), 2002.

At the beginning of the 21st century, the largest global surplus countries in the field of business services were the UK ($ 20.6 bill.), the US, Hong Kong, India and Singapore (followed by China); in computer & information services, the leaders were Ireland, the US, the UK, Canada and Spain. The five largest deficit countries in the field of business information were Korea, Japan, Indonesia, Germany, Ireland; in the field of computer and information services, China, Italy, Germany, Japan and Brazil.

So the picture at the beginning of the 21st century is inconclusive, and one may draw only preliminary conclusions:

- Some EU countries are major insourcers of ICT services
- Some EU countries have a considerable sectoral deficit position in ICT services
- Some Asian countries seem to play a considerable role as successful net exporters of ICT services; from this perspective it will be interesting to observe whether subsidiaries of EU ICT multinationals are among the driving forces of those surpluses. If there were such a sustained phenomenon, one may assume that international ICT outsourcing of EU firms reflects a win-win international division of labor in the digital world economy.

I.2.4.2. ICT and R&D

ICT – broadly defined – is a strong driver of innovation dynamics in OECD countries. According to the European Innovation Scoreboard 2006, electrical and optical equipment and ICT information and communication technologies as well as computer and related activities show the highest ranking of average innovation

156   Paul J.J. Welfens

performance by sector. This indicates a strong relevance of ICT for growth and structural change. R&D activities in ICT are strongly internationalized in some sub-sectors, including software development. (The US, the EU, China and India plus Japan are strong centers of software development; some of the US firms' and EU firms' activities in China and India partly reflect the search for comparative advantage and cost-cutting. There is, however, also pressure by governments of these big countries, namely to give access to markets only under the condition that firms establish a development center.)

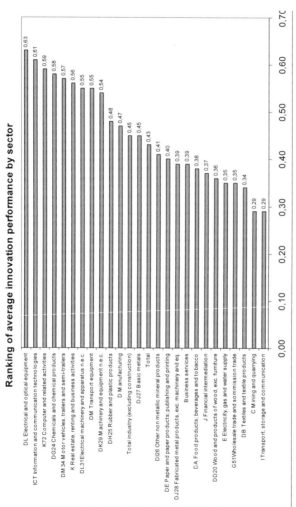

Source: EUROPEAN INNOVATION SCOREBOARD (2005), S. 23.

Fig. I7. Sectoral Innovation Performance in the EU.

As regards links between the US, the EU and Japan, one should emphasize the role of international R&D alliances, which became rather important in the 1980s and 1990s in OECD countries – not only in ICT. As regards international alliances, the emphasis is more on EU15 countries than on EU accession countries. Strategic R&D alliances played an increasing role in the EU in the late 1980s, as globalization and the run-up to the single market programme as well as higher EU funds for cooperative R&D projects stimulated the internationalization of European R&D (NARULA, 2000); the IT sector and biotechnology played a particular role in this respect. Moreover, there have also been renewed dynamics in R&D in the form of both asset-exploiting and asset-seeking FDI in the EU and the US. CRISCUOLO/NARULA/VERSPAGEN (2005) argue that R&D facility's capacity to exploit technological competences is a function not just of its own resources, but also of the efficiency with which it can utilise complementary resources associated with the relevant local innovation system. The empirical analysis indicates that both EU (US) affiliates in the US (EU) rely strongly on home region knowledge sources, although they appear to exploit the host knowledge base as well. The crucial emphasis on home knowledge suggests doubts about a potential R&D strategy of the EU which would neglect the EU countries as prime locations for leading edge R&D in technologically dynamics sectors, in particular the ICT sector. One must also raise the issue as to which extent the expansion of ICT requires reforms of the innovation system and in particular a stronger role of virtual research networks and "Digital Universities." Optimal linkages between R&D facilities and firms in technology-intensive sectors are crucial, which will naturally include foreign investors.

Both the US and the EU belong to the group of major source countries and host countries while Japan is mainly a source country of FDI – at least if one is to believe Japanese statistics (note: according to US FDI outflow statistics, Japan should have high US FDI inflows). In the US and the EU, innovation plays a crucial role for economic growth. The US and several EU countries achieved rather high growth rates of per capita income and total factor productivity in the 1990s, and the expansion of information and communication technologies (ICT) played a particular role. From a theoretical perspective, one may emphasize the endogenous growth model of ZON/MUYSKEN (2005), who highlighted in a refined LUCAS-model the role of ICT in a modern growth model, where the ICT capital intensity has a positive impact on the knowledge accumulation process. ICT is important both in final goods production and in knowledge accumulation. The expansion of knowledge and the rise in ICT capital intensity contribute to higher steady state growth of output. Knowledge accumulation thus plays an important role in economic growth. The implication is that the long run increase in ICT capital intensity in OECD countries and NICs – fuelled by falling relative prices of ICT capital goods – will reinforce the role of knowledge in production. As regards long term dynamics one should, however, not overlook the problems of information markets themselves, which suffer from market imperfections. The special aspects of ICT and growth will not be analyzed here as many special aspects would have to be emphasized, including the considerable role of intangible assets, network effects as a dynamic demand side-effect and static as well as dynamic economies of scale in several sub-sectors. ICT seems to facilitate the outsourcing of services as it supports virtual mobility of the supply-side and the demand side. With the role of digital services increasing in modern economies, one might find that the macroeconomic production function is characterized by economies of scale at the aggregate level; however, there is no clear evidence on this.

The EU adopted the Lisbon Agenda in 2000, emphasizing the need for higher innovation, higher growth and higher employment. According to this agenda, the EU should become the most dynamic knowledge-based economy by 2010. Interim results are rather sobering according to the KOK (2004) report; with EU eastern enlargement the EU faces additional challenges. The EU is moving increasingly towards a digitally networked high technology knowledge society. Western Europe's high-wage countries particularly face the need to adjust to globalization and EU eastern enlargement in a way which requires an increased use of information and communication technology. ICT is one of the most dynamic fields in terms of technological progress in OECD countries and is therefore of prime importance for economic growth, productivity increases and employment. ICT markets in Europe and worldwide are growing at a pace which exceeds both regional and global economic growth.

The ICT sector has also become a major driver of the innovation process and of productivity growth. High Schumpeterian dynamics are not only observed in ICT production but also in the use of ICT. Hence ICT investment relative to overall investment may be expected to grow continuously, not least because falling relative prices of software and hardware stimulate ICT investment. With digital (broadband and narrowband) networks expanding in Europe, North America, Asia and in other regions of the world, one may anticipate a further acceleration in digital knowledge creation and information as well as e-commerce – often associated with favourable network effects as well. With so many changes shaped by ICT, the question arises as to whether traditional economic systems, historically shaped by industry, should adjust in order to optimally support – digital – economic growth. The liberalization of EU telecommunications in 1998 (UK already in 1984) stimulated product innovations and possibly innovations in the overall telecommunications sector. The picture for telecommunication network operators is inconclusive as one finds some firms with rising R&D-sales ratios and other with falling R&D-sales ratios. One cannot, however, overlook that the R&D-sales ratio of the equipment industry has increased, which suggests that in the course of restructuring of telecommunications network operators – in the post-1998 period – R&D activities were effectively shifted to a considerable extent to the equipment industry, which is both knowledge-intensive and scale-intensive. The more competition drives e-communication towards global technological standards, the higher the pressure in the equipment industry to consolidate. It is noteworthy that R&D-sales ratios of telecommunications operators are lower than in the continental EU, where the liberalization of the telecommunications sector occurred only 14 years after the opening of the market in the US.

Taking a broader look at R&D expenditure in ICT – relative to overall business R&D expenditure – one can observe considerable differences across countries.

Ireland and the Scandinavian EU countries were leaders at the beginning of the 21st century. The three top OECD countries – Ireland, Finland and Korea – spent 70, 64 and 50% of total business R&D expenditures on ICT in 2003. Canada, the Netherlands, the US and Japan followed with an ICT share of about 35%; France had 31%, the UK 24 and Germany, Italy and Spain about 22%. Ireland, the UK, Norway, Denmark, Australia, Spain and the Czech Republic had a relatively high share of R&D ICT expenditures in the service sector. The ranking in terms of ICT patents looks rather similar to that in ICT R&D expenditures. The top countries are Singapore, Finland, Israel, Korea, Netherlands and Japan, Ireland the US, Canada and Sweden, which recorded an ICT patent share of close to or above 40% (top scorers Singapore and Finland close to 60%) based on figures at the European Patent Office. These countries were followed by the UK, Chinese Taipei, China, Australia, Hungary France, EU, Russia, Germany, Norway, Switzerland, Denmark, New Zealand, South Africa, Belgium Spain, Austria, Italy, India and Brazil. It is clear that the ICT patent position of US firms – with subsidiaries in many of the top countries – is much stronger than that of the US as a country. Moreover, taking a look at US figures shows a clear US lead even if one assumes that there is a home bias (in the US in favour of US firms, in the EU in favour of EU firms). As regards ICT goods, Japan is very strong in global markets. This also becomes apparent from the fact that Japan's share in EPO patents was very close to the share of the US (see subsequent figures/tables).

As regards ICT employment – narrowly defined – an increase can be seen in most OECD countries in the period from 1995 to 2003. Ireland is a negative example. The share of ICT-related occupations in the total economy was in a range of 3–5%. Sweden was the OECD leader in 2003, and the US was ahead of the EU by almost 1 percentage point. This finding points to a transatlantic lead on the part of the US, which is well ahead of the EU in terms of patenting, R&D-sales ratio and employment. Given the relatively small employment shares, it is impressive to see how important ICT patents are in comparison with other sectors. As regards EU innovation dynamics, one might want to consider a broader coordinated R&D effort in the ICT sector, in particular some form of coordinated international R&D program. The latter should not mean that all EU countries or very many are embarking upon coordinated projects under the heading of EU programmes. Rather it would be desirable for several countries to team up under the heading of a multi-country ICT R&D programme of excellence. The typical EU R&D programme, which effectively requires involving countries/partners from Western Europe, Eastern Europe and the Cohesion countries, makes ICT projects unnecessarily complex and often undermines efficiency. The EU might well want to subsidize employment of R&D researchers from relatively poor countries in leading EU R&D countries. There could be a particular role for EU-funded R&D projects, but overemphasizing EU projects is damaging for European innovation dynamics. Political control of EU R&D policy is rather weak and implies inefficiency risks. The EU might want to consider a special role for the supranational policy level in stimulating diffusion and in financing R&D centres of excellence in the Community. Finally, there is a major inconsistency in the EU R&D projects, which typically require 50% co-financing.

As regards university research institutes, one should expect that national government or special R&D funds with partial government funding would provide the co-financing for successful bidders. This is not the case and indeed is adequate for industrial R&D consortia. However, only a rather limited number of R&D projects are dominated by the business community, namely in applied R&D. Fundamental R&D should be financed mainly by government. In Germany and several other EU countries – including eastern European accession countries – there is no adequate co-financing from governments for projects in fundamental research. Moreover, the broad lack of private universities in most EU countries means that there is insufficient funding of higher education and insufficient R&D activities at the same time (e.g., Germany spends only 1% of its national income on university funding and has very few private universities, which are all very small).

The ICT sector has a special feature which makes adequate financing of innovation projects difficult in the continental EU countries. Many sub-sectors of ICT are characterized by a high share of intangible assets which undermines bank financing. The typical bank will always want collateral, and neither intangible assets (e.g., software) nor computer equipment – whose price absolutely falls over time – can serve as collateral for bank financing. This implies for many Eurozone countries that one has enormous problems in financing innovative young ICT firms. Interestingly, there are some big companies such as Siemens, SAP and Deutsche Telekom which have set up special venture capital funds. However, the general conclusion is that the Euro zone countries should move more towards a capital market system and thus become more Anglo-Saxon in terms of the financial market system. Financial markets are important for growth and structural change (WELFENS/WOLF, 1997). *Mutatis mutandis* this also holds for university financing, where continental EU countries have underdeveloped banking markets for students. Part of EU underfunding of the university system is actually due to a lack of private universities on the one hand and of adequate financing for university study on the other. As one may argue from a theoretical perspective, adequate financial market deepening will contribute to a higher level of growth and potentially to a higher trend growth rate (namely to the extent that the structure of financial markets influences R&D intensity and human capital formation and hence contributes to endogenous growth dynamics). One should make serious efforts in the new EU knowledge society to develop financial institutions that are up to the challenges and opportunities of the digital age. These arguments, however, do not imply that one should underestimate the risks from volatile stock markets.

Slow growth in the Eurozone over many years – in particular in Germany and Italy – should be a wake-up call for many continental EU countries to modernize the innovation system and to put more emphasis on R&D funding; this must at the same time become more efficient. Conditional tax credits should play a larger role than traditional subsidies, which effectively favour large firms that can afford to spend considerable sums of money on active lobbying. R&D tax credits would be less distorting in the sense that large countries and SMEs would act on a more level playing field. Since innovative SMEs are so important in R&D in the ICT sector – and since Germany/the Eurozone is lagging behind the US – one should seriously consider the reform proposals made here (and others made subsequently).

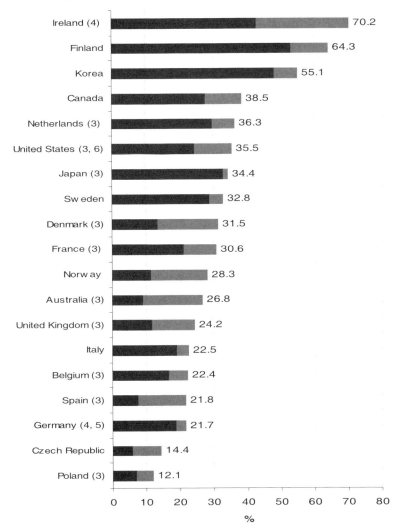

- R&D expenditure in ICT manufacturing industries (1)
- R&D expenditure in ICT services industries (2)

Source: OECD, ANBERD database, March 2005.
Fig. I8. R&D Expenditure in Selected ICT Industries, 2003 or Latest Year Available as a Percentage of Business Enterprise Sector R&D Expenditure.

ICT patents[1] as a percentage of national total (EPO) in selected countries[2]

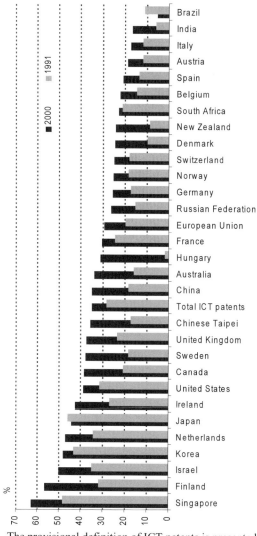

1. The provisional definition of ICT patents is presented in Annex B of the OECD compendium.
2. Cut-off point: countries with more than 100 EPO applications in 2000.
Source: OECD, Patent Database, September 2004.

Fig. I9. ICT Patents as a Percentage of National Total (EPO) in Selected Countries According to the Residence of the Inventors, by Priority Year.

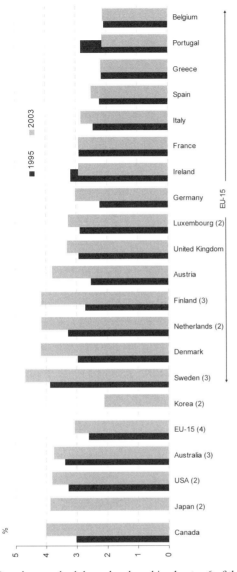

Based on methodology developed in chapter 6 of the Information Technology Outlook 2004. See also van WELSUM, D., and G. VICKERY (2004), New perspectives on ICT skills and employment, Information Economy Working Paper DSTI/ICCP/IE(2004)10, OECD.
2. 2002 instead of 2003.
3. 1997 instead of 1995.
4. Estimates.
Source: OECD Information Technology Outlook 2004.

Fig. I10. ICT Employment Across the Economy- Share of ICT-Related Occupations in the Total Economy in Selected Countries, 1995 and 2003, Narrow Definition (1).

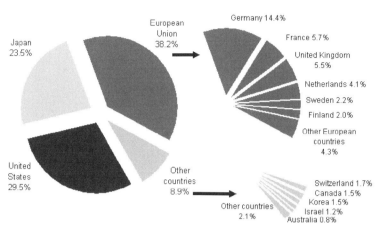

The provisional definition of ICT patents is presented in Annex B of the Compendium of patent statistics 2004.
Note : See table for footnote.
Source: OECD, Patent Database, September 2004.

Fig. I11. Share of Countries in ICT Patents' at the EPO, According to the Residence of the Inventors, by Priority Year.

I.2.5. Regional Integration Dynamics

The international division of labor is changing at a global scale, and changes in competitiveness in ICT sector are of particular interest. This is also an important issue in the context of EU eastern enlargement, namely whether new member countries can reinforce the Community's competitiveness in global ICT markets. This topic can be analyzed by examining the development of RCAs (sectoral export-import balance relative to country's total global export-import balance) in relevant fields, here telecommunications industry and office machinery & computers. An RCA exceeding unity is considered a favorable sign of competitiveness. Those countries with an RCA exceeding unity over a considerable time period are strong competitors in world markets. With respect to RCAs, there is, however, one caveat, namely that the RCA is a sectoral trade ratio relative to an overall export-import ratio where overall exports and imports might reflect rather low technology products; this aspect in turn should be visible in the weighted absolute export unit value for all exports (and import unit value for all imports), which naturally will be much lower than in a high income country in which trade is more concentrated on medium-technology and high-technology products which carry relatively high absolute prices (both export unit values and import unit values). Thus, one may suggest defining a relative price weighted RCA where the respective sectoral RCA is weighted with the relative sectoral export unit value (country I relative to country II in a model or relative to the rest of the world in reality). One could first identify the RCAs exceeding unity and then multiply those with the relative export unit value in order to get an economic weighting of the RCA; in practice relative export unit value could simply mean comparing the sectoral export unit value of country i to that of the respective value of the US. In the perspective suggested here, an RCA in a high income country (with relatively high export unit values) slightly exceeding unity is more impressive than an RCA strongly exceeding unity in an economy with a small relative export unity value. In this perspective, economic catching up requires economic upgrading leading to a long term increase in the weighted export unit value and a increased role of RCAs exceeding unity in those sectors where high Schumpeterian economic rents are earned, namely in scale intensive, technology-intensive and knowledge-intensive goods.

In the following paragraphs, we use "modified" RCA which is the ratio of a countries export share in a sector (for certain relevant markets) to the export share of the competitor's countries in the same market. Here the relevant market is the EU15. An indicator above unity shows a comparative advantage in the respective sector. As regards the telecommunications industry, one may note that the RCA of Japan declined considerably in the decade from 1993 to 2004, yet in 2004 Japan still had a positive RCA. The US has a "negative" RCA (RCA below unity), with its position having deteriorated at the beginning of the 21st century.

RCAs in the Telecommunications Industry

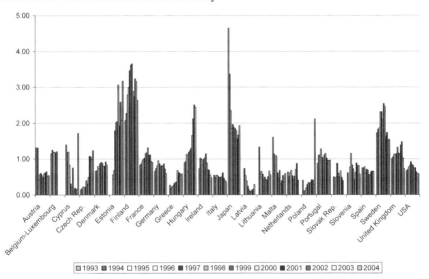

Fig. I12. RCAs in the Telecommunications Industry

Thus it is noteworthy that the Czech Republic, Hungary and Estonia have developed an RCA exceeding unity in the early 21st century. This reinforces the particular strength of leading EU15 countries, namely of the UK, Finland and Sweden, to some extent also of France. As regards office machinery and computers, one may emphasize that this sector has become more price competitive in the early 21st century. Japan's favorable RCA position has strongly eroded in the period 1993–2004, and the country was below an RCA of unity in 2004. The US had a rather stable RCA index which was slightly below unity. Hungary and the Czech Republic have joined Ireland and the UK in their favorable RCA position among EU countries.

The more interesting field here certainly is software whose role is rising relative to that of computers. Software development involves, by and large, much human capital. This statement does not, however, suggest that one could not find useful steps in software development which can be outsourced internationally. Standardized relatively simple tasks in programming can be outsourced conveniently in the internet age. However, the final testing and the high end programming are typically made in advanced OECD countries.

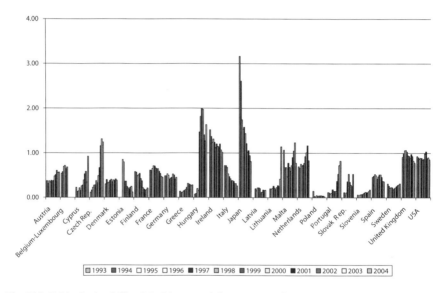

Fig. I13. RCAs in the Office Machinery and Computers Industry.

I.3. Economic Stability: ICT and FDI in a Modified Dornbusch Model

Information & Communication Technology and the Dornbusch Model

A standard model for medium-term exchange rate analysis is the Dornbusch model, which emphasizes the interplay of rapidly reacting financial markets (the nominal interest rate and the exchange rate adjust instantaneously) and the macroeconomic goods market in which the adjustment speed (i.e., the change of the price level) is rather slow. A key feature of the model is an overshooting of the exchange rate, namely that the short-term reaction of the exchange rate is stronger than the medium term equilibrium adjustment would require. In the Dornbusch model (1976), the interest elasticity of the demand for money and the type of exchange rate expectations are crucial for the overshooting problem. Regional monetary integration – as exemplified in the Euro zone – and technological dynamics, particularly the expansion of information and communication technology, signify interesting developments whose implications for economic stability can be highlighted through in the context of the Dornbusch model. How will the expansion of information and communication technology affect exchange rate dynamics and the overshooting/undershooting effects? The speed of price adjustment in the goods market is likely to increase, as the global supply side elasticity in an internationally networked society will be relatively large, in particular in the field of digital services whose share in aggregate demand is likely to increase over time. However, the relative adjustment speed of "digital financial markets" is likely to increase even faster than in the goods markets. To understand the basic problems we consider a modified Dornbusch model, namely a setup which includes foreign direct investment and thus implies a modified interest parity condition (WELFENS, 2006).

Subsequently we consider a simple system of six equations: Equation (1) is a kind of Phillips curve, where Y# is full employment long run equilibrium output: an excess in demand will lead to an increase in price level. Equation (2) is a logarithmically-stated specification of aggregate demand. Though partly following GÄRNTER (1997), we insert several extensions including the impact of product innovations which are assumed to raise net exports; in the original formulation of GÄRTNER there is also a term related to real income, lnY (and a term related to trade and the exchange rate). However, the sign of the parameter of lnY is negative – as we will show – and not positive; this is in spite of hundreds of articles using ad hoc logarithmically stated demand curves where the elasticity of lnY is positive while it actually is negative as the relevant parameter reflects the impact of a change in lnY on real net exports and imports. Moreover, lnG is often in the aggregate demand as well, but we will replace lnG by the ratio G/Y, which is more consistent as will be argued subsequently.

It is assumed that the foreign price level P^* is constant and equal to unity so that $\ln(eP^*/P) = \ln e - \ln P$; we define $q^* = eP^*/P$. To the extent that we consider a model with foreign direct investment, the parameter ψ' does not only reflect the link between trade balance (ψ) and the real exchange rate but also the impact (ψ'') of the real exchange rate on foreign direct investment and hence on the overall investment-GDP ratio. A real depreciation will bring about higher net foreign direct investment inflows – relative to GDP – and hence higher overall investment according to the theoretical arguments and empirical findings of FROOT/STEIN (1991). The perspective suggested here implies that $\psi' = \psi + \psi''$. The variable e is the current nominal exchange rate, and e# denotes the long run exchange rate.

Capital market equilibrium is given by two interacting factors (i is the nominal exchange rate), namely the impact of portfolio investors guided by the interest rate parity ($i = i^* + E(d\ln e/dt)$) and foreign investors who focus on long run differences in the marginal product of capital. As we assume that both the home and the foreign country (* denotes foreign variables) produce according to a Cobb

Douglas function $Y=K^{\beta}(AL)^{1-\beta}$ and $Y^*=K^{*\beta^*}(A^*L^*)^{1-\beta^*}$, respectively, the relevant variable for foreign investors is the difference in marginal products of capita ($Y_{K\#}$, $Y_K^*\#$), namely $\beta Y\#/K$ minus $\beta^*Y\#^*/K\#^*$ where # denotes long run values. From a portfolio-theoretical perspective, real capital and bonds are complementary in terms of risk, as risks faced by holders of K are negatively correlated with that of holding bonds. Hence we state the rather simple equilibrium condition $i+\zeta(\beta Y\#/K\# -Y_K^*\#)= i^*+E(dlne/dt)$. Thus a positive international differential of marginal products in favor of the home country requires that domestic interest rates fall for a given sum i^* +E(dlne/dt). To put it differently, given the domestic and the foreign interest rate the required expected exchange rate depreciation rate E(dlne/dt) must rise along with a positive differential of marginal products since bond investment abroad would otherwise be insufficiently attractive now that holding domestic bonds has become more attractive.

The expected devaluation rate is assumed to be proportionate to the difference between the equilibrium exchange rate e# and the actual exchange rate e; expressed in logarithms, we have equation (6).

Goods Market

$$dlnP/dt= \pi'(lnY^d- lnY\#) \tag{1}$$

$$lnY^d= c+\psi'[lne-lnP]-\Omega lnY\#+[1+\omega]\gamma-[c+\omega']\tau+\eta"lnv+ \Omega^*lnY^* \tag{2}$$

Money Market

$$lnM^d = lnP + \varphi lnY - \sigma'i \tag{3}$$

$$lnM^s = lnM^d = lnM \tag{4}$$

International Capital Market

$$i+\zeta(\beta Y\#/K\# -Y_K^*\#)= i^* + E(dlne/dt)] \tag{5}$$

$$E(dlne/dt) = \theta(lne\#-lne) \tag{6}$$

Note that in the very long run (defined by equality of marginal products of capital across countries), equation (5) results in the standard interest rate parity condition. Here we focus on the short term and the long run, whereby the latter is defined by a response in the price level P.

The long run change of the equilibrium exchange rate lne# with respect to a change of the money supply dlnM is unity. The short run reaction of the exchange rate can be obtained from the following equation (WELFENS, 2006)

(I) $lne=lne\#+[lnM-lnP-\varphi lnY\#]/(\theta\sigma')+i^*/\theta -[\zeta/\theta][(\beta Y\#/K\#-Y^*_{K\bullet}\#)$

Therefore, we have in the short run the following result which confirms exchange rate overshooting:

(II) $dlne/dlnM = dlne\#/dlnM +1/(\theta\sigma') = 1 +1/(\theta \sigma')>1$.

Thus we see that the adjustment parameters relevant for overshooting are θ – the learning speed in the formation of exchange rate expectations – and the semi-interest elasticity of the demand for money (σ'); the smaller both parameters are, the higher the overshooting effect. Both parameters also play a role with respect to the adjustment speed for nominal exchange rate and price level. The adjustment speed is given by the expression $\pi'(\psi'/\sigma'\theta + \psi')=:\alpha"$. ICT will affect some or all of the parameters.

Since ICT facilitates access to various kinds of financial market instruments – as does the creation of the Euro zone (from an EU perspective) –, the interest elasticity of the demand for money may be expected to increase. Monetary overshooting problems should thus be reduced unless the learning speed in the field of exchange rate expectations should decrease. Moreover, ICT might indeed facilitate the learning process in markets and hence ICT expansion will go along with a higher adjustment parameter θ (concerns formation of exchange rate expectations). This implies that ICT will lead to reduced overshooting problems; at the same time, the adjustment speed to the new long run exchange rate equilibrium will slow down. From this perspective, the opportunities of an activist monetary policy have improved, namely in the sense that exchange rate overshooting problems are less severe than in the traditionally industrialized OECD countries. This holds all the more since one has to take into account that ICT expansion is equivalent to a positive supply shock which itself implies a dampening exchange rate movement.

As regards a positive supply-shock we get as a short-term impact
(III) dlne/dlnY# = dlne#/dlnY# – [φ/(θσ')] – [ζβ/θK#]Y# =

$$-\varphi[1+(1/\theta\sigma')] + [(1+\Omega)/\psi'] - [\zeta\beta/\theta K\#]\ Y\#$$

A positive supply-side shock is all the more likely to cause a real appreciation in the short term, the larger the income elasticity of the demand for money is and the higher the output elasticity of capital is (and the lower the capital stock is). A positive supply shock is reinforced by the impact of foreign direct investment which reinforces the tendency towards a short term appreciation.

Moreover, note that the long run exchange rate reaction of a supply-side shock is given by:
(IV) dlne#/dlnY# = $-\varphi + [(1+\Omega)/\psi']$

The short-term reaction of the nominal exchange rate is more towards a nominal appreciation than the long term reaction. The long term real exchange rate (q*=:eP*/P) will depreciate as a consequence of a supply-side shock – whose nature is similar to a process innovation.

(V) dlnq*#/dlnY# = $[(1+\Omega)/\psi']>0$

However, the impact of product innovations (v) imply a real appreciation (q*=:eP*/P):
(VI) dlnq*#/dlnv = $-\eta"/\psi'<0$

Hence the impact of ICT on the long run real exchange rate is ambiguous: If product innovations dominate sufficiently there will be a real appreciation; if process innovations are dominant there will be a depreciation of the exchange rate.

Exchange rate overshooting depends on several parameters, including the learning dynamics of exchange rate expectations and the interest elasticity of the demand for money; the adjustment speed to the new equilibrium is influenced by the responsiveness of the trade balance and foreign direct investment. ICT and

FDI will affect the nominal and real exchange rate dynamics. There are several arguments why FDI could reduce the problem of overshooting. From this perspective, economic globalization – in the sense of a rising share of FDI in overall investment – is likely to contribute to less exchange rate instability. If ICT for technological reasons leads to an increase in the learning speed in the foreign exchange market, the size of overshooting is reduced. At the same time, one might expect that ICT raises the price adjustment speed in the goods markets, which reinforces the speed of adjustment towards the new equilibrium. Monetary policy would then generate less overshooting than in the time of the Old Economy so that a more activist monetary policy could be considered.

From an empirical perspective it would be important to find out more about the effect of the exchange rate regime on innovation dynamics. A fixed exchange rate regime basically transmits the domestic price level to those countries which have pegged the currency to the anchor country. If a fixed exchange rate regime helps to diffuse price stability worldwide – under the assumption that the anchor country pursues a stability-oriented monetary policy leading to a low inflation rate – firms in all countries might find it relatively easy to conduct R&D policies which require a long term perspective; bond maturities (as a proxy for the representative time horizon) are known to be relatively long in periods of low inflation rates. The counter-argument in favour of a flexible exchange rate regime is that it establishes full individual responsibility in monetary policy in each country so that the weighted world inflation rate could be lower under flexible exchange rates than in a system with a fixed exchange rate. However, there are other aspects which are rather unclear: will multinational companies be more active innovators in a system of fixed exchange rates than in a system of flexible exchange rates? More research is needed here.

As regards regional integration several parameters of the (modified) Dornbusch model will be affected. The price adjustment parameter in the goods markets should increase, as this would be natural to expect in a single market – and to the extent that monetary union reinforces this adjustment speed, the argument is even more valid. From a Eurozone perspective there is the crucial issue of whether dollar exchange rate volatility in the sense of overshooting risks will be reduced. Indeed, less overshooting problems should be expected if regional integration – in particular monetary integration – raises the interest elasticity of the demand for money. (In a monetary union one should expect more liquid alternatives to holding money than in fragmented national markets.) Moreover, the learning speed (parameter θ) in the foreign exchange market should also increase. The main problem which arises in a monetary union involving countries with high sustained budget deficits is that there is a considerable risk that tax rates will go up. If such tax increases are not mainly invested in the form of higher public investment – relative to GDP – and higher R&D expenditure-GDP ratios, the impact on GNP could be negative in the long run, not least because an increasing share of GDP will accrue to foreign investors (from country II) who will benefit from a real depreciation through cheaper access to the stock of capital abroad.

Finally, one should notice that the expansion of ICT is likely to reinforce the role of foreign direct investment as firm-internal transaction and management costs are reduced. Thus the findings with respect to FDI are reinforced through the expansion information and communication technology. The logarithmic formulation of the aggregate demand side suggested here should encourage new options to consistently develop macro models. Supply side shocks and product innovations will affect the exchange rate in the long run. In a world economy with increased innovation dynamics, the respective topics need to be further explored and also require additional empirical analysis. While the context of the modified Dornbusch model suggests a reduced risk of overshooting in a digitally networked economy with FDI, this does not rule out that other mechanisms relevant for exchange rate instability could become more relevant through the expansion of ICT. Indeed, if there are two groups of speculators in the foreign exchange market or the stock market – namely group 1, for which expectations are guided by fundamental variables while expectations of group 2, the chartists, follow current market trends –, a temporary dominance on the part of the chartists could bring about instability. With many financial market actors from newly industrialized countries active in a globally networked financial market, one cannot rule out that the influence of chartists could become quite important during periods of market turbulence.

I.4. Challenges: Regulatory Policy and Life-Long Learning

There are three basic challenges for policymakers in a digitally networked European economy:

- actively shaping the global rules for digital trade (this points to the role of the WTO);
- defining adequate rules for competition in telecommunications; national regulatory approaches in combination with the EU framework regulation should bring about sustained competition and a high intensity of innovation in the EU single market;
- maintaining leadership in key fields of ICT, which requires not only adequate R&D government programmes and new initiatives to modernize the university system in a way which combines solid education with innovativeness; it will also be necessary to fully exploit the digital learning opportunities in an ageing EU society.

While the WTO process is a long term challenge whose dynamics are difficult to anticipate, the adjustment of eCommunications rules is a more medium-term challenge for which the European Commission has started a Review Process on the 2002 framework regulation based on market analysis of 18 pre-defined markets and a broad set of rules ranging from universal services to access regulation.

As regards the period 2010–2020, one may anticipate that three major drivers will shape eCommunications:

- digital convergence which already is visible in triple play services (fixed line telecommunications, TV and internet) or quadruple play (triple play plus mobile services);
- mobile telecommunications will increasingly become a substitute for fixed line telecommunications; the majority of calls in EU25 will be from mobile telecommunications. Moreover, there are new options for mobile internet-based phone calls. VoIP – internet-based telephony – will become rather common by 2010 in the business community which is likely to use hybrid network configurations. At the bottom line, international communication costs will continue to fall which should stimulate trade and foreign investment;
- broadband density will increasingly matter for digital modernization of the economy. Here Germany and Italy are two laggards among EU countries, and most Eastern European member countries are rather weak.

As the following graphs illustrate, the cross-country differentials in broadband density are rather large in the EU. If such differentials should be sustained, it will be rather difficult to fully develop a modern digital single EU market – and the innovative applications and productivity improvements that should go along with advanced digital networks and their respective services.

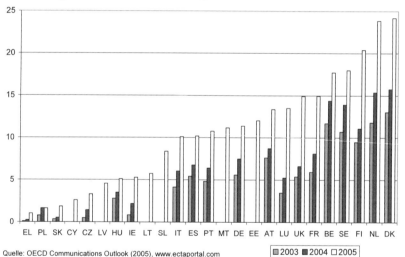

Quelle: OECD Communiations Outlook (2005), www.ectaportal.com   ▨ 2003 ■ 2004 ☐ 2005

Source: OECD Communiations Outlook (2005), www.ectaportal.com

Fig. I14. Broadband Density in Selected EU Countries, 2003–2005 (Density is per 100 Workers).

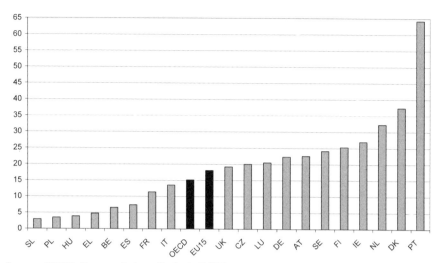

Source: OECD Communiations Outlook (2005).

Fig. 115. Narrowband Densities in EU Countries (per 100 Inhabitants).

From an EU single market perspective, it will be quite important for consolidation in the EU telecommunications market to be facilitated. Compared to the US – with three major fixed network operators and four mobile operators in 2006 – the EU has an amazing number of operators which act in nationally, rather fragmented markets. Anticipating true globalization of communications markets through VoIP services, the EU seems not to be well positioned in comparison to the US. Moreover, it is strange that the European Commission has emphasized in the Lisbon Agenda 2010 the aim of making the EU the most dynamic competitive knowledge-based society by 2010 while the Commissioner responsible for eCommunications is undermining the incentives for telecommunications network operators to invest in innovative networks (e.g., VDSL which is an advanced broadband network). The EU-imposed requirement to give competitors access to the VDSL network on cost-based prices is absolutely inconsistent not only with incentives for innovations in advanced networks and digital product innovations; it also is contradictory to the European Commission's own principle that new markets should not be regulated. Achieving the goals of the Lisbon Agenda without strong national and supranational support for ICT innovation dynamics in general and for modern telecommunications in particular is not possible. If commercial ICT dynamics in the EU are not be fully exploited and national governments are unable to reallocate more funds to complementary higher education, the economic and social opportunities of modern ICT will remain unexploited in critical areas. The traditionally strong role of public universities in Europe lets one expect that even in the university sphere innovative digital opportunities for networked education – teaching and learning – will be exploited rather slowly. The mixed US system – with many private and public universities eager to develop a new digital profile –is apparently better positioned to explore new ICT-related options.

Digital Learning in the Networked Society

If the Community is interested in stimulating economic growth and economic cohesion, the availability of broadband internet access is crucial. The Community might well consider defining broadband universal services and leaving member countries responsible for organizing efficient provision of such services. For the academic community and the business community, Internet 2 – already tested in the US on a large scale in 2006 – will be a major innovation which not only means much more rapid transmission of data but also facilitates national and international cooperation of research institutes. Universities and schools will look different in 2010+, since distance learning and other elements of digital teaching will become a natural element of life-long learning (LLL).

LLL presents four major challenges:

- ageing societies coping with adjustment needs, technological progress and economic globalization can raise the stock of human capital efficiently by including new digital learning features;
- as economic globalization brings with it a tendency towards higher labor market flexibility and reduced tenure in firms, there is a clear need for governments to support retraining and training in firms. With tenure falling in all EU countries, the incentive for firms to invest in human capital formation is reduced – to the extent that training and retraining generate external effects, and governments should provide financial incentives for training and retraining in firms;
- EU member countries show relatively heterogeneous indicators in the field of LLL and it is remarkable that Germany and Italy – two core countries of the Euro zone – are among the relatively weak performers
- LLL will be a particular problem in the context of economic globalization which will not only erode the tax base (in particular with respect to corporate taxation), but also brings pressure towards more flexibility in the labour market which implies – among other things – shorter tenure of workers. In such an environment, the incentive for firms to invest in training and retraining is declining over time. For example, while it is still slightly above ten years in German industry, some of Germany's leading ICT firms have average tenure of workers of less than five years.

Assuming that there are positive external effects from training and retraining, governments should consider subsidizing modern efficient forms of digital learning and teaching.

Drivers of digital learning is ICT expansion, the initiatives in the European education space, the dynamics of the knowledge based society – including the growth of the (digital) services sector – and EU framework programme effects. The Bologna process and the Copenhagen process bring new impulses for digital learning. At the same time, the interaction of innovation, research and development (R&D) as well as the modernization of the education system are crucial drivers of digital learning. The modernization of the education system is largely driven by the increasing need for life-long learning, the rising mobility of people (workers/managers/students/apprentices) and the dynamics in creating new learning spaces. If the interaction of these elements is carefully organized, well managed and to some extent integrated into market mechanisms, the resulting developments would help the EU in meeting the goals of the Lisbon Agenda, reinforce single market dynamics, help in reaching EU policy goals and contribute to avoiding a digital divide within Europe and possibly also beyond the EU (as the EU is an influential actor in many regions of the world – not only in other integration areas such as ASEAN or MERCOSUR); the latter would be in the spirit of the WSIS, the World Summit of the Information Society meeting held in 2006.

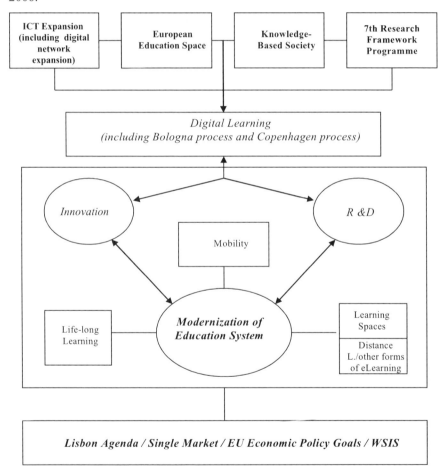

Fig. 116. ICT, Innovation and eLearning.

The internationalization of ICT will continue as falling intra-firm transaction costs coincide with an increasing R&D intensity within the ICT sector. Governments in EU countries should investment more in R&D support. Given the relative innovation differentials within the EU (JUNGMITTAG, 2004), however, the optimum R&D-GDP ratio will certainly differ across countries. Special projects and programs related to the ICT sector could be useful; this approach is particularly valid if positive external effects from ICT innovation projects are relatively large. Encouraging the networking of SMEs in knowledge-intensive and science intensive sectors could also be a crucial policy element. Given the growth of the global knowledge society it will also be important for regulatory policy to encourage the modernization of telecommunications networks. More labor market flexibility in many countries of the Eurozone might also be a requirement to fully exploit the benefit of the digital economy.

Growing internationalization of the ICT sector (including outsourcing) is a natural element of structural change and economic growth. There is hardly a reason for sounding an alarm bell over a hollowing out of German (or EU15) industry; indeed, there is no simple bazaar effect which would be dangerous for economic development and employment. Rather there are imported intermediate products in exports goods, but there are also exported intermediate products in import goods.

As regards Eastern European accession countries it would be desirable for national governments and collective bargaining actors to find ways to reduce the unemployment rates. At the same time, governments would be wise to stimulate both economic modernization and innovation. This should include adequate incentives not only for FDI inflows but also for developing multinational companies which are able to actively use foreign sources of innovation and knowledge abroad. EU structural policies should take some of these aspects into consideration in the future.

Comparing the Eurozone to the US (or ASEAN countries), there might be problems of optimum outsourcing as the resistance of trade unions in countries with high unemployment rates will impair outsourcing which reduces profitability and hence the ability of finance innovation and international marketing campaigns. At the same time one should emphasize that for high wage EU15 countries it will naturally become important in the medium term to specialize more on services which are less exposed to price competition. However, such specialization will indeed require not only flexible outsourcing but also higher expenditures on education in order to have a well-educated workforce. Here the problems of ageing societies will avert increases in the public education budget; ageing societies in Europe might place priority on spending more taxpayers' money on social security, in particular retirement benefits. Globalization at the same time means that the average tenure of workers at the firm is decreasing so that the incentive for firms to invest in human capital upgrading is on the decline. Thus the EU is facing serious risks of losing (relative to the US) two traditional advantages relevant for productivity and growth.

For prosperity, stability and growth, the expansion of ICT will be crucial for the EU in the 21st century. Since EU25 is relatively well positioned in terms of human capital, R&D activities and broadband network expansion, the Community will be able to benefit strongly from ICT. Moreover, the Community should exploit the new democratic opportunities of digital networks and introduce internet-based referenda; this is not to suggest the introduction of a spontaneous political snapshot. Rather, both ICT and the internet make it possible to indeed pose the same question at least twice (say at the beginning and the end of a three-month-period) to the electorate and thereby generate a solid political feedback mechanism which could help to combine a more efficient government with a new digital invisible hand mechanism in the market place.

The global expansion of ICT and particularly of the internet is not without risks. In a political perspective, the internet creates a global public for certain issues. Conflicts which would have remained regional in the 18th or 19th century could quickly expand to a global scale if the respective issue becomes a priority theme in the internet. Speeches of politicians, business leaders or religious leaders that would have received only national attention a century ago – being thus imbedded in a well-known cultural context – will receive global attention in the future in many cases. With information/words absorbed in a heterogeneous global cultural context, the risks of (intended and unintended) misunderstandings are increasing. Thus there is an additional source of conflict with respect to a potential clash of civilizations. This calls for more careful communication policies on the part of politicians and business leaders as well as religious leaders.

From an EU perspective, ICT is quite important not only in economic terms but also in political terms. The internet – as well as mobile communications – allow for the creation of integration in a new manner from below. Digital flexible networking should thus be encouraged through not only adequate infrastructure policies in EU countries, but also through an active digital integration policy by the Commission and the European Council. Making the diversity of the Community more visible and encouraging creative and innovative actors from various member countries to flexibly cooperate through modern networks should be an essential goal of the EU. Finally, considering the opportunities of cooperation among integration areas (e.g., Mercosur, Asean or Nafta), digital global networks create new options not only for policymakers but for cooperation among civil societies as well.

Appendix I.1: Modified Dornbusch-Model (Welfens 2006)

As regards the logarithmic formulation of aggregate demand ($\ln Y^d$) it is not easy to reconcile the commonly used formulation (e.g. GÄRTNER, 1997) $\ln Y^d = a \ln q^*$ + a'$\ln Y$ + a''$\ln$ G (the parameters a, a', a'' all are positive) with the standard expression of the uses side of GDP: $Y = C + I + G + X - q^*J$ where C is consumption, I investment, X exports and J imports (τ is the tax rate, v product innovations, * for foreign variable). One may, however, consider a consistent setup where C= cY(1-τ), G=γY, I=λY; and λ=λ($\ln q^*$, γ, $\ln$v, τ), the net export function is X' = x'($\ln[eP^*/P]$, $\ln$Y, $\ln$Y*, $\ln$v)Y*; we then will use the function $\ln$x'(...). The investment output ratio λ is assumed to be a positive function of the real exchange rate as we follow FROOT/STEIN (1991), who argue that in a world with imperfect capital markets, foreign firms will find it easier to take over companies in country I (host country) since a real depreciation of country I's currency will increase equity capital expressed in terms of the potential host country so that leveraged international takeover will become easier; hence we assume that the overall investment-GDP ratio is a positive function of the real exchange rate eP*/P (or $\ln q^*$); the partial derivative of λ with respect to $\ln q^*$ therefore is positive (ψ>0). With respect to the government expenditure-GDP ratio, γ the partial derivative ω is ambiguous (will be positive if a rise of γ mainly falls on investment goods), with respect to product innovations v the partial derivate is positive (η>0), and with respect to the income tax rate it is negative (in absolute term ω'). We also define 1+ω=:ω''. Furthermore, we assume that $\ln$x' is a function of all the four arguments shown in the function x(...). Thus we can write a consistent version of the aggregate demand side:

(2') $Y^d\{1 - c[1-\tau] - \gamma - \lambda(\ln q^*, \gamma, \ln v, \tau)\} = x'(...)Y^*$

Assuming for simplicity that c[1-τ]+γ+λ is rather small so that we can use the approximization ln (1+z)≈z, we can rewrite the equation as:

(2'') $\ln Y^d - c[1-\tau] - \gamma - \lambda(\ln q^*, \gamma, \ln v, \tau) =$
$= \{\ln x'(\ln q^*, \ln Y, \ln Y^*, \ln v)\} + \ln Y^*$

Using linearized functions λ(...), $\ln$x'(...) we can write – with three positive derivatives $\partial \ln$x'/$\partial \ln q^*$=:ψ'', $\partial \ln$x'/$\partial \ln$Y* =:Ω', $\partial \ln$x'/$\partial \ln$v =:η'and $\partial \ln$x'/$\partial \ln$Y=: - Ω<0 – the equation as follows:

(2''') $\ln Y^d = c - c\tau + \gamma + \psi''\ln(\ln e - \ln P) + \omega\gamma + \eta\ln v$
$+ \omega'\tau + \{\psi(\ln e - \ln P) - \Omega\ln Y + \Omega'\ln Y^* + \eta'\ln v\} + \ln Y^*$

This then leads to subsequent equation (2) where ψ':= ψ''+ψ, η''=η+η' and Ω*=1+ Ω'; we also define 1+ω=:ω''.

The money market is characterized (with φ denoting the income elasticity of the demand for money, σ'the interest semi-elasticity and e' the Euler number) by nominal money demand $M^d = PY^\varphi e'^{-\sigma'i}$ which implies for equilibrium $\ln M = \ln P + \varphi \ln Y - \sigma'i$. While money market equilibrium is fairly standard, the subsequent capital market equilibrium condition is rather unusual as it modifies the interest rate parity condition by taking into account portfolio-theoretical considerations relevant in a setup with foreign direct investment – the latter is not considered in the Dornbusch model. Note that an alternative way to express the aggregate demand in a logarithmically-stated function is based – with j denoting the import – output ratio (imports J=jY) – on $Y^d([1-c-\gamma-\lambda(\ldots)+q^*j(\ln q^*)]$ $=x(\ln Y, \ln q^*, \ln v^*)Y^*$ where we have assumed in the spirit of the gravity equation that exports are not only a positive function of real income abroad but of domestic real output or actually of $\ln Y$ as well (in an empirical context the assumption that $c+\gamma+\lambda-j$ is close to zero is more convincing than assuming that $c+\gamma+\lambda$ is close to zero). Some key equations in the modified Dornbusch model are:

(A1) $d\ln P/dt = \pi'[\psi' (\ln e - \ln e\#) - \psi'(\ln P - \ln P\#)]$

(A2) $\ln e - \ln e\# = (\ln P\# - \ln P)/[\theta\sigma'] - (\zeta/\theta) [\beta Y\#/K\# - Y^*_K\#)$

If we assume that the foreign marginal product of capital is equal to the domestic marginal product we get:

(A3) $d\ln P/dt = - \pi'(\psi'/\sigma'\theta + \psi') (\ln P - \ln P\#) = -\alpha''(\ln P - \ln P\#)$.

Here we have simply defined $\pi'(\psi'/\sigma'\theta + \psi')= \alpha''$; the parameter α'' is crucial subsequently. The above equation is (setting P#=1) a homogeneous differential equation of first order and has the solution

(A4) $\ln P(t) = C_0 e^{-\alpha''t}$

This implies (having solved for C_0 by considering t=0):

(A5) $\ln P(t)= \ln P \# + (\ln P(0) - \ln P\#) e^{-\alpha''t}$

Note that

(A6) $\ln e(t) = \ln e\# +[\theta\sigma']^{-1} (\ln P\# - \ln P) e^{-\alpha''t}$

Thus we can state

(A7) $\ln e(t) = \ln e\# + (\ln e(0) - \ln e\#) e^{-\alpha''t}$

The adjustment speed for the exchange rate variable is therefore the same as for the price level. Obviously, the adjustment speed α'' is faster the higher π' and ψ' are (i.e., the faster goods market react to excess demand and the stronger trade and (foreign direct) investment react to the real exchange rate). The lower the semi-interest elasticity of the demand for money (σ) and the slower the foreign exchange market reacts to divergences between the long run equilibrium value and the current exchange rate (parameter θ), the faster the adjustment process of the price level towards the equilibrium price level. However, we have seen that low parameters θ and σ' imply a large overshooting in case of a monetary supply shock so that these two parameters are ambivalent. If they are low, the overshooting effect will be large, but adjustment to the new equilibrium value will be fast. Foreign direct investment raises the adjustment speed.

References

AGHION, P.; HOWITT, P. (1997a), Capital accumulation and innovation as complementary factors in long-run growth, mimeo, Ohio State University, Columbus, OH.

AGHION, P.; HOWITT, P. (1997b), Endogenous Growth Theory, MIT Press, Cambridge, MA.

AMITI, M.; S.-J. WEI (2005a), Fear of Service Outsourcing, *Economic Policy*, No. 42: 307–348.

AMITI, M.; S.-J. WEI (2005b), Service Outsourcing, Productivity and Employment, *IMF Working Paper*, forthcoming.

AUDRETSCH, D.; WELFENS, P. J. J. (2002), The New Economy and Economic Growth in the US and Europe, Heidelberg and New York, Springer.

BAILEY, M.N.; LAWRENCE, R.Z. (2005), Don't Blame Trade for US Job Losses, McKinsey Quarterly, 2005, 1.

BARFIELD, C. E.; HEIDUK, G.; WELFENS, P. J. J., eds. (2003), Internet and Economic Growth and Globalisation, Heidelberg and New York: Springer.

BARRO, R. J., SALA-I-MARTIN, X. (1995), Economic Growth, New York, MacGraw-Hill Inc.

BRESNAHAN, T. F.; GREENSTEIN, S. (1997), Technological Competition and the Structure of the Computer Industry, mimeo.

BOGDANOWICZ, M.; CENTENO, C.; BURGELMAN, J.-C. (2004), Information Society Developments and Policies Towards 2010 in an Enlarged Europe, Technical Report EUR21407, Sevilla, IPTS, European Commission.

BOGDANOWICZ, M.; BURGELMAN, J.-C.; CENTENO, C.; GOUROVA, E.; CARAT, G. (2003), Building the Information Society in Candidate Countries? A Prospective Analysis on Potential Trajectories to Realise the Lisbon Goals, Report EUR 20754, Sevilla, IPTS, European Commission.

BORBÉLY, D. (2005), EU Export Specialization Patterns in Selected Accession and Cohesion Countries: Tough Competition on the EU15 Market? *Papeles del Este No. 9*, http://www.ucm.es/BUCM/cee/papeles.

COLECCHIA, A.; SCHREYER, P. (2002), ICT investment and economic growth in the 90s: is the United States a Unique Case?, *Review of Economic Dynamics*, Vol. 5, 408–442.

CRISCUOLO, P.; NARULA, R.; VERSPAGEN, B. (2005), Role of Home and Host Country Innovation Systems in R&D Internationalisation: A Patent Citation Analysis, Economics of Innovation and New Technology, Vol. 14, 417–433.

DORNBUSCH, R. (1976), Expectations and Exchange Rate Dynamics, Journal of Political Economy, Vol. 84, 1167–1176.

ECFIN (2005), The EU Economy 2005 Review, REP 55229-EN, Brussels.

EUROPEAN INNOVATION SCOREBOARD (2005), http://trendchart.cordis.lu/scoreboards/scoreboard2005/index.cfm.

FEENSTRA, R.C. (2004), Advanced International Trade: Theory and Evidence, Princeton: Princeton University Press.

FEENSTRA, R.C.; HANSON, G.H, (1996), Globalisation, outsourcing, and wage inequality, *American Economic Review.*

FEENSTRA, R.C.; HANSON, G.H. (1999), The Impact of Outsourcing and High-technology Capital on Wages. *Quarterly Journal of Economics*, Vol. 114: 907–940.

FRAUNHOFER-GESELLSCHAFT (2004), Innovationstreiber Informations- und Kommunkationstechnik, *Fraunhofer Magazin* (2): 8–37.

FROOT, K.A.; STEIN, J.C. (1991), Exchange Rates and Foreign Direct Investment: An Imperfect Capital Markets Approach, *Quarterly Journal of Economics*, November, 1191–1217.

GÄRTNER, M. (1997), Makroökonomik flexibler und fester Wechselkurse, 2nd edition, Heidelberg, Springer.

GORDON, R. (2002), New Economy – An Assessment from a German Viewpoint, Essen: RWI.

GOUROVA, E.; BURGELMAN, J.-C.; BOGDANOWICZ, M.; HERRMANN, C. (2002), Information and Communication Technologies, Enlargement Futures Series 05, Sevilla, IPTS/European Commission.

GROSSMAN, G. M.; HELPMAN, E. (1991a), Innovation and Growth in the Global Economy, Cambridge MA, MIT Press.

GROSSMAN, G. M.; HELPMAN, E. (1991b), Quality Ladders in the Theory of Growth, London: Macmillan.

HEMPELL, T. et al. (2004), ICT, Innovation and Business Performance in Services: Evidence for Germany and the Netherlands, in: OECD, ed., The Economic Impact of ICT – Measurement, Evidence, and Implications, Paris: OECD, 131–152.

HEMPELL, T. (2006), Computers and Productivity, Heidelberg: Physica.

INKLAAR, R., M. O'MAHONY; TIMMER, M. (2003), ICT and Europ's Productivity Performance: Industry Level Growth Accounting Comparisons with the United States. Groningen Growth and Development Centre, Research Memorandum GD-68.

JORGENSON, D. W.; STIROH, K. (2000), Raising the speed limit: U.S. economic growth in the information age, Brookings Papers on Economics Activity (2000), U.S. economic growth and development at industry level, *American Economic Review*, Vol. 90, No. 2.

JUNGMITTAG, A. (2004), Innovations, technological specialisation and economic growth in the EU, *International Economics and Economic Policy,* Vol. 1 (2004), 2/3: 247–273.

JUNGMITTAG, A. (2006), Internationale Innovationsdynamik, Spezialisierung und Wirtschaftswachstum in der EU, Heidelberg: Physica-Springer.

KOK, W. (2004), Die Herausforderung annehmen – die Lissabon-Strategie für Wachstum und Beschäftigung, http://europa.eu.int/comm/lisbon_strategy/index_de.html.

LUCAS, R.E. (1988), On the Mechanics of Economic Development, *Journal of Monetary Economics*, Vol. 22, I. 3–42.

MANN, C. (2000), Import Competition in Germany and the US, Washington DC, mimeo.

MANN, C. (2003), "Globalisation of IT services and white collar jobs: The next wave of productivity growth", International Economics Policy Briefs, no. PB03–11, Institute for International Economics.

MARREWIJK, C. van (1999), Capital Accumulation, Learning and Endogenous Growth, *Oxford Economic Papers*, Vol. 51, 453–475.

NARULA, R. (2000), R&D Collaboration by SMEs in ICT Industries: Opportunities and Limitations, University of Oslo, TIK Centre, mimeo.

OLINER, S.; SICHEL, D. (2002), Information Technology and Producctivity: Where Are We Now And Where Are We Going?, Federal Reserve Board *FEDS Paper* 2002–29, http://www.federalreserve.gov/pubs/feds/2002/200229/200229abs.ttml.

OECD (2002), Measuring the Information Economy, Paris, OECD.

OECD (2003), ICT and Economic Growth – Evidence from OECD Countries, Industries and Firms, Paris, OECD.

OECD (2004), The Economic Impact of ICT – Measurement, Evidence and Implications, Paris.

OECD (2004a), Information Technology Outlook 2004, Paris, OECD.

OECD (2005), Communications Outlook 2005, Paris:, OECD.

PILAT, D. (2005), Growth Differentials in OECD Countries: Some Reflations, contribution to the FORUM Financial Markets, ICT Dynamics and Growth in OECD Countries, *International Economics and Economic Policy,* Vol. 2, 1–6.

PONDER, J.K., MARKOVA, E.N. (2005), Bridging the Eastern European Digital Divide through Mobile Telecommunications: Stimulating Diffusion in Poland and Russia, Communications & Strategies, No. 58, 2nd quarter 2005.

REBELO, S. (1991), Long-Run Policy Analysis and Long-Run Growth, *Journal of Political Economy,* 99, 500–21.

RIVERA-BATIZ, L. A.; ROMER, P. (1991), International trade with endogenous technological change, *European Economic Review*, 35, 971–1004.

ROMER, P. M. (1986), Increasing Returns and Long run Growth, in *Journal of Political Economy* 94, 531–555.

ROMER, P. M. (1987), Crazy Explanations for the Productivity Slowdown, *NBER Macroeconomics Annual,* MIT Press, Cambridge, MA.

ROMER, P. (1990), Human capital and growth: theory and evidence. Carnegie Rochester conference series on public policy: a bi-annual conference proceedings, Elsevier, 251–286.

SAKELLARIS, P.; VISELAAR, F. (2005), Capital Quality Improvement and the Sources of Economic Growth in the Euro Area, *Economic Policy*, No. 42, 267–306.

STIROH, K. (2001), What drives productivity growth?, Federal Reserve Bank of New York, *Economic Policy Review*, 7, 37–59.

VAN ARK, B. (2001), The Renewal of the Old Economy: An International Comparative Perspective, STI Working Papers 2001/5, Paris: OECD.

VAN ARK, B.; PIATKOWSKI, M. (2004), Productivity, Innovation and ICT in Old and New Europe, *International Economics and Economic Poli*cy, Vol. 1, Issue 2+3, 215–246.

VERNON, R. (1966), International Investment and International trade in the Product Cycle, *Quarterly Journal of Economics*, Vol. 80, 190–207.

WELFENS, P.J.J. (2005), Information & Communication Technology and capital market perspectives, *International Economics and Economic Policy,* Vol.2, No: 1, July 2005

WELFENS, P.J.J. (2005), Internationalization of ICT: Theory of Outsouring, Foreign Investment and Competition Dynamics, Paper presented at the workshop "Internationalization of ICT in Europe: Facts, Theory and Empirical Issues", EIIW at the University of Wuppertal, August 26, 2005, revised version for presentation at IPTS Meeting in Brussels, January 18, 2006.

WELFENS, P.J.J. (2006). Innovations in Macroeconomics, Heidelberg and New York, Springer (forthcoming).

WELFENS, P.J.J., PONDER, J.K. (2003), Digital EU Eastern Enlargement, *EIIW Discussion Paper No. 109*, University of Wuppertal.

WELFENS, P.J.J.; WOLF, H.C. (1997) (eds.), Banking, International Capital Flows and Growth in Europe. Financial Markets, Savings and Monetary Integration in a World with Uncertain Convergence, Berlin, Heidelberg, New York 1997.

WORLD TRADE ORGANISATION (2005), Annual Report 2005, Geneva: World Trade Organisation.

ZON, A. VON; MUYSKEN, J. (2005). The Impact of ICT Investment on Knowledge Accumulation and Economic Growth, in: Soete; L; Ter Wel, B., eds., The Economics of the Digital Society, Cheltenham: Edward Elgar, 305–329.

J. The Role of Information and Communications Technology in Improving Productivity and Economic Growth in Europe: Empirical Evidence and an Industry View of Policy Challenges

Axel Pols

J.1. Introduction

There is a broad consensus among economists and policymakers concerning two major phenomena: that the European Union's economic performance has not matched the ambitions formulated in the Lisbon agenda of 2000, and that the EU has not reaped the same benefits from modern Information and Communications Technology (ICT) as has the United States. The EU's economic performance has been particularly disappointing given the strong expansion of the global and US economies in recent years. ICT has not led to productivity improvements and economic growth in the EU to the same extent as it has in the US, thus pointing to one reason for the comparatively weaker economic performance of the EU. Policymakers in Brussels and across Europe have acknowledged this situation and reacted with a number of policy initiatives at both the EU- and national level.

This article aims to contribute to the ongoing discussion about appropriate policies to fully capture the benefits of ICT for the European economy. The focus is on the possible contribution of ICT to economic performance, notably productivity and growth.

The article is organised as follows: Chapter Three reviews the empirical findings with regard to the economic impact of ICT, distinguishing broadly between the effects of ICT production and of ICT adoption (i.e. investment and use). In short, the evidence shows that the EU's challenge is to reap the benefits of both production and adoption, with significant intra-EU variations. Chapter Four briefly discusses some recent policy initiatives that emphasize the role of ICT in strengthening innovation and growth in the EU. Both the EU- and the member-state-level are considered, taking the case of Germany as an example. The major part of the chapter presents some important policy challenges, along with recommendations from the perspective of the European and German ICT industries. The final chapter presents a number of conclusions, emphasising the need for swift and coordinated policy actions in the face of increasing global competition, notably from China and India.

J.2. The Relevance of ICT for Productivity and Economic Growth

Today the importance of ICT's role in fostering innovation and growth is no longer disputed. There is now a broad consensus that ICT has the characteristics of a general-purpose technology, and thus has the potential to enable and accelerate innovation and growth throughout the economy. Conceptually, it is useful to distinguish three channels through which ICT can have an impact on economic productivity and growth:

- ICT production, i.e. through technological progress in the production of ICT products and services
- ICT investment (capital deepening), i.e. through increasing the capital-labour ratio, thus resulting in higher (labour) productivity
- ICT use, i.e. through helping companies increase their overall efficiency and benefit from network effects, such as lower transaction costs

J.2.1. Empirical Evidence Concerning the Productivity and Growth Effects of ICT in the EU as Compared to the US

This section presents some empirical evidence of the productivity- and growth-enhancing effects of ICT, distinguishing between the three channels mentioned above and focusing on the comparative performance of the EU and the US.[1] Some intra-EU differences are also considered.

J.2.1.1. The Contribution of ICT Production to Productivity Growth

Table 1 shows the comparative contribution to labour productivity growth of ICT-producing industries, non-ICT-producing industries and services industries from 1995 to 2003. Two results are particularly noteworthy. First, the absolute magnitude of the ICT sector's contribution to productivity growth was significantly higher in the US than in the EU15. (ICT production was, to be sure, only part of the explanation; the EU15's weaker aggregate productivity growth was in large part due to comparatively slow productivity growth in services.) Second, ICT's relative contribution to productivity growth was similar in both the US and the EU15. From 1995–2000, a period of strong ICT expansion, ICT production in the EU15 accounted for 36% of overall productivity growth. From 2000–2003 this share increased to 45%, while aggregate labour productivity growth slowed down. The comparative figures for the US are 35% and 31%, respectively.

---

[1]   Note that, according to DENIS et al. (2005, p.9), EU living standards as measured by GDP per capita are at roughly 70% the US levels, with about 1/3 of the gap due to differences in labour productivity and the remaining 2/3 due to differences with regard to the utilisation of labour (i.e. hours worked per worker, employment rate).

Table J1. Industry Contributions to Market Economy Labour Productivity Growth, 1995–2003.

	1995–2000	2000–2003	1995–2000	2000–2003
	European Union-15		United States	
Market economy labour productivity growth	2.2	1.1	3.4	3.6
of which:				
ICT production[1]	0.8	0.5	1.2	1.1
Non-ICT production	0.8	0.6	0.5	0.9
Market services	0.6	0.1	1.8	2.0
Reallocation	0.0	-0.1	-0.1	-0.3

[1] Includes ICT manufacturing, telecom and software services.
Source: VAN ARK/INKLAAR (2005, p.31).

To put these figures into perspective, compare them to the shares of ICT value-added in the business sector value-added of both economies. According to OECD calculations, in the EU14, this share increased from 7.2% in 1995 to 8.3% in 2003. In the US, it was 9.6% in 1995 and 10.5% in 2003. The data thus illustrates that the contribution of the ICT-producing sector to overall labour productivity growth was significantly higher than the sector's share in the economy, both in the EU14 and in the US.

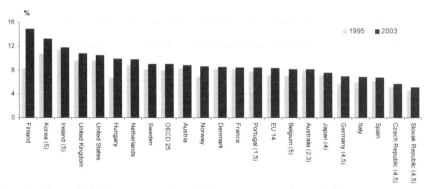

(1) 1996 instead of 1995; (2) 1998 instead of 1995; (3) 2000 instead of 2003; (4) ICT wholesale (5150) is not available; (5) Rental of ICT goods (7123) is not available.
Source: OECD (www.oecd.org/statistics/ICT).

Fig. J1. Share of ICT Value Added in the Business Sector Value Added, 1995 and 2003.

There are considerable intra-EU differences concerning both the size of the ICT sector and related productivity effects. Data available from VAN ARK/INKLAR (2005) for four major EU countries (France, Germany, the Netherlands and the United Kingdom) indicate that from 1995–2003 the contribution of the ICT-producing sector differed significantly, ranging from 0.4 percentage point in the

Netherlands to 0.8 percentage point in Germany. The sector's contribution in Germany appears particularly high when one considers the relative size of the ICT sectors in the various countries (see figure 1 above). One explanation for this could be the significant semiconductor industry in Germany, since this industry has in the past been characterised by particularly rapid productivity growth. Moreover, data available from other studies show that in some EU countries with relatively large ICT sectors, notably Ireland and Finland, the sector's contribution to labour productivity growth from 1996 to 2002 was even higher than in the US (see, for example, PILAT/WÖLFL, 2004).[2]

J.2.1.2. The Contribution of ICT Investment to Productivity and GDP Growth

ICT investment has also been a major driver of productivity and GDP growth in OECD countries. Still, studies have consistently shown that ICT investment's contribution to productivity improvements and growth is higher in the US than in the EU – with ICT investment in the US being driven by a number of service industries, including trade, finance and business services.[3] According to VAN ARK/INKLAAR (2005), ICT investment contributed about twice as much to productivity growth in the US than in the EU15 from 1994–2004. In more detail: from 1995–2000, ICT investment contributed 1 percentage point to aggregate labour productivity growth in the US, compared to a contribution of 0.6 percentage point in the EU15. For the 2000–2004 period the corresponding figures are 0.6 and 0.3 percentage points for the US and EU15, respectively.

There are also significant differences within the EU. From 1995 to 2003, for instance, ICT investment's contribution to labour productivity growth in the Netherlands and the UK was 0.8 percentage points, but just 0.5 percentage points in France and Germany (VAN ARK/INKLAAR, 2005, p.32). These differences are mainly attributable to the larger contribution to productivity growth in the Netherlands and the UK of ICT capital deepening in the services sectors.

The relevance of ICT investment for economic performance can also be gauged from the data presented in figure 2.

---

[2] Note that there is also evidence of the ICT sector's increasing contribution to total factor productivity over the 1990s in a number of countries, including for example Finland and Germany, thus confirming rapid technological progress in the sector.

[3] See, for example, the studies quoted in INKLAAR et al. (2003, p.2).

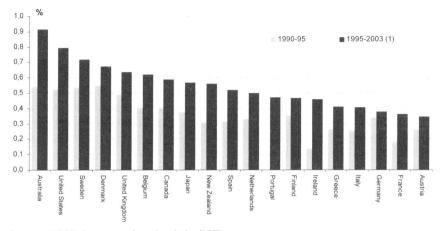

Source: OECD (www.oecd.org/statistics/ICT).

Fig. J2. Contributions of ICT Investment to GDP Growth, 1990–95 and 1995–2003[4] , in Percentage Points.

Two patterns are noteworthy: first, when comparing the first half of the 1990s with the period from 1995–2003, the contribution of ICT investment to GDP growth increased in all countries. This result is easily explained by the take-off of both mobile telephony and the Internet in the latter half of the 1990s. Together with the Y2K effect this led to an unprecedented – and with hindsight clearly unsustainable – investment boom. Second, the contribution of ICT investment to GDP growth in the US was considerably higher than in most European countries. Among EU member states the figures range from 0.3 percentage point (Austria) to 0.7 percentage point (Sweden). Three of the major EU countries are close to the bottom of the list, with ICT investment contributions to GDP growth in Italy, Germany and France reaching just half the US level.

J.2.1.3. The Contribution of ICT Use to Productivity Growth

The use of ICT may help firms increase their overall efficiency of resource use (or total factor productivity) and become more innovative. ICT can also give rise to network effects (or spill-over effects), which can have a positive, if less direct, impact on TFP.5 The efficiency gains of ICT use are more difficult to pin down empirically and the available evidence as yet is mixed. There is evidence of positive spill-over effects of ICT use on TFP, for example, from a number of firm-level studies. The picture emerging from industry-level analyses or macro studies,

---

[4] 1995-2002 for Australia, France, Japan, New Zealand and Spain.
[5] Some of the shortcomings of TFP as a measure of productivity are pointed out by INDEPEN/OVUM (2005, p.22).

however, is less clear.[6] One way to estimate the impact of ICT use on TFP is to compare the respective contributions to TFP growth of ICT-using industries and non-ICT-using industries.[7] Table 2 shows that the contribution of ICT-using industries to aggregate TFP growth from 1995–2000 was more than three times higher in the US than in the EU-4. In the US, the biggest push to TFP growth came from a few ICT-using services industries, notably wholesale trade and retail trade, whereas the TFP impact of these industries was negligible in the EU-4. Moreover, these results are broadly confirmed by a number of studies that analyse the contributions of ICT-using and non-ICT-using industries to either labour productivity growth or TFP growth.[8] PILAT/WÖLFL (2004, p.96) find evidence that ICT-using services have experienced a pick-up in labour productivity growth in some EU countries, notably Ireland, the United Kingdom. They emphasise, however, that the US and Australia are almost the only OECD countries where there is evidence of a positive impact on both labour productivity growth and TFP growth.

This seems to indicate that the EU could significantly increase productivity growth by exploiting the productivity-enhancing potential of ICT in the ICT-using industries, in particular some of the services industries. It needs to be pointed out, however, that there is still some debate as to the exact size of the productivity-enhancing effects of ICT use in specific US services industries.[9]

---

[6] See, for example, OECD (2003, 2004), VAN ARK/INKLAAR (2005), INKLAAR et al. (2003).

[7] To be more precise, note that "ICT-using industries" refers to intensive-ICT using industries, "non-ICT using" refers to industries that use ICT less intensively.

[8] See, for example, VAN ARK (2005), OECD (2004). Note that increases in labour productivity can be due to both capital deepening and TFP growth. Consequently, this measure of productivity does not allow conclusions to be drawn about the relative contributions of either of these two factors.

[9] According to DENIS et al. (2005, p.58-59), "...the evidence for large TFP gains in specific ICT-using industries, such as wholesale and retail trade, was still questionable. These latter gains are perhaps more modest when proper account is taken of measurement issues and of the role of a number of important non-ICT productivity drivers in these specific industries."

Table J2. Contributions to Total Factor Productivity Growth in the EU-4 and US, 1995–2000.

	1995–2000	
	EU-4[1]	US
Total economy	1.07	1.05
ICT producing industries [2]	0.53	0.71
ICT using industries	0.19	0.68
ICT-using manufacturing	0.03	-0.01
Wholesale trade	0.08	0.35
Retail trade	0.03	0.39
Financial intermediation	0.06	0.08
Business services	-0.02	-0.12
Non-ICT industries [3]	0.35	-0.34

[1] Includes France, Germany, Netherlands, UK.
[2] Includes electrical and electronic equipment & instruments; communications.
[3] Includes agriculture, forestry and fishing; mining and quarrying; non-ICT manufacturing; transport & storage; social and personal services; non-market services; other non-ICT.
Source: INKLAAR et al. (2003, p.23).

J.2.2. Explaining the Empirical Evidence

There is still a lack of understanding of the factors that are behind the weaker impact on productivity and growth of ICT in the EU as compared to the US. However, a couple of explanations are frequently quoted as a result of comparative studies.[10] They include the following, which are listed as benefits of the US:

1. A high degree of ICT diffusion resulting from strong ICT investment. In 2001, the share of ICT investment in total non-residential investment was much higher in the US (>25%) than in most EU countries, where the respective shares were in the range of 10–15% in Portugal, France, Austria, Ireland, and Spain, with only the Netherlands, Sweden, and the UK reaching shares of more than 20% (PILAT/DEVLIN, 2004, p.20);
2. A more-flexible economy, with less rigidly regulated product and factor markets. US companies can more easily implement the necessary organisational changes to fully reap the economic benefits of ICT investment. Moreover, a more flexible economy facilitates market-entry and –exit. So ideas and innovation emerge more rapidly;
3. The skill set needed for implementing ICT projects. The US appears to have been more successful in producing and attracting people with the necessary

---

[10] See, for example, the studies quoted in INDEPEN (2006, p.30) and VAN ARK/INKLAAR (2005, p. 16), as well as OECD (2003).

ICT-related skills, while in a number of EU countries ICT uptake has been hampered by skill-shortages (EITO, 2004, 2007);

4. A more-competitive environment. Companies have stronger incentives to invest in ICT to strengthen their performance;
5. A more-developed venture capital market. Innovative entrepreneurs and start-ups have more financing opportunities.

J.3. Unleashing the Growth Potential of ICT in Europe: Policy Challenges and Recommendations from an Industry Perspective

The evidence presented in Chapter 3 makes it clear that the EU and its member states do not fully exploit the potential of ICT at present. The available evidence shows that the EU is lagging behind the US in terms of all three channels through which ICT can foster productivity and economic growth.

From a policy perspective, an important question is whether Europe, in trying to catch up, should give priority to strengthening one of these channels.

While this debate is not yet resolved, it is interesting in this context to note that some analysts have argued that due to falling ICT prices, the main benefits of ICT accrue for the countries that buy ICT goods rather than those that produce them (BAYOUMI/HAACKER, 2002). Similarly, INDEPEN/OVUM (2005, p.24) suggested that the relative contribution of ICT use to productivity growth is likely to grow in the future, partly as a result of declining prices for ICT. Finally, NAHUIS/VAN DER WIEL (2005) argue that the relatively small size of Europe's ICT manufacturing sector is not an important disadvantage and conclude that a European ICT strategy should focus on improving ICT adoption.

Europe certainly has much to gain from improving ICT adoption. The evidence presented in Chapter Three suggests, however, that the relevance for economic performance of the ICT-producing sector should not be neglected.[11]

The sector is an important source of productivity growth and employment in a number of EU countries. Moreover, some major ICT segments, particularly software and IT services, are expected to continue to grow significantly faster than GDP in the foreseeable future. Finally, the performance of some of the non-ICT sectors depends significantly on a strong domestic ICT services sector: geographical and cultural proximity often facilitate the implementation of complex ICT projects.

Consequently, Europe should try to foster the economic performance of its ICT-producing sector and at the same time work on fully reaping the potential benefits of ICT investment and use.

---

[11] Note that DENIS et al. (2005, p. 58) suggest that, due to measurement issues, the sector's contribution to the post-1995 acceleration of productivity in the US should be higher than is commonly assumed.

Section 3.2. already hinted at policy reforms that could help Europe exploit the growth potential of ICT. These reforms include, for example, structural reforms aimed at creating a more flexible economy and increasing the supply of the required skill set. Such reforms are likely to strengthen both the ICT-producing sector as well as ICT investment/use.

In the last several years, major policy initiatives have been launched both by the EU and by individual member states to strengthen ICT production and use.[12] The following sections highlight some of the major recent initiatives and briefly present policy challenges and recommendations as proposed by the ICT industry. Both the EU- and the member-state-level are considered, taking the case of Germany as an example.

It will be argued in particular that there is a need for more emphasis on structural reforms such as labour market and education reforms. Given that these policies fall under the competence of EU member states, those countries with shortcomings in these policy areas need to be particularly active. Otherwise policies addressed more directly at the ICT sector, whether from the EU- or member-state-level, cannot be expected to fully exploit the growth potential of ICT.

J.3.1. The EU Level

Starting with the Lisbon strategy, the EU assigned a leading role to ICT in fostering European competitiveness. As a key component of the renewed Lisbon strategy for growth and employment, the EU launched the i2010 policy package in June 2005. This policy package is intended to support the overall goals of the renewed Lisbon strategy by promoting an open and competitive digital economy. The i2010 initiative rests on three pillars: (1) Creating a Single European Information Space, which promotes an open and competitive internal market for information society and media services; (2) Strengthening innovation and investment in ICT research to promote growth, as well as more and better jobs; (3) Achieving an Inclusive European Information Society (i.e. making sure that ICT benefits all citizens) by improving both public services (through, for example, eGovernment) and quality of life (through, for example, eHealth initiatives).

The policy orientations laid out by the European Commission in these three areas have important implications for both ICT adoption and the performance of the ICT- producing sector. Below, I will provide an industry perspective on these policy orientations, summarizing some of the major policy challenges as perceived by the European ICT industry.[13]

---

[12] The relative emphasis on strengthening ICT production and ICT adoption, respectively, has varied considerably across member states. Ireland and Finland are among the few countries that recognised the potential of the ICT sector early on, promoting its development through various measures.

[13] In particular, the following text draws on two recent publications of the association of the European ICT and consumer electronics industry (EICTA 2006a, 2006b). EICTA is

J.3.1.1. Policy Challenges and Recommendations Related to the Creation of a Single European Information Space

There are a number of policy challenges related to the first pillar of the i2010 initiative, not all of which are given appropriate attention in the EU framework.

Convergence and Regulation

The regulation of electronic communications markets can clearly have a strong impact on the performance of the ICT-sector, notably telecom carriers and network providers, as well as on ICT use (e.g. mobile telephony). One of the key policy challenges is the due reflection of digital convergence in regulatory regimes that traditionally have treated broadcasting, telecommunications, and the Internet as separate vertical markets. Today, the convergence of these markets is a fundamental shift, however, which is shaping new business models and disrupting established value chains and industry structures. Technological developments and market dynamics indicate that, in the future, content and services will be delivered over different types of networks and to a variety of end-user devices, thus resulting in a horizontal market structure with four major layers: content creation, service provision, delivery channel, and end-user devices.

Therefore, regulation must be developed to reflect this emerging market structure. In this context, the creation of a level playing field for all players active in these new markets is particularly important. According to EICTA (2006a, p.11), "this should be done by reducing the level of regulation to the lowest denominator for all relevant technologies."

Allocation of Spectrum

Early decisions on spectrum allocations open the door for the development of convergent services in Europe, with positive implications for both the ICT sector and ICT use. Global or regional decisions on spectrum allocation are creating the opportunity to reap scale effects and are therefore instrumental for the successful introduction of new technologies and services. There may, however, be a need for local variations in the allocation of spectrum due to cultural, demographic or economic differences.[14]

Secure European Information Society

A number of studies have shown that concerns about security and privacy are seriously hampering the adoption and use of ICT and should therefore receive particular attention of policymakers. However, the following trends pose policy challenges not fully accounted for in the i2010 programme. First, the spread of viruses and identity theft is likely to gain further relevance as the number of users

---

composed of 58 major multinational companies and 36 national trade associations from 27 European countries. See www.eicta.org.

[14] For more detail, see EICTA's response to the Radio Spectrum Policy Group – Public consultation on Wireless Access Platforms for Electronic Communications Services (WAPECS), which can be found at http://www.eicta.org.

and citizen services online increases. As a result of increasing fixed-mobile convergence, these threats and attacks will move into mobile and wireless environments. Voice-over-IP services and infrastructures are also likely to be affected by attacks.

The EU should take an active role, promoting, for example, best practices in security and strengthening public-private partnerships on security issues.

Digital Rights Management (DRM)

The traditional copyright levies remuneration system that was justifiable in the analogue world is inappropriate in the digital world. DRM systems that allow control of private copying, thus ensuring appropriate remuneration for copyright-holders, are increasingly available. In contrast to the antiquated copyright levies system, modern DRM systems allow consumers to pay depending on their individual copy requirements. DRM systems therefore facilitate the creation of markets for digital content, with positive repercussions for ICT adoption and use.

The vast majority of EU member states, however, are extending the copyright levies system to digital products. The EU should urge member states to phase out levies for digital products in line with the vision of the 2001 Copyright Directive.

J.3.1.2. Policy Challenges and Recommendations Related to Strengthening Innovation and Investment in ICT Research

Policies to strengthen innovation and investment in ICT research are key for maintaining Europe's current leadership in areas of ICT production such as audio-visual, broadband and mobile communications, enterprise software and embedded systems. Such policies should also encourage development of strong positions in strategic technologies and services that promise to become engines of future growth and employment. These policies are all the more important as new competitors enter the scene, with China and other emerging economies ramping up both their ICT production and their ICT-related R&D capacities.

R&D policy can help ICT companies innovate and thus become more competitive, thereby strengthening the performance of the ICT-producing sector. It can also be argued that such policies often create the basis for successful adoption and use of ICT in Europe as well. The reason for this is that R&D carried out in Europe is more likely to be inspired by or to reflect the particular needs and requirements of European consumers and companies. Consequently, policies in support of ICT R&D may imply a double growth dividend, first through strengthening ICT production and second due to the indirect impact on ICT use.

The suggestions of the European ICT industry with regard to the policy orientations contained in the R&D pillar of the i2010 programme can be summarized as follows:[15]

Given Europe's relative weakness in exploiting its own ICT inventions by developing and introducing marketable products and services, the European Research Council should encourage industry participation.

---

[15] See EICTA (2006b) for more detail.

- European ICT research projects should in general be co-financed at a level of at least 50% (75% for small and medium enterprise projects).
- Reiterating the recommendations of the Aho Report (see AHO, 2006), the role of public procurement and leading-edge markets, for example eHealth, should be given priority.
- State aid, fiscal measures and structural funds all play important roles in boosting industrial R&D and helping bring the benefits of ICT innovations to both urban and rural areas.
- A clear and reliable framework for Intellectual Property Rights (IPR) is an essential pre-requisite for investment in innovation. Therefore, the IPR arrangements embodied in the current Commission proposal for Rules for Participation in the 7th framework programme need to be redressed. The IPR arrangements set out in the current proposal are a drastic deterioration compared with the arrangements in the previous programme and raise major hurdles for industry to participate in projects financed by the new framework programme.
- The Commission's proposals to strengthen the European knowledge base are welcome, notably the initiative to establish a European Institute of Technology (EIT). As envisioned by the Commission, the EIT should be developed organically by leveraging existing activities in universities, research centres and companies.

J.3.1.3. Policy Challenges and Recommendations Related to Achieving eInclusion, Better Public Services, and Quality of Life

This section briefly discusses three policy issues related to the third pillar of the i2010 policy framework: eGovernment, eAccessibility, and Structural and Cohesion Funds. All three have important implications for ICT adoption and use, and the third issue, in particular, impacts the performance of the ICT sector.

eGovernment

A key role for eGovernment policies is reinforcing trust and acceptance for ICT solutions by citizens and business throughout Europe. In this context, an important challenge is developing trusted local solutions while advancing interoperability to ensure that public services can be used without national barriers across Europe. Moreover, at the infrastructural level, there is a need for secure broadband access across the member states. This is the very foundation of successful eGovernment.

eAccessibility

A key challenge is fostering the development of ICT accessible to all people, including those with disabilities, without creating fragmented markets and disproportionate regulatory action and bureaucratic procedures. In particular, one priority should be eliminating unique national requirements and avoiding the introduction of unique regional requirements. As in other areas, technical standards need to be transparent and consensually developed in international fora.[16]

Structural Funds

EU Structural and Cohesion Funds are important instruments for helping less-developed EU regions improve their ICT infrastructure, services and ICT-related education. Public Private Partnerships (PPPs) should be an important element in the use of these funds. Fixed and mobile broadband infrastructures should be categorised as basic infrastructures, in the same way as those for transport and energy. This would help mobilize the resources needed to speed up the development of broadband infrastructures.

J.3.2. The Member-State-Level: The Case of Germany

Over the last couple of years, the German government has promoted ICT through a number of policy initiatives (including, for example, "BundOnline 2005" and "Information Society 2006", initiated in 2000 and 2003, respectively). More recently, the government published the "High-Tech-Strategy" in September 2006, setting out a policy framework to attain leading positions in selected technologies that promise to become increasingly important in the future, including some areas of ICT. A specific programme defining priorities with regard to the support of R&D in the area of ICT, "IKT 2020" is in preparation. Moreover, in response to the i2010 policy framework launched by the EU, the German government is currently drafting iD2010, a national reform programme that will set out policy priorities with regard to the information society in Germany.

J.3.2.1. A Brief Evaluation of the High-Tech Strategy from an Industry Perspective

From the perspective of the German ICT industry, the government's high-tech strategy is a milestone in the reform of the German innovation policy. The following sections highlight some strengths and shortcomings, drawing on the evaluation of BITKOM, the German Association for Information Technology, Telecommunications and New Media.[17]

Strengths of the High-Tech Strategy:

- It correctly analyses the weaknesses of the German innovation system.
- It suggests improvements in the financing possibilities for start-ups and innovative SMEs.
- It commits to continued investment in electronic administration (eGovernment).
- It envisions a stronger reliance on PPPs when modernising ICT infrastructures.

---

[16] For more detail see EICTA's white paper on eAccessibility can be accessed at www.eicta.org

[17] For more detail see STREIBICH (2006).

- It commits to stronger protection of intellectual property rights at the international level.
- It supports the introduction of a bonus for universities and research institutes that attract research contracts by SMEs.
- It includes a special programme for research into security, including IT security.

Shortcomings

- It is not as fully integrated across government departments as is necessary.
- It gives inadequate attention to the role of education as a basic pre-requisite for innovation.
- It fails to fully recognize the valuable role that immigrant experts play in overcoming domestic skill shortages.
- It misallocates funding with regard to various sectors' strategic importance.
- It constructs an inaccurate list of the technologies that should be considered under the umbrella of ICT.
- It fails to improve the current situation of inefficient and insufficient instruments to assess public R&D spending.

Finally, it should be pointed out that the discussion of the factors explaining the greater success of the US economy in reaping the benefits of ICT as compared to the EU (section 3.2.) signals that the high-tech strategy will need to be complemented by a number of structural reforms to fully exploit the growth potential of ICT in Germany.

J.3.2.2. Policy Challenges and Recommendations to Exploit the Potential of ICT in Germany: An Industry Perspective

This section focuses on four policy areas where action is most urgently needed to strengthen the future development of ICT in Germany, based on interviews with ICT companies, market analysts and academics in Germany.[18] Note that these areas include some of the policy challenges mentioned before in the context of the US-EU comparison, notably the creation of a more-flexible economy (labour market reform, reduction of red tape) and the need to produce skill sets required in the ICT sector and the ICT-using sector.

---

[18] The interviews were carried out by Roland Berger Strategy Consultants as part of a study carried out in co-operation with BITKOM in order to identify "strategic" ICT technologies and services providing attractive opportunities for growth for ICT companies in Germany. For more detail see section 3.3 and BITKOM/ROLAND BERGER (2007). Note that, in addition to the four covered here, there are other policy areas that have a major impact on the ICT sector's development, notably regulation of electronic communications and availability of venture capital, See, for example, BITKOM (2005, 2006a).

Education

Education is becoming ever more important in global competition, in particular with regard to highly qualified personnel in technical sciences. Some emerging economies, such as China and India, are producing engineers, IT specialists and other technical graduates at a rapid pace. In contrast, Germany is facing a serious lack of skilled workers, which endangers the domestic capability to innovate and achieve economic growth. Consequently, significant efforts are called for and policy action is needed at all levels of the educational system.

Primary schools should foster interest in the sciences and mathematics, and the number of PCs in schools should be increased.[19] Teachers need to be trained how to better integrate the PC into everyday instruction. Curricula need to me modernised accordingly. Courses offered at institutes of higher education should reflect current scientific developments and have more practical applications. Universities should also provide professionals with opportunities for ongoing education.

Labour Market

Comparative international studies regularly indicate that the German labour market is more rigidly regulated than is the case in most other developed countries. Inflexible labour markets put firms, including ICT firms, at a disadvantage in international competition. Rigid rules for employing new staff and laying off existing personnel, as well as for working hours, hamper ICT companies in particular, as their work is typically project-oriented, which stipulates ups and downs in employment intensity. Moreover, international comparisons provide evidence of a linkage between employment law rigidity and productivity growth in ICT-using industries (INDEPEN, 2006, p.3). The German labour market should therefore move closer to international standards, including facilitating temporary contracts, making job protection laws more flexible, increasing the allowed maximum number of working hours per day and also increasing the number of employees that warrant the establishment of an employee representation council.[20]

Bureaucracy

International comparisons also signal the need to reduce red tape.[21] Recent surveys of both German companies and international investors rank the need to reduce bureaucracy as the most important policy issue.[22] Therefore, the government's decision to put bureaucracy-reduction high on its political agenda is to be

---

[19] According to a 2006 survey of EU schools, 100 pupils, on average, share 9 PCs, putting Germany below the EU average of 11 PCs per 100 pupils and far behind countries like Denmark and the UK, where the figures are 27 and 20, respectively.

[20] Currently the minimum number of employees in Germany is 5, in countries like the Netherlands, Denmark, France, Spain, Belgium, this number varies between 35 and 100.

[21] In the World Economic Forum's Global Competitiveness Report, Germany is ranked 57 concerning the extent of bureaucratic red tape. Finland is in 3rd place, Switzerland 13th, to name just a few other countries. See WORLD ECONOMIC FORUM (2006).

[22] See COMMERZBANK (2006) and ERNST & YOUNG (2006).

applauded. Potential cost savings in both the public and private sector amount to billions of euros. Recommended steps include reducing the time required to start new companies, introducing smart cards like the JobCard and electronic health cards, and maximizing the potential of electronic communication. The new online solution for company data transmission ("eSTATISTIK.core") is a step in the right direction in this respect.

Research and Innovation Policy

As a driver of innovation across the economy, ICT should receive special attention when allocating public support of R&D. In line with the commitments made by EU member states, the German government should increase overall R&D spending by at least 5% annually. In addition:

- The outcomes of current and future public R&D funding should be professionally evaluated, including analyses of the impact of R&D on developing internationally successful technologies.
- Scientific cooperation between the research/academic and private sectors must be improved, aiming at a more effective implementation of research results into new products and services.
- R&D support for ICT should focus on areas of particular strategic relevance, such as embedded systems, biometrics, and DRM systems.[23]

Finally, in addition to the recommendations with regard to specific policy areas (such as education, labour market), BITKOM has emphasised the need to consider the implications for the ICT sector of all major policy initiatives, thus avoiding counter-productive policy actions. The goal should be an ICT-policy that is integrated with other government policies and hence policy actions that are co-ordinated across all relevant government levels (EU, national, federal state) and policy areas (finance, economy, education, etc.).[24]

J.3.3. ICT Meta Trends and Strategic Growth Areas

Based on research carried out by Roland Berger in co-operation with BITKOM, the following table presents a number of technologies and services that were identified as strategic growth areas. These technologies and services are enabling or driving four meta trends that are expected to significantly change companies, business models, and markets in the coming years.

---

[23] For more detail see BITKOM position paper on support of R&D, BITKOM (2006b).
[24] For more detail see BITKOM (2005)

Table J3. ICT Meta Trends and Strategic Growth Areas.

I. Convergence ICT eliminates barriers between historically separated markets	II. Flexibility ICT drives the flexibility of organisations	III. Ubiquity ICT becomes ubiquitous – often not visible but all the more indispensable	IV. Data usability ICT enables effective use of information and digital content
IPTV	Software-oriented Architecture (SOA)	Embedded systems	DRM
Broadband	Utility computing	Biometrics	Data management
Mobile TV	Software-as-a-Service (SaaS)	RFID	Semantic web
Mobile 3.5G+	IT security	Telematics	Knowledge management
Voice over IP		Human-machine interface	Storage
Next generation networks		Optoelectronics	
Online gaming		Ambient intelligence	
Mobile gaming			
Micro payments			

Source: BITKOM/ROLAND BERGER (2007).

The listed technologies and services were evaluated and ranked on the basis of five major parameters, analysing, first, the relevance of the respective ICT technology as an input to other technologies; second, the relevance as an input to other industries; third, the technology's market potential; fourth, the technology's maturity and, finally, the relevance for technology and market developments of political decisions. The growth areas that reached the highest values in the scoring model include embedded systems, SOA and IPTV.

Such an effort in identifying strategic growth areas may be a useful exercise at both the EU- and member-states-level when developing ICT and innovation policies. If member states map their own strengths and weaknesses against the list of particularly promising growth areas, they may concentrate on adopting policies in support of those technologies and services for which they hold a strong position.

J.4. Conclusion

The evidence presented in this paper leads to four major conclusions. First, given that the available evidence shows the EU lagging behind the US in terms of reaping the economic benefits of both ICT production and ICT adoption (i.e. investment and use), the EU is well advised to work on both fronts, strengthening the competitiveness of the ICT sector in the EU as well as promoting ICT investment and use.

Second, intra-EU differences in the relative strength of both ICT production and ICT adoption imply that there is no "one size fits all" policy. In contrast, policy actions at the EU-level need to take account of these differences and, at the same time, national governments should adopt policies that appropriately address the relevant bottlenecks concerning ICT.

Third, there is a need to improve the business environment if Europe is to exploit the growth potential of ICT. In particular, policy initiatives focusing on ICT at the EU- and member-state-level need to be complemented by structural reform policies such as labour market and education reforms – for which the responsibility lies with EU member states. Structural reform policies will typically benefit both ICT production and ICT adoption at the same time. A case in point, for example, would be thorough educational reforms that produce the skill set needed in the production and adoption of ICT.

Finally, globalization and more concretely the rapid emergence of new competitors, notably China and India, make the adoption of these structural reform policies in addition to other policies outlined in this paper all the more urgent, both to maintain or rather enhance the competitiveness of European ICT production and to foster efficiency gains and innovation in ICT-using sectors.

References

AHO (2006), Creating an Innovative Europe, Report of the Independent Expert Group on R&D and Innovation Appointed Following the Hampton Court Summit.

BAYOUMI, T.; HAACKER, M. (2002), IT's Not What You Make, It's How You Use IT: Measuring the Welfare Benefits of the IT Revolution Across Countries, *IMF Working Paper* 02/117.

BITKOM (2005), IT, Telekommunikation und Neue Medien in Deutschland – Status Quo, Perspektiven und politische Handlungsempfehlungen.

BITKOM (2006a), Mittelstandsprogramm 2006.

BITKOM (2006b), Forschungsförderung im ITK-Sektor, Positionspapier, Berlin.

BITKOM; ROLAND BERGER (2007), Zukunft digitale Wirtschaft. Strategische Wachstumsfelder, Empfehlungen an Politik und Untenehmen in Deutschland.

COMMERZBANK (2006), Wirtschaft in Bewegung. Herausforderungen und Strategien am Standort Deutschland.

DENIS, C.; MC MORROW, K.; RÖGER, W.; VEUGELERS, R. (2005), The Lisbon Strategy and the EU's Structural Productivity Problem, European Commission DG *ECFI, Economic Papers* No. 221.

EICTA (2006a), i2010 – A Strategy for Building Digital Europe.

EICTA (2006b), i2010 – Increasing Innovation, Research and Development in Europe for ICT Excellence. An Industry White Paper Addressing the Second Pillar of the i2010 Initiative.

EITO (2004), European Information Technology Observatory 2004.

EITO (2007), European Information Technology Observatory 2007.

ERNST & YOUNG (2006), Kennzeichen D: Standortanalyse 2006 – internationale Unternehmen bewerten Deutschland.

NAHUIS, R.; VAN DER WIEL, H. (2005), How Should Europe's ICT Ambitions Look Like? An Interpretative Review of the Facts, *Tjalling C. Koopmans Research Institute, Discussion Paper Series* Nr. 05–22, Utrecht University.

INDEPEN (2006), Restoring European Economic and Social Progress: Unleashing the Potential of ICT. Main Report.

INDEPEN and OVUM (2005), Achieving the Lisbon Agenda: The Contribution of ICT.

INKLAAR, R.; O'MAHONY, M.; TIMMER, M. (2003), ICT and Europe's Productivity Performance – Industry-level Growth Account Comparisons with the United States, Groningen Growth and Development Centre, Research Memorandum GD-68.

OECD (2003), ICT and Economic Growth, Paris: OECD Publications.

OECD (2004), The Economic Impact of ICT, Paris: OECD Publications.

PILAT, D.; DEVLIN, A. (2004), The Diffusion of ICT in OECD Economies, in OECD, ed., The Economic Impact of ICT, Paris: OECD Publications.

PILAT, D.;WÖLFL, A. (2004), ICT production and ICT use: What Role in Aggregate Productivity Growth?, in OECD, ed., The Economic Impact of ICT, Paris: OECD Publications.

STREIBICH, K.H. (2006), Die Hightech-Strategie aus der Sicht der Hightech-Industrie, Speech delivered at BITKOM Medientag, Berlin.

VAN ARK, B. (2005), Does the European Union Need to Revive Productivity Growth?, Groningen Growth and Development Centre, Research Memorandum GD-75.

VAN ARK, B.; INKLAAR, R. (2005), Catching Up or Getting Stuck? Europe's Troubles to Exploit ICT's Productivity Potential, Groningen Growth and Development Centre, Research Memorandum GD-79.

WORLD ECONOMIC FORUM (2006), The Global Competitiveness Report 2006–2007, Houndsmills: Palgrave Macmillan.

K. Growth, Jobs and Structural Reform in France

Alain Chappert

K.1. GDP per Capita: Poor Apparent Performance, Complicated Contributions

French economic performance had been very satisfactory until the mid 1970s; since that date, however, we have entered a period of much slower economic growth, not only in absolute terms but compared to the US benchmark. Table 1 gives the gap between growth rates of GDP/capita for France and the US. The growth rate for France has been lower than the US in all of the three subperiods 1980–1990, 1990–2000 and 2000–2004.

As is the case for most European countries, this gap is often attributed to differences in growth rates for total labour input, due simultaneously to declining labour force participation rates, a poor employment ratio with a particularly high unemployment rate, and the decline in hours worked per person in employment, which is not necessary a purely negative factor but can result from a political or social choice, namely the preference for more leisure time. The productivity differential, on the other hand, would remain in favour of France, both in terms of levels (according to many data sources, hourly productivity in France would be slightly higher than in the US) and trend.

Table K1. Contributions to the Franco-US Differential of Annual Growth Rates of GDP/Capita.

	Total gap	Demographic ratio (15–64/total population)	Employment rate	Hours worked (per worker)	Hourly productivity
			Contributions		
1980–1990	-0,4	0,4	-1,5	-0,8	1,4
1990–2000	-0,4	-0,1	0,1	-0,6	0,3
2000–2004	-0,2	-0,4	1,1	-0,1	-0,8

As is illustrated in Table 1, the French annual growth rate for GDP/capita between 1990 and 2000 was 0,4 point lower than in the US. Hours worked per worker has contributed to the gap for 0,6 point.

The arithmetical decomposition that is displayed in table 1 shows, however, that things are slightly more complicated. It is true that the declining number of hours worked has systematically contributed to a lower output growth rate in France. Despite this, employment performance has had contrasted effects, negative during the first period, positive during the two other periods (especially due to the very strong recovery that occurred around 2000). The last column shows that while hourly productivity was much more dynamic in France than in the US during the 1980s, this gap was greatly reduced during the 1990s and has even reversed since 2000.

The picture is even more complicated if we take into account interactions between all these components. French hourly productivity has probably been improved by policies of the 1980s that have excluded low-productivity workers from the labour force (e.g., early retirement policies) or by the reduction in working time (if we assume an inverse relationship between hours worked and work intensity). If such is the case, this suggests that the fundamentals of productivity are in fact less favourable in France than is generally believed. Moreover, poor job performance could have been an effect of this low performance in terms of structural productivity.

The conclusion is that a sound explanation of French under-performance must look at both sides of the coin: employment rates and productivity of labour. We shall look successively at these two aspects.

K.2. Low Employment Levels: Reasons and Reforms Implemented or Needed

K.2.1. On the Supply Side

Employment rates are the joint out come of labour supply and labour demand. On the supply side, one is basically concerned with the disincentive effects of social benefits. This question must be raised for two segments of the labour force: less qualified workers who benefit from the general minimum income (RMI) and older workers.

For the first category, there is little doubt that we face a problem of inactivity trap. This problem essentially arises for the choice between complete inactivity and a part-time job paid at minimum wage. This has led to the introduction of a system of negative income tax (PPE) intending to make work pay. However both the magnitude of the problem and the efficiency of this solution remain debated. (According to its detractors, the PPE remains insufficiently targeted to truly be efficient, but measures to improve this efficiency have recently been enacted.)

For the second category of workers, the question is less controversial. Pension rules have certainly encouraged early retirement at age 60 and, in some cases, even earlier. Significant steps have nevertheless been taken to start inverting this trend, first in 1993 followed by the pension reform of 2003. These reforms will progressively impose stronger conditions for getting a normal pension before 65. Incentives were also introduced in 2003 which allowed for postponing retirement beyond the normal retirement age (with a corresponding bonus for each year of postponement).

It is difficult at this stage to know how far these reforms will go toward creating an upward trend for activity and employment rates in the 55–64 age bracket. This depends primarily on the strength of the link between financial incentives and retirement decisions and also on what happens on the demand side.

K.2.2. On the Demand Side

From a general point of view, structural obstacles to employment on the demand side can essentially come from two elements: labour costs and/or excessive regulations on employment lay-offs.

– Concerning labour costs, it is difficult to argue that France is facing a specific problem. One element could be the importance of the socio-fiscal wedge, especially employers' social security contributions. On the average, however, this is compensated by lower net wages. The problem is therefore more specifically concentrated on unskilled workers paid at minimum wage. Wage rigidity is institutional, and the minimum wage per hour worked has actually increased rather significantly relative to the median wage since the 1980s, making this problem increasingly important.

To compensate for this trend, reductions in employers' contributions for low wage workers were introduced at the beginning of the 1990s and have been progressively extended. Currently we have an almost complete exemption of employers' SS contributions at the minimum wage, digressive until 1.6 times this minimum wage. In a first step, these policies have been introduced with the aim of fostering the creation of less-skilled jobs by reducing their total cost. Since these measures took place in a rather unfavourable phase of the cycle, however, they have at best been able to stop the long run decline of the share of less-skilled employment. The second phase took place during working time reduction, where these measures were developed in a more defensive fashion with the purpose of avoiding increases in hourly labour costs. This time around, the policy took place in a very positive phase of the economic cycle: Job creation has been very rapid, but it is difficult to disentangle the cyclical component and the relative roles played by WTR *stricto sensu* (if any) and the role of these reductions in employers' contributions.

Other measures to minimize the adverse effect of social security contributions on labour demand have been recently discussed again, but as is well-known, there is no radical way to remove the economic distortions of taxation.

– Concerning other labour market rigidities, the debate must be clarified: "regular" dismissal costs are not that large in France compared to similar countries, and the labour market presents a strong rate of turnover that seems comparable to other countries (although producing comparable statistics in this domain is relatively difficult). The noteworthy points are rather that:

.Dismissal costs are subject to strong uncertainty. A significant proportion of lay-offs are reexamined by industrial tribunals (*prudhommes*), and costs for the employer can be very high if the lay-off is declared invalid.

.The burden of labour market flexibility is unevenly shared among categories of workers. We have a dual structure combining workers (especially young workers) locked into short-term contracts and unemployment spells, coexisting with insiders for whom the risk of job loss is much more limited.

In this context, propositions for structural reform not only include withdrawing all barriers to firing, but rather homogenizing and stabilizing the rules as well. One of the propositions under discussion is the introduction of a unique labour contract that would not completely suppress the distinction between workers of varying seniority, but that would manage it in a more continuous way with well-defined profiles of dismissal costs.

K.3. What About Productivity?

Any success in reintroducing young, less-skilled or senior workers on the labour market will be paid, at least transitorily, by a productivity slowdown. Some estimates are that a 1% increase in total employment only generates a 0.5% increase of total output (i.e., these categories of workers are about 50% less productive than insiders).

This would definitely bring our productivity performance below that of similar countries by removing the artificial inflation of our apparent productivity level resulting from selectivity in our labour market. Are there possibilities for avoiding this cost of improving access to employment for all of the population? This encourages us to look at some possible determinants of less than average "structural" productivity in France. Here, we shall briefly explore some elements that have been pushed forward in recent literature dealing with the now popular theme of the "French decline":

– This being eventually due to a deficit of R & D, not so much in global terms, but in terms of applied R & D produced by the private sector, one explanation for this problem is, among other reasons, the poor relationship between firms and the academic sector.
– A deficit in terms of education: part of this deficit results from a stock effect (the expansion of mass education occurred later than in some other countries), but could also apply to flows. In particular, some scholars point to an inefficient allocation of education expenditures between secondary and upper levels of education, with an excessive emphasis on the secondary level: This is in some way related to the argument that we lack efficient synergy between universities and firms.
– The lack of a network of dynamic medium-sized firms and the excessive weight of large groups, although this could be debated.
– Market structures are excessively concentrated.
– Beyond labour market regulations that have already been mentioned, it is also common to blame the excessive amount of administrative rigidities imposed on

all kinds of economic activities, and the lack of optimization and coordination of public interventions.

In conclusion, the French situation is not as bad as is sometimes forebode. Important changes have been made to increase the employment rate of older workers and to lower labour costs. Nevertheless, some work must still be done to improve the flexibility of labor contracts. A first step has been made with the so-called CNE in small firms. Political acceptance is not absolutely impossible in this field, if dismissed workers have a temporary but sufficient rate of replacement and a good chance to find another job.

L. Growth, Jobs and Structural Reform in the Netherlands

Kees van Paridon

L.1. On the Importance of Economic Policies

The late 1960s and early 1970s can now be described as the heyday of demand-managed macro-economic policy making. That certainly was the case in the Netherlands. The combination of Keynesian oriented demand management policies, the increasing relevance of the CPB[1], the Dutch Bureau for Economic Policy Analysis, and the use of tailored macro-models had created a climate, within which many economists, policy-makers and civil servants believed they knew how the economic development could be steered in an optimal way. How disappointed it must have been during the 1970s and early 1980s, when it became clear that Keynesian-oriented demand management policies could not prevent the return of a long period with sluggish growth, rising unemployment, high inflation rates and increasing budget deficits. Whatever policy was applied in those years – more government expenditures, lower taxes, investment subsidies and the like –, they all failed in restoring economic development back to its stellar performance of the 1960s. The Keynesian paradigm did not work properly anymore, a message which was, at that time, difficult for many people to accept. For a long time, the old views were still prevailing but at the end of the 1970s new ideas burst through, thereby demolishing much of the confidence people had in economic policies and government interventions in general.

Starting with Reagan and Thatcher, a new orientation towards government intervention unfolded itself. Government and government intervention were not seen anymore as the solution for existing problems, but much more as the basic problem itself. In this view, the best way to bring the economy back on track was by reducing government expenditures, taxes, regulations, in other words government intervention in general. The markets, so the argument, should be liberated from all governmental chains to be able to revive the economy. In many countries this approach was appropriately applied: budget cuts, deregulation, more emphasis on competition policy, more activating social security arrangements, and privatization and so on. The assumption was that in this way, necessary structural

---

[1] CPB actually means Central Planning Bureau, a reminiscence of heavy discussions immediately after the war when the CPB was erected, on the way economic policies should be applied and on the role of the government in that respect. There were strong links with social-democratic ideas in the 1930s with detailed plans, based on macro-economic modelling, about how to combat the heavy economic crisis in that era. See DON/VERBRUGGEN (2006).

changes could be brought about that would improve the long run competitiveness of national economies.

In like manner, ongoing European integration played its role. There was a general feeling that increasing internationalization, not only inside the EU but also at a global level, had reduced national sovereignty and with it the power of national governments to steer their own economy in the desired direction. With the EMS and later the EMU, the possibility to practice independent monetary and exchange rate policies were abolished. To become a member of the EMU, there were also strict requirements regarding budget deficit and the government debt. Once countries were members of the EMU, they had to meet the standards of the Stability and Growth Pact regarding budget and growth; this further restricted the possibilities of a budget policy.

All in all, the impression arises that the government's role regarding economic policies has been reduced considerably; it is not only reduced, but also changed. Much more than in the past, economic well-being has become dependent upon adequate functioning and, therefore, appropriate arrangements of labor market, social security and product markets. While in the past most emphasis was given on macro-economic demand management policies, manipulating budgets, interest rate and/or exchange rate, economic policies are now strongly directed at bringing about necessary structural changes in the aforementioned domains. To bring about these structural changes, the formulation alone of appropriate policies is not enough. To get these policies politically accepted and subsequently introduced and applied, national governments have to create a sufficient level of trust among its citizens and its main social-economic institutions. The differences in economic performance between countries that could be observed in the last 20 years are, in my view, strongly connected to the way certain governments have been better able to create such an appropriate environment.

The main intention of this contribution is to discuss these issues for a relatively small and open economy, that of the Netherlands. While many other continental-European countries showed a difficult economic development pattern, this country was able to generate a process of economic development and change during the 1980s and 1990s, with relatively high growth, low unemployment, a very high employment rate, and fewer taxes and social security premiums as well as fewer budget deficit problems.

L.2. Structural Reform Progress: Some Basic Factors

In recent years a number of studies have been published dealing with the issue of the political economy of reform.[2] Some of them have tried to empirically find out which factors are important in realizing structural changes, or negatively formulated, to discover those which happen to be an obstacle to bringing about

---

[2]   See in this respect for instance DRAZEN (2000). Empirical evidence can be found in HOJ/GALASSO/NICOLETTI/DANG (2006), and in IMF (2004).

such structural changes. Hoj and his coauthors listed a number of factors, namely initial structural conditions, macro-economic conditions, macro-economic policy, political institutions, international influences, demographic changes, technological developments, the sequencing of policy changes and possible interactions between policy changes, and the availability and usefulness of compensation strategies.

Initial structural conditions determine the scope for structural reform[3]. The wider the gap between actual and desired economic performance is, the larger the pressure to bring about necessary changes. In such a situation – normally rather crisis like –, however, strong resistance to change can be expected from those groups that had been beneficiaries thus far and that fear the negative consequences of proposed policy changes.

The sense of urgency to bring about policy changes is increased when there is a severe economic crisis. Under such macro-economic conditions, decision-making can be accelerated, oppositional forces are weakened and the costs of continuing existing arrangements are increase.

A poor budgetary position can hamper reform policies, because sufficient financial means to compensate for possible negative effects of policy changes are not available. It can, however, also stimulate them, as it is then obvious for the general public that alternatives for returning to a more sound budgetary position are no longer available.

The pressure to apply reform policies is certainly greater in case of fixed exchange rates, even more so for the EMU-countries[4]. Besides budget policies, exchange rate policies are impossible as well; now, only appropriate wage rate policies and, in the longer run structural reforms, are available to improve national competitiveness.

Differences in political systems are also relevant. Resistance of (small) interest groups is better dealt with in countries with a presidential political system and majoritarian electoral rules. In these economies, governments have a smaller size and welfare state programs are also smaller[5]. Other political institutional aspects – influential for the pace and direction of reform changes – are: the remaining period in office until the next elections, the political fragmentation in parliament, and the level of ideological polarization. In more general terms, Persson and Tabellini do stress the nexus between political and economic change: The more democratic a political system is, the better both the economic performance and the functioning of the political system[6] are.

A very strong factor for policy reforms involve international influences through several channels: competition from foreign firms in the home market and abroad, peer pressures and imitating successful policies from other countries, and the acceptance of binding agreements and treaties. To remain competitive or to restore national competitiveness, national governments can be forced to bring about these policy changes. There are indications that reforms are easier realized in relatively

---

[3] This paragraph is based on HOJ a.o. (2006).
[4] See DUVAL/ELMESKOV (2005).
[5] See PERSSON/TABELLINI (2001).
[6] See PERSSON/TABELLINI (2006).

small economies, in countries with a more homogeneous population, and in countries with a younger population. Technological developments can be helpful in bringing about structural reforms, especially in product markets.

The sequencing of policy changes is another important factor. Where to start, and with whom to cooperate are decisive aspects. Regarding the labor market, some countries tried to pursue necessary policy changes by attacking unions, other countries tried to bind then, and still other countries used support from "insiders" to start policy changes that initially hurt mainly the "outsiders." The first changes occasionally dealt with social security arrangements, leaving labor market arrangements untouched; sometimes countries started with adjusting the labor market, leaving social security unchanged. On product markets, it is on the whole easier to start with changes in the intermediate product markets.

Finally, changes are easier to bring about with a broader array of policy change measures, and, once initial changes have been implemented and have resulted in changing outcomes, new opportunities for further changes arise.

This is a whole list of factors[7]. It makes clear that bringing about policy reforms at the right moment, with the right content and the right consequences, and last but not least, with the appropriate electoral support and societal understanding, is difficult and delicate. Economic policy certainly has been changed, from a dominant demand-oriented approach towards a stronger supply-side orientation; and it certainly has not become easier. First, the development of a social security system has created not only a group of people dependent on this means of income support, but also of a major group that expects to become dependent in the future, i.e. the future pensioners. Both groups are very sensitive to any changes in these arrangements and also have considerable electoral power due to their size. Second, technological developments and ongoing internationalization are especially detrimental for lower productivity jobs; they have the highest chance to be outsourced abroad. This implies that the labor market position of the lower educated becomes increasingly threatened, again a source of potential resistance to reform changes. And finally, while all incomes have increased, many people are now in the situation that they have accumulated wealth and must therefore take into account the possibility of losses. Again, this creates the risk of resistance to drastic policy changes.

---

[7]   See for a similar overview HENIGER/STRAUBHAAR (2004).

L.3. Structural Reforms in the Netherlands[8]

These insights in the acceptance of, and at the same time resistance to, reform policies are now confronted with the Dutch experience in the last 25 years. There is no doubt that around 1982–1983 important changes were introduced and that these changes have ultimately resulted in a structural improvement in the performance of the Dutch economy. Why then did this change occur, and what happened thereafter?

In 1982, a majority of politicians had finally arrived at the conclusion that the observed gap between actual and possible or desired economic performance was not a short term problem, but rather a development with a structural character. Only structural solutions would be appropriate to change the tide. Because the economic development had already been below expectations since 1973, and the economic situation was quite dramatic – hardly any growth, an unemployment rate of 12%, a budget deficit of almost 9%, and a government expenditure ratio of above 60% –, there was also a sufficient sense of urgency that current problems could only be solved with a new economic policy and with drastic policy changes.

This growing consensus was not only visible at the political level, but certainly also with regard to unions and employers' organizations. This made it possible to include wage moderation as an important element of this reform strategy as well, in addition to strong expenditure cuts, a decoupling of civil servant salaries and social security benefits of the wage development of the private sector (if only modest at first), efforts to deregulate and privatize, major changes in labor market and social security arrangements, and the abandoning of all policies aimed at subsidizing or protecting old traditional sectors. It actually meant the revival of a situation that had already existed in the 1950s. At that time, wage moderation had also been an essential part of the policy package to rebuild the Dutch economy. In 1982, the same instrument was used to revive the Dutch economy once again. The reawakening of this Polder model became quite famous in the 1990s. In my view, bringing about important policy reforms in a small country like the Netherlands – with coalition governments and an important role for social partners – can only be realized if these actors are involved, which mean they must be convinced. That is not always easy, and is most certainly time consuming. The final results of such negotiations are often seen as soft compromises, hardly effective anymore to solve the main problems. Of course, that can happen and has actually happened, but experience shows that many times, constructive pragmatism also with these actors made it possible to usher in major policy reforms. The possible negative aspects of compromises – less strong than maybe some would like, and a time consuming negotiation process – must be confronted with a situation in which social parties are not involved and governments do come up with more drastic proposals. In that

---

[8] The description in this paragraph is rather sketchy. Thorough publications on the economic development have been published in the late 90s. See HEMERIJCK/VISSER (1997), and WATSON (1999). More recent descriptions of economic development and economic policies can be found in OECD economic Surveys of the Netherlands and IMF CONSULTATION REPORTS of the last years.

situation, the societal backlash can also be very time consuming and negative for such policy changes.

This consensus could also arise because of the contribution of independent policy institutions able to come up with policy relevant advice acceptable for government, parliament, social parties and society in general. If these advisory bodies are able to select relevant problematic developments, to distill its negative consequences and to come up with proposals for improvement, stimulating thereby the political and social debate on such issues, they could be very helpful in creating a climate in which policy changes do become more easily acceptable. In the Dutch case, reports of the Dutch Scientific Council for Government Policy[9] and a number of white papers of the Wagner commission[10] played a very influential role in this respect.

There is no doubt that international influences have been important in bringing about these changes. Even though most Western economies were confronted with a harsh economic recession and with quite negative results, Dutch performance was even worse. Of course, the dramatic price increase of oil was an important factor. More crucial had been the loss of competitiveness on the world market due to high wage costs, mainly because of the expanding social security system, and the exchange rate rise, also known as Dutch disease. But equally important were the lack of sufficient new innovations, the absence of sufficient structural changes inside firms and sectors as well as at the national level, and the rise of new competitors in Europe and certainly in Asia. The old products, production methods, and institutions were no longer appropriate anymore at meeting the new standards.

It is not only difficult to come up with policy reform proposals, but maybe even more difficult to stick to such policies over a very long period of time. Political courage and patience are essential, and improvements usually do not appear after merely two or three years. To stick to the new course is difficult, because the population normally perceives only the costs of such changes in the initial years and not the benefits, which appear only in the longer run. In the Dutch case, it took more than ten years before political parties, social partners and the Dutch population in general realized that all these painful changes really had brought about a change in economic development. With some exaggeration, it can be stated that all cabinets after 1982, with different coalitions, have practiced the same economic policy, stressing wage moderation, strict budget rules, deregulation in general and in the labor market and social security in particular as well as a stronger market orientation in general.

It is very challenging for any government to draw a parallel between improving economic performance and the policies it proposed and applied, but in reality, the consequences of almost any policy change are only felt after a longer period of time. There are hardly any strategies that can show a structural improvement after just a few years. Such improvements occur only in the longer run. The better subsequent governments are able to continue a certain economic policy, the better

---

[9]   See WRR (1980).
[10]   See WAGNER COMMISSION (1981).

the possibilities become that the expected positive consequences really can be harvested. As such, they can also benefit from these consequences because it creates new room to maneuver with respect to further policy reforms.

This economic policy should also be as broad as possible. A deterioration of economic performance as seen in the Netherlands in the 1970s and early 1980s cannot be reduced to one single factor or single policy change. The long period of high economic growth during the 1950s and 1960s influenced the behavior of all relevant economic actors, firms, individuals, and government to such an extent that they all did not react properly to new chances and challenges, causing a slowdown in necessary changes and as such in economic performance itself. Only through a broad economic policy can all these actors as well as their behavior be influenced. Furthermore, with a broader economic policy the costs of these policy reforms could be more evenly distributed among the several groups in society, thus reducing the potential resistance to change.

L.4. And What Happened with the Dutch Economy after 1983?

After 1983, eight subsequent cabinets – Lubbers-I, II and III, Kok-I and II, and lastly Balkenende-I, II and III – have been able to pursue an economic policy aimed at bringing about necessary changes and improving the competitiveness of the Dutch economy. As earlier mentioned, the main points have been quite similar, even though these cabinets differed considerably in their composition. Wage moderation, lower budget deficits and lower budget expenditures, lower unemployment and many more people employed have been basic goals of all these governments. They were also quite similar in their striving towards deregulation and privatization, and even more importantly in their policies for adjusting labor market and social security arrangements in such a way that the Netherlands could also be characterized as an emerging welfare state. Of course, due to the actual economic situation, political debates and differences in social resistance, there were periods with more drastic changes and other periods with slower progress. Sometimes it was difficult to start with changes, and only after a few tries could considerable progress be realized. The prime example of this is the debate on the labor disability law. It could have been decided more quickly, but the social battles would also have been much more intense.

And what have been the consequences of all these changes? The table shows the main results after 1983. They show a strong improvement in every indicator.

Table L1. Economic Indicators for the Dutch Economy, 1983–2007.

	BBP in PPP's (EU-15 = 100)	Unemployment	Employ-ment rate in persons	Employ-ment rate in fte	Taxes and premiums (as a per-centage of GDP)	Government expenditures (as a percentage of GDP)	Budget deficit (as a percent-age of GDP)
1983	108.9	10.2	53.9	49.7	43.9	62.2	-5.5
1988	105.9	8.4	55.0	51.0	45.0	60.2	-4.2
1993	111.1	7.5	57.9	53.0	45.3	58.4	-2.8
1998	112.9	5.2	62.0	58.6	39.4	47.2	-0.9
2003	114.4	5.4	65.2	59.6	37.4	45.9	-3.1
2007	116.3	4.5	66.7	60.2	39.1	45.5	0.0

Source: EUROPEAN COMMISSION (2006) and CPB (2006).

The conclusion therefore has to be that the Netherlands has been able to apply an appropriate economic policy strategy aimed at bringing about sufficient economic policy changes for improving Dutch economic performance. At the moment, it seems that the Dutch economy is once again strong enough to continue with necessary policy changes to meet the challenges of the future.

References

ALESINA, A., ARDAGNA, S.; TREBBI, F. (2006), Who adjusts and when? The political economy of reforms, *IMF Staff Papers,* vol. 53, special issue, 1–29.

CPB (2006), MACRO-ECONOMISCHE VERKENNING 2007 (Macro-Economic Forecast 2007), The Hague.

DON, F.J.H.; VERBRUGGEN, J.P. (2006), Models and methods for economic policy: 60 years of evolution at CPB", *Statistica Neerlandica*, vol. 60, no.2, 145–170

DRAZEN, A. (2000), Political economy in macroeconomics, Princeton, Princeton University Press.

DUVAL, R.; ELMESKOV, J. (2005), The effects of EMU on structural reforms in labour and product markets, *OECD Economics Department Working papers* 438, Paris.

EUROPEAN COMMISSION (2006), Statistical Annex of the European Economy, april 2006, Brussels.

HEINIGER, Y.; STRAUBHAAR, TH. (2004), Ökonomik der Reform. Wege zu mehr Wachstum in Deutschland, Orell Füssli, Zürich.

HEMERIJCK, A.C.; VISSER, J. (1997), 'A Dutch miracle': job growth, welfare reform and corporatism in the Netherlands, Amsterdam: Amsterdam University Press.

HOJ, J.; GALASSO V.; NICOLETTI G.; DANG, TH.-TH. (2006), The political economy of structural reform: empirical evidence from OECD countries, *OECD Economics Department Working papers* 501, Paris.

INTERNATIONAL MONETARY FUND (2004), Fostering structural reforms in industrial countries, chapter 4 in World economic Outlook, April 2004, 103–146.

INTERNATIONAL MONETARY FUND, Kingdom of the Netherlands – Netherlands: Article IV Consultation – Staff Report; several editions, Washington.

NICOLETTI, G.; SCARPETTA, S. (2005), Product market reforms and employment in OECD countries, *OECD Economics Department working papers no.* 472, Paris.

ORGANISATION FOR ECONOMIC COOPERATION AND DEVELOPMENT, OECD Survey of the Netherlands, Paris, several editions.

PERSSON, T.; TABELLINI G. (2001), Political institutions and political outcomes: What are the stylised facts?, *CEPR Discussion paper no.* 2872, London.

PERSSON, T.; TABELLINI, G. (2006), Democratic capital: the nexus of political and economic change, *CEPR Discussion paper* no. 5654, London.

WAGNER COMMISSION (1981) Een nieuw industrieel elan (A new enthusiasm for manufactiuring), The Hague.

WATSON, C. M. (1999), The Netherlands: transforming a market economy, *IMF Occasional paper* no. 181, Washington.

WETENSCHAPPELIJKE RAAD VOOR HET REGERINGSBELEID (Scientiofic Council for Government Policy), Industry in the Netherlands, its place and future, report no. 18, The Hague.

M. Growth, Jobs and Structural Reforms in Greece

Daphne Nicolitsas[*]

M.1. Introduction

This short intervention does not present details of the structural reforms that took place in Greece recently. Nor does it include an assessment of these or explanations for why more extensive changes did not take place. Instead, it suggests certain product market reforms that could contribute to decreasing the gap in per capita income between Greece and the EU-15.

M.2. A Broad Picture of Recent Economic Developments in Greece

If one had to summarize recent economic developments in Greece in a single sentence an accurate representation might have been: robust growth rates, certain structural reforms and a moderate degree of job creation. And what about the outlook? Given the speed of technological progress, the intensification of globalization and population ageing, prospects will certainly depend on the continuing pursuit of structural reforms.

The significant growth rate of the Greek economy in the last decade or so is well documented. Figure 1 clearly illustrates the point; in every year since 1996 the growth rate of the Greek economy exceeded the corresponding EU-15 average. The margin averaged 1.7 percentage points over the period 1996–2005, but has, however, widened over time and in some years even exceeded three percentage points.

---

[*] Bank of Greece. Views expressed herein are the author's and do not necessarily coincide with those of the Bank of Greece.

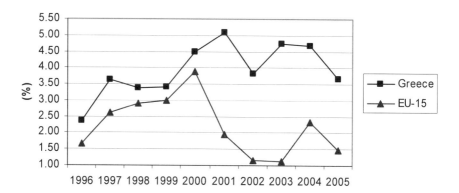

Source: EUROSTAT, NEW CRONOS DATABASE.

Fig. M1. Annual Real GDP Growth Rates in Greece and the EU-15, 1996 -2005.

Domestic demand was the main contributing factor to growth; the significant decrease in interest rates, the inflow of funds from the Community Support Framework (CSF) and to, some extent, one-off events such as the Olympic Games fuelled both investment and consumption. On the supply side, the main driving force was an increase in labour productivity (at an annual average rate of around 2.6% during the period 1996–2005) reflecting both capital deepening and total factor productivity growth. From the data presented above on GDP and labour productivity growth it becomes clear that employment increased at a rate of a little over 1 per cent per annum. This rate of employment growth, however, was only moderate compared to developments in other high growth EU-15 countries (e.g. Ireland, Spain).[1]

A number of structural reforms also took place during the last decade or so; certain sectors (the financial sector, the postal and telecommunications sector, air transport, electricity and gas supply) were (gradually or completely) liberalized. Details of these reforms are documented in the national progress reports (the so-called "Cardiff reports" and the Lisbon National Reform Programme for Growth and Jobs 2005–8) submitted annually, from 1999 onwards, to the European Commission.[2] The degree to which structural reforms actually stimulated economic activity is difficult to ascertain since, as often alluded to in the literature, benefits from structural reforms are widespread and take time to materialise (HOJ et al., 2006). Structural reforms must however have contributed to the robust growth rate as evidenced, by amongst other things, the impressive productivity

---

[1]   The annual average rate of employment growth during the period 1996-2005 was 4.3% in Ireland and 3.5% in Spain.

[2]   Most of the individual country reports can be downloaded from the following two sites:
http://ec.europa.eu/growthandjobs/key/index_en.htm
http://ec.europa.eu/economy_finance/epc/epc_countryexaminations_en.htm.

performance of the sectors in which reforms took place, e.g. financial sector, telecommunications (see, *inter alia*, ECB, 2006).

Despite the recent high growth rates, however, there is still a sizeable gap between the per capita income in Greece and that in the EU-15. In 2005 the gap from the EU-15 average (set at 100) was of the order of 24 percentage points and was mainly due to a lower level of labour productivity (accounting for 14 percentage points of the total gap) while the difference in the employment rate between Greece and the EU-15 accounted for the remainder of the difference (Figure 2).[3]

Per capita Income Gap =   Labour productivity gap   +   Employment rate gap

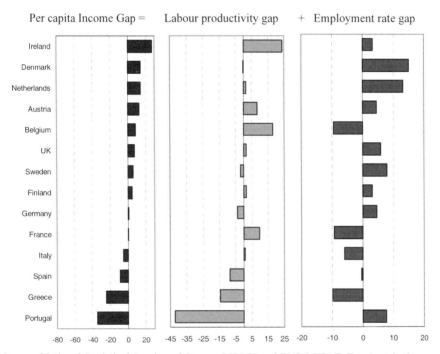

Source: National Statistical Service of Greece (NSSG) and EUROSTAT. For Austria the employment data is from OECD (2006).

Fig. M2. Breakdown of Per Capita Income in its Components, 2005 (Deviations in Percentage Points from the EU–15 average (EU-15 average =100)

A question that arises at this point is what type of structural reforms could address the shortfall in per capita income. The rest of this intervention identifies four types of product market reforms that could potentially, by enhancing both productivity and the employment rate, contribute to closing the gap in the per capita income between Greece and the EU-15.

---

[3] The figures presented herein make use of the data prior to the significant upward revision to the Greek national accounts data announced in the fall of 2006.

The Role of Product Market Reforms in Enhancing Growth Prospects

Notwithstanding the fact that the shortfall in the overall level of labour productivity reflects to a certain extent the difference in the composition of economic activity (a large share of Greece's output is derived from the primary sector) there is room for improvement of labour productivity in most sectors. Four types of reforms that could strengthen productivity and increase the employment rate[4] are those geared towards: (a) reducing administrative burdens, (b) enhancing competition, (c) providing incentives to increase firm size and (d) setting the preconditions for the diffusion of Information and Communication Technology (ICT). To be sure progress has been made on all of these fronts in the last 15 years or so but more needs to be done.

a. Reducing Administrative Burdens:

A number of indices suggest that, despite the improvement that has taken place over time, Greek businesses are burdened to a larger extent than other EU countries by costly bureaucratic procedures; Table 1 presents a couple of indices as evidence on this point. The OECD index provides an assessment of the extent of administrative burdens faced by startups. As the Table suggests Greece is amongst the worst performers in the EU-15. Furthermore, the direct cost of starting a business (i.e. the fees required to start a business) as a percentage of per capita income is the highest amongst the EU-15.

---

[4]   Given that, by definition, an increase in employment with constant output leads to a lower level of labour productivity the impact of reforms on productivity will depend on the relative impact of these on output and employment.

Table M1. Indices of the Administrative Burdens Faced by New Businesses in the EU-15

	OECD index of administrative burdens on startups[1]	Cost of starting a business as a % of per capita income[2]
Austria	2.8	5.7
Belgium	1.7	11.1
Denmark	0.5	0.0
Finland	1.3	1.2
France	1.9	1.2
Germany	1.6	4.7
Greece	2.6	24.6
Ireland	0.5	5.3
Italy	2.4	15.7
Netherlands	1.6	13.0
Portugal	1.7	13.4
Spain	2.8	16.5
Sweden	1.2	0.7
UK	0.7	0.7

[1] The index, which refers to the situation in 2003, varies between 0 and 6 from least to most restrictive. (See CONWAY et al., 2005 for details on the construction of this index).
[2] Refers to the situation in January 2005; see IBRD (2006) for further details.
Sources: CONWAY et al. (2005) and IBRD (2006).

The extent of administrative burdens might, to a certain degree, be one of the factors behind the low level of labour productivity in Greece. In fact, Figure 3 which depicts the values of the OECD administrative burdens index on startups across OECD countries together with the level of hourly labour productivity in 2003 suggests that there is a negative association between the two; countries with fewer administrative burdens have higher levels of labour productivity.

Furthermore, low administrative burdens and a favourable business climate are likely to enhance job creation and hence increase employment rates especially those of women who work predominantly in the service sector for which these procedures are more burdensome.

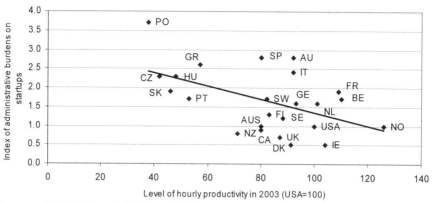

Sources: CONWAY et al. (2005) and OECD (2005)

Fig. M3. Productivity Per Hour and Index of Administrative Burdens on Business Startups in OECD Countries, 2003.

b. Enhancing Competition:

According to economic theory, lack of competition leads to an ineffective distribution of resources in an economy, a reduction in output and lower efficacy of enterprises (see, for example, BROWNING (1997), HARBERGER (1954), NALEBUFF/STIGLITZ (1983).

The lack of competition in Greece is evidenced by *inter alia* (a) the extent of regulations in the economy, (b) the limited liberalization of utilities and (c) the extent of agreements and harmonised practices between companies.[5] Limited competition in the Greek economy does not appear to be caused by *legal barriers* to market entry but rather by the administrative barriers to starting new businesses and by the complexity and frequent changes of the regulatory environment which create incentives for existing businesses to co-ordinate their practices.

c. Incentives to Increase Firm Size:

Firms in Greece, in all sectors of economic activity, are much smaller than in most other EU economies and according to BURTLESS (2002) this is one of the main explanations for Greece's lower level of productivity. A positive association between firm size and the level of productivity, although a controversial point, is often attributed to the ability of large firms to exploit economies of scale. Evidence of the lower productivity of small firms in Greece is provided by the following two facts: (a) average monthly earnings vary positively with firm size even after controlling for both the individual's education level and occupation, well as for industry and region[6] and (b) the level of labour productivity in

---

[5] For more details see Bank of Greece, *Monetary policy 2004-05,* Appendix to Chapter III, February 2005.

[6] These are the results of regressions based on data from the 2002 Structure of Earnings Survey and are available from the author upon request.

manufacturing firms with over 20 employees is around 4% higher than that of all firms with over 10 employees.

d. Diffusion of ICT:
The Greek economy is slower than other economies in adapting to technological change, as shown, for instance, by the relatively limited penetration of new technologies in the production process.[7] In July 2006, the broadband penetration rate in Greece stood at 2.7% (i.e. 2.7 broadband access lines per 100 inhabitants) compared to over 15% in the EU-15. Since, as argued by *inter alia* JORGENSON/ STIROH (2000), there is a positive association between GDP growth and the production and use of new technologies it looks likely that in the case of Greece, where ICT penetration is very low, the adoption of new technologies would help improve productivity, especially if these were to be integrated in a coordinated and globalised manner, with the aim of fully exploiting their "network effects".

M.3. Final Remark

This short intervention did not touch upon labour market reforms for several reasons. First, because it is thought that product market reforms are a precondition for the efficiency of any labour market reforms. Secondly, because the discussion on which specific labour market reforms should be introduced is a long one and invariably linked to a debate on the necessary changes in the education and training systems; a restructuring of the latter is necessary for sustainable growth. Space limitations, however, prevent such a long discussion here.

References

BANK OF GREECE (2005), Monetary policy 2004–05, February.
BROWNING, E. K. (1997), A neglected welfare cost of monopoly and most other product market distortions, *Journal of Public Economics,* Vol. 66, 127–44.
BURTLESS, G. (2002), The Greek labour market, in R.C. Bryant, N.C. Garganas and G.S. Tavlas ,eds., Greece's economic performance and prospects, Bank of Greece & The Brookings Institution, Athens.
CONWAY, P.; JANOD, V.; NICOLETTI, G. (2005), Product Market Regulation in OECD Countries: 1998 to 2003, *OECD Economics Department Working Paper* No. 419.
ECB (2006), Competition, productivity and prices in the Euro area services sector, *ECB Occasional Paper* No. 44.
HARBERGER, A. C. (1954), Monopoly and resource allocation, American Economic Review, Vol. 44, 77–87.

---

[7]   The World Economic Forum Networked Readiness Index for 2005 shows that Greece is the least "prepared" amongst the EU-15 countries.

HOJ, J.; GALASSO, V.; NICOLETTI, G.; DANG, T. (2006), The Political Economy of Structural Reform: Empirical Evidence from OECD Countries, *OECD Economics Department Working Paper* No. 501.

IBRD (2006), Doing Business in 2006: Creating Jobs, Washington.

JORGENSON, D. W.; STIROH, K. J. (2000), Raising the speed limit: US economic growth in the Information Age, *Brookings Papers on Economic Activity*, Vol. 2000, 125–211.

NALEBUFF, B.; STIGLITZ, J. (1983), Information, competition and markets, *American Economic Review*, Vol. 73, 278–83.

NICOLITSAS, D. (2005), Per capita income, productivity and labour market participation: recent developments in Greece, *Bank of Greece Economic Bulletin*, No. 25, 37–60.

OECD (2005), International comparisons of labour productivity levels – estimates for 2005, Paris.

OECD (2006), Labour Force Statistics, 1985–2005, Paris.

N. Economic Catching-Up, Price Levels and Inflation Rates in Central and Eastern Europe

Balázs Égert[*]

N.1. Introduction

It is a long established stylized fact that the price level, expressed in the same currency unit, is lower in less developed countries than in more developed countries. The eight new European Union (EU) Member States of Central and Eastern Europe (CEE) are no exception to this rule. The price level of CEE countries, converted into euro, is well below the price level of the euro area average (Figure 1). At the same time, GDP per capita figures expressed in Purchasing Power Standards (PPS) in CEE show striking similarities with overall price levels in CEE at first glance, given that they are also far below the levels observed in the euro area in 2005. Slovenia and the Czech Republic are the only countries which is close to the level of economic development of the least developed old EU countries such as Greece or Portugal.

A conventional explanation for the observed gap in the price level relates to market-based nontradables and to the absolute version of the Balassa-Samuelson effect, as economists tend to take the position that the overall price level in developing countries is low chiefly because of lower service prices while differences in the prices of tradable goods are unimportant.

Another widely accepted view in the literature is that fast-growing economies record higher inflation rates due to the Balassa-Samuelson effect. This statement needs two qualifications in the case of CEE. First, some of the countries studied here have recently exhibited inflation rates in line with inflation rates in the euro area (Figure 1), partly because the Balassa-Samuelson effect is very low for various reasons. Second, catching-up economies may have so-called structural inflation rates due to changes in the prices of goods and regulated services.

However, considering a number of factors other than the Balassa-Samuelson effect that contribute to lower price levels in CEE, this explanation seems overly simplistic. In particular, the prices of services controlled or influenced by public authorities, housing prices and the prices of tradable goods also have an important role to play in the price level gap.

---

[*] Parts of this study were prepared when the author visited BRUEGEL in 2006. The author thankfully acknowledges excellent language advice by Rena Mühldorf. The opinions expressed in the study are those of the author and do not necessarily reflect the official views of the Oesterreichische Nationalbank or the ESCB.

Against this backdrop, the objective of this paper is to provide the big picture concerning the driving forces of price level convergence and inflation rates in the new EU Member States of Central and Eastern Europe. While this paper is certainly not the first one to look at price level convergence and inflation differentials in the region,[1] it is one of the first studies that considers a very broad range of structural factors relating to economic catching-up that may influence market services, regulated prices, residential property prices and goods prices, and that simultaneously deals with the role of cyclical and external factors in CEE. A contribution of the paper to the previous literature is that it discusses the potential mismatch between price level convergence and inflation differentials in fast-growing economies.

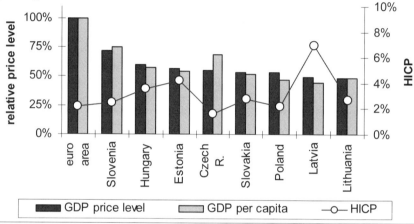

Note: GDP price levels are very comparable to price levels based on final consumption expenditures.
Source: Author's calculations based on data obtained from NEWCRONOS/ EUROSTAT.

Fig. N1. Relative GDP Price Level, Relative GDP Per Capita (Euro Area=1) and HICP

The rest of the paper is structured as follows. Sections 2 to 5 give some stylized facts and review the factors influencing the level of and changes in prices of market services, regulated prices, residential property prices and goods prices. Section 6 analyzes the role of economic structures in business cycle synchronization, the exchange rate pass-through and the impact of oil price developments on inflation rates. Finally, Section 7 concludes and sketches out the potential mismatch between price level convergence and inflation differentials in fast-growing economies.

---

[1] See e.g. BACKÉ et al. (2002) for inflation dynamics in market-based and nonmarket based services and CIHÁK/HOLUB (2001, 2003 and 2005) for relative price adjustments based on data from the international price comparison program. ÉGERT/HALPERN/ MacDONALD (2006) survey the literature on the changes in (but not the level of) real exchange rates (the reciprocal of relative prices) in transition economies but did not address the sources of domestic inflation.

N.2. The Prices of Market-Based Services

Popular wisdom among economists holds that prices in developing economies are lower than in developed economies due to lower service prices in developing economies. At first glance, this is what we indeed see on Figure 2 for the case of Central and Eastern Europe (CEE), where price levels are considerable lower than in the euro area. The usual explanation for lower service prices is given by the absolute version of the Balassa-Samuelson effect developed by BALASSA (1964) and SAMUELSON (1964). Their framework draws on the assumption that a given economy produces tradable and market-based nontradable goods, and that wage levels in the tradable sector are given by productivity in that sector; moreover, that PPP holds for tradables, i.e. the price level of the same good equals in the home and foreign economies. Nevertheless, it can be observed that productivity in developing countries is below levels recorded in developed countries. As a consequence, lower wages in tradables lead to lower wages and lower prices in the nontradable sector if wages equalize across sectors. This implies that while prices are equal for tradables, the prices of market nontradables are lower in low-productivity countries, which decreases the overall price level.

There are two complementary explanations of the Balassa-Samuelson effect. The first one, emphasized by BHAGWATI (1984), claims that prices are lower in poorer countries because these countries specialize in labor-intensive production, where wages are lower, whereas richer countries produce more capital-intensive goods. To turn this argument around, productivity is lower in developing countries because they have lower capital stocks.

The second argument is based on the demand side. BERGSTRAND (1991) shows that the relative price of nontradables depends not only on relative productivity and on the capital-labor ratio but is also crucially influenced by demand-side factors. This implies that richer households consume more services relative to their overall budget, which puts pressure on nontradable prices from the demand side and leads to higher service prices in richer countries.

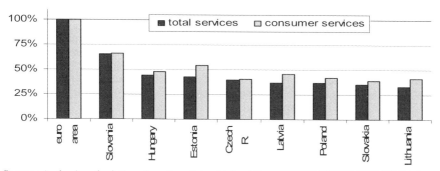

Source: Author's calculations based on data obtained from NEWCRONOS/EUROSTAT.

Fig. N2. Relative Price Level of Market Services (Euro Area=1, 2004)

It is easy to see how changes in the factors underlying the gap in market-based nontradables may make nontradable prices and thus the overall price level converge across countries. For instance, if productivity in the tradable sector increases faster in the developing economy than in the developed country, higher wages in tradables will spill over to the market-based nontradable sector – unless offset by productivity increases in the nontradable sector – , in turn causing an increase in nontradable prices.

A look at productivity data points into the direction of a potentially mighty Balassa-Samuelson effect. Yet large productivity gains in Central and Eastern European countries do not materialize in correspondingly high inflation rates or in a convergence of the price levels to euro area levels. Table 1 below shows that the inflation rates implied by productivity growth are not very high and in fact range between 0% and 2% a year. These figures are particularly low if compared to average productivity growth rates and to the average inflation rate during the past 10 years or so.

Table N1. Annual Inflation Implied by the Balassa-Samuelson Effect in Central and Eastern Europe

	B-3			CEE-5				
	EE	LV	LT	CZ	HU	PL	SK	SI
BURGESS et al. (2003)	0.75	0.75	0.85					
ÉGERT (2002)				0.55	1.75	2.25	-0.35	-0.15
ÉGERT (2005)	1.05							
ÉGERT et al. (2003)	0.85				1.15	2.05	1.25	1.05
FELK et al. (2002)				0.05				
KOVÁCS (2001)					1.85			
KOVÁCS/SIMON (1998)					1.95			
KOVÁCS (2002)				0.45	2.25			
MIHALJEK/KLAU (2004)a					1.55	1.45	0.65	0.65
WAGNER/HLOUSKOVA (2004)	0.25	0.45	0.95	0.55	1.05	1.05	0.15	0.85
ŽUMER (2002)								1.05
Average	0.7	0.6	0.9	0.4	1.7	1.7	0.4	0.7

Note: Figures are average annual changes. Furthermore, figures are average figures of the range given in the original paper. The inflation rate a) = the inflation differential against Germany computed using a Balassa-Samuelson implied inflation rate of 0.35% for the euro area / Germany (SWAGEL (1999), LOMMATZSCH/TOBER (2003) and Égert et al. (2003) put the size of the Balassa-Samuelson effect at 0% (1990 to 1996), at 0.1% (1995–2002) and at 0.55% (1995–2000), respectively.) EE=Estonia, LV=Latvia, LT=Lithuania, CZ=Czech Republic, HU=Hungary, PL=Poland, SK=Slovakia, SI=Slovenia.
Source: Calculations based on ÉGERT/HALPERN/MacDONALD (2006).

There is an array of explanations for the small size of the Balassa-Samuelson effect in the CEE countries. The first reason is that large productivity gains in tradables are offset by substantial productivity growth in nontradables, in particular in the Baltic states. The second explanation relates to the share of market nontradables in the CPI basket. Because market nontradables account for between 10% and 30% of the whole consumer basket (HICP in 2006), the full impact of productivity cannot be felt through the nontradable price channel on the inflation rate. Finally, it may also be possible that the transmission between productivity and nontradable prices is not perfect, i.e. that the impact of productivity is not passed fully on nontradable prices. This may be due to an incomplete relationship between productivity and real wages in the tradable sector, which results from an imperfect wage equalization process across the tradable and nontradable sectors, and finally, from a disproportionate link between wages and prices in the nontradable sector. In addition, large productivity gains in tradables are not necessarily spread evenly across manufacturing sectors. Overall, large productivity improvements may come from very specific sectors. The implications of this are twofold. First, very large productivity gains are unlikely to be fully passed on to wages. Second, the specific sectors may be not large enough to impact on wage developments in the whole economy, i.e. they fail to transmit wage increases to the rest of the economy.

N.3. The Prices of Regulated Services and Goods

The view that only market services are at the root of overall lower price levels in developing countries is not backed by data on nonmarket service prices. As depicted in Figure 3 below, the relative price level of nonmarket services (government and collective services) is very low in transition economies as compared to the euro area average.

Because regulated prices, mostly of nonmarket nontradables, are obviously influenced by (central or local) government interference, the reasons for lower price levels may be different for this segment than for market-based nontradables. While the wage argument may also partially apply here if there is perfect wage equalization across sectors in the economy, a more fundamental factor could be the disconnection between wages and prices in the public sector: price levels might be kept at an artificially low level for some time for political reasons. This was especially true for transition economies, where prices in sectors under the control of public authorities were frozen to compensate for very high inflation rates triggered by price deregulations in other parts of the economy during the early stages of the transition process.

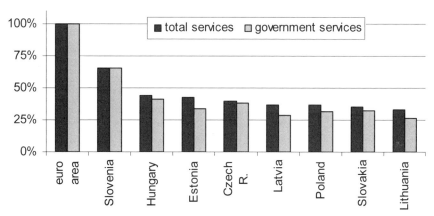

Source: Author's calculations based on data obtained from NEWCRONOS/EUROSTAT.

Fig. N3. Relative Price Level of Nonmarket Services (Euro Area=1, 2004)

Regulated prices are important not only for price levels but also for the evolution of the inflation rates. First, they represent an important portion of the CPI. Table 2 demonstrates this point and shows that the share of regulated prices may reach 27% in Central and Eastern European countries.

Table N2. Share of Regulated Prices in the CPI

	1995	2005
Czech Rep.	17,4	10,9
Estonia	18,0	26,7
Hungary	12,9	17,0
Latvia	16,6	14,3
Lithuania	NA	19,8*
Poland	12,0	1,2
Slovakia	21,8	19,9
Slovenia	22,5	16,7

*2004.
Sources: EBRD Transition Report, based on data reported in ÉGERT/HALPERN/
MacDONALD (2006).

Second, regulated prices are not only important for inflation developments on the grounds of their large share in the CPI but also because they exhibit a specific development over time. Figure 4, which plots year-on-year changes in regulated prices and in headline inflation, shows that changes in regulated prices are infrequent and large, hence jump-like, and changes may occur mostly after rather than before general elections for political considerations.

But perhaps more importantly, regulated prices recorded above-average growth rates over time in most of the transition economies. The explanation for these above-average changes can be traced back to the early days of the transition process. As already noted earlier, the prices of regulated services were kept unchanged while the prices of most goods and market services were freed during the early 1990s. It was possible to keep regulated prices unchanged during this period because the capital stock of the sectors falling under price regulation were inherited "for free" from the socialist regime, as ZAVOICO (1995) puts it. As a result, only operational costs had to be taken into account in the price-setting procedure. However, by the time the main storm of price liberalization was over, two factors had surfaced and had to be considered in setting the price of regulated items: a) capital maintenance costs, and b) the replacement of the capital stock at market prices. This came at the cost of large price increases, given that most of the sectors concerned are very capital intensive.

It is important to emphasize that changes in regulated services may not have any direct link to the Balassa-Samuelson effect even in the medium to long run because public interference in price-setting and the impact of an upgrading of the capital stock on prices may outweigh the effects of wage pressures coming from the tradable sector due to productivity gains in that sector.

234   Balázs Égert

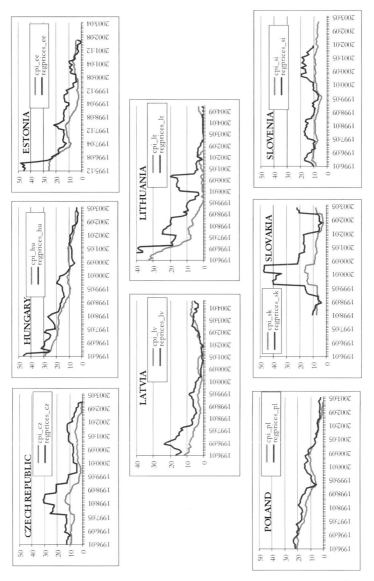

Source: National central banks, based on data reported in ÉGERT/HALPERN/
MacDONALD (2006).

Fig. N4. The Evolution of Regulated Prices (Year-on-Year Changes).

N.4. Residential Property Prices

Generally speaking, like the price of market-based and regulated nontradables, housing prices (in euro per square meter) are substantially lower in Central and Eastern Europe than in the old EU member states (see Figure 5).[2]

Nevertheless, the overall picture becomes a little bit more nuanced if regional differences within individual countries and compared to the European Union are taken into consideration. First, housing prices in capital cities are usually much higher than in the rest of the country. Typically, prices in Prague or Ljubljana are higher than prices in the countryside. Second, the old EU Member States also display a large amount of heterogeneity, with for instance France located at the higher end and Germany having much lower housing prices. As a result, housing prices in CEE capital cities are not far from levels observed in Berlin (Figure 5).

Source: Author's calculations based on data obtained from the European Council of Real Estate Professions.

Fig. N5. Relative Housing Prices (EUR/m2) in Central and Eastern European Capitals.

Housing prices recorded huge growth rates in some CEE economies, such as Bulgaria, Estonia and Lithuania, where year-on-year housing price inflation of close to 60% was not infrequent over the last five years or so. These large increases and the acceleration of the increases in some cases stands in contrasts with overall inflation developments in those economies, with CPI inflation moving from double-digit to low or intermediate single-digit levels.

Housing price inflation was substantially lower in Slovenia and exhibited high growth rates only periodically and decelerated to or even below headline inflation in Croatia, the Czech Republic, Hungary and Poland (Table 3).

---

[2] See OECD (2002) and PALACIN/SHELBURNE (2005) for a description of housing markets and ÉGERT/MIHALJEK (2006) for a detailed analysis of the factors driving house prices in Central and Eastern Europe.

The fact that housing prices have little influence on overall inflation rates is not very surprising if we bear in mind that the share of rents is negligible in the CPI in those economies and that the wealth effects of housing price rises remained largely unimportant in the absence of equity withdrawals from the housing markets.

Table N3. The Evolution of Housing Prices in Central and Eastern Europe

Annual growth rates in national currency units, 2000–2005	
Croatia – Zagreb	0.1
Croatia	0.5
Poland	1.4
Czech Rep.	8.4
Czech Rep. – Prague	11.6
Hungary – Budapest	12.6
Hungary	14.5
Slovenia – Ljubljana	14.1
Slovakia	15.4
Bulgaria	26.2
Lithuania	33.4
Lithuania – Vilnius	23.8
Estonia	55.9

Source: National central banks, data taken from ÉGERT/DUBRAVKO (2006).

In general, housing price developments are viewed as driven by changes in demand and supply conditions. The usual demand-side factors are income, the real interest rate on housing loans, financial wealth, demographic and labor market factors, such as the share of the labor force in total population or the unemployment rate and the expected rate of return on housing. Typical supply-side factors are the real costs of construction, including the price of land, wages and material costs. In particular, the price of land is closely related to the issue of economic concentration and agglomeration. For instance, GLAESER (1998) and QUIGLEY (1998) argue that the increase in concentration of economic activity at given locations leads to the scarceness of land in urban areas, which increases the price of land. Changes in the aforementioned factors, also termed fundamentals, cause housing prices to increase in a sustainable manner.

Against this background, it is useful to spell out the role of some special factors on the housing markets in Central and Eastern Europe.

1. Quality changes: A portion of house price increases may be due to higher construction costs resulting from a huge quality increase in the supply of new residential properties, which are not accounted for in housing price measures. A shift from low quality (low price) toward high quality (high price) housing suffices to produce an increase in overall housing prices even if the construction costs of a given quality do not change. Interestingly, there is scope for further housing price increases, given that the overall quality of the housing

stock in Central and Eastern Europe is still behind Western European standards measured, for instance, in terms of the share of dwellings with piped water and flush toilets as a share of total dwelling stock.

2. Wages: Another factor related to construction costs is the pace of change in wages in the construction sector. This may turn out to be another cost-push factor insofar as the catching-up process drives up wages in the productive sectors, yielding higher wages in construction if there is wage equalization and if productivity gains do not compensate for higher wages in the construction sector.

3. The price of land: The transition process goes hand in hand with the economic reorientation and restructuring of the post-communist countries. This has a clear effect on economic agglomeration. Economic activity tends to abandon regions forcefully industrialized under the communist regime and to move to the centers, i.e. to the capital cities, creating extra demand for land there and thus pushing prices up.

4. Housing price misalignments: Housing price developments can be disconnected from fundamentals, resulting in undershooting or overshooting periods. Initial undershooting and the adjustment from initially low levels to levels predicted by economic fundamentals may have played and may still play an important role in the CEE economies, since housing prices (and their relative prices to other goods and services) were substantially distorted during the early 1990s. Because the housing market was illiquid due to initially high owner occupancy ratios, it took some time to correct the initial undershooting.

More recently, there has been a nonnegligible risk of a housing price bubble developing in countries with extraordinary high house price increase. Transition economies may be particularly prone to housing price bubbles for three reasons. First, during periods of strong growth observed in these countries, economic agents may see future housing price developments excessively optimistically, which can trigger a self-reinforcing housing price bubble. Second, housing price booms can occur on the back of a credit boom, which in turn is caused by financial market liberalization, quite a feat of CEE. Finally, capital inflows related to external demand for domestic property can also feed into private agents' expectations regarding future housing price developments.

N.5. Market-Based Goods Prices

Figure 6 below indicates that goods prices are lower in CEE countries than in the euro area.[3] This observation discredits the view that large differences in relative price levels across countries are only attributable to differences in the price level of services. As a matter of fact, even perfect competition on the product markets

---

[3]   ROGERS (2002) was one of the first observers to note that the price level of tradables is very low in Central and Eastern Europe. However, he did not provide any possible causes of this observation.

cannot eliminate such large differences in goods prices as long as large differences in wages persist across countries. Wage differences matter on several grounds. First, people who earn lower wages buy fewer quality goods. Second, lower wages could incite international companies to set lower prices in poorer markets (pricing to market). Third, lower wages also influence final consumer prices via the local component of goods, such as the distribution sector. Finally, taxes might be used more extensively as a social policy instrument in richer than in poorer countries.

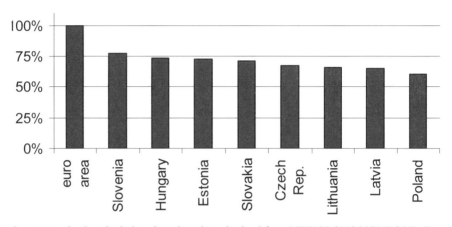

Source: Author's calculations based on data obtained from NEWCRONOS/ EUROSTAT.

Fig. N6. Relative Price Level of Goods (Euro Area=1, 2004).

N.5.1. The Quality of Goods

The prices of goods may differ if their quality does. Note that this could also apply for service pricesIt is a well observed phenomenon that poorer households consume lower-quality and thus lower-price goods than wealthier households. This can be thought of as a generalization of Engel's law, which puts forth than poorer household spend a higher proportion of their disposable budget on foods than richer households. Analogously, wealthier households tend to buy more branded quality and thus more expensive goods than poorer ones.

Quality differences are not taken into account in price level data, and, as a result, the institutions collecting price level data also frequently stress that the timely evolution of such data cannot be interpreted meaningfully as rates of inflation, given that the composition may change over time.

In fact, as households grow richer, they consume more higher quality goods, and this leads to a rise in the overall price level. At the same time, the shift in the composition of the consumed goods should not be reflected in inflation rates (or to a lower extent) given that the statistical offices endeavor to filter out quality changes and the composition effect from the inflation data.

N.5.2. Pricing-To-Market Practices

Price differences may be persistent even for homogeneous goods if producers set lower prices for the very same goods in countries with lower disposable income. The underlying motivation could be to attract more customers who otherwise would not buy the given good because of its high price. Lower prices can generate more sales, partially or even fully offsetting the price effect, and may garner a producer considerable market shares by the time a country has completed the catching-up process. Pricing to market may be encountered e.g. in the 2006 car price data of the European Commission. Figure 7 shows that the prices of small cars such as Ford Fiesta or Opel Corsa are between 10% to 20% lower in Central and Eastern Europe than in the euro area.

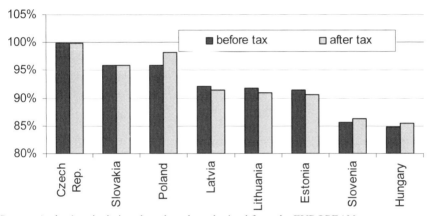

Source: Author's calculations based on data obtained from the EUROPEAN COMMISSION (DG COMPETITION).

Fig. N7. Relative Price Level of Small Cars (Euro Area=1, 2006).

N.5.3. Limited Tradability, Local Tastes and the Importance of Local Inputs

The price gap is most obvious for nondurable goods because this category often includes goods which are produced and consumed in the home country and which are not subject to international competition. Examples are fresh bakery and diary products. A number of nondurable goods are consumed only in the producer country. This prevents the possibility of cross-border arbitrage. As a result, the prices of these goods are determined in the domestic market. Since these goods are labor intensive, the general wage level is a major determinant of their price level. The price level of these goods will be lower in poorer countries than in richer countries, but as countries catch up economically, they will rise in line with overall wage level increases.

In general, a large number of goods are not pure tradables, given that they also contain local nontradable inputs (see e.g. ENGEL, 1999). Consequently, the price of such "composite" goods is to a varying extent driven by local factors. The distribution sector features prominently in this respect, as all final consumer goods have to be wholesaled and retailed to the final costumers. In particular, distribution costs can be decomposed into a) wage costs, b) rents, c) utilities such as water and electricity, d) marketing costs, and e) transportation costs related to the moving of goods to the shops. Clearly, the distribution cost of most of these goods is lower in low-wage economies than in high-wage countries. Yet, distribution costs tend to increase as real convergence progresses, unless they are offset by productivity gains in the distribution sector.

Productivity gains in the distribution sector were substantial in CEE, given the deep restructuring of the sector over the last decade. Most of Europe's established large hypermarket chains and discounters with a German background moved to the region, which brought about considerable efficiency gains. Remarkably, some of the transition economies are among the ones most densely covered by hypermarket and discount stores in Europe (exceptions are Bulgaria, Croatia, Romania and Slovenia). An interesting observation is that while all large European hypermarkets and discounters are fighting for market shares in Central Europe, the Baltic countries are dominated by Scandinavian retailers and home-grown champions.

N.5.4. Tax Systems

A widely recognized factor prohibiting price equalization across countries is the difference in indirect taxes. Nevertheless, this factor seems to have little impact on price differences, since standard VAT rates are fairly similar across the EU-25 (Figure 8) even though taxes may make a difference for specific goods, such as fuel for road transport (Figure 9). This is only a first rough observation given that other kinds of indirect taxes could also have an effect on prices.

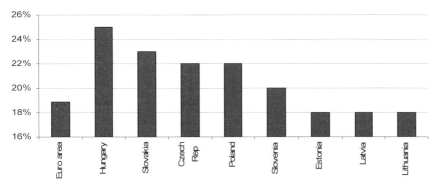

Note: Euro area average is the arithmetic average of the standard VAT rate of the 12 euro area members
Source: EUROPEAN COMMISSION.

Fig. N8. Standard Value Added Tax Rates in Europe, 2006.

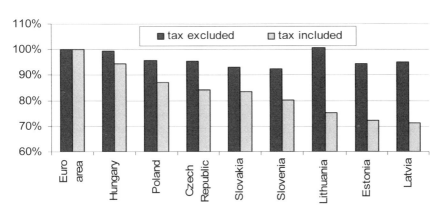

Note: Euro area average is the arithmetic average of the standard VAT rate of the 12 euro area members
Source: EUROPEAN COMMISSION.

Fig. N9. Relative Fuel (Super 95) Prices in 2006:S2 (Euro Area=1).

N.6. Inflation Differentials: Other Structural and Cyclical Factors

N.6.1. Economic Structures and Business Cycle Synchronization

Since the output gap is usually viewed as an important determinant of inflation rates (see e.g. LANE/HONOHEN, 2004 and ANGELONI/EHRMANN, 2004 for the euro area), one possible reason for diverging inflation rates can be sought in diverging output gaps and business cycles. Factor mobility, labor market flexibility, trade openness and similar economic structures are usually listed in the literature on optimal currency areas (OCAs) as promoting business cycle synchronization if the exchange rate is fixed.

In addition to the traditional OCA criteria, FRANKEL/ROSE (1998) shed some light on the important role of intraindustry trade in business cycle harmonization. They argue that more intraindustry trade leads to more business cycle synchronization, with the business cycle in one country affecting the business cycle of the trading partner. Furthermore, business cycle synchronization can occur endogenously because even though business cycles are not synchronized today, they will be synchronized in the future if the share of intraindustry trade in total trade is sufficiently high.

Numerous attempts have been made to determine the degree of business cycle synchronization between transition economies and the euro area. FIDRMUC/ KORHONEN (2006) analyze the results of 35 papers by means of metaanalysis and find that Hungary, Poland and Slovenia are the countries most synchronized with the euro area business cycle, while the Baltic countries, the Czech Republic and Slovakia are less correlated with the euro area business cycle. This is to be expected if the share of intraindustry trade in total trade is looked at: Hungary, Poland and Slovenia are the countries with the highest shares of intraindustry trade in total trade. Notwithstanding very high intraindustry trade, business cycle synchronization is low between the Czech Republic and euro area countries. Yet synchronization may happen in the future according to the endogeneity argument.

The implications of these observations are that diverging inflation rates between the Baltic states and the euro area may be a result of different positions in the business cycle, while a lack of business cycle synchronization is probably not causing large inflation differentials between the other countries and the euro area.

N.6.2. External Factors: Oil Prices and the Exchange Rate

Two external factors, namely oil price developments and exchange rate fluctuations, may manifest themselves in different inflation rates in CEE countries and in the euro area. Let us consider oil prices first. While differences in the price of fuel are mainly a result of different tax rates, as we have seen earlier, changes in oil prices corrected for tax adjustments may affect countries in an asymmetric way. Oil price increases can be passed on to consumer prices more easily under strong economic conditions. As a result, changes in the price of oil could affect inflation in a different manner if business cycles are not synchronized across countries. Moreover, CEE economies are still more energy intensive than their Western European counterparts, and they import more oil per GDP unit than the euro area average. The upshot of this is that changes in world market prices feed into oil prices more quickly in the CEE economies (and also because of the lower buffer role of taxes) and affect production prices more than in old EU Member States. Nonetheless, real convergence also implies a further convergence of economic structures and a fall in oil intensity, leading to more symmetric reactions to changes in oil prices.

Looking at the role of exchange rate fluctuations second, exchange rate pass-through could generate asymmetric responses in inflation rates for a number of obvious reasons. First, asymmetry exists between euro area and the CEE economies because the exchange rate matters much less for the euro area than for CEE countries with flexible rates. In particular, extra-euro area openness is much lower in the euro area than total trade in the CEE economies (except for those CEE countries with a currency board arrangement vis-à-vis the euro, like Bulgaria, Estonia and Lithuania). A second asymmetry, advocated by LANE/ HONOHEN (2004), concerns differences in the degree of overall openness rates across countries. Third, exchange rate movements could be larger for CEE economies than for the euro area. Individual economies face different changes in the exchange rate simply because they have different exchange rate arrangements (pegs, managed or free floating) and because the development of the economic factors affecting the exchange rate diverges across economies.

All things being equal, the size of the exchange rate pass-through can be different in the CEE economies and in the euro area. The literature scrutinizing the reasons for a different exchange rate pass-through identifies two factors, namely a) the macroeconomic environment: the exchange rate pass-through is lower in a low-inflation environment, and b) the composition of imports: the higher the share of differentiated goods (with a low pass-through) is, the lower the overall pass-through is. Evidently, these two factors may differ across countries. Yet economic catching-up would imply a move toward more differentiated imported goods in the CEE economies and a more uniform pass-through at some point in the future.

N.7. Conclusion

In this paper, we provided an overview of the most important structural and cyclical factors that determine price levels and that drive inflation rates in the eight new EU Member States of Central and Eastern Europe. We emphasized the role of structural factors other than the Balassa-Samuelson effect. Lower wages in Central and Eastern Europe not only influence market-based nontradable prices but also have an effect on the prices of goods and for housing. The general wage level matters for these prices. Wages matter for labor-intensive domestically produced and consumed goods and affect goods prices via wages in the wholesale and retail distribution sectors. Housing prices also incorporate wages as part of construction costs. But wages also matter for two additional reasons. First, multinational firms may set lower prices for poorer countries because of the higher price elasticity of demand for goods in poorer countries. Second, the level and evolution of wages are reflected in the composition of final household consumption. To the extent that households grow richer, they consume more goods of better quality, which leads to a rise in the overall price level. Richer households also demand higher housing quality. Hence, higher wages also mean an increase in the quality of residential property.

When comparing price level convergence and inflation differentials, it becomes evident that price level convergence is not necessarily reflected in higher inflation rates and that positive inflation differentials do not imply price level convergence. The first reason is the difference in weights applying to the GDP price level and the inflation rate. For instance, the GDP price levels contain a higher proportion of nontradables than the inflation basket (CPI or HICP) does. Hence, low Balassa-Samuelson effects in the inflation rates may go hand in hand with a fast catching-up of the price levels. A similar problem arises for housing prices. While changes in housing prices have a full impact on the price level in practice, their influence on the inflation rate transits through rents, the weight of which usually depends on the share of households renting their home. Second, quality changes are reflected in different price level and inflation developments. While quality changes are supposed to be mostly filtered out from inflation rates, they are not corrected for in the calculation of the price levels. Hence, increasing quality implies price level convergence without corresponding inflation rates. Finally, the exchange rate also has an asymmetric effect. If the exchange rate pass-through is incomplete, changes in the exchange rate will have little effect on the inflation rate, while they will lead to a change in the price level of the home country.

References

ANGELONI, I.; EHRMANN, M. (2004), Euro area inflation differentials. *ECB Working Paper* No. 388.

BACKÉ, P.; FIDRMUC, J.; REININGER, T. ; SCHARDAX, F. (2002), Price dynamics in Central and Eastern European EU accession countries. *Oesterreichische Nationalbank Working Paper* No. 61.

BALASSA, B. (1964), The Purchasing-Power-Parity Doctrine: A Reappraisal. *Journal of Political Economy* 72(6). 584–596.

BERGSTRAND, J. H. (1991), Structural determinants of real exchange rates and national price levels: Some empirical evidence. *American Economic Review* 81(1). 325–334.

BHAGWATI, J. (1984), Why are services cheaper in poor countries? *Economic Journal.* 94(374). 279–286.

ČIHÁK, M.; HOLUB, T. (2001), Convergence of relative prices and inflation in Central and Eastern Europe. *IMF Working Paper* No. 124.

ČIHÁK, M.; HOLUB, T. (2003), Price convergence to the EU: What do the 1999 ICP data tell us? *Czech National Bank Working Paper Series* No. 2.

ČIHÁK, M.; HOLUB, T. (2005), Price convergence in EU-accession countries: Evidence from the international comparison. *Economie Internationale.* 102(2). 59–82.

ÉGERT, B. ; MIHALJEK D. (2006), Determinants of house prices in Central and Eastern Europe. Oesterreichische Nationalbank. Mimeo.

ÉGERT, B.; HALPERN, L. ; MACDONALD, R. (2006), Equilibrium exchange rates in transition economies: Taking stock of the issues. *Journal of Economic Surveys.* 20(2), 253–324.

ENGEL, C. (1999) Accounting for US real exchange rate changes. *Journal of Political Economy,* 107(3). 507–538.

FIDRMUC, J.; KORHONEN, I. (2006), Meta-analysis of the business cycle correlation between the euro area and the CEECs. *Journal of Comparative Economics.* 34(3). 518–537.

FRANKEL, J. A.; ROSE A. K. (1998) The endogeneity of the optimum currency area criteria. *Economic Journal.* 108(449). 1009–1025.

GLAESER, E. L. (1998) Are Cities Dying, *Journal of Economic Perspectives.* 12(2). 139–160.

LANE, P.; HONOHAN, P. (2004), Exchange rates and inflation under EMU: an update. *CEPR Discussion Paper* No. 4583.

OECD. 2002. Housing finance in transition economies. Paris.

PALACIN, J.; SHELBURNE R. (2005), The private housing market in eastern Europe and the CIS. United Nations Economic Commission for Europe. *Economic Analysis Division Discussion paper* No. 6.

QUIGLEY, J. M. (1998), Urban diversity and economic growth. *Journal of Economic Perspectives.* 12(2). 127–138.

ROGERS, J. H. (2002) Monetary union, price level convergence and inflation: how close is Europe to the United States? Board of Governors of the Federal Reserve System. *International Finance Discussion Papers* No. 740.

SAMUELSON, P. (1964), Theoretical Notes on Trade Problems. *Review of Economics and Statistics* 46(2). 145–154.

ZAVOICO, B. (1995), A brief note on the inflationary process in transition economies. IMF. Mimeo.

O. On the Value and Need for Revising the Economic Policy Framework in the Union

Andrew Hughes Hallett

O.1. Introduction

If I had to pick the three problems that have caused the European Union the greatest problems over the past thirty years, I would pick the constitutional issue, enlargement and the problem of settling on a coherent economic policy framework. Many citizens miss an effective system of economic governance in the Union in its current form, and most would argue that this is of more direct relevance to them than adding extra layers to the governmental structures that they already have. What matters to them is the effectiveness and coherence of their economic policies; a clearer case for market and structural reforms that could be used to enhance those economic policies; and a more effective way of handling enlargement when the new member states are increasingly different from the existing members in their economic and social structures.

O.2. Background

My comments are mostly concerned with the framework for setting fiscal and monetary policies in the European Union, although I do consider the difficulties caused by how those policies interact with programmes of structural reform, with labour market deregulation efforts, and with the enlargement of the European Union.[1]

Second, I am concerned with the policy making framework as such rather than with the detail of how different policies might be constructed in particular circumstances. We use that framework to show how different policy institutions may be allowed to retain different priorities, and hence individual policies that are internally consistent, while also maintaining a degree of flexibility that allows them to deal with problems as they arise. At the same time, I recognise that policy makers need to remain independent of external influences and political pressures in particular, so that their policies remain consistent with the goals that they, or the public, have set for them.

The received position in the existing European policy framework is that the central bank should be independent of outside forces and political pressures, and that national fiscal policies should be left free to address the particular economic

---

[1] See HUGHES HALLETT/JENSEN (2004); HUGHES HALLETT et al. (2005); HUGHES HALLETT/WEYMARK (2006).

circumstances in each member state. The difficulty with this is that an independent monetary authority necessarily means an independent fiscal authority – which, in this European context, means a fiscal authority subject to political and electoral pressures.[2] That in turn means fiscal policy will increasingly cater for the preferences of local populations since monetary policy by definition (being common to all) cannot. In addition, fiscal policy will be increasingly called upon to reflect the population's legitimate interest in seeing that public money is spent on the goals that they themselves determine. In a democratic society, the electoral mechanism must be the driving force behind this. As a result, fiscal and monetary policies are likely to, if not conflict, at least blunt the impact of the other on their own assigned targets. That will lead to poor and possibly unstable outcomes. Indeed, that appears to be the story of the Stability and Growth Pact (SGP). In fact, the SGP was first put in to rule out such un-coordinated and undisciplined behaviour. But under popular pressure, it was violated widely as this argument suggests it would; and few counties now show any genuine commitment to adhering to it, even in the new and revised version.

Something has to happen in the general policy framework therefore. The answer seems obvious at a theoretical level. We need to reduce the encouragement to self-interest that is implied by the one-to-one, policy to target assignments in the current policy framework when there is no corresponding one-to-one separation of their effects within the economy. That suggests we need to find a way to create greater coordination (consistency) between the fiscal and monetary policy makers, without introducing the need for direct negotiations over the precise measures to be taken in any particular case that could compromise the independence of the policy makers to take whatever actions they regard as necessary.

One way to do that would be to provide a less than exclusive *intertemporal* assignment of policy goals to policy makers – in place of the one-to-one assignments (policy separations) within each period. The reason is that within period assignments mean that policies must compete to satisfy their own priorities at that particular moment, increasing the degree of conflict between them. Inevitably, each will end up offsetting the effects of the decisions of the other, in a vain attempt to reach their own goals, since they know they have no other opportunity to do so without a further conflict with their rival.

But if there is temporal separation, such as would happen if fiscal policies prioritise long term expenditure goals and monetary policy concentrates on cyclical stabilisation and inflation control, then there will be less conflict and each policy maker can start to take account of the existing or predicted stance of the other. There is also the threat that an undisciplined (or inappropriately selfish) move by one player will be punished by the subsequent actions of the other, and (more important) will be anticipated to be punished according to the preferences of the other. Yet each player gets their chance to implement their own preferred

---

[2]   With the implication that rational voters will drive governments to pusher harder for what they elect those governments to do, even if it conflicts with the policies pursued by the central bank (DEMERTZIS et al., 2004).

policies without direct opposition of the other. The implied process of action and threat of counteraction, a form of "negotiation over time", leads policies to an equilibrium in which the policies are better coordinated than they would be when the resolution is achieved through a straight-forward conflict. One convenient way to set this implicit negotiation process up is to impose a debt target on fiscal policy making. Being a stock not a flow, a debt target implies a significant carry over (persistence) from period to period, and therefore forces a temporal difference (a longer term view) on the fiscal planning of governments which will not be evident in the making of monetary policy. But there is no compromise on the independence of the central bank to make monetary policy as it sees fit. Similarly, there are no physical restrictions on fiscal policy makers to interfere with the legitimate priorities of the societies that elected them.

Fiscal-monetary interactions like these are just one example of where interactions between the impact of policies can change the outcomes you would expect from the analysis of the individual policies one by one – and hence change how you would use them from what may have appeared best when you analysed them as if they were separate. We touch on other examples here: the interaction between fiscal policy and the ability to carry out structural reforms; or between labour market policies and social security, or between labour market reform and supply side policies (R&D, competition policy etc.). This is an old theme, but I am giving it new European Union clothes as a suggestion for improving the policy making framework in Europe. Both TINBERGEN (1956) and COOPER (1968), in their contributions to the theory of economic policy, have stressed the difficulties that arise when policies cannot be coordinated properly and that the consequence of not doing so will be greater instability and a worse economic performance as each policy maker tries to cope with the unanticipated spillovers from the decisions of others, while also trying to get the best for his own targets in the current period. That means: larger deviations from target, more time spent away from target and a slower return to the target path. The framework outlined above allows for better coordination without any loss of independence for individual policy makers.

O.3. Structural Reforms

Structural reform is perhaps the leading economic policy issue in Europe today. Indeed, it is widely argued that structural reform is a prerequisite for a successful monetary union. Moreover, since the European economies appear to be less reformed and less flexible than their American and Asian counterparts, initiatives to restore economic performance vis-à-vis the US economy have been associated with the need for higher productivity, lower costs and more flexible labour markets in Europe. This argument formed the basis for the Lisbon Agenda.

Since structural reforms are widely regarded to have strong cross-country repercussions although they are treated as a matter of national responsibility. The question therefore arises as to whether a lack of co-ordination among supply-side policies is particularly wise. But it is not only within the domain of supply-side initiatives (such as R&D, skills and training, competition policy, etc.) that co-ordination may be insufficient. Within the more conventional demand-side policy framework, one may ask whether the monetary and fiscal policies of Europe are sufficiently co-ordinated with each other and with the reform agenda. This question seems particularly relevant in the light of the recent enlargement of the EU. It is also important to stress that it is not just co-ordination between countries that might be desirable, but also across different institutions of policy-making as well; e.g., between fiscal and monetary policy, between structural reforms and fiscal policy, or between labour market or social security institutions and fiscal policy.

O.4. Greater Internal Coordination

Co-ordination involves a negotiated policy bargain in which the outside option – the point to which the participants can threaten to return if negotiations break down – is a narrowly self-interested, uncoordinated solution. Bargaining power, the inverse of how much one would lose if the bargain broke down, will likely determine how much of each policy maker's private interests are satisfied in the final coordinated solution. To take place, and to command assent, these coordinated policies must be *incentive compatible*, i.e., offer some gains to each participant individually (rather than just on average) over the best that each could hope to achieve on their own.

Co-ordination will be at its most effective when the spillovers of policy between economies or onto non-assigned targets are strongest; or where one policy maker has comparative advantage for reaching the targets with one instrument, and another has comparative advantage with another. In the latter case, co-ordination brings gains because it allows the reallocation of policy effort to those with comparative advantage, even if that means less effort at home using the comparatively ineffective instrument. Co-ordination is most effective, therefore, when the economies are different (including different dynamics); or when the policy arenas in which the instruments are being used involve different transmission mechanisms, so that comparative advantages and policy effectiveness can be exploited more fully.

Harmonization is not the same as co-ordination. Indeed, harmonisation may not be helpful because it does not allow comparative advantage to be exploited correctly when countries are different in structures or policy responses. Indeed, it is entirely possible that harmonisation could lead governments to enact policies sufficiently far from what would be efficient for themselves that those policies become incentive incompatible compared to what those governments would have chosen for themselves. If that were to happen, the government or country in question would inevitably want to withdraw from the joint decision making regime. Only if countries are all the same, or the effectiveness of different instruments on each of the targets is roughly the same, will harmonisation look attractive. But that is also the case where co-ordination brings little benefit.

Hence, in Europe, to arrange coordination between policies operating in different policy arenas [for example, between monetary, fiscal, labour markets or structural reform policies nationally or Europe-wide] is likely to prove more effective and important than coordination between countries in any one of those arenas.

O.5. Monetary Policy

At present we have a monetary union covering about 70% of EU GDP, inflation targeting in the UK and Sweden (plus Poland, Slovakia, the Czech Republic and possibly Hungary among the new member countries) and either ERM-II or currency pegs elsewhere. Since a single monetary policy in the Eurozone is a form of co-ordination, and those outside are either effectively floating or are too small to influence the stability of the Euro, this arrangement would appear to be sustainable.

Hence, if there are problems with monetary policy, they will come from instability in the external value of the Euro; or from the asymmetric effects of a common monetary policy because different countries have different transition mechanisms and are at different phases of their cycle.

The first problem would perhaps call for better co-ordination with US policies and those in Asia. The second is really a matter of how well the asymmetric effects can be compensated for locally by suitably flexible fiscal policies or suitably flexible market adjustments. Therefore, they are better dealt with under the headings of fiscal policy and structural reform.

O.6. Fiscal Policy and the Stability Pact

The Stability and Growth Pact, introduced in 1997, has not been successful. It remains operative on paper – complete with its excessive deficit procedure, sanctions for violators and other enforcement procedures. But it remains ineffective in practice for at least two fundamental reasons.

The first is that it has proved to be unenforcable in practice. The Amsterdam treaty defines a country to have an excessive fiscal deficit if *both* that country's deficit exceeds 3% of its gross national product, *and* if the Council of Ministers meeting in Brussels judges it to have done so. In that context, the two most telling facts to emerge since the Stability Pact was introduced were: a) That deficits are to a large extent endogenous – which gives plenty of scope for arguing that a deficit is temporary, mis-measured or beyond one's control. And b) to get the Council of Ministers to declare a country to be in violation of the excessive deficit procedure involves "potential sinners sitting in judgement on current sinners" since the

Council will necessarily include representatives of the violating government. There is very little incentive for countries to vote to support an excessive deficit decision and sanctions when they may very well be the next in line and the current sinner is sitting right next to them (even if unable to vote on this occasion). Policy coalitions build up, and it appears that this was exactly the case when the European Commission referred France and Germany to the European Court of Justice in 2004 and lost because the Council of Ministers had declined to declare them to be in violation of the 3% deficit limit.

O.7. Does Enlargement Affect the Need for Coordination?

The short answer to this question is, no. There are three reasons. First, none of the enlargement countries has an economic performance that differs substantially from the existing Eurozone countries in a way that would be damaging. Growth is significantly faster, and inflation (but based on a significantly lower price level) a little above the Eurozone average in some of those economies – but not by enough, given the small size of the enlargement economies, to have any real influence on Europe-wide outcomes. Indeed, given the lower prices in those countries, Eastern enlargement and the expansion of trade will exert downward pressure on existing European price levels, while faster growth will (if anything) help expand growth in the rest of the EU. If there is a problem with enlargement, it will be that slowing growth rates and falling inflation rates will make it harder to restrain the growth in their fiscal deficits and public sector debt ratios (HUGHES HALLETT/LEWIS, 2006). But that is a problem for the accession countries, not for the EU.

The second reason why enlargement is unlikely to affect growth and fiscal stability in the EU is that the accession countries are all committed (as part of their accession treaties) to join the Euro, and hence to satisfy the Maastricht convergence criteria. Since the sanction of being kept out of the Eurozone has proved the most effective force for policy reform and convergence so far, and since the experience of Slovenia and Lithuania show that these criteria will be enforced in practice, one can expect these countries to converge on the Eurozone of their own free will.

The remaining question is whether these economies are likely behave differently after having joined the Eurozone, and whether it would matter if they did. The answer to that is they may continue to grow faster than average, and inflation and the fiscal balances could remain a little higher than the Euro average while price levels remain below. But it none of this would be a matter of concern to the remaining Eurozone, any more than it is in the case of Ireland who shares many of the same characteristics. These economies are simply too small: at present they amount to less than 5% of EU-GDP in total.

O.8. Fiscal Policy

The logic of these comments suggests the big issues for fiscal policy are:
- should fiscal policies be more closely coordinated between countries (towards a common fiscal policy: harmonization)?
- should fiscal policies, taken as a group, be better coordinated with monetary policies (inter-institutional co-ordination) across the union?
- should fiscal policies be restricted in order to prevent spillovers on others, or to prevent them undermining the ECB's inflation policies, or to prevent public debt becoming unsustainable when there is no national monetary policy to bail governments out? Or
- should fiscal policies become more flexible to cope with the asymmetric effects of a common monetary policy on economies with differing structures, or economies that are out of cycle with each other?

Evidently, the logic of a currency union suggests that harmonization is *not* appropriate. The need for extra flexibility at a national level could be supplied by greater wage and price flexibility in the markets of course, in which case fiscal flexibility is less important. That implies structural reform. Consequently, there is a need for inter-policy co-ordination between the two arenas, similar to that operating within the fiscal and monetary policies.

1. Debt Targeting: Many other possible solutions to the Stability Pact problem – setting debt targets (a debt rule), the golden rule (balancing the budget for non-investment expenditures only), using cyclically adjusted budget deficits, and substituting "soft" for "hard" targets – have been considered. These turned out to be nice ideas but too weak numerically to make any appreciable difference – debt targets excepted. Debt targets have the extra advantage of being a stock and not a flow. That implies a degree of persistence -- especially in those countries with high levels of public debt. Debt targets can therefore be used to good effect to pre-commit fiscal policies, all the more so in countries where fiscal policies have been lax in the past, to a path consistent with the expected stance of the independent monetary policy and hence to achieve the goals of sustainability and limited spillovers on others.

2. Fiscal Leadership: A natural way to precommit fiscal policy, to prevent excessive deficits or debt, in such a way that it can be combined with an independent monetary policy, but without any explicit negotiations that might bind or compromise that independence, is to make fiscal policy lead – in the sense of going first. It is easy to operationalise this suggestion by giving the fiscal authorities an explicit debt target so that we get a precommitment technology with a long term aim and a slowly moving target variable (debt being a stock rather than a flow). That particular mechanism could therefore provide a convenient solution since the fiscal authorities will be obliged to make their longer term plans first. Coordination would then follow because, once the monetary authority knows what the (now credible) long run path of fiscal policy is going to be, it is free to choose a monetary policy that "fits best"

in terms of achieving the Bank's objectves. Moreover, should the fiscal policies deviate from their chosen path, the monetary policies can adapt to counter-act or cut out any unwanted effects. That punishment threat, in the context of a strategic game, should be enough to persuade fiscal policy makers to stick to their previously announced path.

O.9. Labour Market Policies and Structural Reform

It is obvious that flexible labour markets, and the labour market policies which influence employment, wages or non-wage costs, are an important component of policy design in a currency union where transmissions and national economic structures differ. Since market flexibility has not been a feature of European markets, structural reforms will be needed to ensure that sufficient price and wage flexibility can be brought to bear. Hence market flexibility measures and structural reforms are a substitute for imperfect co-ordination elsewhere (especially when national fiscal policies lack flexibility and/or are constrained).

The trouble with structural reforms is that, once in the currency union, no country has much incentive to carry them out. Such reforms inevitably carry significant short run costs. They will increase unemployment in the short run while they are being carried out; and they may well require fiscal subsidies and transfer payments while that is happening, and because development grants, tax relief and retraining prog-rammes to induce the investment in new plant, equipment and skills are required for the reforms to take place. And that is before the policy makers face the special interests that will be damaged by the changes in market regulation, employment protection or social support arrangements. As a result, it is very likely that the short run costs will loom large, and make the policy makers/population reluctant to engage in any reform whatever the long run benefits (especially if those benefits seem uncertain or distant). Consequently, it will always be more attractive to persuade your neighbours undertake such reforms so that you can free ride on the rise in flexibility that they have introduced. If the partners do reform, you can benefit from the adjustments in their markets (to which you have unlimited access) without actually having to bear the cost of carrying out any reforms yourself. Thus, no country has any real incentive to carry out reforms or become more flexible that the others, unless the others are guaranteed to reform at the same time. This is a "Groucho Marx theorem": no country will want to be in a union that is less flexible than itself, and no country will want the other members to be as inflexible as it is.

Moreover, if this move to greater market flexibility is not to damage the welfare state, much of the cost of social security (financed to a large extent from payroll taxes and other contributions by employers) should be transferred to regular tax payers. If the burden of contributions is on employers, then their costs will increase and the flexibility of unit labour costs must fall. The key for employment, for example, will not be policies that expand the supply of labour or the level of demand. Instead, it will be policies that expand the demand for labour

within the existing configuration of policies. Hence, labour market policies need to be coordinated.

It is also worth pointing out that fiscal restrictions may conflict with structural reform. If it is true that reforms impose significant costs in the short run, then any risk that those costs might push a government's deficit up towards or beyond 3% of GDP, would cause that government to abandon its reform plans rather than risk being sanctioned for violating the Stability and Growth Pact. In other words, it will be important to be able to coordinate reform efforts and fiscal policies properly. The idea of an independent "sustainability council", which has been floated recently, would be a possible agency to monitor this kind of co-ordination. Principally in the fiscal area: all it would have to do is set debt targets, monitor progress, and make discrete statements to the financial press that so-and-so is likely to exceed what is safe so that they get penalised by risk premia in the markets. But such an agency could also monitor structural reforms, pointing out who is doing it right, who is backsliding or free riding on the others, and whose fiscal limits could be relaxed (and by how much) in order to help get the reforms done.

References

COOPER, R. (1969), Macroeconomic Adjustment in Interdependent Economies, *Quarterly Journal of Economics*, 83, 1–24.

DEMERTZIS, M.; HUGHES HALLETT, A.; VIEGI, N. (2004), An Independent Central Bank Faced with Elected Governments, *European Journal of Political Economy*, 20, 907–22.

HUGHES HALLETT, A.; JENSEN, S. E. H. (2004), On the Enlargement of Currency Unions: Incentives to Join and Incentives to Reform, in *European Macroeconomic Policies after Monetary Unification: Fiscal Policies, Monetary Policies and Labour Markets*, edited by R BEETSMA and others, Cambridge University Press, 2004.

HUGHES HALLETT, A.; JENSEN, S. E. H.; RICHTER, C. R. (2005), The European Economy at the Cross Roads: Structural Reforms, Fiscal Constraints, and the Lisbon Agenda, *Research in International Business and Finance*, 19, 229–50.

HUGHES HALLETT, A.; LEWIS, J, (2006), Debt, Deficits and the Entry of the New Accession Countries into the Euro, forthcoming in the *European Journal of Political Economy.*

HUGHES HALLETT, A; WEYMARK, D. (2006), Fiscal Leadership and Central Bank Design, to appear in *the Canadian Journal of Economics.*

TINBERGEN, J. (1956), *Economic Policy: Principles and Design*, North-Holland, Amsterdam.

P. An Alternative Route to Europe – An Alternative for Europe?

Christian Müller

P.1. Perspectives for Switzerland and the EU (A Pamphlet)

This note briefly describes the current degree of integration of Switzerland in the EU and argues that the reasons for it not becoming a full member any time soon may be at the heart of the current stagnation of the EU constitutional process. However, Swiss membership may come about under conditions that would promote the European idea in an alternative way, emphasising the role of democratic participation of its citizens and more federalism.

The Swiss electorate could be regarded as an electorate a standard EU government could only but dream of. It is generally positive about the EU objectives, its common market, and the four freedoms. The Swiss are fully aware of the economic benefits of the EU, both current and prospective, and they have manifested their support for Switzerland's EU policy in many general votes, approving among other things the free movement of labour within EU and Switzerland. This development, however, comes at the end of a long and winding road leading Switzerland to Europe.

In 1992, the Swiss electorate rejected the proposal to enter the European Economic Area (EEA). At that time, Switzerland had already been a member of the European Free Trade Agreement (EFTA), and it was anticipated that they consecutively join EEA as did some of the other EFTA members. The 50.3% of voters casting their NO ballot have not, however, been opposed to the European idea as such. Instead, they weighed the political implication of a membership against the economic benefits. The latter seemed not to exceed the costs of the former. Interestingly, what first appeared to be the end of a process really kicked things off. By 2004 more than a dozen bilateral treaties had been signed and later approved by the electorate on two occasions.[1] These treaties generate large benefits for Switzerland in that they provide access to a huge market helping to achieve the benefits of the division of labour as already promised by (SMITH, 1776 and RICARDO, 1817) and more recently argued by (GROSSMAN/ HELPMAN, 1991). The EU offers relatively cheap production factors including labour, ensuring low costs of production. Finally, the participation in the Schengen and Dublin treaties as well as harmonisation of technical standards provide public goods which can be supposed to generate endogenous growth dynamics (BRETSCHGER/STEGER, 2004). As of today major gaps with respect to

---

[1] A thorough account of the bilateral treaties is available in (KOBEL ROHR/MÜLLER, 2006).

economic integration remain only in the service sector, including banking and the trade of processed food. There are, however, shortcomings within the EU itself in this regard. As a result, Switzerland trades more than 62 percent of its exports and 81 percent of its imports with the EU. There is no other country in the world for which the Union plays a bigger role on that account. Moreover, due to the fact that the Swiss franc has been regarded a safe heaven for many investors, the interest rate level is on average one percentage point below the Euro (Deutsche Mark) rates, which provides a comfortable investment environment. Therefore, adding the bilateral treaties and the absence of the Euro, the alternative integration strategy can be deemed successful from the Swiss perspective.

Nevertheless, there are also significant drawbacks to this policy. Most importantly, Switzerland cannot participate in formulating and deciding on EU policy. Its bargaining power in future negotiations is probably even becoming ever lower. It is thus not difficult to imagine that future agreements will not easily become as attractive for Switzerland as the ones already achieved. On the other hand, since most agreements are static there will for sure be more need to negotiate in the years to come. A recurring question therefore is whether the alternative, Swiss way of integration is a promising route. The probably surprising answer to this question is yes. The reason for this answer dates back to 1992 and continued through to the 2005 defeat of the EU constitution at the French and Dutch polls.

As argued, the 1992 rejection of EEA membership cannot be seen as a rejection of the economic spirit of the EU. At its core is political reasoning instead. This is why the Swiss and the EU citizens have much more in common than is widely believed. They both long for an alternative to the current political, institutional design of the community. Looking back to 1992, three important factors contributed to the NO vote: first, Swiss neutrality; second, Swiss federalism; and finally, Swiss direct democracy. The first factor has meanwhile lost part of its importance due to the breakdown of communism, Swiss membership in the UN and its participation in military peace keeping missions. The second and the third reasons, however, are as significant as ever. Swiss federalism has a tradition dating back to 1291 when the first Swiss cantons joined forces. Until today the federal government has far less power than it has in virtually any other EU country. This fact is reflected for example in the fact that the federal budget is only half as large all the budgets of all the regions. On the other hand, despite Switzerland's four languages and despite its strong cantons, it has enjoyed a high degree of political and constitutional stability over the past 200 years. One of the main reasons why this is the case is very likely related to the third factor, direct democracy. Almost every law which passes the parliament (e.g., EEA membership) may be challenged by a group of voters. In addition, citizens may suggest an amendment to the constitution. Both will lead to a public vote on the issue under consideration. The effect is threefold. First, politics becomes comparatively pragmatic as every policy maker must take into account the possibility of finding himself in a minority position. Second, the electorate is supportive of the final decision as a sign of respect for the majority opinion. Finally, the Swiss electorate is very well informed about the issues at stake, politically active and articulate.[2] Taken together, this is why the Swiss electorate is an electorate many other EU governments desire. The 1992 NO thus foreshadowed the recent decline of the EU constitution proposal in that it confronted the political leaders with the fact that their voters had a different perspective for the future of Europe in mind. The tale of Switzerland's development in the aftermath of 1992 may consequently provide a hint as to how to proceed.

Prior to any further decision, the vision of the future Europe must be discussed by the EU citizens themselves that is. the very basis of political power. Such a discussion has to be open to a failure of the current proposal as that would provide the opportunity to move on. A useful means of achieving this is the imperative of a public vote on a constitution, for example, or on a set of agreements as an alternative way to "re-found", or, better, revitalise the EU. As in the Swiss case, a sideway of 12 years and more may in the end prove more beneficial than avoiding the dire prospect of not having reached the final objective within one's legislature. The EU member states' electorates certainly also want to maintain and emphasize the federal structure of the EU while joining forces whenever sensible. The example of Switzerland tells that more democracy by more direct participation is not an obstacle but a promoter of this aim. Therefore, more elements of direct democracy seem desirable, not in the least as they would also help to restrict the EU budget and the flood of regulations. On the other hand, Switzerland has more than 150 years of experience with a strong federalism, a highly diverse population and direct democracy. This experience helped Switzerland turn the initial weakness of not joining the EEA into a strength in the long run, as it appears stronger and internally more united than before in its European integration policy. Being a small country with such an exceptional history also means that it cannot simply be used as a blueprint. It can, however, serve as an encouragement to think beyond the prevailing structures. The next 50 years of EU dynamics should thus see the formation of a truly European vision that should adapt the principles of a genuinely subsidiary federalism and lively democratic participation of its citizens. In this manner, an alternative to the current EU can provide the missing link between yesterday's rejection of the EU constitution and the Europe we wish to live in tomorrow.

References

BRETSCHGER, L.; STEGER, T. (2004), The dynamics of economic integration: theory and policy, *International Economics and Economic Policy*, Vol. 1, 119 – 134.
GROSSMAN, G.M.; HELPMAN, E. (1991), The comparative advantage and long-run growth, American Economic Review, Vol. 80, 769–815.

---

[2] Interestingly, the federal government hardly ever loses in those referenda, the EEA decision being an exception.

KOBEL ROHR, R.; MÜLLER, C. (2006), A Swiss perspective on European integration, *Comparative Law Review,* Vol. 14, 67–88.

RICARDO, D. (1817), On the principles of political economy, and taxation, Düsseldorf: Verlag Wirtschaft Und Finanzen, 1988, facsimile of the 1st. edition London, 1817.

SMITH, A. (1776), An inquiry into the nature and causes of the wealth of nations, Mclean Virgina: Indypublish.com, 2002, 1st. edition London, 1776.

Q. Remarks on the Future Challenges of the European Union[1]

András Inotai

Q.1. Introduction

In recent years, many experts and politicians have started talking about a "crisis" in Europe. This view has been supported not only by the latest negative developments in the European Union represented by the refusal of the Constitutional Treaty both by the majority of the French and the Dutch citizens or the unholy and unproductive debate on the next financial framework covering the period between 2007 and 2013. Protracted sluggish growth in the key member countries, stubborn and high level unemployment, the lack of and unwillingness to reform as well as the emerging new protectionism in some member countries provide evidence which seems to strengthen the arguments and the general feeling of a "crisis." Moreover, the latest enlargement, the really historical development in Europe in the last decade, has also been assessed responsibility for the deadlock of the integration process, the new challenges and the declining importance of the European economy.

As an economist, I would not use the word "crisis" when trying to describe the current situation in Europe in general and in the European Union in particular. Namely, several key developments indicate that a process of restructuring in Europe and the EU is well under way, even if details cannot always be identified and, not less importantly, some of the changes do not fit into the status quo mentality of some Member States and are difficult to be digested or adjusted to by parts of the respective societies. Sooner or later, this restructuring will force political leaders, policy-makers and academic experts to redefine Europe's tasks and role both in its closer "domestic" environment and in the rapidly changing global setting.

Q.2. Lacking but Wanted: Identity, Vision and Leadership

Three issues have to be revisited and recreated: identity, vision and leadership. In none of these three areas can conventional values and thinking be helpful. The redefinition has to take into account the dramatic changes that happened and are

---

[1] Modified version of the lecture held in the framework of the Seventh Summer Seminar for Young Public Administrators from the Southeastern European countries, organized by the Economic Policy Institute, Sofia, Albena, June 01-05, 2006.

happening both in the continent and in its wider environment. In the second half of the 20th century, European identity became exclusive mainly for the new geopolitical reality. It was fundamentally based on the enlarging community of Western (later Southern and Northern) European countries but did not include the "other" part of the continent that – even in the most difficult times of its recent history – considered itself a part of Europe, not only in geographic but also in historical and cultural terms. With the fall of the iron curtain and the Berlin wall as well as a result of the unprecedented political and economic transformation started after 1989/1990, the exclusivity of European identity has been questioned and could not be sustained. However, the crystallization of a new identity based on the new realities of Europe did not make any quick progress. Certainly in some areas, Europe became more united. Political barriers were largely eliminated, visa-free travel for the citizens of most countries became a reality, and economic (re)integration as expressed in statistical figures on trade and capital flows developed rapidly. Even the qualitative jump of institutional integration occurred when the EU experienced the biggest enlargement in its history. The 2004 enlargement will soon be followed by the joining of two other countries in 2007. In addition, this process cannot be considered finished, since all Western Balkan countries have been given the concrete promise of European perspective (i.e., membership), and negotiations on accession with Turkey have officially started. Still, there is a marked and sometimes growing polarization in the public perception of the new European realities, many times fuelled by narrow-minded and irresponsible political demagogy. Evidently, Europe became more heterogeneous, not only as a result of the joining of new countries but also as a consequence of different national (and sub-regional) answers and attitudes towards external and European challenges. Heterogeneity, in itself, cannot be used as an excuse for why identity building cannot happen. The new European identity has to be built on new realities in a world that is not only characterized by globalization (homogenization) but, at the same time, indicates fresh and powerful tendencies of new, open regionalism. "European values", if they exist, must be identified, determined, constructed and implemented in this new framework. Needless to say, each European country can and has to contribute to this image-building process on equal footing. Any new (or old-fashioned) form of exclusion would be highly counterproductive and might threaten the security and stability of the continent.

Identity-building is closely connected with vision. There is interdependence between them, since identity helps formulate clear visions, the fulfillment of which is based on time-related concrete tasks and instruments of how objectives can be achieved. In turn, visions clarify identity and make it stronger and more deeply-rooted. Europe's goals must be determined in a longer perspective by taking into account both possibilities and limits, chances, and risks of European developments in the global context. In order to make full use of the European potential, in political, security, economic, social and cultural terms, the continent and the enlarging EU must not miss a vision on the "mission" of Europe in the world.

Although any European strategy must be based on the fundamental feeling of identity and shared visions, it can only be implemented if Europe has unquestionable leadership. Here, too, a mental and psychological breakthrough is required. Old patterns that may have worked adequately in the past, under different conditions, can no longer be used. New leadership has to be collective and inclusive, with the pioneering role of those countries, political groups and representatives of the wider society that not only share the key future-oriented goals of Europe but are also ready and able to work for it. In key strategic areas, leadership is likely to be composed of different countries and interest groups. This must not necessarily drive the EU into a more heterogeneous or fragmented situation, if two basic principles are observed. First, leadership must remain open to each Member State wishing to act for the implementation of shared objectives. Second, any rebuilding of past leadership patterns, based on the historically privileged position of some large countries (starting from the Vienna Congress in 1815 up to the French-German alliance in the last decades within the EU) must strictly be avoided. The new and viable leadership has to be based on those countries and interest groups seeking to build a dynamic, competitive, solidarian and future-oriented Europe.

Q.3. The New External Framework of European Integration

According to historical experience, the large majority of successful strategies that used to shape world and European developments were not only based on clear objectives (vision), adequate instruments and resolute leadership, but needed external pressures as well. In fact, the history of European integration witnesses three such basic building stones.

First, the European integration is a product of "benign" (but evident) US pressure and conditions after World War Two. In fact, US economic support of the reconstruction of (Western) Europe was linked to Franco-German reconciliation and the building of a Europe without wars. The economic potential of previous wars has been pooled from the very beginning between the Western European countries (Coal and Steel Community). The US considered successful economic reconstruction not only in the context of creating new markets for American companies in Europe but also in the light of emerging strong Communist movements in France and Italy.

Second, European integration had a visible and clearly identified enemy, the Soviet Union that, as an expansionary power with nuclear arsenal, was considered a threat to European stability. In addition, European integration had to provide protection against the spread of some Communist ideas that might have enjoyed wide support in parts of the Western European societies. Actually, the establishment of the social market economy cannot be separated from the competition of different economic and social models in Europe.

Finally, the generation creating the European integration was fully aware of the physical destruction and unique material and personal losses caused by consecutive wars in Europe. Based on personal experience and sufferings, this generation wanted to eradicate the roots of any open hostility in the (Western part of the) continent and considered integration the most convenient means of achieving sustainable peace and stability.

Examining the current situation, none of these factors are any more valid. The US pressure was replaced by trans-atlantic cooperation and competition, with a more assertive Europe in several global and bilateral issues but still characterized by a huge gap in the mentality and capacity to implement military power. The Soviet Union, together with the palpable threat of expansion no longer exists. Instability based on potential military interventions gave way to enhanced stability in large parts of the continent. At the same time, however, several power vacuums and black holes have also been created. They can represent a source of danger and insecurity but cannot be unambiguously linked to one dominant military power. Finally, for demographic reasons, the generation with its own memories of the world at war is slowly fading away. The new generation takes stability and (even relative) prosperity for granted and is not aware of the vital importance of peace and the extremely high price Europe had to pay for it over generations.

Of course, there are new external pressures which may be able to mobilize the forces acting in favour of European integration. However, they are of a different character and less easily identified and presented to the societa in order to shape public opinion in favour of further integration. To be sure, international terrorism is such a factor, but it is difficult to be detected; it does not have just one clear source, rather is spreading under the surface and is absolutely incalculable. (Despite its huge military power, the Soviet Union was much more "predictable.") Thus, the external threat is there, but its form of appearance cannot mobilize in the same way as anti-Communism could several decades ago. In addition, globalization can rightly be considered a major challenge to Europe(an integration). It would definitely need a clear and strong European answer, in political, economic and social terms alike. However, instead of uniting the European potential, it seems to generate different national answers, including a new wave of protectionism and national „economic patriotism".

These instruments are certainly not the adequate tools facing global challenges successfully. Even less are they able to strengthen future-oriented common European strategies. Finally, there is a "perception gap" rooted in the different experience of the new generation, most importantly in Western Europe but increasingly also in the Central, Eastern and Southeastern European countries, where their own experience with a divided Europe, economic shortcomings, low living standard and foreign domination should have remained more vivid in the memory of the elderly but to a large extent is still active part of societies. In this light, it is no surprise that the internal pressure to restructure the European integration is (still) stronger in the new (and future) Member States than in the "old" ones. There is, however, a real risk that further stagnation or slow and contradictory progress in European integration could also convert new members into status quo-oriented and mainly rent-seeking societies. This situation could result in two negative scenarios. On the one hand, Europe in general, and European integration in particular, would be deprived of the internal driving forces capable of shaping a competitive and forward-looking Europe. On the other hand, a new conflict potential could emerge if and when some of the old Member States wished to jump over their own shadow and take the future of Europe seriously in order to survive in the new global environment. However, they may meet substantial resistance by the new members which believe to be just accommodated under the protective shelter of integration and wish to reap the benefits of financial transfers that other member countries experiences for decades. In order to avoid such traps, the European integration requires fundamental reshaping despite the low level of open and manifest external pressures that are interpreted differently from country to country.

Q.4. Three Levels of Reform Pressure

In the early 21st century, the enlarged and enlarging Union faces different levels of reform pressure.

First, new challenges are reaching the EU from global developments to which the Union and its Member States have to adjust. Since the EU is a global economic actor, this adjustment is by far not one-sided. In fact, the EU can shape and is shaping global trends in several areas (trade and capital flows, trade and other external economy-related bilateral and multilateral agreements, aid policy, WTO negotiations, international environmental standards, etc.). Increasingly, however, the EU is not only imposing its rules on other countries but has to meet developments launched by other players. In this context, a fundamentally new phenomenon has to be mentioned, since it will decisively influence the future of Europe. For the first time since the early Middle Ages, Europe is no longer part of the global growth centre. For centuries, Europe, and different countries or geographic regions within the continent, were the undisputed engines of global growth. Italian cities, German banks, discoveries and colonization, and, finally, the English industrial revolution shaped the growth pattern of the continent (and of the world as it was known at that time). The growth centre had to be shared with the United States from the late 19th century on, but remained stable over almost one century. Large fluctuations due to two world wars have been ironed out either in negative terms by the big depression, or positively by surprisingly rapid and successful reconstruction in Europe. In the last decades of the 20th century, the world economy was managed by the triangle, in which Europe had its adequate place. In the last decade, however, the European economy ceased to be a major actor of global growth[2]. Most probably, for a longer time, and for the first time in several centuries, the international growth centre has shifted to Asia (and the

---

[2]   In this context, a clear difference has to be made between the low growth performance of the key EU economies and the partly very dynamic development of large multinational firms originating in the same countries.

Pacific). Thus, Europe has to redefine its role in the changing global situation and find its way to higher and sustainable growth (even without regaining a leading role as far as growth rates are concerned).

Second, successful adjustment to global challenges requires the urgent revision of traditional community-level policies (e.g., agriculture, budget, decision-making) and the development of new ones in critical areas of global competition (such as fiscal coordination, social policies, migration issues, common foreign and security policy). Key importance has to be given to the restructuring of the Western European "welfare model"[3] in order to find a new equilibrium between international competitiveness and social justice. Over the last several years, the Scandinavian countries have shown that there such possibilities exist by combining the liberal approach applied by the respective economic policies (less state intervention, more flexible labour markets) and the maintenance of adequate (although reformed) social protection. However, the Scandinavian system requires three clarifications. First, it was preceded by a huge economic (and social) crisis in the early nineties as could be seen in Sweden and Finland. Second, the key role of the State is by far not limited to the redistribution of growth based on social considerations. More and more, the State became an active agent of future-oriented development by concentrating centralized resources on research and development, education and health (all of them connected with the reproduction of human resources, the key element of current and future global competitiveness). Finally, the implementation of the "model" required a high level of solidarity among the Scandinavian societies, in which mutual support and overriding social considerations, including some sort of egalitarianism and social solidarity have a strong historical legacy.

Another key challenge comes from the demographic development of Europe. Declining native population in most countries, accompanied by accelerated ageing and the dramatic shift between active and inactive people (both for labour market and tax revenue reasons) push for a new development pattern for which migration policy, to be coordinated on the EU level, is of the utmost importance.

Third, no successful EU policies can be carried out without essential reforms in some of the key member countries (Germany, France, Italy). In fact, the geographical map of European growth reveals a strong difference between relatively rapidly growing small countries at the geographic periphery of the continent (including the new members) and sluggish economic growth in the geographic centre. Due to national differences in the volume of GDP, Europe can only stop its decline in world output and catch up to other countries and regions with higher growth, if the core countries can substantially enhance their growth performance. This, however, is dependent upon the speed and scope of

---

[3] It is a common mistake to think that (Western) Europe has just one social model, which is called the "European social model." In fact, there are at least three basic patterns, the Anglo-Saxon, the continental European (Rhineland model) and the Scandinavian one. In addition, the Mediterranean approach (similar to the continental European model) and the evolving Central-Eastern European pattern (likely to follow the continental model but without the necessary financial resources) have to be mentioned.

implementing far-reaching reforms. While there is widespread agreement that such reforms (mainly in the labour market, the regulatory environment of enterprises, research and development, education, social policies, etc.) are indispensable, the reform willingness and ability of the governments is modest (if available). Of no less importance, most societies are highly resistant to major changes and try to flee back to the increasingly illusory and hollow world of status quo, including social welfare and national protectionism.

Q.5. Selected Areas of Challenges and Policy Imperatives

This paper is not aimed at providing a detailed analysis of all areas to be reformed. Instead, it focuses on some key issues that are likely to be at the centre of public discussion and policy-making in the next decade.

Imbalance between the Economic and Political Weight of the EU

It is not difficult to draw the conclusion that the EU is a global economic actor, but it is hardly present in global politics (this role is, less and less efficiently, still played by selected Member States). The European history knows such imbalances – the case of the Federal Republic of Germany over decades being the latest – before the overcoming of political division of Europe. However, there is a fundamental difference between the two imbalances. For Germany, it was an externally imposed imbalance, since the country was deprived of developing a genuine foreign policy following its defeat in World War Two. In turn, most of its energy could be channeled into economic development. This imbalance could be partly overcome after reunification, although German foreign (and EU-level) policy still does not play the role many countries would like to see, experience and cooperate with. The European imbalance is not imposed by anyone in particular, but it represents a growing burden for the EU. If Europe wishes to remain a global economic actor, it must substantially upgrade its common foreign (and security) policy and become a more influential global player in the political context as well. If the current gap cannot be narrowed over the next several years, the EU is threatened by a loss in part of its global economic power. In order to pave the way toward positive developments, the EU is challenged in several policy areas (from foreign and security issues over migration to enlargement and budget).

The Dilemma of Deepening and Widening

Until the last round of enlargement, each widening of the European integration was preceded by a process of deepening. Such an approach ensured the development of integration even in the event of embracing new members with different or special interests and structures. In addition, the new community policies represented a further test of the adjustment capacity of the new countries. The first enlargement happened in the context of enforcing the common trade policy (starting in 1975), and the Mediterranean enlargement was accompanied by the launching of the internal market program (1985). A decade later, Austria,

Finland and Sweden joined a Union that was already well on the way to the Economic and Monetary Union and a common currency.

Surprisingly, the last enlargement bringing not less than ten countries into the EU, lacked such a deepening process. Just the opposite, even those areas that were expected to advance before enlargement (as a condition for preparing integration to be able to incorporate new members without serious internal conflicts) were not in a position to carry out the necessary reforms. In most cases, half-hearted initiatives could be observed that were further diluted in the process of decision-making and implementation (e.g., common agricultural policy, institutional reforms, budget). Programs such as giving the EU a new Constitution could not be considered as a step towards deepening, even if the French and Dutch referenda had been successful. Much more, the whole approach could be seen as a sidestep in order to do something when no fundamental policy area seemed to be able to carry out fundamental restructuring. The Lisbon strategy could have been more promising, but its initial record is modest and the open coordination method chosen for its implementation is hardly able to deepen the integration process, at least not in the first and critical years of an enlarged EU.

The most success at deepening the Union in light of the latest round of enlargement could have been expected by the quick establishment of the internal market in those critical areas for which liberalization became the hostage of the special interests of some Member States. Unfortunately, instead of experiencing a breakthrough, more and more anti-liberalization moves could be observed in the first two years of the EU-25. Nevertheless, it has to be stressed that the most critical element of the success of widening the EU is its capacity to deepen. This factor is at least as important as the excellent preparation of new members. Further enlargement(s) without simultaneous deepening in various fields of community policies produce(s) the real danger that European integration thereby remains blocked. Such a situation, however, would mean a slow, or more rapid but unstoppable, backward development of integration with more and more internal conflicts and the diluting of current and future community policies. This risk is all the more evident, because the dynamism of enlargement is further nourished by global and European political and security considerations, unclear EU policies, as well as (largely exaggerated) expectations of candidates. In turn, it is difficult to identify the driving forces of deepening, let alone the critical mass necessary for the relaunching of the European integration according to the new global and internal requirements. Thus, the obvious answer of the EU to the challenge of widening cannot be a longer "reflection period" (i.e., the closing of the doors to further enlargement) that would almost immediately generate social instability and serious security risks in selected European regions and countries. The only justified and viable strategy is the urgent acceleration of the process of deepening.

Coping with Shifting Internal Balances in the Enlarged EU

The 2004 enlargement has caused several shifts in the internal balance of the EU. Some of them have become immediately visible, others are expected to exert their impact in the medium or longer term. First, a geographic shift must be mentioned. All new members, with the exception of the Czech Republic, have become the new external border of the EU. At the same time, the previous external borders of Germany, Austria and Italy became internal borders which, with the enforcement of the Schengen agreement, will practically disappear from the map and from the mind of the citizens.

Second, the centre of economic growth clearly shifted towards the Northeast and the East of the "old" EU-15. Unfortunately, due to the modest economic weight of the new members, higher growth affects figures and prospects of the enlarged EU only marginally. However, its impact on structural change, new market opportunities and future EU policies may be more relevant. Moreover, if the new high growth region of the enlarged EU can sustain its current performance and continue with the catching up process to reach the income level of richer Western European countries, the region's weight in total EU performance, and accordingly its economic importance, will increase.

Third, the enlargement process had been accompanied for more than a decade by gradual shifts in trade and capital flows. As of today, the four new Central European members (Czech Republic, Hungary, Poland, Slovakia) export meaningfully more to Germany as their main trading partner than Germany purchases from France, its number one trading partner. Geographic reorientation was accompanied by relevant structural changes, mainly in exports but also in imports. In addition, international capital has not only discovered Central and partly Eastern and Southeastern Europe, but has developed production and service capacities narrowly incorporated into the global and European network of transnational companies. Western European firms have developed leading positions in new and some of the future Member States in key economic sectors such as banking and insurance, public utilities, telecommunications or selected business and personal services. This shift has not been the product of accession; it started much earlier and, most probably, accession has consolidated and further accelerated this process, with new trends and a modified economic map of Europe emerging in the next decade.

Lastly, enlargement dramatically changed the distribution pattern between "large" and "small" countries. Instead of a proportion of 10 to 5, the EU-25 contains 19 "small" and only 6 "large" countries. In addition, further enlargements are expected to bring new "small" countries into the Union (before Turkey's accession may realistically come on the enlargement agenda). This development has clear implications on the decision-making process, since small countries are regularly "overrepresented" in their voting share and the number of their seats in the European Parliament. However, one should not count on a strong alliance of small countries, since their interests, as those of the large countries as well, are rather differentiated. What can be realistically expected is a much more flexible building of tactical and strategic alliances and a more active role of smaller countries in a discussion on shaping the future of Europe. Certainly, special (traditional) alliances built on the leading role of some large countries will be even less accepted in the future. In turn, a relatively large number of small countries can be interested and become increasingly active in alliances to be constructed with one or more large countries in critical policy areas of the European integration.

Critical Issues of the Budget (Financial Framework)

After heated discussions, very different starting positions of the member countries, and substantial delay, the financial framework for the period between 2007 and 2013 has been approved both by the Council and the Parliament. In itself, the fact that a compromise could be found can be interpreted as a success of integration, or at least as a step that had prevented a major crisis. Still, there are few reasons to celebrate. On the one hand, the way the compromise was reached is reminiscent of more a narrow-minded horse-trading than a mutually acceptable balance of representing and implementing enlightened self-interests. On the other hand, major issues of restructuring the budget have been postponed.

However, it is well known that the future of the budget cannot be based on the same pillars and considerations as was the case in the past. First, the new budget, for which serious discussions will soon start, must replace the past-oriented structure with a future-oriented one. If Europe wishes to remain a global economic player and increase its global political influence, the budget has to reflect and support these objectives in an efficient and convenient way. Therefore, the structure must be dramatically changed, with a much lower role of financing the common agricultural policy. In turn, future-oriented activities, both economic and political ones, have to enjoy larger amounts of money. Second, the balance between financing competitiveness and solidarity (internal cohesion) must be revisited, and not only in the context of future members on (much) lower levels of income and with serious regional imbalances. Sustainable development and cross-border (really European) projects should be given priority. Third, the size of the budget (currently 1.045 per cent of GNI of the Member States) should not be determined on the basis of the payment willingness of the members but should be based on the identification of key objectives to be achieved on the European level. It is not the "offered" money that has to determine which and how many different objectives can be financed, rather clearly defined and shared European projects should present financial needs. Fourth, in order to achieve a breakthrough both in financing the budget and in its future structure, the system of resources for the EU must be based on a solid foundation. There have been several proposals for how a just and solidarian system of national contributions to the common budget can be created. However, there is no clear formula available at the moment, and important negotiations are forthcoming. Within this uncertain situation, the only clear issue is that the EU needs a new system for its own resources in order to finance future budgets.

Economic Policy Coordination and the Future of the Monetary Union

According to many experts, one of the few big success stories of the EU in the last decade was the introduction of the common currency. Without denying the importance of the monetary union in the context of European integration, it has to be noted that, to a large extent, its establishment can be traced back to a political compromise between Germany and France. France was ready to accept German unification at the price that Germany get rid of its strong and successful national currency and enter a monetary union with France and some other smaller, and more importantly, economically weaker and less stable countries. Moreover, the monetary union has not been accompanied by adequate fiscal policy harmonization, since the latter remained almost completely in the competence of the nation-states (and of the national parliaments, as national budgets are concerned). Moreover, the latter was unable to contribute to the stronger political cooperation within the EU despite expectations on the contrary at the moment of launching the idea of monetary union.

As a consequence, the few years of existence of the monetary union reveal an increasing differentiation process among Member States due to diverging developments in cross-country competitiveness. For example, German unit labour costs declined over the last several years by about 7 per cent in total, while Italian unit labour costs increased by more than 10 per cent. As a result, a cumulative competitiveness gap started to emerge, since no member country can change its relative competitive position by devaluation (as it used to be a traditional and also socially-supported instrument of "regaining" competitiveness in Italy and some other countries). It is unknown how long such gaps can be tolerated and, if not, what kind of national policy measures should be applied to restore the balance (e.g., longer working time, increases in productivity, new taxes, lower wages and wage-related costs). If, however, such instruments will not be consequently applied (to a large extent due to social opposition or the long time some instruments require to demonstrate positive impacts), the cohesion of the monetary union may be seriously challenged. In this situation, the introduction of a special compensation mechanism would be possible or even imperative. However, it would have a sizeable impact on the EU budget, in a volume that could hardly be compared to the rather modest "costs" enlargement(s). It seems not to be an exaggerated hypothesis that such a situation could become the real lacmus test of European integration and Member State commitment to the "European project."

This perspective should not remain unnoticed when the new member countries prepare to adapt the Euro. In this "race," the individual countries show substantive differences. Slovenia has successfully applied for membership an will be allowed to introduce the Euro in 2007. Two Baltic countries, Estonia and Lithuania, had the same plan but will have to wait at least one more year due to their inflation figures.[4] Other countries, particularly the larger Central European member states, are more cautious or are less prepared to enter the monetary union with the current state of their budget, structural policies or inflation rates. Certainly, they do not comply with all Maastricht criteria and have been subject to extremely tight examination.

It seems that the EU has selected this field in which it wants to apply the conditions of entry in a very strict sense. In principle, this approach may be

---

[4] While Estonia withdrew its application in April 2006, Lithuania sought to test the EU despite several warnings, leading eventually to its refusal. In both cases, the main stumbling stone was officially the inflation rate that surpassed the Maastricht level. In fact, the real reason was the rising trend of inflation, as an obvious consequence of fixed exchange rate systems with structural inefficiencies and rigidities as well as the high level of exposure to Russian energy price building.

justified on the basis of the Maastricht criteria, but it can hardly be accepted because of other reasons. First, the new member countries cannot be measured with the same standards, for they have to narrow the income and development gap that requires heavy investments in selected sectors of the economy (e.g., physical infrastructure). The Maastricht criteria were elaborated for countries that had already fulfilled these important tasks one or two decades earlier (otherwise also accompanied by huge budget deficits and heavy indebtedness). In addition, those relatively less developed countries that were involved in such developments (Spain, Portugal, Greece, Ireland) had got access to the Cohesion Fund that was created at the moment of launching the project of monetary integration in order to alleviate the development burdens of the national budget and facilitate its adjustment to the respective Maastricht indicator. Second, as of mid-2006, only three member countries fulfill all Maastricht criteria (Austria, Finland and Ireland), while the others fail to comply with one or more of them. Still, nobody talks about excluding them from the "club." Third, Lithuania's failure of getting access to the „Euro club" highlights a construction problem of the Maastricht criteria. Its membership depended on 0.1 percentage point of inflation difference (2.7 per cent as compared to 2.6 per cent of the Maastricht indicator). More interestingly, this Maastricht criteria is not calculated on the basis of the Eurozone countries, but it includes all EU members. In fact, two of the countries with the lowest level of national inflation that have shaped the average figure of 2.6 per cent (1.1 per cent of inflation plus 1.5 per cent of maximum divergence), do not belong to the Eurozone (Sweden and Poland). In sum, Lithuania was "disqualified" not as a result of the performance of the Eurozone it wanted to join, but on the basis of an indicator that includes all EU member countries.

Q.6. Concluding Remarks

At the beginning of the 21st century, European integration has reached a critical stage. Its further success, a key element of continental stability and sustainable growth, as well as an important factor of international security, fundamentally depends on its answers to global challenges, the capacity to deepen and extend community-level policies, finding a careful balance between deepening and widening as well as the capability, willingness and political courage of the key member countries to implement fundamental domestic reforms.

Blaming enlargement and/or globalization for the domestic problems of sluggish growth, high level of unemployment, social (and also ethnic) tensions and declining competitiveness are unproductive responses. Similarly, it is a mistaken approach to try to remedy deeply-rooted structural problems with old-fashioned, outdated and, more importantly, counterproductive instruments such as protectionism, blocking the liberalization of the internal market, trying to impose outdated "social welfare models" on more competitive members, supporting the idea and practice of "economic patriotism" or stopping the process of further enlargement of the Union.

However, it must be acknowledged that social support and public opinion are rather hostile to facing the most important problems of the European economy with a future-oriented attitude. Just the opposite arguments are spreading: narrow-minded nationalism, the strengthening of outdated or never-proved stereotypes, generation of (largely unjustified) fears and anxieties instead of mobilizing social support to a forward-looking, offensive and competitive strategy have been gaining ground in the last years, not without the "effective" but highly irresponsible and dangerous support of political demagogy and populism. Normal transactions among "old" Member States have been blocked several times, with poisoning effects not only for the liberalization of the internal market and the strategic decisions of companies, but also for the public opinion of the new member countries, which find themselves much more liberalized (and „dominated" by old member countries with clear nationalistic attitudes) at a (much) lower level of economic development, welfare and bargaining capacity. After half a century of European integration, European arguments and priorities hardly find their way in presenting the necessity of national reforms or in important decisions to be taken at the EU level.[5]

The growing disappointment of citizens from several Member States with the functioning of European integration is particularly harmful. This topic has a rich literature basis, thus only one recent experience will shortly be mentioned here. In the last months, mainly the Western European media as well as politicians began contending that the EU suffers from "enlargement fatigue," a good argument to stop not only further enlargement but to exclude new members from the "inner circle" of integration (e.g., different plans of "enhanced cooperation" and "integration at different speeds" interestingly put forward by countries and interest groups that hope to protect the status quo and have nothing or very little to do with the shaping of a forward-looking Europe based on the new realities as described in this study).

It must be stated unambiguously that the EU, in general, and some of its members, in particular, cannot be "captured" by "enlargement fatigue." First, the process of enlargement covered more than one decade, in which each country could prepare itself adequately (as most business circles did by benefiting largely from trade and capital liberalization, market-conform privatization and the like in the new Member States). Second, there is not the slightest evidence that the 2004 enlargement produced any problem in the normal functioning of integration. The

---

[5] For instance, the long discussion on the necessity of implementing several reforms in Germany was full of justified arguments for why reforms were inevitable. However, in no case has the argument been used that reforms in Germany (as well as in other Member States), as the most important economy within the EU-25, are imperative in order to spur economic growth in the EU. Similarly, in the decision-making process, all politicians look at their public opinion, short-term party-political interests and (re)election considerations instead of giving more attention and support to the European relevance of the outcome of the decisions. On the average, there are national elections every second month in the EU-25, and narrow-minded national approaches thus can easily and lastingly block any meaningful development of the integration process.

adjustment process of the new members has been running at a normal (almost unaverted) pace. Certainly, there were some deficiencies and delays or slow and inadequate interest implementation, but they did not affect the everyday life and activities of the integration. If problems were produced, they represented additional costs to new members only. Third, and based on the previous points, the issue of "enlargement fatigue" should urgently be clarified before it starts to contaminate the minds of broad sectors of (Western) European society. The real problem behind the erroneous (but rather comfortable) perception of „enlargement fatigue" is the unwillingness, unpreparedness or inability of selected (Western) European governments and societies to finally face the challenges of globalization and reconsider the basic pillars of their economic growth and competitiveness.[6]

For the Central, Eastern and Southeastern European countries it was self-evident, therefore never fundamentally discussed, that they wanted and still want to enter and participate in a forward-looking, future-oriented, competitive and solidarian European integration capable of remaining or becoming a global player both in economic and political terms. Optimistically, we can still assume this basic attitude has not changed radically. However, there are growing signs that status-quo mentality and rent seeking (although still at the initial and a much lower level than in many other "old" EU countries) are advancing. Protectionist, nationalistic ("patriotic") statements and actions as well as new efforts to constrain the activities of new Member States within the EU framework (also by neglecting their justified interests and, in some aspects, special situation) can certainly contribute to the fostering of similar attitudes also in the "new" part of the EU. If these trends become stronger and future-oriented mentality is replaced by short-term "national interest"-based protection and implementation, Europe's future is evidently bleak or at least highly uncertain.

A future-oriented breakthrough not only requires clear objectives and bold politicians (as on the eve of European integration). It definitely needs public support and societies with forward-looking mentality as well. At the moment, this seems to be the most important obstacle for implementing a positive trend at the turning point of modern European history. The large majority of the public, practically in most Member States, is not mentally prepared for the challenges of the 21st century. Since these challenges affect them each day, they are nevertheless forced to give an answer. As they do not have adequate answers – in conformity with the requirements of the 21st century as an involuntary, but deeply-rooted, reflex –, however, they look back to experiences gathered in the 19th century. This is a most dangerous path, the consequences of which Europe had to experience several times in the last century. To avoid this blind alley and to create a modern and competitive Europe is the common task and responsibility of all Member and would-be Member States and their citizens.

---

[6]   In this comparison, Western European business is very much ahead of most politicians and a large part of the public opinion (or already on a different qualitative track).

R. Applying a Comprehensive Neo-Schumpeterian Approach to Europe and Its Lisbon Agenda

Horst Hanusch and Andreas Pyka

R.1. Introduction

In March 2000, the EU Heads of States and Governments agreed on the so-called *Lisbon Agenda* to make the EU "the most competitive and dynamic knowledge-driven economy by 2010". This goal must be considered extremely challenging and extraordinarily difficult to be accomplished. From the point of view of economics, the following major issues have to be addressed:

1. First of all the decisive economic elements and forces responsible for the achievement of the agenda must be identified.
2. An adequate economic approach should be developed which explicitly includes these elements.
3. For the application of this theoretical approach on the empirical realm the right methodological concept must be found.
4. The fourth major issue is to apply this operationalization to Europe. A severe difficulty here stems from the fact that Europe is not a unity composed of homogenous components but a collection of heterogeneous countries. Accordingly, the method chosen should focus on detecting patterns of similarities and dissimilarities among the countries under investigation.
5. This discovery of patterns is a necessary step for a further analysis which focuses on the manifestation of success in the sense of the Lisbon Agenda and compares patterns of similarity with patterns of performance.

These five points also structure the content of our paper. In the first section we derive the economic substrate of the Lisbon agenda. It can be shown that the Lisbon Agenda is mainly based on innovation and the resulting future orientation. We then elaborate Comprehensive Neo-Schumpeterian Economics (CNSE) as an adequate theoretical framework suitable for the enforcement of the Lisbon agenda. In order to apply CNSE, we develop an indicator based 3-pillar model in the following section, composed of an industry, a financial and a public sector part. This 3-pillar concept is applied to 14 European countries encompassing the old member states of the EU (excluding Luxemburg); the new accession countries are not included.

We then focus on dissimilarities and similarities of the various economies and their pillars. This analysis allows for the detection of whether there is variety in the composition of the three pillars for the different countries or whether one finds a convergent structure of groups of countries especially in Europe. This allows us to get a first hint on the convergence and divergence of structures in geographic areas in Europe. This study is done by a cluster analysis.

After having discovered patterns for the pillars and having grouped the countries into clusters with similar pillars, we perform a ranking analysis within the cluster, i.e. only comparable countries are compared according to their pillar performance. This is done by a linear benchmarking program. Then as a crude representation of macro-economic success, the cluster composition is sorted by the average growth rates of the economies for the period from 1996 to 2000. This allows a first correlation of pillar composition and growth performance. In a final step, we stress the pattern dynamics by comparing the situation of the period 1996 to 2000 with the consecutive period 2001 to 2005. Our paper ends with some conclusions and the agenda for future research.

R.2. The Economic Substrate of the Lisbon Agenda

One of the most frequently cited statements of the famous Lisbon agenda claims that *Europe should become the most competitive and dynamic knowledge-based economic region in the world.* What does this mean in economic terms?

Today, economists widely agree that technological progress is the central determinant of growth and dynamics in modern economies. These dynamics are propelled by innovative activities in all parts and spheres of the economy and the society as the main driving force of change and development. Behind innovation understood as a process of unpredictable and discontinuous crowding out of established and appearance of new products, production technologies and organizational solutions, we most importantly find knowledge generation and diffusion processes. As a consequence, looking at the competitiveness of firms, regions, countries or even a union of countries, it is no longer price-competition which plays the central role, but the competition for innovation which really counts (SAVIOTTI/PYKA, 2007). Under this angle, the dynamics which are relevant and have to be observed include not only quantitative features of economic growth but also qualitative features of economic development and structural change. Obviously, dynamic processes understood and analyzed in this vein are fed by multiple sources which also mutually influence each other in a co-evolutionary way. These sources encompass actors like entrepreneurs, firms and households as well as financial actors as banks, venture capitalists and private equity firms. Public actors and institutions like governments, universities, schools, research institutes, patent offices and regulatory authorities also play a role.

Keeping in mind this comprehensive innovation-oriented view of the Lisbon Agenda, which economic approach might be suited for its enforcement?

R.3. Comprehensive Neo-Schumpeterian Economics

The Lisbon agenda formulates a strategy for keeping and even improving the competitiveness of the European Union. Therefore, its overall goal must be seen in securing the welfare for European citizens. Without doubt, economics is the science which focuses on economic welfare and the ability to increase it. This can be stated as a goal for all schools in economics, among the most important being the Neoclassical school, the Neo-Keynesian approach and Neo-Schumpeterian economics. But the angle of analysis differs sharply among these various approaches. Boiling down the Neoclassical approach to its essentials, it can be characterized by rational individuals acting on markets where the price mechanism is responsible for an efficient allocation of resources within a set of given constraints. Neo-Keynesian Economics, briefly characterized, turns out to be a demand-oriented macro approach based primarily on short term processes occurring in non-perfect markets. Accordingly, the knowledge-driven and the ensuing innovation-driven processes characterizing long run development are by far not central to both of these approaches.

One of the decisive differences of Neo-Schumpeterian Economics with respect to other approaches in economics can be found in its emphasis on different levels of economic analysis and their particular interrelatedness. Due to the dominance of the Neoclassical School in the 20th century, the approach of a micro foundation of macroeconomics has wide appeal. The aggregation from micro to macro becomes possible because of the idea of representative households and firms. Although this approach may seem convincing due to its analytical stringency, its mechanistic design may lead to difficulties when it comes to the analysis of dynamic phenomena endogenously caused by the economic system.

Neo-Schumpeterian economics, by contrast, seeks to get a grip on these dynamic phenomena of economic reality. In order to do this, important meso-level aspects between the micro and the macro level of economic analysis are considered (e.g. DOPFER/FOSTER/POTTS, 2004). It is the meso-level of an economic system in which the decisive structural and qualitative changes take place and can be observed.

To understand the processes driving the development at the meso-level, Neo-Schumpeterian economics puts a strong emphasis on knowledge, innovation and entrepreneurship at the micro-level. Innovation is identified as the major force propelling economic dynamics. In this emphasis on innovation, the major difference in the Neo-Schumpeterian approach with respect to alternative economic approaches can be identified. Generally, one may say that novelty (i.e., innovation) is the core principle underlying the Neo-Schumpeterian approach. Innovation competition takes the place of price competition as the coordination mechanism of interest. Of course, prices are also of significance, but concerning the driving forces of economic development, they are by far not central. Whereas prices are basic concerning the adjustment to limiting conditions, innovations are responsible for overcoming previous limiting conditions and – as in economic reality, everything has an end – setting new ones.

The focus on novelties is thus the most important distinctive mark of Neo-Schumpeterian economics. By its very nature, innovation, and in particular technological innovation, is the most visible form of novelty. Therefore, it is not very surprising that Neo-Schumpeterian economics today is most appealing in studies of innovation and learning behavior at the micro-level of an economy, in studies of innovation-driven industry dynamics at the meso-level, and in studies of innovation-determined growth and international competitiveness at the macro-level of the economy (e.g. HANUSCH/PYKA, 2007c).

To summarize, in Neo-Schumpeterian Economics the central actor under investigation are entrepreneurs and entrepreneurial firms, the most important process under investigation is innovation and the underlying knowledge creation and diffusion processes. Here, in sharp contrast to Neoclassical Economics, the notion of innovation focuses on the removal and overcoming of limiting constraints and the setting of new ones.

However, Neo-Schumpeterian Economics, in its present shape, restricts itself to the dynamics of the industry side only. Even with this shortcoming, Neo-Schumpeterian Economics seems to be the most adequate approach in tackling the enforcement of the Lisbon Agenda. Nevertheless, to fulfill its extreme challenges, namely to successfully hold ground in global innovation-oriented competition with the aim of enforce a development which makes *Europe to the most dynamic knowledge-based economic region in the world*, the Neo-Schumpeterian approach has to be put in a broader conceptual basis.

For this purpose, we suggest Comprehensive Neo-Schumpeterian Economics (CNSE) as elaborated in HANUSCH/PYKA (2007a). CNSE has to offer a consistent theory which encompasses all realms relevant to an improved understanding of economic processes involving change and development. This becomes even more pressing in cases in which the different realms are in close relation, mutually influencing each other, which is very likely the case for economic development. In other words, a comprehensive understanding of economic development must inevitably consider the *co-evolutionary* processes between the different economic domains.

Consequently, we argue that it is high time for Neo-Schumpeterian economics to devote considerable attention to the role of the financial and public sector with respect to economic development. In particular, we introduce the Comprehensive Neo-Schumpeterian approach as a theory composed of 3-pillars: one for the real side of an economy, one for the monetary side of an economy, and one for the public sector. Economic development then takes place in a co-evolutionary manner, pushed, hindered and even eliminated within these 3-pillars (figure 1).

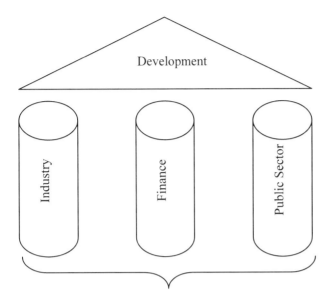

Orientation towards the Future: Uncertainty

Fig. R1. The Three Pillars of Comprehensive Neo-Schumpeterian Economics.

In order to understand the crucial co-evolutionary relationship, one must explore the bracket encompassing all 3-pillars, namely their orientation towards the future which introduces uncertainty into the analysis. The relationships between the 3-pillars drive or hinder the development of the whole economic system in a non-deterministic way. Consider, for example, the case of the financial sector, exaggerating the developments taking place in the real sector and leading to dangerous bubble effects which might cause a breakdown of the whole economy. Or think of the case in which the public sector cannot cope with the overall economic development, and areas such as infrastructure and education become the bottlenecks of system development.

A comprehensive Neo-Schumpeterian economic theory focusing on innovation driven qualitative development should offer theoretical concepts to analyze the various issues of all 3-pillars: industry dynamics, financial markets, and the public sector. Innovation and, as a consequence thereof, uncertainty, are ubiquitous phenomena characteristic of each of these pillars and are also intrinsically interrelated. An improved understanding of the development processes can only be expected when the co-evolutionary dimensions of the three pillars are taken into account. This is illustrated within the concept of a Neo-Schumpeterian corridor shown in figure 2.

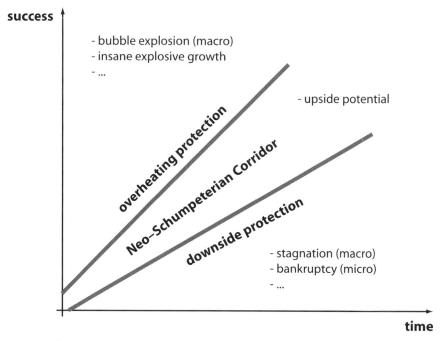

Fig. R2. The Neo-Schumpeterian Corridor.

In a CNSE-perspective, there exists only a narrow corridor for a prolific development of socio-economic systems. Profound Neo-Schumpeterian development takes place in a narrow corridor between the extremes of uncontrolled growth and exploding bubbles, on the one hand, and stationarity (i.e., zero growth and stagnancy) on the other hand. Economic policy in the sense of CNSE strives to keep the system in an upside potential including both overheating-protection (i.e., on the macro-level bubble explosions and on the micro-level insane explosive growth) and downside-protection, that is on the macro-level stagnation and on the micro-level bankruptcy.

To summarize: The essence of CNSE is captured by the following definition: CNSE deals with dynamic processes causing qualitative transformation of economies driven by the introduction of novelties in their various and multifaceted forms and the related co-evolutionary processes. These processes are not merely restricted to industry but also include the financial and public sphere of an economy and thereby encompass all spheres of economic and societal issues.

R.4. The Indicator Based 3-Pillar Approach

It is a central aim of this empirical study to gain new findings as regards the structural characteristics and the functioning as well as the competitiveness of economies in 14 highly developed countries belonging to the EU from a Neo-Schumpeterian angle.

R.4.1. Data

To achieve this objective, our analysis is grounded on a comprehensive set of indicators (HANUSCH/PYKA, 2007b). In total, more than sixty variables have been collected, reflecting many different activities in the various EU economies which are related to innovation. In dependence of data availability, the indicator sets comprise different years in the two periods investigated in this paper, 1996 to 2000 and 2001 to 2005.

Above all, the set of variables reflects structural specifics, yet the data are also comprise of several indicators for the functioning of the economies, including outputs of the innovation process such as patents or the commercialization of technology- and knowledge-intensive goods and services on international markets. To summarize, the data we draw upon must reflect all types of activities for the three pillars introduced above, immediately entailing the future-oriented characteristics.

The utilized indicators originate from various sources, the most important one being the OECD, especially its *Main Science and Technology Statistics*, its *Educational Database* and its *Patents Database*. From these three OECD databases, patent statistics, R&D expenditure data as well as several indicators of national education systems and of qualification structures of national workforces have been extracted. The main data sources are the World Economic Forum and the UN.

R.4.2. The Indicators for the 3-Pillars[1]

The crucial feature of the *industrial pillar* in a CNSE conception is its orientation towards the future. In order to comprise this dimension structurally as well as from a process perspective, the indicators we use for the industrial pillar encompass various patent information with a particular focus on knowledge intensive industries in order to cover the sectoral composition of the pillar (Biotech, ICT, knowledge-intensive services) as well as cooperation (co-patenting). Furthermore, international orientation is depicted by a couple of indicators such as FDI and foreign trade.

The *financial pillar* we emphasize examines its future orientation as well, which therefore must be expressed in the selection of indicators. A first set of indicators reflects the financing of innovative activities in particular venture capital involvement in the various stages (founding and expansion phase, VC availability) of the entrepreneurial innovation process. A second set of indicators covers the organizational dimension of financial markets (soundness of banks,

---

[1] A complete listing of all utilized data sources can be found in Appendix 1 and 2.

etc.) and their degree of sophistication. Finally, we include the difference between short- and long-term macro-economic interest rates to consider the transformation process between the monetary and real sphere of an economy.

The future orientation of the *public pillar* is divided into five groups of indicators covering public revenues and expenditures, the knowledge and information infrastructure, education and science as well as the institutional framework governing development. In addition to public expenditures on R&D, the expenditures for programmes of technology policy are covered by indicators (GOVERD, etc.) as well. Infrastructural information is contained in indicators describing, for example, the quality of internet access. Indicators describing the education sector encompass quantitative information (e.g., HERD) as well as qualitative information (e.g., class room size) stemming mainly from the OECD PISA study. The science sector is included by indicators like number of publications. Indicators concerning the framework conditions of development include such factors as an index of regulatory quality and political stability.

R.5. Pattern Detection: Similarities and Dissimilarities

By using the conceptual framework of our Comprehensive Neo-Schumpeterian Approach, the specific targets of the study are to detect and then to analyze cross-national (dis-)similarities in the structure and composition with the respect to the future orientation and innovativeness of the economies.[2]

To meet these objectives, cluster analysis techniques are applied to the data (see, e.g. JOBSON, 1992). The general rationale behind this analytical tool is to test a sample for the degree of structural commonalities between the units of analysis. Its outcome is a categorisation of the analyzed units so that the coherence of each group (or cluster) as well as the heterogeneity across different clusters is maximized. To determine the coherence of a certain cluster and to calculate the existing diversity of different clusters, distance values between the units of analysis need to be determined on the basis of the characteristics of each entity. From the various methods to calculate distances between the entities, the squared Euclidean distance measure is applied, because it is a frequently applied distance measure of metric data. Furthermore, it more strongly accounts for differences between entities than the linear Euclidean distance does.

Hence, the distance between two countries i and j can be calculated as follows:

$$d(i, j) = \sum_{k=1}^{m} (a_{ik} - a_{jk})^2$$

Here, a_{ik} represents the parameter value of characteristic $k=1,...,m$ for country $i=1,...,n$.

---

[2] A similar approach has been applied in BALZAT/PYKA (2006) in an analysis of national innovation systems.

Thus, the entire quantitative data matrix is $A = (a_{ik})_{m \times n}$

The determination of distances between entities is a crucial but at the same time preliminary step in the entire cluster analysis. It needs to be completed by the application of a classification algorithm. Depending on the quality of the underlying data and on the research target, various classification procedures exist.

The data are characterized by a relatively small number of units of analysis (i.e., fourteen countries in total) and at the same time by a relatively large number of variables (more than sixty variables in total) as well as by a cardinal data level.

Given these specifics of the underlying data and the country sample, a hierarchical, two-step cluster method (which rests upon the average-linkage principle of cluster membership) is applied to the sample.

The determination of the inter-cluster diversity between two classes K and L, $v(K, L)$, can thus be described formally as follows:

$$v(K, L) = \frac{1}{|K| \cdot |L|} \sum_{\substack{i \in K \\ j \in L}} d(i, j),$$

with both distinctive classes K and L (i.e. $K \neq L$) belonging to the entire classification **K**.

Since it is not intended to impose a given, pre-determined classification of countries ex ante, an agglomerative classification method is utilized. This method starts with single-country clusters and entails a step-wise concentration of countries according to their degree of structural similarities. Given that it is intended to attach all countries in the sample to a certain cluster and that cases in which a certain country belongs to several clusters shall be ruled out, the selected clustering method yields an exhaustive as well as a disjunctive classification. A classification is exhaustive

if $\qquad \bigcup_{K \in \mathbf{K}} K = N$,

with N being the total amount of analyzed objects. A disjunctive partition meets the condition that $K, L \in \mathbf{K}, K \neq L$, so that $K \cap L = \phi$.

The clustering method is applied to each pillar of the countries under study.

In order to determine the optimal number of clusters, the so-called elbow criterion (see HANUSCH/PYKA, 2006b) is applied. The elbow-criterion is a commonly employed measure in cluster analysis that guarantees intra-cluster homogeneity and at the same time inter-cluster heterogeneity. Countries grouped within one cluster show strong similarities concerning the future orientation of the different pillars, whereas countries allocated to different clusters are structurally heterogeneous in this respect.

R.6. Empirical Results

The following sections deal with the description of detected clusters, a ranking of countries within a single cluster as well as a correlation of cluster composition with macro-economic success approximated by average growth rates. The final section is about pattern dynamics between the periods 1996–2000 and 2001–2005.

R.6.1. Country Pillar Groups 1996–2000

In order to represent the country clusters graphically, the figures 3 a, b, c are organized as follows: The upper line includes the country codes (the meaning of the abbreviations for the different countries is explained in the appendix 3). The lower line includes the mapping of the countries to the various clusters which is expressed by numbers and colours.

	NL	UK	E	EL	P	DK	A	B	F	D	I	Fin	Ire	S
industrial	1	1	1	1	1	1	1	1	1	1	1	2	3	4

Core European industrial pillar group

Fig. R3.a. Country Clusters of the Industrial Pillar 2000.

A central result concerning the industrial pillar is a large cluster including 11 countries labelled as the *core European industrial pillar group*. This might be interpreted as a hint on strong structural similarities within European countries concerning the innovativeness and future orientation prevailing in the industrial sphere during this five year period. This result does not mean that the different countries are characterized by the same quantitative values, rather only the structural composition is similar. Not surprisingly, the tremendous catch-up process of the Finish industry in the 1990s leads to a single cluster solution which justifies stressing the particular role of the country often coined as the "Nokia-effect". The large engagement of foreign firms in production activities together with framework conditions supporting entrepreneurial activities in Ireland also leads to a single country cluster. This obviously corresponds to a widely used description of this country as the "Celtic Tiger". Finally, the industrial pillar of Sweden with respect to the core European cluster as well as the other single country clusters is different enough to form its own pillar group. As such, one might place a strong orientation towards knowledge-intensive industries (Biotech, ICT) in the Swedish economy at that time.

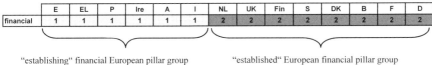

	E	EL	P	Ire	A	I	NL	UK	Fin	S	DK	B	F	D
financial	1	1	1	1	1	1	2	2	2	2	2	2	2	2

"establishing" financial European pillar group   "established" European financial pillar group

Fig. R3.b. Country Clusters of the Financial Pillar 2000.

Concerning the financial pillars, we find two clusters in Europe which surprisingly do not coincide with the Euro-zone. Due to the strong emphasis of the future orientation in our indicator-based model, a pattern instead emerges which might correspond to different development stages of national financial industries. Whereas one cluster labelled the "established European financial pillar group" includes the countries of the so-called "blue banana" in northern and central Europe, the other cluster labelled the "establishing financial European pillar group" encompasses mainly Mediterranean countries as well as Ireland and Austria. This might reflect a different orientation of the financial industries, with stronger emphasis towards traditional business and less knowledge intensive industries (agriculture, natural resources, etc.).

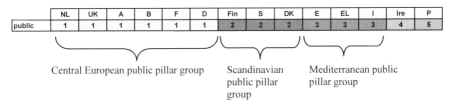

	NL	UK	A	B	F	D	Fin	S	DK	E	EL	I	Ire	P
public	1	1	1	1	1	1	2	2	2	3	3	3	4	5

Central European public pillar group   Scandinavian public pillar group   Mediterranean public pillar group

Fig. R3.c. Country Clusters of the Public Pillar 2000.

The pattern of clusters in public pillars shows this to be strongly geographically determined. We find three larger clusters, a central European, a Scandinavian and a Mediterranean public pillar group. For the group of Scandinavian countries, a common alignment in one cluster clearly follows the idea of the Scandinavian welfare state which shapes the design of the public sector even visible with regard to the future orientation. This holds particularly for the education and science sector and the importance which is attached to a highly developed public infrastructure.

Obviously different enough to the Scandinavian strong welfare-orientation, the clustering algorithm identifies a Central European public pillar group. Here the social responsibility of the public sector is also pronounced, but the particular public areas with a high future orientation (e.g., the education system and the knowledge infrastructure) seem to play a minor role.

Concerning the Mediterranean public pillar group encompassing Spain, Greece and Italy, the public sector has a different influence on economic life compared to the Scandinavian and Central European cluster. One can assume a less dominant role in the social domain as well as in the domains of futurity. Of particular note, the education and knowledge system as well as the future-oriented public infrastructure seems to be less important.

Ireland and surprisingly also Portugal form their own country clusters and are therefore identified as structurally different to the other three European clusters.

R.6.2. Similarity Patterns and Performance 1996–2000

The cluster analysis has generated pillar groups of countries which show strong structural similarities and which are sufficiently heterogeneous compared to other pillar groups. In the following section, we begin with an intra-cluster comparison by performing a ranking analysis of cluster performance. In the following section we compare the particular cluster composition of the various countries under study with their respective macro-economic performance referring to average growth rates of the years 1996 to 2000.

a) Pillar Performance Ranking 1996–2000

The ranking analysis is done by drawing on the indicators of the different pillars. In a first step, the empirical information of the single indicators is normalized between 0 and 1 in order to be linearly aggregated in a second step. The figures 4 a, b and c show the results of the rankings of the countries for the different clusters and pillars.

	NL	UK	E	EL	P	DK	A	B	F	D	I	Fin	Ire	S
industrial	1	1	1	1	1	1	1	1	1	1	1	2	3	4
ranking	4	5	9	11	8	3	7	1	6	2	10	1	1	1

Fig. R4.a. Country Rankings of Performance for the Industrial Pillars 2000.

	E	EL	P	Ire	A	I	NL	UK	Fin	S	DK	B	F	D
financial	1	1	1	1	1	1	2	2	2	2	2	2	2	2
ranking	3	6	2	1	5	4	1	2	3	5	9	8	7	4

Fig. R4.b. Country Rankings of Performance for the Financial Pillars 2000.

	NL	UK	A	B	F	D	Fin	S	DK	E	EL	I	Ire	P
public	1	1	1	1	1	1	2	2	2	3	3	3	4	5
ranking	1	3	5	4	6	2	1	2	3	2	1	3	1	1

Fig. R4.c. Country Rankings of Performance for the Public Pillars 2000.

The comparison of the country rankings in the various clusters and the 3-pillars leads to some revealing insights. For instance, Germany is ranked second in the large European industrial cluster, and also holds the second place in its public pillar cluster, the Central European public pillar group. However, the results concerning the financial pillar of the "established" European financial pillar group are comparatively bad; Germany ranked only fourth, which means that future orientation here is only moderately pronounced compared to countries like the Netherlands and the United Kingdom, ranked 1 and 2 respectively. From this, one can conclude that major bottlenecks for the development of the German economy with respect to other European economies in its clusters are rooted to a high degree in the composition of its financial pillar during the period under investigation (1996 to 2000).

A similar case is Denmark, which is ranked third in its industrial and public pillar groups, but holds only the ninth place in its financial pillar group. Also here, the financial pillar shows an underdeveloped orientation towards the future, restricting its developmental potentials.

An interesting example can also be seen in the UK, which is ranked third in its public pillar group and second in its financial pillar group. However, the strong trend towards de-industrialization since the 1980s is only partly compensated by the creation of a strong knowledge-intensive service industry. This has thus left its mark in the British industrial pillar, where the UK holds only the fifth rank in its group. Accordingly, our method suggests a relative weak future orientation of the British industry pillar compared to other European countries in its cluster.

In the large Central European clusters, the Netherlands is an impressing case: It holds first rank in their public and financial pillar clusters and is also third in its industrial pillar cluster. Accordingly, the Netherlands seems to be well prepared concerning the future orientation of its economy in the sense of CNSE.

The Italian economy gives an example in the other direction: Italy holds nearly the last rank in all its pillar clusters. It is ranked fourth in its financial pillar cluster, ranked as next to last in its industrial pillar cluster and last in its public pillar cluster. This clearly indicates that the Italian economy had serious deficiencies in its future orientation at this period in time.

So far, our results are restricted to the performance of the 3-pillars of countries in their different clusters. Although the advantage is that in this case only structurally similar and not heterogeneous countries are compared, the particular rankings tell nothing about coherent pillar compositions with respect to macro-economic success. This will be done in the next section.

b) Pillar Constellations and Growth Performance 1996–2000

In figure 5 the countries are ordered according to their macro-economic success approximated by the average growth rates of the years 1996 to 2000. To establish a relation to our concept of the *Neo-Schumpeterian Corridor*, we introduce four different growth classifications. They range from "very high" (vh) which means an average growth rate higher than 4 percent, to "high" (h) with an average growth rate between 3 and 4 percent, "medium" (m) with an average growth rate between 2 and 3 percent and "low" (l) with an average growth rate below 2 percent.

	Ire	Fin	P	E	NL	EL	S	UK	F	A	B	DK	I	D
public	4	2	6	3	1	3	2	1	1	1	1	2	3	1
financial	1	2	1	1	2	1	2	2	2	1	2	2	1	2
industrial	3	2	1	1	1	1	5	1	1	1	1	1	1	1
growth	vh	vh	h	h	h	h	h	h	m	m	m	m	l	l

Countries with hyperdynamics?   Countries within the Neo-Schumpeterian Corridor?   Countries dropped out of the Neo Schumpeterian Corridor?

Fig. R5. Growth Performance and Pillar Composition 2000.

Ireland and Finland are those countries with "very high" average growth rates. In this group one might ask the question whether the countries have left the Neo-Schumpeterian Corridor in the upper direction and run the risk of potential hyper dynamics. Interestingly, the pillar compositions of these three, with respect to their growth performance most successful, countries are completely different. A similar result also shows up for the other growth clusters with lower performance.

At the other end of the growth performance scale we find two countries, namely Italy and Germany. For these countries, one might ask the question whether they have left the Neo-Schumpeterian Corridor in downwards direction and find themselves in an area of stagnation. Again, a look at the pillar composition of these two countries shows that it is completely different.

The country groups with "medium" and "high" performance are integrated, and we suggest placing them within our Neo-Schumpeterian Corridor. Again, no specific pattern of pillar composition responsible for a specific growth performance can be detected.

This observation becomes even more puzzling, when countries with similar pillar compositions are compared according to their average growth rates as is shown in figure 6.

	NL	UK	F	B	D
public	1	1	1	1	1
financial	2	2	2	2	2
industrial	1	1	1	1	1
growth	h	h	m	m	l

Fig. R6. Similar Pillar Compositions and Varying Growth Rates.

Figure 6 displays five countries which in all 3-pillars are allocated in the same clusters. This means that there are pronounced structural similarities concerning their future orientation. In this case one would also expect comparable growth performances. However, a look at figure 6 shows that is not the case, but that almost every growth performance becomes possible.

A potential explanation for this surprising case might be found when the results of the intra-pillar-cluster-rankings are additionally considered. If countries with lower performances are ranked behind those with higher average growth rates, the reason behind our observation would be obvious. In order to see whether this is true, figure 7 displays the rankings of the five countries under consideration together with their average growth performances.

	NL	UK	F	B	D
public	1	3	6	4	2
financial	1	2	7	8	4
industrial	4	5	6	1	2
growth	h	h	m	m	l

Fig. R7. Growth Performance and Pillar Rankings.

Figure 7 illustrates that the relationship between the intra-cluster-ranking and growth performance is less trivial. This is strongly illustrated in the special case of France and Germany: Germany's growth performance is the worst in this group of five countries with similar pillar composition. However, within all pillars France is ranked behind Germany. Nevertheless, the growth rates of France are almost 1 percent above those of Germany within the observed time span. What might be an explanation for this unusual finding?

To give a first answer to this question, we refer again to our CNSE approach. Besides the design of the 3-pillars, an important dimension of economic development is constituted by the co-evolutionary relations between the 3-pillars. Accordingly, complementarities and harmonised relations between the different pillars are also an essential prerequisite for prosperous economic development. In the case of France and Germany, we can conclude that a further deficiency of the German economy has to be seen in an imbalanced relationship between the industrial, financial and the public sectors. Instead, France seems to be a case for which the disadvantages shown in the ranking analysis are compensated by a relatively higher degree of balance, harmony and integration between the 3-pillars. The higher consistency among the French pillars might have led to hidden co-evolutionary forces which are supportive and benevolent with respect to the macro-economic performance.

R.6.3. Pattern Dynamics: A Temporal Comparison of 1996 to 2000 and 2001 to 2005 Pillars

From the viewpoint of Comprehensive Neo-Schumpeterian Economics, it is obvious that the patterns of pillar future orientation are not stable but subject to change in the course of time. In order to detect these dynamics, we perform a similar cluster analysis as the one already described, using data from the period 2001 to 2005 and compare the results with those generated for the time span 1996 to 2000. Ideally one should use the identical structure of data stemming from the same data sources to avoid any artificial shifts in the cluster patterns. Due to data availability as well as irregularly published data we succeeded only partially and have approximately 90% coincidence with the data set used for the period 1996 to

2000. The remaining 10 % of the indicators were substituted by other information reflecting similar features concerning the future orientation of the underlying economies and their respective pillars. A complete list of the indicators can be found in the appendix 2.

- Industrial Pillar

For the industrial pillar between 2001 and 2005, we find the following clusters displayed in figure 8a:

	NL	UK	E	EL	P	DK	A	B	F	D	I	Fin	Ire	S
industrial	1	4	2	2	2	1	1	1	1	1	2	1	3	1

Fig. R8.a. Country Clusters of the Industrial Pillar 2005.

We see two larger clusters, a Mediterranean Cluster and a cluster comprising the Middle European as well as the Scandinavian countries. The industrial pillars of United Kingdom and Ireland are in a way exceptional, as they constitute their own single country clusters.

As we are most interested in cluster shifts between the two periods we compare patterns of 1996 to 2000 with 2001 to 2005 in figure 8b).

industrial	NL	UK	E	EL	P	DK	A	B	F	D	I	Fin	Ire	S
2000	1	1	1	1	1	1	1	1	1	1	1	2	3	4
2005	1	4	2	2	2	1	1	1	1	1	2	1	3	1

Fig. R8.b. Industrial Pillar Cluster Comparison 2000 and 2005.

Whereas in the early period the two Scandinavian countries Finland and Sweden were identified as different enough to create their own clusters, in the recent period a certain convergence with respect to the future orientation of the industrial pillars between these countries and the Middle European countries can be observed, as Sweden as well as Finland are now located in the large Middle-European group (cluster 1). However, besides this trend towards an assimilation of the industry pillars, divergent developments also took place. Most visibly, the Mediterranean economies no longer belong to the "core European industrial pillar group", but build rather their own group (cluster 2). The United Kingdom is also identified as different enough to now constitute its own cluster; it seems therefore that the de-industrialising trend already visible in the 2000 data still holds in 2005. Ireland is the only economy which in both periods is not allocated to other economies concerning its industrial pillar.

	D	Fin	S	DK	NL	A	F	B	I	E	EL	P	Ire	UK
industrial	1	1	1	1	1	1	1	1	2	2	2	2	3	4
ranking	1	2	3	4	5	6	7	8	1	2	3	4	1	1

Fig. R8.c. Country Rankings of Performance of the Industrial Pillars 2005.

Concerning the ranking within clusters of the industrial pillar in the period 2001–2005 (fig 8c) a not expected result is that Germany is ranked even ahead of Finland in first place within its cluster. These results may suggest that the future orientation within the German industrial pillar has grown in recent years and is much more present and vivid as is commonly expected. In particular, emerging sectors like biotechnology, renewable energies and nanotechnologies are already visible, even if, as we see below, the impact on the economic success measured by growth rates is not yet significant. For Finland, however, the often-cited "Nokia-effect" seems to have vanished in recent years.

Within the Mediterranean cluster, the future orientation of the Italian industry has improved and is clearly pronounced when compared to the other countries in this group.

- Financial Pillar

The next pillar under investigation between the period 2001 and 2005 is the financial pillar. In total we find three different clusters shown in figure 9a. One cluster is constituted mainly by economies outside the Euro-zone. The future orientation of the financial pillars of the United Kingdom, Denmark and Sweden shows similar developments which might be traced back to their own national currencies. Only Finland as a member of the Euro-zone is also included in this group. An explanation for the Finland case might be its geographical closeness and integration in Scandinavia.

The second large pillar group comprises all other European economies with the exception of Greece and Italy, which together constitute their own cluster.
Country clusters of financial pillars 2005.

	E	EL	P	Ire	A	I	NL	UK	Fin	S	DK	B	F	D
financial	1	3	1	1	1	3	1	2	2	2	2	1	1	1

Fig. R9.a. Growth Performance and Pillar Rankings.

What has changed between the two periods under consideration (see fig. 9b)? With respect to the earlier period where we find only two clusters labelled the "establishing financial European pillar group" and the "established financial European pillar group", the new pattern is rather different. The previous line of distinction no longer seems to be relevant. Whereas most of the economies previously belonging to the establishing financial pillar converge into the group of the established financial pillar, only Italy and Greece remain in a separate group. Furthermore, within the established financial pillar group, the future orientation of the Non-Euro-group together with Finland shows a divergent development justifying their classification in a cluster all their own.

financial	E	EL	P	Ire	A	I	NL	UK	Fin	S	DK	B	F	D
2000	1	1	1	1	1	1	2	2	2	2	2	2	2	2
2005	1	3	1	1	1	3	1	2	2	2	2	1	1	1

Fig. R9.b. Financial Pillar Cluster Comparison 2000 and 2005.

Within the Non-Euro financial pillar group, the United Kingdom and Sweden occupy the first two ranks (see fig. 9c). In the other cluster, the Netherlands keeps their leading position and the future orientation of the financial pillar in Germany again is ranked at lower levels. Worth mentioning is the considerable improvement of the ranking of France in this cluster; its financial pillar has moved from lower ranks towards the top group within this cluster.

	NL	F	Ire	B	D	A	E	P	S	UK	Fin	DK	EL	I
financial	1	1	1	1	1	1	1	1	2	2	2	2	3	3
ranking	1	2	3	4	5	6	7	8	1	2	3	4	1	2

Fig. R9.c. Country Rankings of Performance of the Financial Pillar 2005.

- Public Pillar

Finally, we look at the clusters of the public pillar of the European economies in the period from 2001 to 2005 displayed in figure 10a.

Here we find the most heterogeneous pattern: The large European economies – United Kingdom, France and Germany – make up one cluster, whereas the smaller economies – Denmark, the Netherlands, Belgium and Austria – are incorporated into another cluster. It seems as if the size of the economies influences the future orientation of the public pillar. A third larger cluster is composed of the Mediterranean countries with Italy, Spain, Portugal and Greece. The other three clusters are single country clusters including Finland, Ireland and Sweden.

	NL	A	B	DK	F	D	UK	Fin	E	EL	I	P	Ire	S
public	1	1	1	1	2	2	2	3	4	4	4	4	5	6

Fig. R10.a. Country Clusters of the Public Pillar 2005.

Also for the public pillar clusters the comparison between the different time periods is revealing (fig. 10b). Only the Mediterranean cluster is characterized by certain stability. In a way, the consistency of this cluster is even strengthened as Portugal has now joined the group of the other Mediterranean economies with respect to the future orientation of its public pillar. However, the other geographic consistency concerning the public pillar which we detected in the 2000 pattern, namely the clustering of the Scandinavian countries is no longer visible. Finland and Sweden constitute single country clusters, and the future orientation of Denmark's public pillar is identified as being similar to the one of the smaller European countries. Interestingly, the size effect visible in the pattern composition of 2001–2005 is not observable in the pattern of 2000.

public	NL	UK	A	B	F	D	Fin	S	DK	E	EL	I	Ire	P
2000	1	1	1	1	1	1	2	2	2	3	3	3	4	5
2005	1	2	1	1	2	2	3	6	1	4	4	4	5	4

Fig. R10.b. Public Pillar Cluster Comparison 2000 and 2005.

Concerning the ranking displayed in figure 10c, Denmark takes over the leading position in the group of smaller European countries, where its efforts with respect to a modern public sector design seem to be most advanced. Within the group of large European economies, the United Kingdom is in a leading position followed closely by Germany and by France on the last rank. Although the Mediterranean public pillar group is stable in its composition between the years observed, the ranking positions between the included countries is subject to considerable change. Greece fell from its leading position to last place, whereas the other countries slightly improved their positions.

	DK	NL	B	A	UK	D	F	Fin	E	I	P	EL	Ire	S
public	1	1	1	1	2	2	2	3	4	4	4	4	5	6
ranking	1	2	3	4	1	2	3	1	1	2	3	4	2	1

Fig. R10.c. Country Rankings of Performance of the Public Pillar 2005.

- Pillar Constellation and Growth Performance 2005

The period between 2001 and 2005 is characterized by a considerable slow down in economic growth compared to the previous five years. Again, no simple relationship between pillar composition and average growth rates can be postulated, as very different growth results appear with similar cluster compositions (see figure 11). Nevertheless, the following points seem to be obvious. Among the extraordinarily successful countries, only Ireland is still in the upper part of the Neo-Schumpeterian corridor with a very high average growth rate of about 6 % in the years under observation. Ireland shows a unique pillar composition, which might be the secret of its economic success. Greece is also characterized by a very high average growth rate. This is not too surprising, because we have seen already a high average growth rate in the previous period of our investigation. This also holds for Spain and its average high growth rates over the last 10 years. What might be an explanation for this extraordinary success? The particular pillar composition of these two countries might not be the one and only reason; two other countries, namely Italy and Portugal, are characterized by the same pillar composition but by low average growth rates in the last period. The growth success of Greece and Spain might be partly traced back to an effect which we would label *asset price inflation*, based on hyper-dynamics on the real estate markets.

	Ire	EL	E	UK	S	F	Fin	B	A	NL	DK	P	I	D
public	5	4	4	2	6	2	3	1	1	1	1	4	4	2
financial	1	3	1	2	2	1	2	1	1	1	2	1	3	1
industrial	3	2	2	4	1	1	1	1	1	1	1	2	2	1
growth	vh	vh	h	m	m	m	m	l	l	l	l	l	l	l

Fig. R11. Growth Performance and Pillar Composition 2005.

The cluster composition of Germany now resembles the particular composition of only France. Concerning average growth rates, France again is clearly ahead of Germany. Now, however, the ranking in the pillars have changed. Germany no longer holds better positions in all the pillars, but has lost the relative lead in its financial pillar where France has considerably improved its ranking. This again underscores our presumption that the most severe bottlenecks for the success of the German economy may be found in the future orientation of its financial pillar.

R.7. Conclusions

Innovativeness and orientation towards the future are central elements of the Lisbon Agenda. CSNE offers an appropriate theoretical approach for the enforcement of the Lisbon Agenda. Our cluster analysis demonstrates that from an empirical point of view, CNSE can be operationalized without major difficulties. It is central to maintain future orientation as a common feature of both the Lisbon Agenda and our 3-pillar approach. This target can be achieved by relying on a comprehensive set of indicators reflecting different activities related to innovation.

Of course, due to its composition of very heterogeneous member countries, Europe will not come up with a simple pattern of pillar compositions. Does this mean that each country needs a specific policy design to achieve the Lisbon strategy? Our results show that this is not the case. Instead similarities in the composition of the pillars as well as dissimilarities in their composition allows for a sorting of groups of countries. These groups of countries with similar pillar compositions can then be analyzed according to their performances in such areas as patenting, growth, employment in order to identify bottlenecks as well as catalysers of economic development. This has the advantage that only comparable countries are used for comparisons in the sense of benchmarks concerning their future orientation and innovativeness. This avoids a major problem of all international comparisons, namely neglecting the complex interdependencies and complementarities stemming from two sources: First, countries composed of very different pillars (e.g., the Swedish vs. the Greek public pillar) are not used for comparisons and for deviating policy conclusions. Second, within groups of countries with similar structures of pillars, one can analyze the joint functioning of the industrial, the public and the financial pillars. Besides the design of the 3-pillars, one can thus demonstrate that an important dimension of economic development is constituted by the co-evolutionary relations between the 3-pillars.

Our methodology of pattern detection allows for a fine-grained analysis of the composition of the main institutional and structural components of an economy (the 3-pillars: industry, finance and public sector) in the various countries with a particular orientation towards the future. The results show that there is no single and unique solution with respect to sound macro-economic growth and development; the same compositions of the 3-pillars allow for high as well as low growth rates. It seems that pillar performance within a cluster also influences macro-economic success; at least bottlenecks or weak points for growth can be identified. Furthermore, our methodology also highlights the importance of the interrelatedness between the 3-pillars. This concerns not only the composition but also the qualitative amalgamation of the 3-pillars at the organizational, institutional and political levels of an economy.

Finally, the patterns of pillar composition are not stable but subject to change over the course of time. In all of our three pillars we find considerable shifts. A general trend underlying the pattern dynamics is not observable. However, it seems that the size of the economies, in addition to their geographical locations, has become relevant as a major ordering principle in the recent past.

This empirical analysis of the capabilities of the EU countries in achieving the goals of the Lisbon Agenda allows for the design of a sound, well balanced and differentiated policy. This policy design, on the one hand, avoids being too general in the sense of neglecting the heterogeneity of countries in the European Union. On the other hand, it considerably reduces the complexity which stems from this heterogeneity by grouping countries with similar pillar compositions. This allows for a well-adapted design of policy measures according to the specificities of the various country groups identified in Europe and differing according to their innovativeness and future-orientation (i.e., their capabilities to achieve the goal of the Lisbon Agenda). The development of policy designs following CNSE is certainly on the agenda for future research.

Appendix R1: The Indicator-Based Pillar Model 2000

Industrial Pillar:
BERD (Business Expenditure on R&D) in percent of value added of industry, 2000
BERD, average 1991 to 2000
Indirect labour costs in Euros (reciprocal values), 2000
Number of researchers per 1,000 labour force, 2000
USPTO patents per million population, 1999
EPO patents per million population, 1999
R&D personnel per 1,000 labour force, 1999
Triadic patent families per million population, 1999
Percentage of patents with foreign co-inventors, 1995–1997
Students going abroad in percent of all students, 2001
FDI in percent of gross domestic capital formation, average 1997–1999
FDI inward stock in percent of GDP, 1999
FDI inflows in percent of global total FDI inflows, average share between 1996 and 2000
Share in total OECD high- and medium-high-technology exports, 2001
Growth of high- and medium-high-technology exports (based on the corresponding OECD classification), 1992–2001, average growth rate per annum
Number of patents in biotechnology per million population, 2001
Number of co-patents in biotechnology per million population, 2001
Number of firms in biotechnology-based industries, 2003
Number of ICT patents per million population, 2001.
Exports of services in percent of GDP, 2001
Imports of services percent of GDP, 2001
Employment in ICT sectors, in percent of total national employment, 2001
Balance of trade in communications equipment, 2001
Financial Pillar:
Soundness of banks, 2001
Sophistication of the national financial market, 2001

Average level of short-term interest rates 1997–2001
Average level of long-term interest rates 1997–2001
Local equity market access, 2001
VC investment (founding phase) in percent of GDP, 1995–1999
VC investment expansion phase in percent of GDP, 1995–1999
Perceived VC availability, 2001
Locals' access to foreign capital markets, 2001
Access of foreigners to the local capital market, 2001
Public Pillar:
GOVERD (Government Expenditure on R&D) in percent of GDP, 2000
GOVERD, average 1991 to 2000
GERD (Gross Domestic Expenditure on R&D) in percent of GDP, 2000
GERD, average 1991 to 2000
Tax burden for companies (corporate income tax, highest level, on non-distributed gains, reciprocal values), 2001
Tax burden for households (highest level of income tax, reciprocal values), 2001
Index of political stability, 2002
Index of regulatory quality (higher values indicating lower regulatory burden), 2002
Quality of internet access, broadband penetration rate, 2001
Number of personal computers per 100 inhabitants, 2001
Internet users per 100 inhabitants, 2001
Business internet penetration, number of internet hosts per 10,000 inhabitants, 2001
Number of secure internet servers per million inhabitants, July 2001
Employment rate of the population that has attained tertiary education and is aged 25–64, 1999
Perceived R&D subsidies, 2001
Perceived R&D tax credits, 2001
Tax treatment of R&D for large manufacturing firms, 1999–2000
Tax treatment of R&D for small manufacturing firms, 1999–2000
Number of scientific publications per million population, 1999
Percentage of scientific publications with a foreign co-author, 1995–1997
Percentage of the population of 25- to 34- year-olds that has attained tertiary education, average 1993–2000
Total expenditure on non-tertiary education in % of GDP as of 2000
Total expenditure on tertiary education in % of GDP, 2000
HERD in % of GDP, 2000
Teaching staff per 1,000 students in primary and secondary educational establishments, 2001
Graduation rates at PhD level, 2001
Total public expenditure on education, all educational levels combined, 2000
Change in expenditure on educational institutions (1995, 2002)

Appendix R2: The Indicator-Based Pillar Model 2005

Industrial Pillar:
BERD (Business Expenditure on R&D) in percent of value added of industry, 2003
BERD, average 1994 to 2003
Number of researchers per 1,000 labour force, 2003
USPTO patents per million population, 2001
EPO patents per million population, 2001
R&D personnel per 1,000 labour force, 2003
Triadic patent families per million population, 2003
FDI inward stock in percent of GDP, 2003
Share in total OECD high- and medium-high-technology exports, 2003
Growth of high- and medium-high-technology exports (based on the corresponding OECD classification), 1997–2002, average growth rate per annum
Number of patents in biotechnology per million population, 2003
Number of ICT patents per million population, 2002.
Exports of services in percent of GDP, 2004
Imports of services percent of GDP, 2004
Employment in ICT sectors, in percent of total national employment, 2004
Financial Pillar:
Soundness of banks, 2005
Sophistication of the national financial market, 2005
Average level of short-term interest rates 2001–2005
Average level of long-term interest rates 2001–2005
Local equity market access, 2003
VC investment (founding phase) in percent of GDP, 2001–2004
VC investment expansion phase in percent of GDP, 2001–2004
Perceived VC availability, 2003
Locals' access to foreign capital markets, 2003
Public Pillar:
GOVERD (Government Expenditure on R&D) in percent of GDP, 2003
GOVERD, average 1994 to 2003
GERD (Gross Domestic Expenditure on R&D) in percent of GDP, 2003
GERD, average 1994 to 2003
Tax burden for companies (corporate income tax, highest level, on non-distributed gains, reciprocal values), 2005
Tax burden for households (highest level of income tax, reciprocal values), 2005
Index of political stability, 2002
Index of regulatory quality (higher values indicating lower regulatory burden), 2002
Quality of internet access, broadband penetration rate, 2004
Number of personal computers per 100 inhabitants, 2004
Internet users per 100 inhabitants, 2004

Employment rate of the population that has attained tertiary education and is aged 25–64, 2003
Perceived R&D subsidies, 2004
Perceived R&D tax credits, 2004
Tax treatment of R&D for large manufacturing firms, 2000–2004
Tax treatment of R&D for small manufacturing firms, 2000–2004
Number of scientific publications per million population, 2003
Percentage of the population of 25- to 34- year-olds that has attained tertiary education, 2003
Total expenditure on non-tertiary education in % of GDP as of 2003
HERD in % of GDP, 2003
Total public expenditure on education, all educational levels combined, 2003

Appendix R3: Country Abbreviations

A   Austria
B   Belgium
D   Germany
DK   Denmark
E   Spain
EL   Greece
F   France
FIN   Finland
I   Italy
IRE   Ireland
NL   the Netherlands
P   Portugal
S   Sweden
UK   United Kingdom

References

BALZAT, M.; PYKA, A. (2006), Mapping National Innovation Systems in the OECD Area, *International Journal of Technology and Globalisation*, Vol. 2, Nos. 1/2 2006, 158–176.
DOPFER, K.; FOSTER, J.; POTTS, J. (2004), Micro-meso-macro, *Journal of Evolutionary Economics*, Vol. 14, 263–279.
HANUSCH, H.; PYKA, A. (2007a), The Principles of Neo-Schumpeterian Economics, *Cambridge Journal of Economics*, Vol. 31 (forthcoming).
HANUSCH, H.; PYKA, A, (2007b), The Troika of Economic Growth and Development – Applying a Comprehensive Neo-Schumpeterian Approach to OECD countries, *Galileu Revista de Economia e Direito*, Vol. XII, 2007 (forthcoming).

HANUSCH, H.; PYKA, A. (2007c) (eds.), The Elgar Companion to Neo-Schumpeterian Economics, Cheltenham UK: Edward Elgar Publishers (forthcoming March 2007).

JOBSON, J.D. (1992), Applied Multivariate Data Analysis: Volume II: Categorical and Multivariate Methods, New York, Berlin, Heidelberg: Springer.

SAVIOTTI, P.P.; PYKA, A. (2007), Product Variety, Competition and Economic Growth, *Journal of Evolutionary Economics*, Vol. 17 (forthcoming)

S. Ageing and Economic Growth in Europe Assessing the Impact of Systemic Pension Reforms

Werner Roeger[*]

S.1. Introduction

The expected declining population of working age and the increase in the dependency ratio in Europe is likely to have serious consequences for the growth of per capita income in the next decades. The macroeconomic consequence of demographic pressure is exacerbated by a PAYG pension system, which currently is the dominant source of intergenerational income transfer in the EU. Currently ten workers finance two and a half retirees, in 2050, ten workers will have to finance five retirees with their pension contributions. This has serious consequences for wage costs in coming decades if no reforms are undertaken. As shown previously, leaving the generosity of the PAYG system unaffected would require an increase in pension contribution rates from currently about 16% to about 27%[1] in 2050, taken as given the demographic trends currently projected for the EU. Given the still high levels of unemployment in the EU and the fact that non wage labour costs are partly blamed for low employment rates in Europe, letting the current pension system in place does not seem to be an attractive policy option since it drags down the employment rate. There are two radically alternative fiscal strategies of financing additional pension expenditures if one wants to avoid ever increasing pension contributions. A first alternative could be seen in a switch to debt financing of additional ageing related pension expenditure requirements and freezing the replacement rate at current levels. An alternative strategy would be to partially move to a funded system, with a government guarantee of accrued pension rights for current pensioners and certain well defined age cohorts within the pool of current workers. It will be assumed that the transition costs are financed via an increase in government debt.

Obviously, the first option is not a true long run solution but rather a strategy of postponing reforms, since it will eventually lead to exploding debt levels. Nevertheless it is interesting to show the debt dynamics implied by that strategy and the implied macroeconomic effects. The second option would certainly be preferable from a debt sustainability point of view, however, the short to medium

[*] European Commission, DG ECFIN/Research Directorate.
I am grateful to Volker Clausen for very helpful comments. The views expressed in this paper are those of the author and not necessarily those of the European Commission.
[1] See, The EU Economy Review 2001 Review, Reforms of Pension Systems in the EU – An Analysis of the Policy Options, pp. 171-222.

term budgetary costs, in terms of deficits, are likely to be larger, because of immediate and large transition costs due to a fraction of accrued pension rights guaranteed by the government. However, unlike with the first option, the transition costs would be temporary. The duration would be limited by the age cohorts who are chosen to be eligible for government transfers. Nevertheless, given the voting power of age cohorts older than 40 years in Europe, it is likely that any transition to a funded system in Europe would be accompanied by a fairly generous compensation of current retirees and older workers.

This paper compares these two stylised strategies to each other and to a baseline PAYG scenario where the current generosity of the pension system is retained, financed by increasing pension contributions. In particular it asks the following questions. What are the macroeconomic and fiscal consequences of retaining the generosity of the present PAYG system? What would be the macroeconomic impact of the two strategies for stabilising social security contributions? And what would be the level of debt the EU would end up in 2050 under the two alternative strategies?

The quantitative analysis is conducted with a five region version of the 'QUEST model', where we distinguish between EU15, US, Japan and the rest of the World divided into fast and slow ageing regions (FA, SA). We regard the international dimension as useful since ageing and pension reforms are generally associated with changes in national savings and have implications for international capital flows. This model is an extension of DG ECFINs macro model, allowing for a disaggregated household sector, split into worker and pensioner households along the lines suggested by GERTLER (1999). The paper is structured as follows. Section 2 presents the model, followed by a section discussing the calibration of the most crucial structural parameters. Section 4 presents standard simulations on debt and pension reforms in order to show the basic magnitudes of crucial multipliers in the model. Section 5 compares the alternative scenarios to each other and the paper ends with some concluding remarks.

S.2. The Model

An identical good is produced in each region with a constant returns to scale production function. The technology in each region is identical up to the level of TFP. We allow for capital mobility across regions but restrict international migration to zero. In order to allow for demographic effects on savings within a life cycle framework and at the same time keep the model tractable we distinguish three age groups in each region and adopt the GERTLER (1999) specification of consumer preferences and make similar assumptions concerning population dynamics, insurance arrangements and preferences.

Individuals go through three distinct stages of life: youth (0 – 14 years), work (15 years – retirement age), and retirement (retirement age+1 – expected end of life). The number of children in period t is given by N^y. Each period bN^y children are born and average duration in childhood is $1/\lambda^y$ where λ^y is the fraction of young people turning age 15. Child population dynamics is given by

$$N_{t+1}^y = bN_t^y + (1 - \lambda_t^y)N_t^y \qquad (1)$$

The working age population in period t is given by N^w. Each period $\lambda^y N^y$ children enter the working age population cohort. The mean duration of staying in this cohort is $1/\lambda^w$ where λ^w is the fraction of the population in working age which goes into retirement in the current period. Thus the population of working age evolves over time as follows

$$N_{t+1}^w = \lambda_t^y N_t^y + (1 - \lambda_t^w)N_t^w \qquad (2)$$

There are λ^y pensioners at date t. they are joined by $\lambda^w N^w$ new retirees, while a fraction $(1- \lambda^y)$ incumbent retirees survive to the next period. This gives the following law of motion for the retiree population

$$N_{t+1}^r = \lambda_t^w N_t^w + (1 - \lambda_t^r)N_t^r \qquad (3)$$

Population dynamics imply that individuals face certain probabilities of switching into different stages of their lives. Each child faces a probability λ^y of becoming a worker, each worker has a probability λ^w of becoming a retiree and each retiree faces an uncertain time of death. Following BLANCHARD (1985) a perfect annuities market is introduced which provides life insurance for retirees. Each worker faces an idiosyncratic income risk each period of loosing wage income and receiving pension income for the rest of his life. This type of uncertainty is dealt with analytically by restricting preferences, i. e. by employing a special class of nonexpected utility functions proposed by FARMER (1990). The so called risk neutral constant elasticity of substitution (RINCE) preferences separate a household's attitude toward income risk from its intertemporal elasticity of substitution. In particular they restrict individuals to be risk neutral with respect to income risk but allow for an arbitrary intertemporal elasticity of substitution. Notice, income risk is introduced artificially because it allows to simplify the analysis and not because there is a real income risk. Therefore it seems reasonable to mitigate the impact of the stochastic income variation of individuals between work and retirement by assuming risk neutrality. Children are assumed not to make any economic decisions. Extending population dynamics to include children is nevertheless useful since it allows to take care of different birthrates and initial youth dependency ratios.

The decision problem of retiree and workers can now be formulated by postulating value functions V^y and V^w over consumption for retirees (r) and workers (w) respectively as follows

$$V_t^z = \left\{ C_t^\rho + \beta^z E_t (V_{t+1}|z)^\rho \right\}^{1/\rho} \qquad (4)$$

with z=(r, w). The value function is non-linear in the two arguments. However, instead of complicating the analysis it is exactly this type of non-linearity of the value function which generates risk neutrality with respect to stochastic income and which allows the derivation of closed form decision rules which are functions of first moments of income only.

Consumption of retirees:

Each retiree j consumes out of pension income w_t^y and financial wealth A_t^{rj}. Because of the life insurance contract pensioners receive a premium on top of the interest rate which is equal to the probability of death. Thus the budget constraint is given by

$$A_t^{rj} = (1 + r_t + \lambda_t^r)A_{t-1}^{rj} + w_t^r - C_t^{rj} \wedge \wedge \tag{5}$$

Maximising (10) subject to (20) yields the consumption Euler equation

$$C_{t+1}^{rj} = (1 + r_t)\beta C_t^{rj} \tag{6a}$$

From this first order condition together with the intertemporal budget constraint the following decision rule for retiree consumption can be derived

$$C_t^{rj} = \varepsilon_t \pi_t \left[A_t^{rj} + S_t \right] \tag{6b}$$

where the marginal propensity to consume out of wealth is given by the following difference equation

$$\varepsilon_t \pi_t = 1 - \left((1 + r_t)^{\sigma-1}\beta^\sigma (1 - \lambda_t^r)\right)\frac{\varepsilon_t \pi_t}{\varepsilon_{t+1}\pi_{t+1}} \tag{7}$$

and the present value of retirement income is given by

$$S_t^j = \frac{1 - \lambda_t^r}{(1 + r_t)}S_{t+1}^j + w_t^r \tag{8}$$

Consumption of the population of working age:

Each member of the labour force j can either be employed or unemployed. Employed workers receive net wage $w_t^e = (1 - t_t - ssc_t)w_t$ where w_t is the gross wage. The unemployed receive unemployment benefits w_t^u. An unemployed worker finds a new job with probability p_t^u while a currently employed worker looses his job and becomes unemployed with probability p_t^e. Both employed and unemployed workers can expect the same pension. The budget constraint of both types is given by

$$A_t^{wj} = (1 + r_t)A_{t-1}^{wj} + w_t^w - C_t^{wj} \tag{9}$$

where the superscript $w=\{e,u\}$ indicates the employment status of worker j. The FOC of worker ej is given by

$$(1 - \lambda_t^w)\left((1 - p_t^e)C_{t+1}^{ej} + p_t^e C_{t+1}^{uj}\right) + \lambda_t^w \Lambda_{t+1}C_{t+1}^{rj} = \left((1 + r_t)\Omega_t \beta\right)^\sigma C_t^{ej} \tag{10}$$

The FOC of unemployed worker uj is given by

$$(1 - \lambda_t^w)\left((1 - p_t^u)C_{t+1}^{uj} + p_t^u C_{t+1}^{ej}\right) + \lambda_t^w \Lambda_{t+1}C_{t+1}^{rj} = \left((1 + r_t)\Omega_t \beta\right)^\sigma C_t^{uj} \tag{11}$$

Where $\Lambda_t = \varepsilon_t^{\frac{\sigma}{1-\sigma}}$ is the marginal rate of substitution of consumption across work and retirement and Ω_t is a factor that adjusts the rate of time preference for the fact that the worker can be in a different state next period. It is given by

$$\Omega_t = (1 - \lambda_t^w) + \lambda_t^w \varepsilon_t^{\frac{1}{1-\sigma}} \tag{12}$$

The worker determines the level of consumption in period t such that the ratio of the marginal utility of consumption tomorrow vs. today is equal to the difference between the real interest rate and the rate of time preference. The expected marginal utility of consumption in the next period is a weighted average of consumption in the two possible states. Notice, because of risk neutrality only the mean of consumption in the two states matters. A closed form decision rule for workers consumption can be derived and is given by

$$C_t^{wj} = \pi_t \left[A_t^{wj} + H_t^{wj} + S_t^{wj} \right] \tag{13}$$

where the marginal propensity to consume out of wealth is given by

$$\pi_t = 1 - \left(((1+r_t)\Omega_t)^{\sigma-1} \beta^\sigma \right) \frac{\pi_t}{\pi_{t+1}} \tag{14}$$

The term H^w is the present discounted income of an employed or unemployed worker. Because workers can switch employment status randomly in the next period, H^e and H^u are best represented by the following arbitrage conditions

$$H_t^{ej} = \frac{(1-\lambda_t^w)}{(1+r_t)\Omega_t} \left((1 - p_t^e) H_{t+1}^{ej} + p_t^e H_{t+1}^{uj} \right) + w_t^e \tag{15}$$

$$H_t^{uj} = \frac{(1-\lambda_t^w)}{(1+r_t)\Omega_t} \left((1 - p_t^u) H_{t+1}^{uj} + p_t^u H_{t+1}^{ej} \right) + w_t^u \tag{16}$$

The capitalised future pensions of workers S^w also enter the consumption rule. To simplify the analysis we assume that pensions of workers and unemployed are identical. This does not seem to be too strong an assumption since we assume that each member of the labour force has identical characteristics they will spend equal proportions of their working life in unemployment. The expression for the present value of future pensions is given by

$$S_t^{wj} = \frac{\lambda_t^w \varepsilon_{t+1}^{\frac{1}{1-\sigma}}}{(1+r_{t+1})\Omega_{t+1}} S_{t+1}^j + \frac{(1-\lambda_t^w)}{(1+r_{t+1})\Omega_{t+1}} S_{t+1}^{wj} \tag{17}$$

Notice, the marginal elasticity of substitution between consumption during working life and during retirement enters this expression, because workers value consumption in the two states differently. Aggregation across workers, unemployed and retirees is straightforward and yields the following aggregate consumption rule

$$C_t = \pi_t \left[(1 - s_t) A_t + H_t + \varepsilon_t \left(s_t A_t + S_t \right) \right] \tag{18}$$

where s is the share of total assets held by retirees and H is the present discounted value of net wages and unemployment benefits.

Notice also, like in the standard finite horizon model the dynamics of aggregate consumption differs from the dynamics individual consumption. While the change of individual consumption is only a function of the difference between the real rate of interest and the rate of time preference, the aggregate rate of time preference becomes a positive function of financial wealth because households belonging to different age cohorts have different financial wealth positions. This implies that in the steady state the rate of interest will exceed the rate of time preference, because high interest rates are needed in order to induce newly created worker households to save.

The life cycle feature also has consequences for the dynamics of assets and interest rates in open economy models. With infinitely lived consumers the steady state requires the same rate of time preference in all regions. In contrast with the life cycle model of consumption the effective rate of time preference becomes a positive function of financial wealth, i. e. an endogenous distribution of wealth will be generated in steady state equilibrium which equalises the effective rate of time preference across regions. In other words those regions with above average rates of time preference will, everything else equal, end up with a lower asset stock.

It is also instructive to compare consumption in this model to the standard infinite consumption model. A first difference applies to permanent income. Permanent income consists of discounted labour income throughout the expected working life as well as the expected present value of pension income. Adjusting the discount factors of H and S with the respective probabilities of staying in the two states takes care of the finite durations of work and retirement. Thus there is saving for retirement.

There is another important feature of the utility function which can potentially work in the other direction. Workers value the marginal utility of a unit of consumption differently between their working life and retirement. This valuation depends crucially on the intertemporal elasticity of substitution. For $\sigma > 1$ the marginal utility of consumption in retirement exceeds the marginal utility of consumption during work and vice versa. Especially the case $\sigma < 1$ has the interesting consequence that workers prefer consumption during working life. Intuitively this phenomenon can be related to the preference for income smoothing implied by a low intertemporal elasticity of substitution. Effectively this increases the rate of time preference of workers.

Total financial wealth A_t consists of three types of assets, government bonds B_t domestic equity $q_t K_t$, where q_t is the share price and K_t are units of real capital owned by the household. Households can also store wealth in the form of internationally traded bonds F_t issued by private agents in both countries.

$$A_t = q_t K_t + B_t + F_t. \tag{19}$$

Imperfect international capital mobility is introduced via a trading friction for internationally traded bonds expressed as a function which captures the cost for the domestic household of undertaking positions in the international capital market. As borrower, the household is charged a premium on the foreign interest rate and as lender he receives a remuneration which is below the foreign interest rate. Effectively this implies that uncovered interest parity does not hold between the domestic and the foreign economy where the spread between the domestic and foreign interest rate depends on whether the home country is a borrower or a lender in the market for international bonds. We specify the interest differential as a linear function of the net foreign asset position of the respective country

$$r_t^F = r_t - \psi\left(\frac{F_t}{Y_t}\right), \psi \geq 0 \tag{20}$$

The corporate sector in each region operates under perfect competition. Output is produced with a constant returns to scale Cobb Douglas production function

$$Y_t = F(K_t, L_t)\Gamma_t = K_t^{1-\alpha} L_t^{\alpha} \Gamma_t \tag{21}$$

where Γ_t is total factor productivity. Capital stock changes according to the rate of fixed capital formation J_t and the rate of geometric depreciation

$$K_t = J_t + (1-\delta)K_{t-1} \tag{22}$$

Total investment expenditures are equal to investment purchases plus the cost of installation. The unit installation costs are assumed to be a linear function of the investment to capital ratio with a parameter ϕ. Total investment expenditure is therefore given by

$$I_t = J_t\left(1 + \frac{\phi}{2}\left(\frac{J_t}{K_t}\right)\right) \tag{23}$$

The corporate sector in country i maximises the net present value of its cash flow

$$V_t = E_t \sum_{j=0}^{\infty} \prod_{k=0}^{j} (1+r_{t+k})^{-1} \left\{ (1-t_c)\left[Y_{t+j} - w_{t+j}L_{t+j}\right] - I_{t+j} \right\} \tag{24}$$

subject to the technology, the adjustment cost and the capital accumulation constraint. Define with λ^k the multiplier associated with the constraint on capital respectively. Differentiating the objective function with respect to K_{t+j}, J_{t+j}, L_{t+j} ($j=0,1....$), gives the following system of stochastic Euler equations (subject to the transversality condition)

$$(1-t_c)(1-\alpha)\frac{Y_{t+j}}{K_{t+j}} = (r_{t+j}+\delta)\lambda_{t+j}^k - \frac{\phi}{2}\left(\frac{J_{t+j}}{K_{t+j}}\right)^2 - E_{t+j}\left[\lambda_{t+j+1}^k - \lambda_{t+j}^k\right] \tag{25}$$

$$\left(\phi\frac{J_{t+j}}{K_{t+j}} + 1\right) = \lambda_{t+j}^k \tag{26}$$

$$\alpha\frac{Y_{t+j}}{L_{t+j}} = w_{t+j} \tag{27}$$

Equation (25) is the equation of motion of the marginal shadow value of capital λ^k. Equation (26) is the first order condition for total investment and it implies that the cost of a marginal unit of capital, including both its purchase and adjustment costs, must equal the shadow value of capital λ^k. It has been shown by HAYASHI (1980) that marginal and average value of Tobin's Q coincides under the technology and market structure assumed here, i. e. λ^k = q. The cost of capital includes both the pure rental price and adjustment costs. Equations (27) defines labour demand

Unlike in the goods market we assume imperfect competition in the labour market in both countries. Instead of deriving a labour supply equation from the household optimisation problem we assume a standard wage rule which can be derived from various labour market models. As discussed by PISSARIDES (1998) for example, the following generic wage rule

$$w_t^e = (1-\chi)w_t^u + \chi \left(\alpha \frac{Y_t}{L_t} + \frac{v_t}{LF_t / L_t - 1} \right) \tag{28}$$

could be derived from a search model, a union bargaining or an efficiency wage model of the labour market. According to this rule, net wages are a weighted average of the reservation wage (w^u) labour productivity plus an additional mark-up term that depends positively on labour market tightness.

The government provides three types of transfers to households: it pays unemployment benefits $(LF_t - L_t)w_t^u$, subsidises pension transfers at the amount $(TRPEN_t)$ and provides lump sum transfers (TR_t). In addition the government purchases goods and services (G_t). Expenditures are financed by labour income and company taxes plus taxes on consumption. The tax rates on wages (T_l) and corporate income (t_c) as well as the consumption tax rate (t_v) are assumed to be constant. Alternatively, the government can issue debt. Thus the government budget constraint is given by

$$B_{t+1} = (1+r_t)B_t + (LF_t - L_t)w_t^u + G_t + TR_t + TRPEN_t - t_l w_t L_t - t_c(Y_t - w_t L_t) - t_v C_t \tag{29}$$

Since we allow the government to subsidise the PAYG pension system, the financing constraint is given by the following equation

$$w_t^r part_t^r N_t^r = ssc_t w_t L_t + TRPEN_t \tag{30}$$

The left hand side gives current pension expenditures which are determined by the number of persons older than 65 eligible for a pension. Eligibility criterion is past labour force participation $(part^y)$ and N_t^y is the total number of persons in retirement age. Pensions (w_t^r) are determined as a percentage of current wages. Pensions are financed from two sources, social security contributions of current workers plus government subsidies.

Lump sum transfers are adjusted proportionally to the gap between the debt to GDP ratio and its target level b_0 according to the following rule

$$\Delta T = -\psi_1 \left(\frac{B_t}{Y_t} - b_0 \right) - \psi_2 \left(\frac{B_t}{Y_t} - \frac{B_{t-1}}{Y_{t-1}} \right) \tag{31}$$

Equilibrium

There is a homogeneous good which is traded internationally, therefore world supply is equated to world demand in each period and the market clearing condition is given by

$$\sum_{i=1}^{5} Y_{it} = \sum_{i=1}^{5} \left(C_{it} + I_{it} + G_{it} \right)$$ (32)

All bonds and equity supplied by the domestic government and the corporate sector are held by domestic households. The market clearing condition for internationally traded bonds is

$$\sum_{i=1}^{5} F_{it} = 0$$ (33)

Output price serves as numéraire. The competitive equilibrium of this economy consists of a sequence of real interest rates (r_{it}) and allocations (C_{it}, I_{it}, G_{it}, K_{it}, F_{it}, B_{it}) that satisfy the first order conditions of households and firms, the budget constraints of households, governments and firms and goods and bond market equilibrium conditions. Real wages (w_{it}) are determined by the wage contracting rule (28) and firms set employment optimally according to the first order condition (27). The labour market equilibrium can coexist with involuntary unemployment. Furthermore, the evolution of the economy is subject to initial conditions (K_{i0}, F_{i0}, B_{i0}, Γ_{i0}, N^y_{i0}, N^w_{i0}, N^y_{i0} , N^y_{i0}) and a sequence of fiscal instruments (t_y, t_l, t_c, t_y, b_0, g_0) as well as a debt targeting rule that ensures intertemporal solvency of governments.

Because the initial position of the economy is far from the steady state, the solution of a model, which is linearised around the steady state may give imprecise results. Therefore we have opted for a solution procedure developed by LAFFARGUE (1990), BOUCEKKINE (1995) and JUILLARD (1996) to solve the dynamic non-linear forward looking model by Newton-Raphson. The simulation horizon must, however, be chosen long enough such that the solution is close to the steady state at the final date. We set the simulation horizon to 500 years. ROEGER/IN'T VELD (1997) provide a more detailed technical discussion of this solution method as well as some sensitivity analysis in the context of permanent shocks.

S.3. Model Calibration

We select parameters such that the model fits some basic economic ratios both within and across regions. The objective of this exercise is to limit the international variation of structural parameters as much as possible and to explain divergences of economic development by the exogenous shocks and institutional differences. To select parameter values we largely follow standard procedures, *i.e.* we base these values on evidence from growth observations and some microeconometric evidence.

Demographics: We calibrate the model such that it can closely replicate the most recent EUROSTAT projections until 2050[2]. Because we make some simplifying assumptions on the evolution of the birth rate and life expectancy and because we do not consider migration our demographic projections in the model are not identical to the EUROSTAT projection. However, as can be seen from Table 1, using the old age dependency ratio as a summary measure of the demographic trend, the model projections follow the fundamental trends of the EUROSTAT projection. The survival probabilities in the three age groups are chosen such that the mean duration in each group is consistent with the age classification (0–14), (15–64) and (65-life expectancy). The demographic trend is fundamentally determined by two features, namely a decline in the fertility rate from 2.4 in 1970 to 1.6 in 1990. Since 1990 the decline has slowed down and has reached a value of 1.3 in 2004. The projections assume that it will slightly increase to 1.6 in 2050. More important for the dependency ratio is the development of life expectancy, which is supposed to increase from currently 81.7 to 86.7 for women and from 76.0 to 86.7 for men.

Table S1. Old Age Dependency Ratio.

	2004	2010	2020	2030	2040	2050
EUROSTAT	24.5	26.2	31.9	39.7	47.4	51.4
Model	25.5	27.3	31.4	38.1	45.7	52.0

Preferences: Consumption and savings behaviour is characterised by three parameters, the intertemporal elasticity of substitution, the rate of time preference and the elasticity of substitution between domestic and foreign assets. Most studies using household survey data (see e.g. ATTANASIO/WEBER, (1993), ATTANASIO/BROWNING, (1995)) tend to find estimates for sigma which are below one. We choose a value of .5 which is compromise between a value of one which is often used in the business cycle literature and smaller values often used in micro simulation studies. For the rate of time preference we choose a value of 1% per year. This is at the lower end compared to existing studies. This value is necessary for the model to generate a realistic level of the real interest rate. As discussed above, the effective rate of time preference is higher since it is a function of financial wealth. In selecting values for the rate of time preference we also take into account household savings rates across regions. An outstanding feature is the relatively low US household savings rate. To better capture this phenomenon we set the US rate of time preference to 1.5%.

Production: The output elasticity of labour is set equal to an average wage share across OECD countries. An annual depreciation rate for capital of 6% is assumed. The adjustment cost parameter is difficult to pin down on the basis of first moments of the data. It has been shown in the business cycle literature, however, that this parameter is crucial for determining the relative volatility of

---

[2]   We use United Nations (2000) and US Census (2001) data for the other regions.

investment (see, for example, MENDOZA (1991)). It is therefore set in such a way as to make investment about 3 times as volatile as GDP.

Labour market: Wage setting is characterised by three parameters, the level of the unemployment replacement rate, the parameter χ which determines "bargaining strength" of workers and the elasticity of wages w. r. t. unemployment. Since our starting point is 1970 where we observe low unemployment rates across the world we assume identical parameters for wage setting for all regions. Unemployment benefits are set such that they amount to roughly 30% of gross wages, which is around the order of magnitude found for a weighted average of EU countries and the US. The elasticity of wages with respect to unemployment is set to .5 which again corresponds to a weighted average of elasticity estimates found for the EU and the US. The bargaining strength is set to .5. The indexation of unemployment benefits to gross wages is chosen such that an increase in labour taxes or social security contributions by 1% leads to an increase of the unemployment rate of around .3% in the long run. This is about the average value reported by various empirical studies with values ranging from practically zero (BLANCHARD/WOLFERS, 2001) to a value of .5 obtained by DAVERI/TABELLINI (2000) for example.

International financial markets: Little is known about the degree of international capital mobility. Earlier simulation exercises have, however, shown that full capital mobility between EU15, US and Japan on the one hand and the ROW would have led to net foreign asset positions which would by far exceed the observed international imbalances. It is assumed that international financial markets are incomplete by introducing a risk premium which depends on the net foreign asset position of the respective region. We impose a small risk premium. Previous research (ROEGER, 2003) has shown that higher risk premia for the non OECD regions are necessary such that the model approximately fits the observed net foreign asset position of the fast and slow ageing RoW. For example, without risk premia, the fast and slow ageing RoW economies would exhibit net foreign debt ratios in the order of magnitude of about 120%, which is nearly ten times larger than the observed level in 2000.

S.4. Standard Policy Experiments

The scenarios analysed below will be combinations of changes in government debt combined with changes in social security contributions (combined with changes in the generosity of the pension system). In order to better understand the total effect it is useful to look at the individual effects separately by conducting two standard simulation experiments. This also allows us to see how the effects in this model relate to results in the literature. We analyse two experiments, a permanent increase in government debt and a reduction in pensions.

1. An Increase in Government Debt

Because of finitely lived households Ricardian equivalence does not hold in this model. In this experiment we show the degree in which Ricardian equivalence is violated by showing the real interest rate response of an increase in the debt to GDP ratio in Europe of 10% points. ENGEN/HUBBARD (2004) provide a summary of recent research (in the US case). Their reported estimates for a 1% point increase range from zero to 24 basis points. Their preferred estimate lies between 2 and 3 basis points. Our model is more Ricardian than the results obtained by ENGEN/HUBBARD. A 1% increase in the debt to GDP ratio increases the long run real interest rate by slightly less than 1 basis point. Notice this result is obtained by increasing government debt in Europe only. The results obtained in standard regression analysis are probably biased upwards because the debt dynamics are positively correlated internationally over the sample period used for the regression analysis.

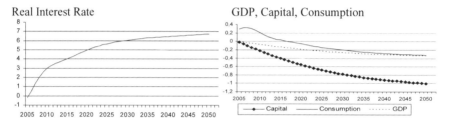

Share of Financial Wealth of Pensioners

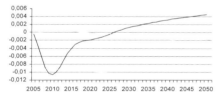

Fig. S1. Increase in Government Debt (10% points).

After 50 years the real interest rate increases by about 7 BP and the capital stock declines by about 1% and GDP by around .3%. The effects on the intergenerational wealth distribution are minor. This compares to Gertler's closed economy case where a 10% increase in government debt leads to an increase in interest rates of about 25 BP and reduces the capital stock by roughly 2.5%.

2. A Reduction in Pensions

In 2005, the share of pensions in total GDP is roughly 11%. What would happen if the pension system would become less generous? In this experiment it is assumed that the share of pensions in total GDP would be reduced by 2.5% points (gradually phased in over a period of 10 years). This corresponds to the pension experiment conducted by Gertler for the US. The most important question is, how such a reform would increase financial wealth and in particular capital accumulation. A less generous pension system in the EU would increase savings and reduce interest rates by about 60 BP in the long run and lead to an increase in the capital stock of about 7%. Notice, however, a significant part of the additional savings would flow abroad. Foreign wealth as a per cent of GDP would increase by about 10% points, while domestic capital as a per cent of GDP would only increase by 7% points. Associated with the reform is a redistribution of financial wealth from pensioners to worker households. These results compare to a reduction of the real interest rate of 275 BP in the closed economy model of Gertler, accompanied by an increase in the capital stock of 20%.

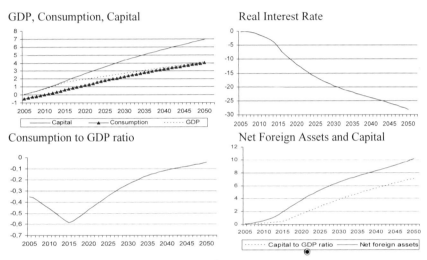

Fig. S2. Reducing PAYG Pensions (2.5% of GDP).

One striking feature of this comparison is the relatively small crowding out effect of both government debt and the PAYG social security system. Two features of the model are probably crucial for this result. First unlike GERTLER who models the US as a closed economy, we model the EU economy as having access to international capital markets. Second, we assume a higher intertemporal elasticity of substitution (σ), namely .5 vs. .25 in GERTLER's paper. Both features tend to reduce the crowding out effect. The openness assumption implies that interest rates are essentially determined by world savings and investment. A higher σ induces a stronger response of savings to the initial wealth shock and does therefore require a smaller long run interest rate response.

S.5. EU Pension Scenarios

We conduct three policy experiments. The first (baseline) experiment leaves the generosity of PAYG system in place and explores its economic and budgetary consequences. The second scenario looks what happens if EU governments resort to debt financing of additional age related expenditure and the last scenario analyses a partial transition to a funded system, with deficit financing of transition costs. All three alternatives face certain trade offs between fiscal sustainability and macroeconomic efficiency. The PAYG system does not pose a particular fiscal sustainability problem. However ever increasing social security contributions are likely to generate negative labour supply incentives. Along with it goes an erosion of the tax base. The debt solution could reduce the macroeconomic costs especially in environments characterised by near Ricardian equivalence. However, sustainability of the government budget will certainly become an issue in this scenario. The third option is likely to yield the best long term economic and budgetary outcome, however transition costs are potentially large, leading to high permanent but sustainable debt burden as well.

S.5.1. The Baseline Scenario: Letting the PAYG System in Place

Without reforms, the share of pensions financed via the PAYG system will nearly double until 2050 from currently 9.7% to more than 17%. This is accompanied by an increase in pension contributions in the EU from 16 to 27%. The demographic trend is leading to permanently lower GDP (per capita) growth rates in the EU over the coming decades. Reduced labour supply is likely to cut GDP per capita growth by one third in 2050. Notice, rising social security contributions will reinforce the labour supply pressure. With the significant increase in social security contributions, a further rise in structural unemployment by nearly 5% points seems possible. Though higher savings and increased capital formation will somewhat alleviate the demographic pressure, the current pension system does not provide sufficient investment incentives to compensate the decline in labour input by increased productivity generated via higher capital intensity.

Table S2. Baseline Scenario: Keeping Generosity of PAYG.

	2004	2010	2020	2030	2040	2050
GDP per capita	1.7	1.7	1.6	1.5	1.3	1.2
Private Investment/GDP	15.5	16.5	18.1	19.3	19.3	19.0
Unemployment Rate	8.1	8.3	9.0	10.0	11.3	12.8
Real Interest Rate	4.9	4.6	4.0	3.4	3.0	2.9
Retiree Cons./Worker Cons.	1.8	1.7	1.7	1.6	1.6	1.6
Pension/GDP	9.7	10.3	11.6	13.3	15.4	17.3
Social Security Contributions	14.9	15.8	17.8	20.4	23.5	26.5

GDP per capita: % deviation from baseline levels. The remaining figures are percentage point deviations from baseline levels.

S.5.2. Scenario 1: Debt Financing of Additional Pension Spending After 2005

The government guarantees the 2005 pension replacement rate and at the same time freezes the pension contribution to the current level. The difference between contributions and actual pension expenditure is financed via an increase in government debt[3]. With a constant contribution rate (of currently 16%) the share of pensions covered by the PAYG contribution would decline from 100% to about 66% in 2050. In other words the pension contributions of workers would only finance a replacement rate of about 50% in 2050. After 2050 debt accumulation is stopped via an increase in lump sum taxes. As shown in figure 3, debt is on an explosive and clearly unsustainable path.

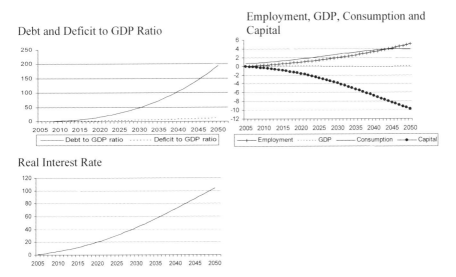

Fig. S3. Debt Financing of Additional Pensions.

In 2050 the debt to GDP ratio would reach about 250%. However, debt financing is less distortionary than financing via social security contributions. Thus relative to the baseline scenario, employment increases, leading to an increase in GDP. Since households perceive government debt partly as net wealth, consumption rises as well. Initially, debt accumulation would be relatively slow because of the positive employment effects resulting from keeping pension contributions constant. However, the macroeconomic gains would be small. The employment gains would largely be compensated by a crowding out of the domestic capital stock, due to the increase in real interest rates.

---

[3]   Technically this is achieved by disregarding the debt rule until 2050 and setting the new debt target to the debt to GDP ratio reached in 2050.

S.5.3. Scenario 2: A Partial Move to a Funded System

In this scenario the government makes an effort to reduce current pension contributions and the generosity of the PAYG system such that the ageing induced increases in pension contributions will lead to a rate in 2050 equal to the current pre reform rate. This essentially means a reduction of the generosity of the current first pillar by about 50%. In terms of rates, the replacement rate is reduced from 75% to 37.5% and social security contributions are reduced from 16% to 8% and will gradually rise to 16% in 2050. The government respects the entitlements of current pensioners fully but only partially the entitlements of workers older than 40 years in 2005 by providing subsidies to individual age cohorts at a (linearly) declining rate according to the following formula.

$$
w_t^r(age) = \begin{cases} wold_t^r - \left(\dfrac{retage - age}{retage - 40} \right)(wold_t^r - wnew_t^r) & for\ age \in (40, retage) \\ \\ wnew_t^r & for\ age < 40 \end{cases}
$$

where wold^y is the pension paid under the pre-reform rule while wnew^y is the pension consistent with the new contribution rate. Workers below 40 years of age at the year when the reform is introduced only receive wnew^y. The pension subsidies for those cohorts fulfilling the eligibility criteria are financed via issuing new debt. Notice, this transition is not actuarially fair for current workers, since the government only partially compensates current workers for their pension contributions and does not compensate at all workers younger than 40 in 2005. Nevertheless the government provides old age income support in such a way that a change in savings allows individual age cohorts to adjust smoothly to the new institutional environment. Also taking into account the life expectancy this policy implies increased government transfers for more than 40 years to come.

Even under this restrictive compensation scheme, the transition burden would be large. As can be seen from figure 4, government debt would increase by 80% of GDP over the next 40 years and would only decline afterwards. Government deficits would increase by about 4% points initially and decline gradually until the subsidies to older age cohorts are terminated after about 40 years.

These simulation results show that a transition to a funded system is most likely not self financing via increased economic activity. Because of the transition burden, the question can be raised when to expect positive economic effects from such a reform. There are at least two arguments in favour of a positive effect. First, because of a reduction in social security contributions positive employment effects should emerge and second there should be increased savings and higher capital formation to build up a second pillar. However, the build up of government debt accompanying the transition could dampen or even offset the positive savings effect.

As can be seen from the following figures, there is indeed a level increase of GDP, however this is mostly explained by the increase in employment. Additional effects from increased capital accumulation only arrive gradually. Over the first 15 to 20 years, the transition does not lead to additional savings.

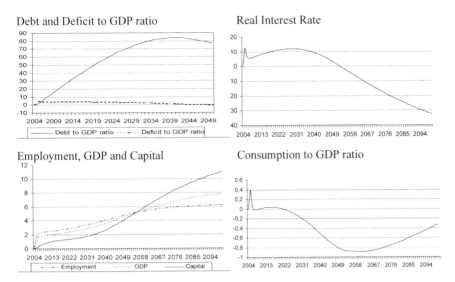

Fig. S4. Partial Move to a Funded System.

S.6. Conclusions

This paper has provided a projection on the likely macroeconomic impact of leaving the current PAYG system in place and has analysed a number of alternative strategies of avoiding an increase in non-wage labour costs. Special emphasis was laid on the question whether a partial move to a funded system could be a feasible option from a budgetary perspective under the constraint that age cohorts older than 40 must be subsidized by the general public over a transition period. At least for the transition as outlined in this paper, the fiscal costs appear to be rather large and hardly feasible from a budgetary perspective.

Apart from the generosity in which older worker cohorts are compensated, the crucial question is, what are the growth effects of such a reform and what is happening to growth of the tax base. In this paper it is found that the macroeconomic benefits from a transition to a funded system are limited, initially because the build up of government debt is crowding out private investment activities. Higher savings occur in the longer term. However, in an ageing open economy it is likely that a substantial fraction of savings will be invested abroad. The question arises whether it will be possible to tax the returns from foreign assets.

Thus all the options discussed in this paper will have to be supplemented by other measures in order to keep the budgetary and macroeconomic costs within some limits. At the end it appears unavoidable to also consider other measures such as an increase in the retirement age as a means to cushion demographic pressure.

References

ATTANASIO, O. P.; BROWNING, M. (1995), Consumption over the Life Cycle and over the Business Cycle, *American Economic Review*, 85, 1118–37.
ATTANASIO O. P.; WEBER, G. (1993), Consumption Growth, the interest Rate and Aggregation, *Review of Economic Studies*, 60, 631–49.
BLANCHARD, O.; WOLFERS, J. (2000), The Role of Shocks and Institutions in the Rise of European Unemployment : The Aggregate Evidence. Harry Johnson Lecture, *Economic Journal*, 110, 462, 1–33.
BLANCHARD, O. J. (1985), Debt, Deficits and Finite Horizons, *Journal of Political Economy*, 93, 223–247.
BOUCEKKINE, R. (1995), An Alternative Methodology for Solving Nonlinear Forward-Looking Models, *Journal of Economic Dynamics and Control*, 19, 711–34.
DAVERI, F.; TABELLINI, G. (2000), Unemployment, Growth and Taxation in Industrial Countries, *Economic Policy*, 15, 30, 49–104.
ENGEN, E. M.; HUBBARD, R. G. (2004a), Federal Government Debt and Interest Rates NBER Macroeconomics Annual 2004, Cambridge, MA.
EUROPEAN COMMISSION (2001A), The EU economy: 2001 review.
FARMER, R. (1990), Rince preferences, *Quarterly Journal of Economics*, 105, pp. 43–60.
GERTLER, M. (1999), Government debt and social security in a life-cycle economy, Carnegie-Rochester Conference Series on Public Policy Vol. 50. pp. 61–110.
JUILLARD, M. (1996), DYNARE: A Program for the Resolution and Simulation of Dynamic Models with Forward Variables Through the Use of a Relaxation Algoritm, *CEPREMAP Working paper no.* 9602.
LAFFARGUE, J.P. (1990), Résolution d'un Modèle Macroéconomique avec Anticipations Rationnelles, *Analyses d'Economie et Statistique*, No. 17.
MENDOZA E. (1991), Real business cycles in a small open economy, *American Economic Review*, p. 797–818.
PISSARIDES, C. A. (1998), The Impact of Unemployment Cuts on Employment and Wages: The Role of Unemployment Benefits and Tax Structure, *European Economic Review*, 42, 155–84.
ROEGER, W.; IN'T VELD, J. (1997), Quest II – A multi country business cycle and growth model, *EC DG ECFIN Economic Papers No* 123.
ROEGER, W. (2003), Explaining Long Term International Capital Flows, Paper presented at the annual meeting of the European Economic Association. Stockholm.

T. The EU Emissions Trading System and Its Sustainability Impact on European Industry[*]

Raimund Bleischwitz and Katrin Fuhrmann

T.1. Introduction

In this contribution we explain the mechanism of the EU Emissions Trading System (ETS) for greenhouse gases and explore into its likely sustainability impact on European industry. In doing so, we focus on energy-intensive industries like cement, steel and aluminium production as well as on the emerging hydrogen economy. Our hypothesis is that while the impact of the EU ETS on energy-intensive industries is severe and likely to be negative, the impacts on the emerging hydrogen economy are almost negligible. If that proves to be correct, the ETS would have a bias towards cost-increases for industry without fully exploiting the potential to stimulate innovation. Our interest thus is an analysis of expected structural changes in the European economy as a whole, where industries are scrutinized to adapt to climate policy while keeping core competences of energy intensive production along value chains, and others are challenged to radically innovate and to invent a new energy carrier such as hydrogen within existing energy markets.

Our article is structured as follows: the following section 2 briefly explains the mechanism and the political background of the EU ETS. Section 3 looks into real developments since the system started in early 2005. Section 4 analyses the impacts on EU energy-intensive industries. Section 5 assesses in a preliminary way the impacts on radical innovation towards the hydrogen economy – seen as a technological proxy for a more sustainable energy system and as a radical innovation. Section 6 draws conclusions.

T.2. The EU ETS: Political Background and the Mechanism

According to economic theory, an Emissions Trading Scheme is an economic instrument that enables the meeting of emissions targets in a cost effective manner (BAUMOL/OATES, 1998). It reduces the cost of reaching a specific target by taking advantage of the different marginal abatement costs of participating actors

---

[*] Draft as of Jan 30, 2007. We wish to thank Ralf Schüle and Bettina Wittneben for useful comments on an earlier draft. Edited by WELFENS/TILLY/HEISE.

with different emission sources. Cost savings are particularly big if mitigation costs differ significantly between sources covered by a scheme. This cost differential creates an economic incentive to trade. The task therefore is to build up a scheme that includes as many emission sources as possible and, if necessary, to link different domestic trading schemes. The economic theory of comparative advantages demonstrates that countries benefit and prosper economically from trade, relative to no trade. This can also be applied to the trading of emissions units. Against this theory it will be interesting to test how the EU ETS realizes the potential cost savings, whether the compliance costs resulting from additional bureaucracy outweighs the benefits and whether there might be undesired side effects.

With the Kyoto protocol signed in 1997 the European Union committed itself to reduce its GHGs by 8% in 2012 compared to the level of 1990. However, in the late 1990s the EU implementation of climate policy instruments has been rather lackluster and international credibility suffered. To address the reduction challenge cost-effectively, the EU established the European Climate Policy Program (ECCP) in 2000 in order to find the most promising climate policy measures. The results of the ECCP were to support the European Commission in developing an overall EU climate strategy (ECCP 2001). Yet, the overall progress of this strategy is up till now limited, except for the development of an Emissions Trading Scheme. At the time, this has been rather surprising, since usually the EU had been critical of market mechanisms and preferred fiscal and regulatory measures. NGOs were in general critical, since no recognizable "green" action was occurring, as in other measures such as promoting renewable energies. Industry and their lobbyists refuse caps and prefer voluntary approaches.

One reason for the quick start of emissions trading in the EU was the attempt of some pioneering member states to introduce national emissions trading schemes. The UK and Denmark started one and others such as the Netherlands and Germany had established working groups dealing with such an idea. The Commission thus feared a patchwork of systems, since the already established ones and the ones existing on paper were not at all compatible with each other.

Parallel to the ECCP, the Commission analyzed whether emissions trading on the level of installations might be an appropriate policy to meet the Kyoto target. In March 2000 the "Green Paper on Greenhouse Gas Emissions Trading in the EU" was published. Emissions trading was seen as the best instrument to deliver the proposed target in time – certainly an advantage over Eco-taxes – and at lowest possible costs since large emitters could be identified easily. According to the Commission's own assessment, the EU's own annual costs of the system would be in the order of 2.3 to 3.7 Mio € compared to 6.8 Mio € necessary to meet the same objective with other instruments (ENDRES/OHL, 2005: 20). After intense consultation with the European Parliament, the Council and several lobbying groups, several opinion papers and draft directives, a compromise on emissions trading, for CO_2 only, came out on October 13, 2003 (EC, 2003). The EU was set to become the world's largest market for company-level emissions trading (IEA 2003).

If the EU emissions trading scheme (EU-ETS) proves successful, there may be bilateral interest in linking it to the domestic schemes of other non-EU countries. Several non-EU countries have plans to introduce domestic emissions trading schemes, and according to economics, there are benefits to creating a larger market by linking such schemes. The broader the coverage of an emissions trading scheme, the greater the potential for economic efficiency gains of the scheme in terms of lowering overall compliance costs. However, the extent to which these benefits are realized will depend on the details of their design and the similarities of the schemes (SCHUELE et al., 2006, ANGER et al., 2006)

T.2.1. Main Characteristics of the EU ETS

The EU emissions trading scheme EU-ETS takes place on the level on installations[1], thus targeting the emitters themselves. The Directive 2003/87/EC which establishes the scheme was issued in September 2003, with a start date set for the 1st January 2005. The scheme initially specifies two periods, the first from 2005–2007, the second from 2008–2012 (corresponding to the first commitment period of the Kyoto Protocol). Compliance is required on an annual basis within these periods, but the allocation of allowances will be decided separately for the two periods. The Directive sets out some of the key design features of the emissions trading scheme. One of the key elements defined by the Directive is the unit of trade.

The EU-ETS cap – and – trade system came into force in January 2005 and also applies to the accession countries. Each participating installation needs a general *permit* to emit CO_2 and gets an allocation of *allowances* representing its initial absolute emissions budget for a year or compliance period. Where emissions exceed allowances, operators will need to either invest in abatement or buy more allowances on the market. It has a mandatory three year start-up phase from 2005–2007 and a five year mandatory Kyoto Phase from 2008 -2012. The following table gives an overview of the basic characteristics of the size of the emissions trading market in the first phase from 2005–2007. The EU ETS is based on six basic principles (EEA 2005):

1. Cap and trade system
2. Initial focus is on CO_2 emissions
3. Implementation will take place in phases with reviews and possibilities for expansion of additional sectors and gases
4. Allocation plans for emission allowances are decided periodically
5. Compliance framework
6. EU-wide system that taps reduction opportunities in the rest of the world through the other mechanisms of the Kyoto Protocol (Joint Implementation and Clean Development Mechanism).

---

[1] Art. 3 of directive: "An installation is stationary technical unit where one or more activities listed in Annex I are carried out."

EU Member State	Allocated CO_2 allowances (million tonnes)	Share in EU allowances (%)	Installations covered [1]	Kyoto target (%)
Belgium	188,8	2,9	363	− 7,5 [2]
Czech Republic	292,8	4,4	435	− 8
Denmark	100,5	1,5	378	− 21 [2]
Germany	1497,0	22,8	1849	− 21 [2]
Estonia	56,85	0,9	43	− 8
Greece	223,2	3,4	141	+ 25
Spain	523,3	8,0	819	+ 15
France	469,5	7,1	1172	0 [2]
Ireland	67,0	1,0	143	+ 13 [2]
Italy	697,5	10,6	1240	− 6,5
Cyprus	16,98	0,3	13	—
Latvia	13,7	0,2	95	− 8
Lithuania	36,8	0,6	93	− 8
Luxembourg	10,07	0,2	19	− 28 [2]
Hungary	93,8	1,4	261	− 6
Malta	8,83	0,1	2	—
Netherlands	285,9	4,3	333	− 6 [2]
Austria	99,0	1,5	205	− 13 [2]
Poland	717,3	10,9	1166	− 6
Portugal	114,5	1,7	239	+ 27 [2]
Slovenia	26,3	0,4	98	− 8
Slovakia	91,5	1,4	209	− 8
Finland	136,5	2,1	535	0 [2]
Sweden	68,7	1,1	499	+ 4 [2]
United Kingdom	736,0	11,2	1078	− 12,5 [2]
Total	**6572,4**	**100,0**	**11428**	

Notes:
[1] Please note that the figures do not take account of any opt-ins and opt-outs of installations in accordance with Articles 24 and 27 of the emissions trading directive.
[2] Under the Kyoto Protocol, the EU-15 (until 30 April 2004 the EU had 15 Member States) has to reduce its greenhouse gas emissions by 8 % below 1990 levels during 2008–12. This target is shared among the 15 Member States, marked with (2), under a legally binding burden-sharing agreement (Council Decision 2002/358/EC of 25 April 2002). The 10 Member States that joined the EU on 1 May 2004 have individual targets under the Kyoto Protocol with the exception of Cyprus and Malta, which have no targets.

Fig. T1. Trading Period 2005–2007 Indicative Data from the Commission Based on National Allocation Plans (EC 2005a).

T.2.1.1. Coverage and Duration

The EU ETS covers no other greenhouse gases other than CO_2. Annex I of the directive defines the activities that are obliged to participate. The following are some of the variety of sources (EC 2003):
- Combustion installations with a rated thermal input >20MW
- Mineral Oil refineries

- Coke ovens
- Iron and steel production >2.5 t per hour
- Cement > 500 t per day and lime >50 t per day production
- Glass production > 70 t per day
- Ceramics >75 t per day
- Pulp and paper >20 t per day.

Even with this limited scope, about 12000 installations are taking part. This accounts for 45% of EU's CO_2 emissions. Energy-intensive sectors have not been included in general because they are energy users rather than producers, e.g. the chemical sector, waste incineration, aluminium and other metal industries are not included. The chemical sector's direct emissions of carbon dioxide are not very significant (less than 1% of EU's total Carbon Dioxide emissions). Additionally the number of chemical installations (ca. 34.000) would increase the administrative complexity significantly (EEA 2005). The issue of competitiveness also can be raised.

Looking at the scope from a polluter-pays viewpoint, one has to keep in mind that in EU policy the non-covered sectors and/ or entities should be subject to other, equivalent policy instruments to avoid inequitable treatment. For the second National Allocation Plans the European Commission tries to be especially strict on this point (EC 2005b). In doing so however, one needs to be careful with the installations covered, in so far as they might face a double burden with other national climate policies such as energy taxes which would lead to rising abatement costs.

T.2.1.2. Allocation

The Emissions Trading Directive determined that the Member States allocate at least 95% of allowances free of charge. For the second period starting in January 2008 the amount is reduced to 90% free allowances. Such 'grandfathering' has been criticized by many economists for being not in accordance with the polluter pays principle (MICHAELOWA/BUTZENGEIGER, 2006). Member States are obliged to develop National Allocation Plans (NAP), which gives details about the total quantity that member States intend to allocate to the trading sector and how they propose to allocate them. To assist the Member States with the process of writing the NAPs, the European commission issued a guidance paper. Also for the second period, the Commission issued a new and stricter guidance paper in order to achieve higher harmonization between the different NAPs, to promote benchmarking and auctioning and to make sure that the Member States reach their Kyoto Targets. In the first period most Member States opted for full grandfathering on the basis of historical emissions whereas the proportion of benchmarking and the use of auctioning is likely to be increased for the second trading period. A lot of Member States were late to submit their NAPs for the first period. The same can be witnessed at the moment for the second trading period.

In the first phase Member states were allowed to "opt out" (exempt) individual installations from emissions trading. This has been done by some Member States especially to exclude some of the smaller installations and to reduce their administrative burden.

T.2.2. Linkage

In 2004 the Council of Ministers and the European Parliament agreed on a text for the linking directive (EC 2004 / LANGROCK and STERK, 2004). Its core is the recognition of credits obtained with Joint Implementation and the Clean Development Mechanism. CDM credits were eligible from 2005 onwards, whereas Joint Implementation credits may only be used from 2008 onwards. This means the system not only provides a cost-effective means for EU-based industries to cut their emissions but also creates additional incentives for businesses to invest in emission-reduction projects elsewhere, for example in Russia (JI) and developing countries (CDM).[2] In turn this spurs the transfer of advanced, environmentally sound technologies to other industrialized countries and developing nations, giving tangible support to their efforts to achieve sustainable development (EC 2005a). Some Member States had preferred a directive that had allowed companies participating in the scheme to gain credits by investing in emission reduction projects at home or other European countries. The European Parliament did not agree and therefore the provision was deleted (EEA, 2005).

The relationship between the EU ETS and other policies and measures that pursue the same objective is most obvious in the case of taxes levied on energy products and electricity, which are harmonised by Council Directive 2003/96/EC (the "Energy Tax Directive"). Greenhouse gas emissions trading and energy taxation are different economic instruments, operating by different legal means but partially pursuing the same objectives, in particular as concerns internalisation of externalities via market-based instruments i.e. CO_2 taxes targeting industry. The energy tax directive foresees that under certain conditions taxation can be fully or partially replaced, in particular for energy intensive companies, by some other instrument, including tradable permit schemes. This possibility is subject to the applicable State aid provisions. The EU ETS limits the emissions of covered installations in the EU collectively, and until 2012 the Directive requires most allowances to be allocated free of charge.

In line with its commitments, the Commission will consider further the interplay of the EU ETS with other measures pursuing the same objectives, and in particular with energy taxation. An occasion for this will be the beginning of the discussion on the review of the Emissions Trading Directive and the planned Green Paper on the use of indirect taxation and other market instruments.

---

[2] Joint Implementation projects can be pursued in countries that themselves have a Kyoto reduction target, whereas Clean Development Mechanism projects can be organized in developing countries without reduction targets under the Kyoto Protocol, such as China, Brazil and India.

T.3. EU ETS: The Development

Since the official start of the European Emissions Trading scheme and even before one could notice a dynamic institutionalisation around the idea of emissions trading, trading platforms, such as Noordpool, EEX, ECX or EXAA have been created and brokers and banks have started to get involved in the subject. Since the EU ETS introduction there has been a need for new institutions and new administrations also at the Member State Level. Some Member States have established specialised agencies specialised in the implementation of the EU ETS and to manage the nation's emission registry. Institutional changes give rise to administrative costs which in principle should be kept as low as possible. Such analysis is in line with new institutional economics (e.g. ZERBE, 2001), but not often reflected in textbooks on tradable permits.

Before the official start of the Scheme experts were unsure about the price developments of the newly developing carbon market. Some observers expected that prices would not be very high due to over allocation, especially in the new Member States, but also some "old" Member States. However, the prices started to climb immediately after the introduction of the EU ETS in January 2005 up to a level of above 20 € per tonne of CO_2 emissions in June 2005. Such a price was above all expectations and is not easily explainable. The main reasons are:

- The *immature market* is one factor that came into discussion, as only low volumes and a few players were active in the market. Even if liquidity was increasing slowly it was for a long time not sufficient as especially large players (many allowances) were hard to identify.
- Another reason could be *uncertainty* about the rules of the system in the future. Liquidity in this market is largely driven by emission reduction efforts that would free up allowances to then be traded on the market. Some companies fear that emission reduction efforts could be sanctioned (by possible changes) in the next allocation plan, so they refrain from reducing emissions in the current period. This impacts liquidity in the CO_2 market negatively (MCKINSEY/ ECOFYS, 2005).
- The market participants were slowly getting more *experience*. In the beginning, energy companies that are used to trading in the energy market and also leading in factoring costs, were active in the market. Accordingly, a lot of companies, especially smaller players, did not have a thorough understanding of the market and allowances were rather perceived as licenses to produce and not as an economic asset with opportunity costs.
- *Other energy markets*: During the period of high energy prices the coal – gas price spread has been moving to the advantage of coal as one can depict from the following figure. The increasing demand for coal thus has triggered the rising of the price of allowances.

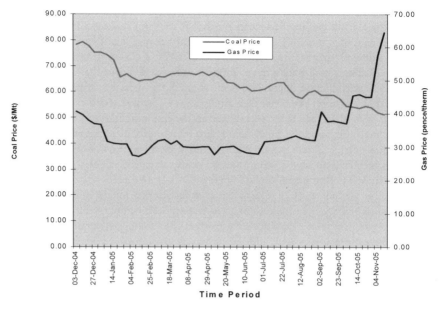

Source: CONVERY (2006)

Fig. T2. Coal – to – Gas Spread.

Higher gas prices relative to coal moves coal up the dispatch order and is used more frequently relatively to gas. However, this required the purchase of more allowance certificates as coal emits more CO_2 than gas fired power plants. Prices stayed at this level with high volatility though until some Member States announced their emissions data mid 2006 before the European Commission's deadline. The content of those announcements were that a lot of countries had more allowances than the industry needed, meaning a surplus of emissions. When this became obvious, the result was an immediate drop in CO_2 prices from €33 to only 10 € per tonne of CO_2 emissions (POINT CARBON/EEX 2006). Later on, prices increased again, but they never reached their pre-crash level. They remained rather low and tended to decrease further (January 2007: € 3.50). Thus it seems that, firstly, the market for carbon proves to be flexible and, secondly, information and expectations are explanatory factors for price developments.

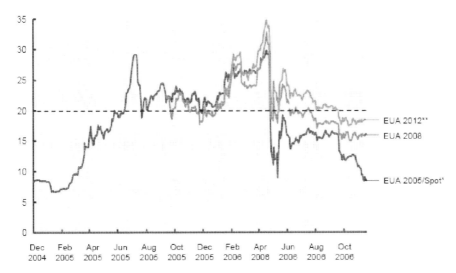

* Spot since Sept 2005, before Sept 2005forwards on EUA 2005
** EEX futures
Source: POINTCARBON, EEX

Fig. T3. CO_2 Prices in the Years 2005 and 2006.

A lot of industry representatives made the CO_2 prices responsible for increasing power prices. Future contracts for power prices do indeed show a high degree of correlation with forward allowance prices. However, correlation does not necessarily imply any immediate causation. Oil prices have almost doubled during the time of high CO_2 prices and therefore power prices have not only increased in Europe (CONVERY 2005). Emissions Trading is certainly but one factor when looking at energy prices. In fact one needs to take into account that changing relative prices in favour of less greenhouse gas emitting technologies is central to any serious climate change policy. Emissions trading, because it is a cost-effective way of reducing emissions, will mean most probably lower price changes than any alternative – but higher prices for CO_2-intensive activities compared with business as usual. One should also not forget the fact that other policies have impacts upon prices in the electricity sector too. Emissions trading, or more accurately, taking action to tackle climate change, is just one of many factors potentially influencing the power markets.

Pricing in allowances as opportunity costs in the cost calculation following the free allocation of CO_2 allowances was an expected scenario. Counting the allowances as assets in the company reports means that they are placed on the asset side of the company balance sheets with their market value. Since they are handed out free of charge, this in essence represents a windfall profit for the participating companies! The incomplete liberalisation of the European Energy Market however, allows power companies to pass on a high proportion of those opportunity costs – quite relevant for energy intensive industrial users. It is thus important to keep an eye on a possible misuse of market power. From today's perspective though, discussion regarding high power prices due to Emission Trading should not be on the top of the agenda as allowance prices are decreasing (see above).

The system is working, even if there is an over allocation at the moment. Prices do react to market developments and information given out to the public. However, there are still a lot of issues that can be kept in mind for an improved system:

- *Allocation*: Grandfathering cannot be the future of the scheme as it brings along adverse incentives when the base year needs to be changed. Auctioning and also free allocation on the basis of benchmarking should be taken into account when looking at the period from 2013 onwards (MICHAELOWA/ BUTZENGEIGER, 2005).

- *Complexity* and *transaction costs* are too high. Various interests have different objectives and as the regulator is trying to meet all demands the system tends to become more complex, less efficient and it looses market effectiveness (EEA, 2005).Transaction costs should be kept down e.g. via establishing an EU wide new entrants reserve or an EU wide registry and, later on, a European agency. Of course, information should be freely available for all market actors in the same manner and at the same time.

- The *trading periods* are regarded to be too short for any serious investment decision. Asset lifetimes in capital intensive industries are roughly between 20 to 60 years with several years of construction time. Most companies are therefore pleading for a trading period of at least 10 years and if necessary with adjustments (MCKINSEY, 2005), which is analytically in line with the concept of asset specificity (WILLIAMS, 1985).

- In general a higher degree of *harmonisation* in all architectural aspects has been asked for by all actors involved in order to exclude inequality between the same sectors across Europe (MCKINSEY, 2005).

- Also, an *inclusion of further greenhouse gases and sectors* as soon as the EU ETS has stable rules has advantages. Especially as other sectors, such as transportation are responsible for a high proportion of total greenhouse gases and have in particular grown in the last years as can be seen in the following graphic.

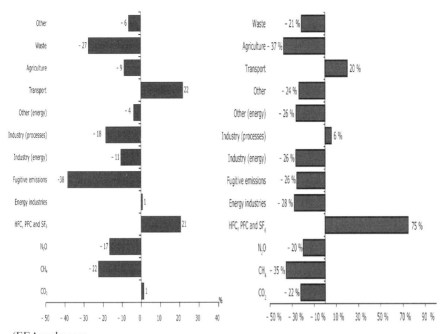

(EEA webpage:
http://dataservice.eea.europa.eu/atlas/available2.asp?type=findtheme&theme=climate).

Fig. T4. Change in EU-15 (left) and EU-10 (right) Emissions of Greenhouse Gases by Sector and Gas 1990–2003

To tackle part of the transport emissions, in December 2006, the European Commission issued a legislative proposal to include CO_2 emissions from aviation into the EU ETS from 2011 onwards (EC, 2006b). Even though the emissions from aviation account for only 3% of total EU greenhouse gas emissions, they are rapidly increasing (87% since 1990), as air travel has been becoming relatively cheaper compared to other travel possibilities. Air travel is not yet regulated by other parts of EU climate policy. For example, someone flying from London to New York and back generates roughly the same level of emissions as the average person in the EU does by heating their home for a whole year (EC, 2006b). Some issues in the debate on including aviation in the EU-ETS are:

• Whether or not to include *international flights from 2012 onwards* in the scheme. The US especially has made clear that such an action could result in trade sanctions as a consequence. The Commission plan maintains the idea of including international flights in the scheme, but proposes exempting them until 2012, while intra-EU flights will have to come under the scheme in 2011.

• How to take *other greenhouse gases* into account, including Nitrogen oxides (NOx) and the water vapour in aircrafts' condensation trails which also contributes to global warming. The Intergovernmental Panel on Climate Change (IPCC) has estimated that the total impact of aviation on climate change is currently about 2 to 4 times higher than what stems from CO_2

emissions alone. NOx had been in the initial proposal by the European Commission, but for political reasons it was taken out.

T.4. Impacts on Energy-Intensive Industries

The case of the energy intensive industries is important for several reasons: firstly, competition intensity in general is higher than in energy production with its inherent natural monopoly (the grid). Secondly, energy intensive industries are an essential supplier to many other industries downstream and, thus, form a vital part of the European economy. Thirdly, if energy intensive industries would relocate, not only the environmental relief would be questionable (assuming that other countries would not have stricter environmental policies), but also sustainable value chain management would become more difficult. Assessing the impacts of the ETS on these industries therefore is of high importance for economic research.[3]

One impact is quite clear: the choice of allowance allocation does affect the international factor mobility as well as the location of new companies. That is especially true for sectors that are competing in a world wide market. This could even be true within the European Union, as companies situated in relatively well endowed accession countries, such as Poland, might have an advantage over companies that are situated in countries such as Spain or Portugal which have limited surplus allowances (KLEPPER/PETERSON, 2003).

Energy intensive industry, covered by the EU ETS or not, is affected directly by the cap that is set on their CO_2 emissions or indirectly by increasing electricity prices. In general one can say that three factors determine the impact of Emissions Trading on the industry sector (CARBON TRUST, 2004):

1. Energy intensity,
2. Ability to pass on costs to the customer,
3. Abatement possibilities.

The ability to pass on costs depends again on three factors and differs substantially across sectors. Firstly the price elasticity of customers in the sector is essential when determining the degree of pass through ability of costs. The nature of competition is important as well. A sector with fierce competition has less opportunity to pass on costs to its customers. The third factor – abatement possibilities – not only depends upon technology choices: any substitution of energy intensive materials downstream certainly is a desired steering effect. But abatement costs also relate to the geography of the market, meaning whether companies being affected by the scheme are competing on a global scale or in a

---

[3]   There have been different analyses on the impact on industry due to the introduction of the EU ETS. One is for example a study conducted by KLEPPER/PETERSON in 2003. Carbon Trust examined different sectors in 2004 and a more recent one is done by McKinsey&Company and Ecofy in 2005/2006 commissioned by the European Commission/DG Environment. See also SZABO et al. 2006.

regional/national market. Companies outside the EU will not experience any direct cost increase as a result of the EU ETS. However other countries which have signed the Kyoto Protocol will start to put in place national policies and, therefore, companies in those countries might be affected by other domestic policies.

Abatement possibilities have different costs depending on the sector. With CO_2 emissions having a price, investment in abatement, such as energy efficiency, should offer opportunities that limit exposure to the EU ETS. Although some design features and uncertainty could hamper such a development.

The Carbon Trust has tried to characterise the different sectors according to those factors as illustrated in figure 5.

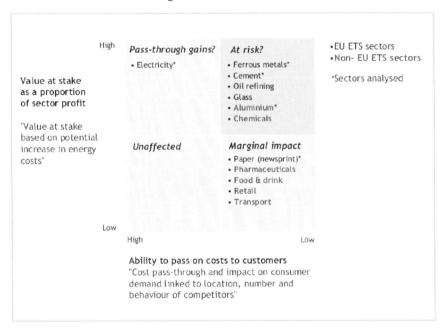

Fig. T5. Classification of Industry Sector by CARBON TRUST (2004).

In general, an economic analysis can say with confidence that electricity generators (i.e. utilities) are gaining or at least are not loosing from the introduction of the European Emissions Trading system, especially nuclear power plants. Fossil fuel power plants will incur a huge increase in direct costs, but are still able to pass through costs. This is partially due to the fact that the liberalisation of the European Energy market is not yet finalised and moreover a lot of incumbents still have strong market power in their respective market. For example, EDF can still be considered a quasi monopolist in France and Germany is characterised by an oligopoly with only four main players dominating the market. This paper will now look into the characteristics of selected energy intensive sectors.

T.4.1. The Cement Industry

The Cement Industry, included in the EU ETS, is the basis for every construction project and is therefore important for every economy. More than 50% of European cement production is accounted for by five major players, while the top 10 players hold about a 76% market share. It must also be mentioned that the top five players hold a large share in the global cement market of around 30% (MCKINSEY and ECOFYS, 2006).

Regarding the location of the cement industry, production usually takes place where the basic material is available. Transport costs are relatively high compared to the end price of cement, which results in low international trade. Recently marine transport is becoming more and more attractive and therefore international trade is increasing (CEMBUREAU, 2006).

Cement production costs will approximately increase by 36% due to Emissions Trading according to the McKinsey Study (2006) that assumes an average CO_2 price of 20 €/ton CO_2 emissions. Most of this cost increase is due to direct emissions, indirect impact from higher electricity prices make up only a small share of overall cost increase. Thus, depending on the ability to pass on costs to customers, the European cement industry on average will face a cost increase – moderate or neutral if the costs can be passed through. Potential cost increases will probably be seen close to seaports or EU borders (Greece, Spain, southern France, Italy) where the possibility of importing cement is the highest (MCKINSEY/ECOFYS, 2006) and therefore costs cannot easily be passed on to final consumers.

Experience during the first phase of the scheme shows that there is significant capacity to cut back emissions by reducing clinker input and by using more non-fossil fuel (CARBON TRUST, 2006). Thus some environmentally benign innovation effects seem to take place. The Carbon Trust (2004 and 2006) study that is mainly looking at the UK cement industry does not see major risks for the UK cement industry as there is hardly any international competition in the sector. However, both studies note that with higher carbon prices and the possibility that the allocation will be auctioned, the situation might change in the long term. Under these conditions and with increasingly low-cost marine transportation, the cement industry will have an incentive to relocate at least parts of their production capacities.

T.4.2. The Steel Industry

The steel sector is a highly energy intensive industrial sector included in the EU ETS. When looking at the impact of Emissions Trading on the steel sector one has to take into account the two different main processes for steel making: Basic Oxygen Furnace (BOF), producing mainly flat products and Electric Arc Furnace (EAF) production mainly long products from scrap steel (MCKINSEY and ECOFYS, 2006). Nearly 100% of emissions in the EAF process are indirect emissions whereas only 10% are indirect in the BOF process. Products produced by the EAF process compete mostly in regional markets and are therefore able to pass through more costs than products (cold rolled flat steel) from the BOF process, which are competing on the global market (CARBON TRUST, 2004).

Especially in the BOF process the long term industry margin of about 5% might come under pressure if China is to become a steel exporter instead of importer in the near future. Given the additional costs on marginal production of BOF products there is a possible incentive to stop producing in Europe and to shift production to countries without carbon costs.

Therefore, one could expect a shift from the BOF process towards the EAF process in Europe. Such a shift might also be influenced by high prices for iron ore. Currently however there is a scarcity of scrap steel, caused by high demands from China, which is not expected to decrease in the future (MCKINSEY and ECOFYS, 2006). The steel industry is therefore faced with high input prices anyway.

T.4.3. The Aluminium Industry

The Aluminium Industry is a sector that is not included in the European Emissions Trading scheme, but will probably still see an increase in production costs due to the indirect impact of rising electricity prices because of the EU ETS. Half of the EU's aluminium is produced by primary smelting whereas half is produced by secondary smelting/recycling. The process of smelting aluminium consumes over 15Mwh of electricity per ton of aluminium. In comparison to i.e. steel production (300kwh/tonne of steel) this is extremely high (CARBONTRUST, 2006). Recycling on the other hand or secondary smelting consumes about 0.7Mwh/ton of steel.

If Aluminium smelters do not generate their own electricity (as a lot of them across Europe do not) they will be exposed to increasing electricity prices after their long term contracts with electricity companies run out and they will have to buy their electricity from the grid or purchase it at less favourable conditions via new contracts.

Due to intense competition both inside and outside of Europe (high international trade) none of the cost increases can be passed on to customers. All studies expect the shut down of primary smelting in Europe in the next 20 years. However, the scheme is only one more reason to focus investment outside of Europe. Most probably this development would happen irrespective of the EU ETS due to the general development of the energy markets and the fact that aluminium smelters already operate at the high cost end of the commodity. Secondary aluminium smelters will probably not be affected by higher electricity prices.

To conclude, our brief analysis reveals that the EU ETS is possibly having negative economic effects in the energy intensive industries. Those industries have – at least in parts – an incentive to relocate their production outside the EU. Even the cement industry where transportation costs are significant, may decide to use marine transportation from outside the EU. Assuming that those other countries do no meet the high environmental standards set by Europe, this should become an issue. One option would be to design sectoral agreements where long term perspectives are formulated and some short term exemptions from climate policy are combined with sustainability innovation in those sectors, supported by border tax adjustments to compensate industry producing in regions with high CO_2 costs. In that context, WTO provisions would need to be assessed.

T.5. Impacts Towards Sustainable Energy Supply Systems

If one takes the climate issue seriously (STERN, 2006), the European Union needs to radically innovate and to change energy supply systems in the long run. Assuming that all GHG emissions need to decrease by at least 20 % by 2020 and by 50 – 80 % in the long run, there has to be a massive restructuring of the energy supply system. Despite these requirements however, both energy and electricity production is likely to increase from 2,963 TWh to 3,666 TWh till 2020 according to current EU forecasts and the McKinsey European Power Model (MCKINSEY, 2006). The challenges therefore are enormous and aggravated by the global nature of the problem and rising emissions elsewhere (IEA WORLD ENERGY OUTLOOK 2005).

The European Commission launched its energy package in January 2007. The main aspect of the proposals is a binding target to slash the EU's greenhouse gas emissions by 20% in 2020 compared with 1990 levels (EC, 2007). Against this background, economic analysis assesses the consistency and the impacts of current incentives. To what degree does, for instance, the EU ETS spur investments towards more sustainable energy supply systems?

Up to now the international agreements such as the Kyoto Protocol do not give a clear long term perspective. One could of course assume that the energy world will need to become less and less carbon intensive, but this is a normative assumption and there have been no intermediate and long term goals set. A promising energy carrier such as hydrogen, which is at the stage of demonstration projects but well below any deployment, needs long term forward looking politics with a system of clear time perspectives (CARRARO/EGENHOFER, 2003; BLEISCHWITZ/FUHRMANN, 2006).[4]

Analysing the Emissions Trading Scheme, it partly encourages the uptake of climate-friendly technologies by rewarding businesses investing in energy efficiency and some green technologies, thus turning their investments into quick, short term profits. But given the uncertainties about its future characteristics, it can hardly encourage investments into long term solutions. The risk of sunk costs is still too big and the coordination costs are too high for many investors. This is aggravated by the limited playing field for the ETS: the automobile industry and

---

[4]   See the articles in the special issue on hydrogen edited by BLEISCHWITZ/ FUHRMANN 2006 or the ,Hydrogen and Fuel Cell Platform' www.hfpeurope.org for further information.

oil industry, both of whom have an interest in investing into mobility after the oil age, are not covered by the EU ETS. Surrounded by many constraints, the EU ETS can only provide narrow incentives to discover new technical solutions. According to ENDRES/OHL (2005: 29) the ETS will display the push generally expected from market forces only to a limited extent. The European Emissions Trading Scheme in itself thus does not give the incentive to invest in such disruptive technologies and it is also not its aim to start with.

Also given other barriers such as;

- Lack of seed money and venture capital for start ups,
- split incentives between users and investors,
- biased calculation and underestimated payback times not favouring investments into more efficient technologies,
- existing market power, in particular in the energy sector,
- general information deficits.

A dynamic push towards sustainable energy systems would require both an improved ETS system and more targeted programs for business development and market entry of new energy sources and carriers. One could, for example, imagine that companies invest in emission reducing projects within the EU and get credits for it, comparable to JI or CDM projects.

Some technologies can already be seen as key technologies for mitigating global warming and to ensure a less dependent energy supply in the European Union. Some are already being actively encouraged by EU policies (e.g. renewables) while others are still subject to further research (e.g. hydrogen, CO_2 sequestration). A few options on how an improved ETS might be part of a larger policy package aimed at long-term innovation should be mentioned here:

1. More strategic policy coordination between different parts of the European Commission, such as DG Environment, DG Research and DG Transport and Energy is at stake. Quite often, steps are undertaken without sufficiently taking into account other policy areas. The regulatory impact assessment might be a tool for better policies, but communication and strategic policies should also be improved.

2. More focussed action: the Hydrogen and Fuel Cell Platform (HFP) aims to facilitate and accelerate the development and deployment of European hydrogen and fuel cell based energy systems and component technologies for applications in transport, stationary and portable power. Major challenges can be seen in a) disseminating the knowledge and b) to speed up the deployment strategy. Currently not only the hesitation of the financial markets to support long term investments in new infrastructures or public acceptance, but also the lack of coordination between the EU programmes themselves and between EU and national programmes are a serious barrier to deployment. A focussed action could include HFC demonstration projects at the sites of energy intensive industries and exemptions from energy taxation and feed-in laws for renewable energies only if those energy intensive industries adopt credible strategies for sustainable energy use.

3. Financing innovation: If policy makers would adopt auctioning as the preferred allocation method one could use part of the generated revenues to put into a fund that is investing in research, demonstration and implementation projects such as hydrogen technology. An auctioning scheme would also create a uniform and transparent price signal for the costs of carbon, whereas allocation based on grandfathering creates manifold distortions and inconsistencies. As the transport sector is not yet included in the EU ETS, research could develop scenarios to indirectly decrease emissions from that sector in the long term with carbon free produced hydrogen/fuel cell vehicles. In order not to create additional bureaucracy, those revenues could support EIB programmes or the EU regional funds targeted to co-finance hydrogen communities.

This section has not been written down to fully describe incentive schemes towards a sustainable energy supply in the EU. Many economic and legal aspects need to be assessed thoroughly. But with proper analysis, a reformed EU ETS might become part of European policies that might turn challenges into opportunities.

T.6. Conclusions

The implementation of the EU ETS is the largest experiment in environmental policy in the world. Never before has such a market-based environmental policy instrument been created that has a comparable coverage, both in geographical terms and with regard to the emissions and the market volume. The EU ETS is foremost a working system that – with some improvements – has the potential to become a pillar for effective and efficient climate change policy that also gives incentives for investment into climate friendly policies. With a range of lessons being learnt and still to be learnt, emissions trading in the EU can move from a new instrument with teething problems to a mature instrument that allows the meeting of targets at the lowest cost, when compared to other policy options.

Current weaknesses of the EU ECTS can be summarized, with regard to the scope of our paper, as follows: at the moment it is still very inconsistently implemented and has a fairly narrow scope regarding greenhouse gases and involved sectors. The distribution of allowances to sectors and installations was seen as purely a distributional problem for a long time. However, the initial experiences of effective implementation show that some key provisions were implemented that create disadvantages which will have significant effects on the environmental effectiveness of the scheme in the medium and long term for the EU as a whole.

The EU ETS creates incentives to relocate for energy intensive industries – at least the three industries analysed here (cement, steel, aluminium) are faced with higher production costs and cannot fully pass on those costs to their customers. If prices for allowances skyrocketed (say above 30 €/t) those industries would be at a disadvantage compared to their competitors from outside the EU. Incentives to innovate within the EU and downstream of their value chain certainly are an option, but this is not yet discussed in depth at the European level.

As of today, the EU ETS does not yet properly facilitate long term innovation dynamics such as the transition to a hydrogen economy. This may not come as a surprise, because the EU ETS has not been set up to do that in the first place. It encourages low cost emissions reduction measures but does not provide the support needed to bring about structural change. An improved EU ETS should definitely facilitate the agreement of new long-term targets with mid-term reviews. Further options to be analysed in more depth include flexible regulatory approaches and long term innovation programmes.

Additional to the technology pull via the Emissions Trading Scheme a technology push should be considered as the United States and Japan are promoting already. It is time to design an energy system for after the "oil age" and to deploy technology options able to meet the challenges ahead. The European Emissions Trading System might be able to help in this regard if the right incentives are set into its future architecture and if a policy package is designed on the basis of sound economic sustainability impact analysis.

References

ANGER, N.; BROUNS, B.; ONIGKEIT, J. (2006), Economic Impacts and Emission Effects of Linking the EU Emissions Trading Scheme in the Context of Post 2012 Reduction Targets, JET-SET Project Report. (available at:
http://www.wupperinst.org/de/info/detailseite_mit_datum/index.html?&beitrag_id=36 0&projekt_id=97&bid=66&searchart=)

BAUMOL, W.; OATES, W. (1988), The Theory of Environmental Policy. Second edition, Cambridge Univ. Press, Cambridge.

BLEISCHWITZ, R.;FUHRMANN, K. (2006), Introduction into the special issue on hydrogen, in: *Energy Policy,* 34, pp. 1223 – 1226.

CARBON TRUST (2004), The European Emissions Trading Scheme – Implications for Industrial competitiveness, Carbon Trust, London.

CARBON TRUST (2006), Allocation and Competitiveness in the EU Emissions Trading Scheme – Options for Phase II and beyond, Carbon Trust, London.

CARRARO, C.; EGENHOFER, C. (Eds.) (2003), Firms, Governments and Climate Policy. Incentive-Based Policies for Long-term Climate Change, Edward Elgar.

CEMBUREAU (2006), Activity Report 2005, Brussels.

CONVERY, F. (2003), Issues in emissions trading- an introduction, Policy Brief, 1, Environmental Institute, University College Dublin.

CONVERY, F. (2005), European Emissions Trading- A first assessment and the way ahead, Commentary by Frank Convery, Presented at: Future European Challenges conference, organised by the Toyota Chair of the College of Europe, Bruges and the European Policy Centre, 12th January, 2005, Crown Plaza Hotel, Brussels.

ECOFYS (2006), Auctioning of CO2 Emission Allowances in the EU ETS – Report under Review of the Emissions Trading Scheme, Brussels.

ENDRES, A.; OHL, C. (2005), Kyoto, Europe? – An economic evaluation of the European Emission trading directive, in: *European Journal of Law and Economics*, 19, pp. 17 – 39.

EUROPEAN COMMISSION/EC (2005a), EU action against climate change- EU emissions trading scheme, an open scheme promoting global innovation, Brussels.

EUROPEAN COMMISSION/EC (2005b), COMMUNICATION FROM THE COMMISSION "Further guidance on allocation plans for the 2008 to 2012 trading period of the EU Emission Trading Scheme", COM (2005) 703 final, Brussels.

EUROPEAN COMMISSION/EC (2006a), Communication from the Commission to the council, the European Parliament, The European Economic and Social Committee and the Committee of the Regions-Building a global carbon market – Report pursuant to Article 30 of Directive 2003/87/EC, COM(2006)676 Final, Brussels.

EUROPEAN COMMISSION/EC (2006b), Climate change: Commission proposes bringing air transport into EU Emissions Trading Scheme, Press Release, IP/06/1862, Brussels.

EUROPEAN COMMISSION/EC (2007), Commission proposes an integrated energy and climate change package to cut emissions for the 21st Century, Press Release, IP/07/29, Brussels.

EUROPEAN ENVIRONMENT AGENCY/EEA (2005), Market Based Instruments for Environmental Policy in Europe, EEA Technical Report No 8/2005 ISBN: 92-9167-782-5, Copenhagen.

EUROPEAN ENVIRONMENT AGENCY/EEA (2006), Application of the emissions trading directive by EU-Member States, EEA Technical Report No 2/2006, ISBN1725-2237, Copenhagen.

IEA/OECD (2004), Linking Non-EU Domestic Emissions Trading Schemes with the EU Emissions Trading Scheme, IEA/OECD Paper, Paris.

IEA(2005), World Energy Outlook, IEA, Paris.

KLEPPER, G.; PETERSON, S. (2003), International Trade and Competitive Effects, Policy Brief, 6, Environmental Institute, University College, Dublin.

LANGROCK, T.; STERK, W. (2004), Linking CDM & JI with EU emission allowance trading, Wuppertal Institute for Climate, Environment and Energy, Wuppertal.

LEVERE, J. (2003), Linking emissions trading and project based mechanisms, Policy Brief, 5, Environmental Institute, University College Dublin.

MCKINSEY and ECOFYS (2005), Review of Eu Emissions Trading Scheme-Survey Highlights, Brussels.

MCKINSEY and ECOFYS (2006), EU ETS Review- Report on International Competitiveness, Brussels.

MICHAELOWA, A.; BUTZENGEIGER, S. (2005), EU emissions trading: navigating between Scylla and Charybdis, *Climate Policy*, 5, p.1–9.

PAOLELLA, M.; TASCHINI, L. (2006), An Econometric Analysis of Emissions Trading Allowances, *Swiss Finance Institute Research Paper Series*, N°6 – 26, Zürich.

SCHÜLE, R. et al. (2006), Linking Emissions Trading Schemes: Institutional, Economic and Environmental Effects of Policy Scenarios, JET-SET Project Report.

STERN, N. (2006), The Economics of Climate Change: The Stern Review, Cabinet Office – HM Treasury, Cambridge University Press. (available at: http://www.hm-treasury.gov.uk/independent_reviews/stern_review_economics_climate_change/stern_r eview_report.cfm)

WILLIAMSON, O. E. (1985), The Economic Institutions of Capitalism: Firms, Markets, Relational Contracting, New York (Free Press).

WIT,R.; BOON, A., VAN VELZEN, A.; CAMES, M.; DEUBER, O.; LEE, D. (2005), Giving wings to emission trading – Inclusion of aviation under the European Emission Trading System (ETS): Design and impacts, CE, Delft.

ZERBE, R. O. (2001), Economic Efficiency in Law and Economics, Cheltenham: Edward Elgar.

U. Is a European Constitution for an Enlarged European Union Necessary? Some Thoughts Using Public Choice Analysis[1]

Friedrich Schneider

U.1. Introduction

After successfully implementing the European Economic and Monetary Union, we are currently realizing the failure of implementing a European constitution due to the selfish behavior of politicians and the rejection of this constitution in popular referenda by a vast majority of the French and Dutch voters in spring 2005. A year earlier, ten mostly former transition countries (e.g. Poland, Czech Republic, Hungary, Slovenia) entered the EU in May 2004 establishing a European Union of 25 members. Given this development, the following basic question arises:

Which essential constitutional reforms (possibly ending in a European Federal Constitution) are needed? Due to the rejection of the European Constitution by the French and Dutch voters and due to the enlarged EU with 25 members, the "old" EU arrangements do not guarantee a smooth functioning of the institutions of the European Union with 25 quite different members, mainly different with respect to their economic development. Hence new institutional arrangements have to be developed and one possible reform step is a new but much less ambitious European Constitution[2]. In order to avoid a major crisis of the functioning of this larger EU, the author proposes the idea, that some (albeit, minimal) European federal union will be necessary[3].

---

[1] Written version of a dinner speech at the conference "Financial Market Integration Structural Change and Growth: 50 Years of EU Dynamics", July 6-7, 2006, Frankfurt/M., Germany. This paper is a shortened and revised version of SCHNEIDER (2005).

[2] The idea of a European Constitution is also discussed and mostly supported by various other researchers like PIRIS (2000), FELD (2003, 2005), FELD/KIRCHGÄSSNER (2004). BLANKART/MUELLER (2004a, b), VAUBEL (2004).

[3] Such a much less ambitious, smaller constitution, which takes the preferences of the European voters into consideration, has been developed by the European constitutional group, compare BERNHOLZ/SCHNEIDER/VAUBEL/VIBERT (2004).

The author is convinced that a 25 member EU needs major reforms and even a minimal constitution, which can of course be debated (see e.g. PIRIS, 2000; FELD, 2005 BLANKART/MUELLER, 2004a, b). The author of this paper supports the value judgment, that the EU should be transformed from a confederation into a minimal

In this paper some ideas of a federal European constitution, like subsidiarity, federalism, and direct democratic institutions are developed with the help of constitutional economics. In part 2, six basic elements of a European constitution are introduced and in parts 3 to 5 an attempt is made to scientifically justify these propositions, like the design of European legislation (part 3), the subsidiarity and federalism principle (part 4), and direct democratic institutions (part 5). Finally part 6 provides a summary and gives some conclusions.

U.2. Six Basic Elements of a Future European Constitution

After the successful completion of the European Economic and Monetary Union a number of efficiency gains were achieved, and also economic growth of EU countries was stimulated. Furthermore, competition has been promoted between Member States by having a single currency and by weakening state-owned monopolies (like power plants and telecommunication systems). However, there is also the danger that these positive influences would be weakened if national regulations were replaced by EU regulations, and even more importantly if a 'new federal' government at the EU level is 'created' without operating in a carefully designed institutional framework with the consequence that it might grow and adopt responsibilities from EU Member States, which they possibly do not want to shift to this federal level[4]

It has already been stressed in SCHNEIDER (1993, 1996) and others (e.g. MUELLER, 2003) that democratic systems with market economies, if unchecked, show a strong tendency towards increasing state activity and interest group influence at the highest level.[5] As a consequence, the motivation of individuals to work efficiently, to engage in risky productive activities and to innovate is dampened. Whereas the removal of intra-European barriers to the movement of people, goods, capital, and services might weaken the influence of special interest groups and bureaucracies in EU Member States, a growth of the size of expenditure at the federal European level has to be expected as soon as Europe-wide interest groups and parties have been fully established. A European constitution must thus contain provisions to counterbalance such tendencies. In the current political debate it is clearly argued that the functioning of this enlarged

---

federation. Consequently this paper is a shortened and revised version of SCHNEIDER (2002, 2005), where the idea of a European Federal Union has been developed.

[4] Compare ALESINA/PEROTTI (1994), ALESINA/RODRIK (1992), KIRCH-GÄSSNER/POMMEREHNE (1995), VAUBEL (1996), VOIGT (2003), FELD (2005); consider also the current discussion about a European Constitution like in the European Constitutional Group (2003).

[5] Compare the studies by OLSON (1965), BERNHOLZ (1990a,b), SCHNEIDER/FREY (1988), PEDEN/BRADLEY (1989), WEEDE (1986, 1990), DE HAAN/SIERMANN (1995, 1996).

Union depends on the European Union's ability to reform its institutional framework in order to maintain efficiency as well as to regain the support of European voters.[6]

A European Constitution is also needed, so that a European identity can slowly grow or be formed. So far a European identity is rather weak if it exists at all. It has begun to grow since the creation of the Euro but on average the European citizens consider themselves primarily French, Italian or German and not European. This is one of the major difficulties when making suggestions about a European Constitution, because such a Constitution can only last and will only be accepted by European voters (citizens) if they think in a European way and are convinced that such a Constitution is needed and helps to strengthen their rights.[7] It is also difficult to create or strengthen a European identity as long as the European voters have little or no influence in either changing the government or participating in major decisions of the European Union like widening the European Union and a change in finances. Therefore, the following constitutional elements will support the idea of a slowly growing (and/or creating) European identity, e.g. by introducing direct democratic elements in such a constitution.[8]

The following elements could be an essential part of such a constitution:[9]

1. The European Commission should be turned into a European government with strictly limited tasks (for instance, the ones set up in element 2), the Council of Prime Ministers and Presidents into a second chamber (European Council), where each country has the same voting power. The simple majority approval of both chambers (the European Parliament and the European Council) is necessary for any legislation passed. Obviously, the European Parliament and the second chamber should solely have the full authority and responsibility for all European budgetary and federal decisions. If the two chambers cannot agree on a legislative or budgetary item, the parliament can overrule the decision of the second chamber by a qualified (for instance, 2/3) majority.

2. The jurisdiction of the European federal government should consist of defense, foreign policy, foreign trade policy, the enforcement of free intra-community movement (of people, goods, services and capital), anti-cartel and anti-monopoly policy and environmental policy concerning community-wide environmental problems. All these policy issues should only be taken over by the new European government, if there is consensus between Member States

---

[6] Necessary reforms of the EU are discussed in KÖNIG/BRÄUNINGER (1999); they concentrate on two aspects of institutional reform and functional as well as parliamentary integration. See also TABELLINI (2003a, 2003b) and VAUBEL (2003).

[7] Compare e.g. FELD (2003, 2005) and ABROMEIT (1998).

[8] Compare FELD (2003, 2005), FELD/KIRCHGÄSSNER (2004), BLANKART/MUELLER (2004a, b).

[9] The justification of these six elements is given in the following sections. But for a detailed discussion of constitutional issues, see also GWARTNEY/WAGNER (1988), VANBERG/BUCHANAN (1989), SCHNEIDER (1993), KIRCHGÄSSNER (1994) and HOLZMANN (1996); for fiscal federalism, OATES (1985), BLÖCHLIGER/R.L. FREY (1992), EICHENBERGER (1994), FELD (2005), VAUBEL (2004).

that the highest federal unit should do it and if a referendum over these issues is approved by simple majority of the European voters and by simple majority of the Member States.

3. For the federal European government, it should not be possible to run or accumulate deficits on its (current) budget over a legislative period. If a budget deficit still occurs at the end of a legislative period, either expenditures should be cut or revenues should be increased, given that the political conditions for a tax rate increase are fulfilled (compare elements 4 and 5) so that the budget will again be balanced. Longer (than a legislative period) lasting public debt at the European federal level should only be allowed for financing investment expenditures and only if the federal government has the financial capacity to pay the interest and amortization of the debt out of its current budget.[10]

4. The activities of the Community should be financed by one specifically labeled tax, like a proportional (indirect) tax. Changes of the rate of this tax should be subject to a 2/3 majority of the European parliament and of the second chamber, and to the approval of a popular referendum.

5. The institution of a popular referendum should be introduced for major policy issues (like a change of the European constitution, change of tax rate, etc.). Furthermore, a popular referendum should be held if a certain number of voters ask for it and if at least a certain percentage of all people entitled to vote participate[11] The issue over which the referendum is held is only accepted if it is approved by simple majority of the European voters and by simple majority of the Member States.

6. EU Member States should have the right to secede from the European federal union. A member state should, by qualified (2/3 or 3/4) majority vote of their population, be able to leave the European federal constitution to become an independent state once again. If a EU member state fails to reach such a qualified majority, the next attempt should be possible after 20 years.

U.3. The Design of European Legislation

As the first element in Section 2 proposes the formation of a European government with a two chamber system, and obviously the control of both chambers over all federal decisions which are delegated to the European Union, some general remarks will be made to justify this proposition. In a review article, POSNER (1987) argues that the separation of powers increases the transaction costs of governing. This would hold for welfare-enhancing as well as for

---

[10] Whether the European economic and monetary integration provides incentives to increase public deficits is investigated in HORSTMANN/SCHNEIDER, (1994). Compare also FELD/KIRCHGÄSSNER, (1999).

[11] The precise figures under which conditions a referendum has to be held and is accepted have to be specified. The only important point is that the option exists to force the European government to hold a referendum over a certain issue.

redistributive or even exploitative measures. The concept of separation of powers can be classified into horizontal separation (legislature, executive, judiciary) and vertical separation (federalism). Some progress has been made in analyzing the effects of separation of powers and political accountability. For example, PERSSON, ROLAND/TABELLINI (1997) show in a formal principal-agent model, that the separation of powers improves the accountability of elected officials, and thereby the utility of voters, but only under appropriate checks and balances. Two central provisions are needed: (1) there must be a conflict of interest between the executive and the legislative. (2) Moreover it must be impossible to implement any policy unilaterally, i.e. without the consent of both bodies. The application of these results to the European Union makes it necessary for institutions to be created, which leave only limited leeway for selfish actions of European Politicians.

The various effects of unicameral and bicameral legislators were first analyzed from a public choice perspective by BUCHANAN/TULLOCK in their famous book *Calculus of Consent* in 1962. One of the major conclusions in their analytical framework is that the optimal decision rule is the one leading to a minimum of the sum of external and decision costs (interdependence costs). BUCHANAN/TULLOCK (1962: p.235) conclude that in comparison with unicameral systems, bicameral systems have higher decision costs and continue: "On the other hand, if the basis of representation can be made significantly different in the two houses, the institutions of bicameral legislature may prove to be an effective means of securing a substantial reduction in expected external cost of collective action without incurring as much added decision making cost as a more inclusive rule would involve in a single house."

In a more recent study LEVMORE (1992) investigated the advantages and disadvantages of a bicameral versus a unicameral system. He concludes that a bicameral system might be better suited to reduce the power of the agenda setter (mostly the government) than a corresponding qualified majority in a unicameral system. Bicameral systems are often interpreted as a 'break' against overly active legislatures. Summarizing the effects of bicameral systems, I conclude that the legislative activities in a bicameral system are indeed lower than in a unicameral one, and this should be reflected in a lower government consumption of economic output and in higher growth rates.[12]

Some papers in constitutional economics (see, for instance, MOSER/SCHNEIDER, 1997) try to give an analysis of the consequences of a change in the procedure on the power of the European government organs.[13] Within the European Union, the strengthening of the European parliament can be attributed as a further safeguard in addition to the second chamber. A bicameral system is also demanded, since it reduces the capability of rent seeking, because it is much more difficult to get a majority in both chambers than in only one. This is

---

[12] A similar conclusion is reached and preliminary empirical evidence is given by the studies of FELD/KIRCHGÄSSNER (1996), FELD/SAVIOZ (1997), and for a more general view of this aspect see WEINGAST (1995).
[13] Compare PETERS (1996a, b) and STEUNENBERG (1994).

especially important after the widening of the European Union, because the more Member States the European Union has, the more likely rent seeking might occur. The draft report of the European Constitutional Group (1993, 2003, 2004) stresses the importance of competition as a mechanism to best fulfill consumer and/or voter preferences. Competition, however, is not only crucial for the working of economy; it is also needed in political markets, and the concept of institutional competition has a long tradition (starting with Tiebout's 'voting with the feet'). The introduction of a bicameral system not only reduces attempts for rent seeking but is also an important element to strengthen the federal structure of the EU. The second chamber can be seen as an institution which solely represents the interests of the EU member countries, like the German *Bundesrat* or the Swiss *Ständerat*. It might especially help to take care of the interests of a larger number of smaller EU member countries.

U.4. The Subsidiarity and Federalism Principles as Safeguards Against Government Growth and Centralization Tendencies

U.4.1. The Subsidiarity Principle

One key element of a European constitution is a fixed set of tasks for the European federal government, which has to be carefully defined. This basic proposition comes from the idea of using the subsidiarity principle. VANBERG (1994) argues that this principle is meant to provide a criterion for what can be considered a desirable constitutional order, a criterion that concerns an allocation of political authority in a multi-layer system of states/governments. To put it simply, the subsidiarity principle requires that in a multilevel polity, the distribution of power should be in favor of lower level governments and hence smaller jurisdictions. In other words, it demands that political authority always be located at the lowest possible level, that is as close as possible to the citizens, the ultimate sovereign.

Judgements on the preferability of particular constitutional arrangements (for instance, using the subsidiarity principle in a strict way) over others always refer to somebody to whom these alternatives are claimed to be preferable. In other words, all such judgements are directed to an addressee's particular interests. In democratic systems, the ultimate addressees of constitutional proposals are, of course, the citizens who constitute this union. If the subsidiarity principle is claimed to be a desirable constitutional norm for the European Union, this means that such claims must be supported by arguments that can convince its citizens that it would be in their interest, if efforts in the constitutional construction were guided by this principle.

What kind of arguments could one put forward in support of the subsidiarity principle as a constitutional norm? In other words, what kind of arguments could be made in favor of this principle, when designing a federal European constitution? One major argument for this principle is the central concern on part of the members of any democratic organization about the principal-agent problem, that is the issue of how one can ensure that power delegated to agents can, on the one hand, be used to the benefit of the principals and, on the other, be prevented from being used against the principals' interests. As far as democratic politics is concerned, there is a long tradition of inquiry, in political economy as well as in other social sciences, into the advantages of decentralization in political organizations. The results of this inquiry are of direct relevance to the subsidiarity principle.

However, it is obvious that the subsidiarity principle alone neither constitutes a basis to regulate the intergovernmental relations in an enlarged European Union, nor does it protect the collectivities at the grass roots (FELD/KIRCHGÄSSNER, 1996)[14] Moreover, the authors argue that the introduction of the subsidiarity principle in the Maastricht Treaty has in fact shifted the burden of proof at least somewhat more toward the centralists; the notion of subsidiarity nevertheless remains very general and open to many interpretations. Hence, the use of the subsidiarity principle does not solve the dynamic organizational problem, under which conditions, competencies or 'rights' should be given to lower governmental units. From a Public Choice point-of-view, there is a need for constitutional rules, which might prevent the 'misuse' of instruments by politicians, bureaucrats, and interest groups. Therefore the subsidiarity principle must be 'filled with life' and the theory of federalism may represent an operational means to regulate the horizontal and vertical relationship between governmental units in the light of a potential Leviathan.

U.4.2. Fiscal Federalism in a European Constitution

Federalism is an important institution that serves to establish competition within the political arena. Costs rise for the voters as taxpayers if certain groups are able to appropriate the benefits of a publicly supplied good, but do not have to pay the price for it. This group can be the politicians and/or the bureaucrats, who are self-interested rent seekers, or special interest groups, who try to attain their selfish goals. Although it is not argued here that politicians and bureaucrats always maximize their own utility up to the extent of actively exploiting the citizens and taxpayers, politicians and bureaucrats will do it from time to time if they have the opportunity. Thus federal competition provides another 'safeguard' against political decision makers taking unfair advantage of their discretionary power.

---

[14] In this context it is not surprising that DELORS (1992, p.12) argues that 'subsidiarity does not enact any restriction for the Commission to take political action' and he continues to argue 'solely on the basis of the Maastricht Treaty subsidiarity is not judiciable'. See also Sachverständigenrat zur Begutachtung der gesamtwirtschaftlichen Entwicklung (1992), VAUBEL (1993, 1995) and MÖSCHEL (1993, 1995).

Federal competition and federal institutions might also be a very crucial argument in a future European constitution. As has been discussed, the highest federal unit in the European Union should only be given those tasks that bring additional benefits (for instance, due to EU-wide spillovers) to voters/citizens, such as foreign or defense policy. The restriction of these tasks is necessary so that a more-or-less automatic centralization of tasks (especially in the area of redistribution) at the highest federal level will be avoided. All other tasks should be provided by the EU Member States.[15]

In order to guarantee that the central power does not take over either fiscal or other items from the EU Member States, BUCHANAN (1995) suggests the exit/secession option in the following way: the EU Member States must be constitutionally empowered to secede from the federal European Union. The secession, or the threat thereof, represents the only means through which the ultimate powers of the European federal government might be held in balance. In the absence of the secession issue, the federal European government may, by overstepping its constitutionally assigned limits, extract surplus value from the citizenry almost at will, because there would exist no effective means of escape.[16] With an operative secession threat on the part of the EU Member States, the European federal government could be held roughly to its assigned constitutional limits, while the EU Member States could be left to compete among themselves in their capacities to meet the demand of citizens for collectively provided goods and services. The (threat of) secession should be seen here as an ultimate 'weapon' for every EU member country in order to avoid a development that is not wanted by EU Member States or their citizens.

U.5. The Tax Base of the European Government

In KIRCHGÄSSNER (1994) and SCHNEIDER (1993, 1996), it is argued that the activities of the European government should only be financed by a proportional (indirect) tax. The rationale behind this idea lies in the different control possibilities which exist on different governmental levels.

First, any government will act more in accordance with the preference of the individuals/voters, the more the citizens are able to control it. At the lower

---

[15] One could go a step further and put forward the idea of federal competition between and within EU Member States when providing goods and services, but also financing them. As has been shown in the extensive research for Switzerland by KIRCHGÄSSNER/ POMMEREHNE (1996), POMMEREHNE, KIRCHGÄSSNER/FELD (1996) there is extensive tax competition in Switzerland, for instance, between the cantons at very small local distances. This tax competition did not result in a breakdown of public good supply in Switzerland and there is no indication of an under-provision of public goods. A critical view of the issue of tax competition is given by GENSER (1992) and SINN (1990).

[16] Compare here the path-breaking study by BRENNAN/BUCHANAN (1980), and the pioneering work of BUCHANAN/FAITH (1987) and BUCHANAN (1991, 1995).

governmental levels with smaller communities, the citizens have better possibilities to force the government to act according to their preferences.

Second, as FELD/KIRCHGÄSSNER (1996) argue, it implies that tasks as well as financial means that are easier to control are more suited to a higher governmental level than those that are difficult to control. Such proportional taxes leave relatively little room for Leviathan behavior of a European federal government, especially if an increase in the tax rate has to be subject to a two-thirds majority in both chambers of the European parliament and approval in a popular referendum. Therefore, at the European federal level only the revenues from this indirect tax should be available.

U.6. Institutions of Direct Democracy in a Future European Constitution

Beside the important issues of federalism and subsidiarity, institutions of direct democracy such as popular initiatives and (obligatory) referenda could also be a crucial factor in a future European constitution. They should be seen as a necessary supplement for the institutions of the representative democracy such as the proposed two-chamber system and the European government.[17]

There is a second crucial institutional feature when introducing institutions of direct democracy. Referenda do not simply consist of a choice between given alternatives, but should also be seen as a quite important 'political education' process over time. According to FREY (1994) and FREY/BOHNET (1994 a, b), three stages can be differentiated:

The first stage is the pre-referendum stage, in which the possibility of undertaking a referendum encourages discussion both among citizens and between politicians. Pre-referendum discussion produces a number of important effects. Preferences are articulated, enabling mutually beneficial bargaining and exchange. Moreover, the agenda of alternatives is to a great extent determined by citizens, thus constituting the relevant decision space. The pre-referendum stage screens the alternatives to be voted upon and reduces the number of relevant alternatives (quite often to only two).

The second stage is the formal decision situation, in which it can be seen that voters clearly express their content or discontent with a proposed referendum and quite often give a government a clear task to do.

Third, in the post-referendum stage, the government on the one hand has a clear task to do, and on the other hand, quite often, initiators of a referendum force the government to change their policy by only threatening to bring an issue into a popular referendum. But in some cases the government can also undertake

---

[17] Compare FELD (2003), FELD/KIRCHGAESSNER (2000, 2001a, 2001b).

unpopular measures (like tax increases), if they are supported in a popular referendum.[18]

The institutions of direct democracies also have other important means, such as their possible use by the voters to break politicians' cartels directed against them. As FREY/BOHNET (1994a) proposed, rent seeking theory argues that representatives have a common interest in forming a cartel to protect and possibly extend political rents.[19] Referenda and initiatives can be means to break the politicians' coalition against voters. Initiatives require a certain number of signatures and if the initiators obtain these signatures, they can force the government to undertake a referendum on a given (mostly disputed) issue. They are a particularly important institution, because they take the agenda setting monopoly away from the politicians and enable outsiders to propose issues for democratic decision, including those that many elected officials might have preferred to exclude from the agenda. As has been demonstrated in public choice theory, the group determining which propositions are voted on and in what order has a considerable advantage, because it decides to a large extent the issues that will be discussed when and which ones will be left out.[20]

If one summarizes these findings, two conclusions can be drawn. Cumulating research on the properties of a popular referendum has revealed two major aspects on which institutional economics has to focus. One is the importance of discussion in the pre-referendum state (FREY, 1994). This implies that the number of propositions and the frequency of ballots must be low enough that the voters have an incentive and the opportunity to collect and digest the respective information in order to participate actively in the decision. The second element is that direct democratic institutions enable voters to break politicians' and parties' coalitions directed against them. Direct participation serves to keep the ultimate agenda-setting power with the voters. Initiatives and referenda are effective means by which the voters might regain some control over the politicians.

Hence, introduction of direct democratic institutions like the referendum at the highest European federal level in the European constitution is an absolute necessity, especially if the European federal government wants to change the tax structure or wants to take over a new policy field.[21] The introduction of direct democratic elements in a future European Constitution is supported by various other researchers, like FELD (2003), FELD/KIRCHGAESSNER (2004), BLANKART/MUELLER (2004a, b).

Moreover, the introduction of direct democratic elements can be seen as an excellent tool in creating a European identity. If European voters have a "say" (e.g., to decide about European Union matters), they will be better informed about

---

[18] For instance, a referendum might help the government undertake unpopular measures in environment policy, compare FREY/SCHNEIDER (1997).

[19] The literature on rent seeking was developed by TULLOCK (1967) and one of the latest surveys is by TOLLISON (1982).

[20] Compare DENZAU (1995) and MUELLER (1987, 1989).

[21] Such a conclusion is also reached by BERNHOLZ (1990b), FELD/KIRCHGÄSSNER (1996) and VAUBEL (1993 and 1995).

European affairs, discuss those of significance, learn about them and after some time will reach decisions in a European way, and not only in a way that is good for their "home" country.

U.7. Conclusions

In this paper I have proposed some basic elements of a future European federal constitution in order to provide the necessary framework for a functioning the European Union with now 25 members. Six basic elements have been put forward, for example, turning the European Commission into the European government, the Council of Ministers into a second chamber, providing full control and responsibility over all federal items together with the chamber to the European Parliament. The jurisdiction of the European federal government should consist of a few specific items which are best suited for the highest federal level, like foreign defense and environmental policy. The activities of the federal European government should be financed by one proportional (indirect) tax, and direct democratic institutions should be introduced in a European federal constitution such as the possibility to force the European government to set up a referendum. These elements are then justified by arguments dealing with the subsidiarity principle, the idea of federalism, and with the effects of direct democratic institutions. As has been demonstrated, such elements are best suited to limit the domain of central European authority in the long run, even in the face of a strong tendency toward centralization in nearly all federal states in recent decades.

With respect to the actual crisis of the European Union in 2006, which resulted in a rejection of the proposed European constitution on the part of the French and Dutch voters, much simpler and much less ambitious constitutional items could help to overcome the fears of the majority of European citizens. Since according to DOWNS (1957), rational voters are rationally ignorant, it is necessary to build the European Union in a way that advantages other than simply the monetary union can be perceived by the ordinary citizens as well, even if they are not well informed.

Up to now, however, the advantages of the European Union are very indirect and often not at all obvious for the citizens, while the public discussion focuses on the interests of producer interest groups and the influence of Brussels bureaucracy. Thus, today the political opinion of ordinary citizens about the European Union varies between apathy and refusal. If such a simple constitutional perspective could be provided, which is understood and accepted by the majority of the European citizens, then the actual political crisis could be overcome. However, this is a long way away and needs a quite drastic political change. European member state governments and EU political actors have to take European issues (unemployment, (illegal) immigration, etc.) that are of great concern to European voters much more seriously and must thereby convince their voters that they are able to solve these problems with the help of a minimal European Constitution.

References

ABROMEIT, H. (1998), Democracy in Europe: Legitimising Politics in a Non-State Polity, New York.

ALESINA, A.; RODRICK, D. (1992), Distribution, political conflict, and economic growth: A simple theory and some empirical evidence, in A. Cukierman, Z. Hercowitz, and L. Leiderman (eds.). Political economy, growth, and business cycles. Cambridge (Mass.): MIT Press: pp. 23–50.

ALESINA, A.; PEROTTI, R.(1994), The political economy of growth: A critical survey of the recent literature, *World Bank Economic Review* 8/3: 351–371.

BERNHOLZ, P. (1990a), The completion of the European market: Opportunities and dangers from an institutional perspective, in: C.E.P.S. (eds.). The Macroeconomics of 1992. Bruxelles: *C.E.P.S. Paper No.* 42.

BERNHOLZ, P. (1990b), Grundzüge einer europäischen Verfassung: Ein Bundesstaat mit begrenzter Zentralgewalt?, in: Frankfurter Institut (ed.). Argumente zur Europapolitik 3: 2–12.

BERNHOLZ, P. (1993), Institutional aspects of European integration, in: S. Borner and H. Grubel (Hrsg.). EC after 1992: Perspective From the Outside. London: McMillan Publishing Company.

BERNHOLZ, P.; SCHNEIDER, F.; VAUBEL, R.; VIBERT, F.(2004), An alternative constitutional treaty for he European Union, *Public Choice* 118/3–4: 451–468.

BLANKART, C. B.; MUELLER, D. C. (eds.) (2004a), A Constitution for the European Union. London: MIT Press.

BLANKART, C. B.; MÜLLER, D. C. (2004b), Welche Aspekte sollen in einer Verfassung der EU berücksichtigt werden, und welche nicht? Eine ökonomische Betrachtung, IFO Schnelldienst 56/1: 5–15.

BLÖCHLIGER, H.-J.; FREY, R. L. (1992), Der Schweizerische Föderalismus: Ein Modell für den institutionellen Aufbau der europäischen Union?, *Außenwirtschaft* 47/3: 515–548.

BRENNAN, G.; BUCHANAN, J. (1980), The power to tax: Analytical foundations of a fiscal constitution, New York: Cambridge University Press.

BUCHANAN, J. M. (1990), Europe's Constitutional Opportunity, Fairfax: Virginia Center for Study of Public Choice, George Mason University.

BUCHANAN, J. M. (1995), Federalism as an ideal political order and an objective for constitutional reform, Publius: *The Journal of Federalism* 25/2: 19–27.

BUCHANAN, J. M.; TULLOCK, G. (1962), The calculus of consent: Logical foundations of constitutional democracy, Ann Arbor: University of Michigan Press.

BUCHANAN, J.; FAITH, R. (1987), Secession and the limits of taxation: Toward a theory of internal exit, *American Economic Review* 91/5: 1023–1031.

COMMISSION REPORT TO THE EUROPEAN COUNCIL on the adaptation of existing legislation to the subsidiarity principle, Com (93), Bruxelles, 1993.

DE HAAN, J.; SIERMANN, C.L.J. (1995), A sensitivity analysis of the impact of democracy on economic growth, *Empirical Economics* 20/1: 197–215.

DE HAAN, J.; SIERMANN, C.L.J. (1996), New evidence on the relationship between democracy and economic growth, *Public Choice* 86/2: 175–198.

DELORS, J. (1991), The principle of subsidiarity: contribution to the debate, European Institute of Public Administration, pp. 7–18.

DENZAU, A. T. (1985), Constitutional change and agenda control, *Carnegie Papers on Political Economy* 47: 183–217.

DOWNS, A. (1957), An Economic Theory of Democracy, London: Harper & Row.

EUROPEAN CONSTITUTIONAL GROUP (1993), A Proposal for a European Constitution, Report by the European Constitutional Group, ed. by European Policy Forum, London.

EUROPEAN CONSTITUTIONAL GROUP (2003), A Basic "Constitutional" Treaty for the European Union – with Comments, unpublished manuscript, Berlin, June, 8., 2003.

EICHENBERGER, R. (1994), 'The benefits of federalism and the risk of overcentralization', *Kyklos* 47/3: 403–420.

FELD, L. P. (2003), Eine Europäische Verfassung aus polit-ökonomischer Sicht, *ORDO*, 54: 289–317.

FELD, L. P. (2005), The European Constitution project from the perspective of constitutional political economy , *Public Choice* 122/34: 417–448

FELD, L. P.; KIRCHGÄSSNER, G. (1996), Omne agends agendo perficitur: The economic meaning of subsidiarity. In: R. Holzmann (ed.), Maastricht: Monetary Constitution Without a Fiscal Constitution?, Baden-Baden: Nomos Publishing Company, pp. 195–226.

FELD, L. P.; KIRCHGÄSSNER, G. (1999), Public Debt and Budgetary Procedures: Top Down or Bottom up? Some Evidence from Swiss Municipalities. In: J.M. Poterba and J. von Hagen (eds.), Fiscal Institutions and Fiscal Performance, Chicago University Press, Chicago 1999, 151–179.

FELD, L. P.; KIRCHGÄSSNER, G. (2000), Direct Democracy, Political Culture and the Outcome of Economic Policy: A Report on the Swiss Experience, *European Journal of Political Economy* 16: 287–306.

FELD, L. P.; KIRCHGÄSSNER, G. (2001A), The Political Economy of Direct Legislation: Direct Democracy and Local Decision-Making, *Economic Policy* 16 (33): 329–367.

FELD, L. P.; KIRCHGÄSSNER, G. (2001b), Does Direct Democracy Reduce Public Debt? Evidence from Swiss Municipalities, *Public Choice* 109: 347–370.

FELD, L. P.; KIRCHGÄSSNER, G. (2004), The Role of Direct Democracy in the European Union. In A Constitution for the European Union, eds. Charles B. Blankart und Dennis C. Mueller. Cambridge/London: MIT Press, pp. 203–235.

FREY, B. S. (1994), Direct democracy: Politico-economic lessons from Swiss experience, *American Economic Association Papers and Proceedings* 84/2: 338–342.

FREY, B. S.; BOHNET, I. (1994a), The Swiss experience with referenda and federalism, IDIOMA, Revue de linguistique et des traductology 10/2: 147–160.

FREY, B. S.; BOHNET, I. (1994b), Direct democratic rules: The role of discussion, *Kyklos* 47/3: 341–354.

FREY, B. S.; SCHNEIDER, F. (1997), Warum wird die Umweltökonomik kaum angewendet?, *Zeitschrift für Umweltpolitik und Umweltrecht* 20/2: 153–170.

GENSER, BERND (1992), Tax competition and harmonization in federal economies, in: Hans-Jürgen Vosgerau (ed.). European Integration in the World Economy. Heidelberg: Springer Publishing Company, pp. 184–205.

GWARTNEY, J.D.; WAGNER, R. E. (1988), Public Choice and Constitutional Economics, Greenwich (Conn.): J. A. I. Press.

HOLZMANN, R. (ed.) (1996), Maastricht: Monetary Constitution without a fiscal constitution?, Baden-Baden: Nomos-Publishing Company.

HORSTMANN, W.; SCHNEIDER, F. (1994), Deficits, bailout and free riders: fiscal elements of a European constitution', *Kyklos* 47/3: 355–383.

KIRCHGÄSSNER, G. (1994), Constitutional economics and its relevance for the evolution of rules, *Kyklos* 47/3: 321–339.

KIRCHGÄSSNER, G.; POMMEREHNE, W. W. (1996), Tax harmonization and tax competition in the European Union: Lessons from Switzerland, *Journal of Public Economics* 60: 351–371.

KÖNIG, T.; BRÄUNIGER, T. (1999), The institutional policies of enlargement: Diverging goals for reforming EU legislation, in Steunenberg, Berhard (ed.). Enlargement and new membership of the European Union. Kluwer academic publishers, pp. 145–172.

LEVMORE, S. (1992), Bicameralism: When are two decisions better than one?, *International Review of Law and Economics* 12/1: 145–162.

MÖSCHEL, W. (1993), Eine Verfassungskonzeption über die Europäische Union, in: Gröner, Herbert, and Andreas Schüller (eds.). Die Europäische Integration als ordnungspolitische Aufgabe. Stuttgart: Verlag Gustav Fischer, pp. 21–39.

MÖSCHEL, W. (1995), Subsidiaritätsprinzip im Zwielicht, *WiSt Heft* 5: 232–236.

MOSER, P.; SCHNEIDER, G. (1997), 'Rational choice and the governance structure of the European Union: An introduction', *Außenwirtschaft* 52/1–2: 64–82.

MUELLER, D. C. (1987), 'The growth of government: A public choice perspective', Washington D.C. *IMF-Staff papers* 34/1: 115–149.

MUELLER, D. C. (2003), Public Choice III, Cambridge: Cambridge University Press.

MUELLER, D. C. (1989), Public Choice II, Cambridge: Cambridge University Press.

OATES, W. E. (ed.) (1977), The Political Economy of Fiscal Federalism, Lexington (Massachusetts).

OATES, W. E. (1985), Searching for Leviathan: An empirical study, *American Economic Review* 75/4: 578–583.

OLSON, M. (1982), The Rise and Decline of Nations: Economic Growth, Stagnation and Rigidities, New Haven: Yale University Press.

OLSON, M. (1983), The political economy of comparative growth rate, in: Dennis C. Mueller (ed.). The Political Economy of Growth. New Haven: Yale University Press, pp. 222–247.

PEDEN, E.A.; M. BRADLEY (1989), Government size, productivity and economic growth: The post war experience, *Public Choice* 61/3: 229–245.

PERSSON, T.; ROLAND, G.; TABELLINI, G. (1997), Separation of Powers and Political Accountability', Center for Economic Studies at the University of Munich, *Working Paper* No. 136, June 1997.

PETERS, T., (1996a), Decision-Making after the EU-Intergovernmental conference, *European Law Journal* 2/3: 251–266.

PETERS, T., (1996b), Voting Power after the enlargement and options for decision making in the European Union, *Außernwirtschaft* 51/11: 223–243.

PIRIS, J.-C., (2005), Does the European Union have a constitution? Does it need one?, Jean Monnet Center NYU School of Law, European University Institute, www.jeanmonnetprogram.org/papers/00/000501.html,

POMMEREHNE, W. W.; KIRCHGÄSSNER, G.; FELD, L. P. (1996), Tax harmonization and tax competition at the state-local levels: Lessons from Switzerland, in: G. Pola, R. Levaggi and G. Francke (eds). New Issues in Local Government Finance: Theory and Policy. Aldersshot: Edward Elgar, pp. 201–255.

POSNER, R. (1987), The constitution as an economic document, *George Washington Law Review* 56/1: 4–38.

SACHVERSTÄNDIGENRAT ZUR BEGUTACHTUNG DER GESAMTWIRTSCHAFT-LICHEN ENTWICKLUNG (1992), Für Wachstumsorientierung gegen lähmenden Verteilungsstreit, Jahresgutachten 1992/93, Stuttgart: Verlag Poeschl.

SCHNEIDER, F.(1993), The federal and fiscal structures of representative and direct democracies as models for a European federal union: Some ideas using the public choice approach', European Economy Report and Studies 5, Bruxelles: 191–212.

SCHNEIDER, F. (1996), The design of a minimal European federal union: Some ideas using the public choice approach, in: José Casas Pardo and Friedrich Schneider (eds). Current Issues in Public Choice. Cheltenham (UK): Edward Elgar, pp. 203–222.

SCHNEIDER, F. (2003), A Federal European Constitution for an Enlarged European Union? Some Insights from Constitutional Economics', in: B. Steunenberg (ed.). Widening the European Union: The politics of institutional change and reform. Dordrecht: Kluwer Academic Publishers.

SCHNEIDER, F. (2005), Is a Federal European Constitution for Enlarged European Union Necessary? Some Preliminary Suggestions Using Public Choice Analysis, *Swiss Political Science Review* 11/4, pp.203–225.

SCHNEIDER, F.; FREY, B. S. (1988), Politico-economic models of macro economic policy: The political economy of money, inflation and employment, in: Willett Thomas (ed.). The Political Business Cycle. Durham & London: Duke University Press, pp. 239–275.

SINN, H.-W. (1990), Tax harmonization and tax competition in Europe, *European Economic Review* 34/4: 489–504.

STEUNENBERG, B., (1994), Decision-Making under different institutional arrangements: Legislation by the European Community, *Journal of Institution and Theoretical Economics* 150/3: 642–663.

TABELLINI, G. (2003a), Will it Last? An Economic Perspective on the Constitutional Treaty, Unveröffentlichtes Manuskript, Università Bocconi, Mailand.

TABELLINI, G. (2003b), Principles of Policy-Making in the European Union: An Economic Perspective, *CESifo Economic Studies* 49, 75–102.

TOLLISON, R. D. (1982), Rent-seeking: A survey, *Kyklos* 25/4: 575–602.

TULLOCK, G. (1967), The welfare costs of tariff, monopolies and theft, *Western Economic Journal* 5/3: 224–232.

VANBERG, V. (1994), Subsidiarity, responsive government and individual liberty, in: Knut Wolfgang Nörr & Thomas Oppernmann (eds). Subsidiarität: Idee und Wirklichkeit zur Reichweite eines Prinzips in Deutschland und Europa. Tübingen: Publishing Company J.C.B. Mohr, pp. 253–269.

VANBERG, V.; BUCHANAN, J. M. (1989), Interests and theories in constitutional choice', *Journal of Theoretical Politics* 1/1: 49–62.

VAUBEL, R. (1993), Perspektiven der europäischen Integration: Die politische Ökonomie der Vertiefung und Erweiterung, in: Siebert, Horst (ed.). Die zweifache Integration: Deutschland und Europa. Tübingen: Verlag J. C. Mohr, pp. 3–31.

VAUBEL, R. (1995), Constitutional safeguards against centralization in federal states: An international cross-section analysis, *Discussion Paper 532/95*, Beiträge zur Angewandten Wirtschaftsforschung, Universität Mannheim, Mannheim (Germany).

VAUBEL, R. (1996), Constitutional Saveguards against Centralisatzion in Federal States: An International Grors-Section Analysis, *Constitutional Political Economy* 7/1: 79–102.

VAUBEL, R. (2003), Europa droht eine Regulierungsspirale: Der Verfassungsentwurf begünstigt die Ausweitung europäischer Gesetzgebung auf Kosten der Bürger, *Frankfurter Allgemeine Zeitung* Nr. 157 vom 10. Juli 2003, p.12.

VAUBEL, R. (2004), Reformen der Europäischen Politikverflechtung, 3. revidierte Fassung, Walter Eucken Instiut, Universität Feiburg.

VOIGT, S. (2003), Towards ever more confusion? The convention's proposal for European Constitutions, *Intereconomics* 38/4: 185–198.

WEEDE, E. (1986), Catch-up distributional coalitions and government growth or decline in industrialized democracies, The British Journal of Sociology 37/2: 194–220.

WEEDE, E. (1990), Wirtschaft, Staat und Gesellschaft, Tübingen: Publishing Company J.C.B. Mohr.

WEINGAST, B. (1993), Constitutions as governance structures: The political foundations of secure markets, *Journal of Institutional and Theoretical Economics* 149/3: 286–311.

List of Figures

List of Tables

List of Contributors

Richard Tilly	Westfälische Wilhelms-University, Münster
Thomas Gries	University of Paderborn
Lucas Papademos	European Central Bank, Frankfurt am Main
Hans-Helmut Kotz	Deutsche Bundesbank, Frankfurt am Main
Ansgar Belke	University of Hohenheim
Daniel Gros	Center for European Policy Studies, Brussels
David Dickinson	University of Birmingham
Michael Heise	Allianz Group and Dresdner Bank, Frankfurt
Freddy van den Spiegel	Fortis Bank, Brussels
Paul J.J. Welfens	EIIW at the University of Wuppertal
Axel Pols	BITKOM, Berlin
Alain Chappert	INSEE, Paris
Kees van Paridon	Erasmus University, Rotterdam
Daphne Nicolitsas	Bank of Greece, Athens
Balázs Égert	Austrian National Bank, Vienna
Andrew Hughes Hallett	Vanderbilt University, Nashville
Christian Müller	ETH Zürich
András Inotai	Institute for World Economics of the Hungarian Academy of Sciences
Horst Hanusch	University of Augsburg
Andreas Pyka	University of Bremen
Werner Roeger	DG ECFIN, European Commission
Raimund Bleischwitz	Wuppertal Institute for Climate, Enviroment and Energy/College of Europe
Katrin Fuhrmann	College of Europe, Bruges
Friedrich Schneider	Johannes Keppler University, Linz

Further Publications by *Paul J.J. Welfens*

M.W. Klein, P.J.J. Welfens (Eds.)
**Multinationals in the New Europe
and Global Trade**
1992. XV, 281 pages. 24 Figs., 75 Tab.,
Hardcover, ISBN 3-540-54634-0

P.J.J. Welfens (Ed.)
Economic Aspects of German Unification
Expectations, Transition Dynamics and
International Perspectives
1996. XV, 527 pages. 34 Figs., 110 Tab.,
Hardcover, ISBN 3-540-60261-5

R. Tilly, P.J.J. Welfens (Eds.)
**European Economic Integration
as a Challenge to Industry
and Government**
Contemporary and Historical
Perspectives on International
Economic Dynamics
1996. X, 558 pages. 43 Figs.,
Hardcover, ISBN 3-540-60431-6

P.J.J. Welfens (Ed.)
Economic Aspects of German Unification
Expectations, Transition Dynamics and
International Perspectives
2nd revised and enlarged edition
1996. XV, 527 pages. 34 Figs., 110 Tab.,
Hardcover, ISBN 3-540-60261-5

P.J.J. Welfens
European Monetary Integration
EMS Developments and International
Post-Maastricht Perspectives
3rd revised and enlarged edition
1996. XVIII, 384 pages. 14 Figs., 26 Tab.,
Hardcover, ISBN 3-540-63305-7

P.J.J. Welfens (Ed.)
European Monetary Union
Transition, International Impact
and Policy Options
1997. X, 467 pages. 50 Figs., 31 Tab.,
Hardcover, ISBN 3-540-63305-7

P.J.J. Welfens, G. Yarrow (Eds.)
**Telecommunications and Energy
in Systemic Transformation**
International Dynamics, Deregulation
and Adjustment in Network Industries
1997. XII, 501 pages. 39 Figs.,
Hardcover, ISBN 3-540-61586-5

P.J.J. Welfens, H.C. Wolf (Eds.)
**Banking, International Capital Flows
and Growth in Europe**
Financial Markets, Savings and Monetary
Integration in a World with Uncertain
Convergence
1997. XIV, 458 pages. 22 Figs., 63 Tab.,
Hardcover, ISBN 3-540-63192-5

P.J.J. Welfens, D. Audretsch, J.T. Addison,
H. Grupp
**Technological Competition, Employment and
Innovation Policies in OECD Countries**
1998. VI, 231 pages. 16 Figs., 20 Tab.,
Hardcover, ISBN 3-540-63439-8

P.J.J. Welfens, G. Yarrow, R. Grinberg,
C. Graack (Eds.)
Towards Competition in Network Industries
Telecommunications, Energy and
Transportation in Europe and Russia
1999. XXII, 570 pages. 63 Figs., 63 Tab.,
Hardcover, ISBN 3-540-65859-9

P.J.J. Welfens
**EU Eastern Enlargement and the Russian
Transformation Crisis**
1999. X, 151 pages. 12 Figs., 25 Tab.,
Hardcover, ISBN 3-540-65862-9

P.J.J. Welfens
**Globalization of the Economy,
Unemployment and Innovation**
1999. VI, 255 pages. 11 Figs., 31 Tab.,
Hardcover, ISBN 3-540-65250-7

P.J.J. Welfens, J.T. Addison,
D.B. Audretsch, T. Gries, H. Grupp
**Globalization, Economic Growth and
Innovation Dynamics**
1999. X, 160 pages. 15 Figs., 15 Tab.,
Hardcover, ISBN 3-540-65858-0

R. Tilly, P.J.J. Welfens (Eds.)
**Economic Globalization,
International Organizations
and Crisis Management**
Contemporary and Historical Perspectives on
Growth, Impact and Evolution of Major
Organizations in an Interdependent World
2000. XII, 408 pages. 11 Figs., 20 Tab.,
Hardcover ISBN 3-540-65863-7

P.J.J. Welfens, E. Gavrilenkov (Eds.)
**Restructuring, Stabilizing
and Modernizing the New Russia**
Economic and Institutional Issues
2000. XIV, 516 pages. 82 Figs., 70 Tab.,
Hardcover, ISBN 3-540-67429-2

P.J.J. Welfens
**European Monetary Union
and Exchange Rate Dynamics**
New Approaches and Applications
to the Euro
2001. X, 159 pages. 26 Figs., 12 Tab.,
Hardcover, ISBN 3-540-67914-6

P.J.J. Welfens
Stabilizing and Integrating the Balkans
Economic Analysis of the Stability
Pact, EU Reforms and International
Organizations
2001. XII, 171 pages. 6 Figs., 18 Tab.,
Hardcover, ISBN 3-540-41775-3

P.J.J. Welfens, B. Meyer, W. Pfaffenberger,
P. Jasinski, A. Jungmittag
Energy Policies in the European Union
Germany's Ecological Tax Reform
2001. VII, 143 pages. 21 Figs., 41 Tab.,
Hardcover, ISBN 3-540-41652-8

P.J.J. Welfens (Ed.)
**Internationalization of the Economy
and Environmental Policy Options**
2001. XIV, 442 pages. 57 Figs., 61 Tab.,
Hardcover, ISBN 3-540-42174-2

P.J.J. Welfens
Interneteconomics.net
Macroeconomics, Deregulation,
and Innovation
2002. VIII, 215 pages. 34 Figs., 30 Tab.,
Hardcover, ISBN 3-540-43337-6

D.B. Audretsch, P.J.J. Welfens (Eds.)
**The New Economy and Economic Growth
in Europe and the USA**
2002. XII, 350 pages. 28 Figs., 59 Tab.,
Hardcover, ISBN 3-540-43179-9

C.E. Barfield, G. Heiduk, P.J.J. Welfens
(Eds.)
Internet, Economic Growth and Globalization
Perspectives on the Digital Economy
in Europe, Japan and the U.S.
2003. XII, 388 pages. 34 Figs., 6 Tab.,
Hardcover, ISBN 3-540-00286-3

J.T. Addison, P.J.J. Welfens (Eds.)
Labor Markets and Social Security
Issues and Policy Options in the U.S.
and Europe, 2nd edn.
2003. X, 402 pages. 56 Figs., 52 Tab.,
Hardcover, ISBN 3-540-44004-6

T. Lane, N. Oding, P.J.J. Welfens (Eds.)
**Real and Financial Economic Dynamics
in Russia and Eastern Europe**
2003. XII, 293 pages. 50 Figs., 63 Tab.,
Hardcover, ISBN 3-540-00910-8

J.E. Gavrilenkov, P.J.J. Welfens, R. Wiegert (Eds.)
Economic Opening Up and Growth in Russia
2004. IX, 298 pages. 61 Figs., 70 Tab.,
Hardcover, ISBN 3-540-20459-8

P.J.J. Welfens, A. Wziątek-Kubiak (Eds.)
**Structural Change and Exchange
Rate Dynamics**
The Economics of the EU Eastern
Enlargement
2005. VI, 288 pages. 26 Figs., 58 Tab.,
Hardcover, ISBN 3-540-27687-4

E.M. Graham, N. Oding, P.J.J. Welfens (Eds.)
**Internationalization and Economic Policy
Reforms in Transition Countries**
2005. XI, 340 pages. 77 Figs., 28 Tab.
Hardcover, ISBN 3-540-24040-3

P.J.J. Welfens, A. Wziątek-Kubiak (Eds.)
**Structural Change and Exchange Rate
Dynamics**
2005. VI, 288 pages. 36 Figs., 58 Tab.
Hardcover, ISBN 3-540-27687-4

P.J.J. Welfens, F. Knipping,
S. Chirathivat, C. Ryan (Eds.)
Integration in Asia and Europe
Historical Dynamics, Political Issues
and Economic Perspectives
2006. VI, 284 pages. 32 Figs., 30 Tab.,
Hardcover, ISBN 3-540-28729-9

H.G. Broadman, T. Paas, P.J.J. Welfens (Eds.)
**Economic Liberalization
and Integration Policy**
2006. VI, 358 pages. 93 Figs., 52 Tab.,
Hardcover, ISBN 3-540-24183-3

P.J.J. Welfens, M. Weske (Eds.)
Digital Economic Dynamics
2007. V, 209 pages. 29 Figs.,
Hardcover, ISBN 978-3-540-36029-2

P.J.J. Welfens
Innovations in Macroeconomics
2007. XIV, 432 pages. 99 Figs.,
Hardcover, ISBN 978-3-540-32859-9

P.J.J. Welfens
Digital Integration, Growth and Rational Regulation
2008. XVI, 186 pages. 31 Figs.,
Hardcover, ISBN 978-3-540-74594-5

Printing: Krips bv, Meppel, The Netherlands
Binding: Stürtz, Würzburg, Germany

2008 11 04